## Advance Praise for *The Elizabeth Keckley Reader*

*The Elizabeth Keckley Reader*, a magnificent collection of creative and scholarly works, examines and honors the heroic life of a courageous and defiant African American woman who overcame slavery, economic privation, and brutal physical punishment to free herself, own her being, speak with her own voice, and lead an independent life as entrepreneur, educator, and civic leader. Elizabeth Keckley's remarkable autobiography reveals the anguished connection between black and white lives in nineteenth-century America with focus on her uncommon relationship with President Abraham Lincoln's wife, Mary Todd Lincoln. This evocative and erudite collection speaks to women everywhere for it lays bare the soul of an unforgettable woman whose indomitable spirit caused her to rise again and again to face whatever comes, to take the journey, to show the way, and to make her contribution to life and to history.

—Barbara Paul-Emile, PhD, Maurice E. Goldman Distinguished Professor of Arts and Sciences, Professor of English, Bentley University

The writer has produced the first of her two-part work on Elizabeth Keckley, resulting in a compelling account of a strong and determined slave girl whose contributions in later life sealed her legacy. As Sheila Smith McKoy notes, Keckley refused to be "erased" from history and became an entrepreneur of enduring fame. She also takes her place among the nineteenth-century black women writers of acclaim.

—Jessie Carney Smith, Dean of the Library and Camille Cosby Distinguished Chair in the Humanities, Fisk University

Presented in a series of two volumes, the *Elizabeth Keckley Reader* breaks new ground in recovering late nineteenth-century texts and contexts, and promotes literary historical inquiry by way of essays, poetry, and drama contributed by an impressive group of scholars. Indeed, the *Keckley Reader* is an innovative project, a crucial contribution to ongoing studies of African American autobiographical acts and American culture.

—Jerry W. Ward Jr., author of *The Katrina Papers: A Journal of Trauma and Recovery, Trouble the Water, Black Southern Voices*, and *The Richard Wright Encyclopedia*

Elizabeth Keckley's *Behind the Scenes* constitutes an invaluable snapshot of the Lincoln White House, the Civil War, and her close kinship with Mary Todd Lincoln, which was ruptured when the seamstress's memoir appeared. Sheila Smith McKoy has expertly edited new and existing essays by leading scholars. Her superb introduction provides a valuable portal to the treasures that follow, which illuminate a fascinating woman and the era she helped shape.

—John Wharton Lowe,
Barbara Methvin Distinguished Professor, University of Georgia

THE ELIZABETH KECKLEY READER

# The Elizabeth Keckley Reader

VOLUME ONE
**WRITING SELF, WRITING NATION**

Dr. Sheila Smith McKoy, editor

The Elizabeth Keckley Reader: Volume One
Editor Sheila Smith McKoy
© Eno Publishers 2016
All rights reserved

Each selection herein is the copyrighted property of its respective author or publisher, if so noted on the Permissions page, and appears in this volume by arrangement with the individual writer or publisher.

Eno Publishers
P.O. Box 158
Hillsborough, North Carolina 27278
www.enopublishers.org

ISBN: 978-0-9896092-5-8
Library of Congress Control Number: 2015960648
First edition, second printing

Cover photograph of Elizabeth Keckley is courtesy of the photography collection of Moorland Spingarn Research Center at Howard University.

Design and production by Copperline Book Services, Hillsborough, North Carolina

EDITOR'S ACKNOWLEDGMENTS

This work would not have been possible without the rare grace and presence of Elizabeth Hobbs Keckley (Keckly), who proved that neither race, rape, slander, nor sorrow could prevent her from living an extraordinary life.

I thank Elizabeth Woodman for hatching the wonderful plan of creating a reader focused on the life and life's work of Keckley whose work has not received the critical attention it deserves and whose life is a telling cultural commentary on the politics of power. I offer special thanks to the graduate assistants, Rinita Banerjee and Sheena Young, who worked tirelessly with me to produce the reader. At Eno Publishers, I extend my thanks to two hard-working editorial interns, Madeline Farlow and John Fate Faherty, and to Marketing Director, Laura Lacy.

Thanks also to my colleagues at North Carolina State University, especially Juliana Nfah-Abbenyi and Marc Dudley; to Helen Houston, Sandra Govan, John Lowe, Barbara McCaskill, Jessie Carney Smith, Jerry Ward, Barbara Paul-Emile, my son, Raymond Smith McKoy, John Berard, and all of my family members—those related by blood and by love.

Above all, thank you to the contributors to this volume without whose support, critical insights, and creative vision this project would not have been possible.

CONTENTS

xi  Introduction | Dr. Sheila Smith McKoy
    Writing Self, Writing Nation
    Reconsidering Thirty Years a Slave, and Four Years in the White House

**EXISTING CRITICISM**

1   ONE | Jill Jepson
    Disruption and Disguise in Black Feminine Entrepreneurial Identity
    Mary Ellen Pleasant, Elizabeth Keckley & Eliza Potter

21  TWO | William L. Andrews
    Reunion in the Postbellum Slave Narrative
    Frederick Douglass and Elizabeth Keckley

34  THREE | Frances Smith Foster
    Autobiography after Emancipation
    The Example of Elizabeth Keckley

60  FOUR | Lynn Domina
    "I Was Re-Elected President"
    Elizabeth Keckley as Quintessential Patriot in *Behind the Scenes: Or, Thirty Years a Slave, and Four Years in the White House*

74  FIVE | Michael Berthold
    Not "Altogether" the "History of Myself"
    Autobiographical Impersonality in Elizabeth Keckley's *Behind the Scenes: Or, Thirty Years a Slave, and Four Years in the White House*

90  SIX | Janet Neary
    Behind the Scenes and Inside Out
    Elizabeth Keckley's Revision of the Slave-Narrative Form

**NEW CRITICISM**

125 SEVEN | Regis M. Fox
Behind the Scenes of American Liberalism

142 EIGHT | Aisha Francis
Stepping Beyond the Formal Lines
Elizabeth Keckley, Gertrude Mossell, and the Cost of Transgression

163 NINE | Nanette Morton
Private Spaces, Public Meanings

183 TEN | Janaka Lewis
Elizabeth Keckley and Lessons of Freedom

**EXISTING CRITICISM CONTINUED**

203 ELEVEN | Clarence W. Tweedy
Splitting the "I"
(Re)reading the Traumatic Narrative of Black Womanhood
in the Autobiographies of Harriet Jacobs and Elizabeth Keckley

220 TWELVE | Michele Elam
Dressing down the First Lady
Elizabeth Keckley's *Behind the Scenes: Or Thirty Years a Slave, and Four Years in the White House*

247 Elizabeth Hobbs Keckley Timeline

251 Further Reading

255 About the Editor

257 About the Contributors

261 Permissions

263 Index

# INTRODUCTION

**SHEILA SMITH McKOY**

## Writing Self, Writing Nation
Reconsidering Thirty Years a Slave, and Four Years in the White House

The labor of a lifetime has brought me nothing in a pecuniary way. I have worked hard, but fortune, fickle dame, has not smiled upon me. If poverty did not weigh me down as it does, I would not now be toiling by day with my needle, and writing by night, in the plain little room on the fourth floor of No. 14 Carroll Place. And yet I have learned to love the garret-like room.... Though poor in worldly goods, I am rich in friendships, and friends are a recompense for all the woes of the darkest pages of life. (330)
—Elizabeth Keckley, *Behind the Scenes: Or, Thirty Years a Slave, and Four Years in the White House*

My life has been an eventful one. I was born a slave—was the child of slave parents—therefore I came upon the earth free in God-like thought, but fettered in action. (1)

WHEN I FIRST ENCOUNTERED Elizabeth Keckley and her unusual narrative, *Behind the Scenes: Or, Thirty Years a Slave, and Four Years in the White House*, almost thirty years ago, I wondered about the young Keckley depicted with her sewing stool, her hair properly managed by a bun: Why was her story so different from those of other formerly enslaved writers?[1] What were the circumstances that almost erased her and her memories from our cultural and literary histories? I wondered if she saw herself as writing herself into our history while writing about a nation on the precipice of race rights and cultural change. Or, if she knew that the textile art that she created would both outlive her and outlast the legacies of the women for whom she created. What was it about her enslavement in North Carolina that gave her the courage to fight back? And why, knowing as she must have known about the fickle bonds of friendship across racial lines, did she leave her thriving business to attempt to salvage Mary Todd Lincoln's financial and public reputation?[2] I have lived with her memories, haunted by her indomitable courage, for years, having first discussed the possibility of producing a Keckley reader in 2012. As a scholar of African American literature and, like Keckley, a creative spirit, I could not give up on this project any more than Keckley gave up in her life. As the editor of *The Elizabeth Keckley Reader* series, I have had the wonderful opportunity to revisit those questions that were seminal to my understanding of the importance of Keckley and her narrative so many years ago. This project is, so to speak, a visitation of the spirit of Elizabeth Keckley that "rebelled against the unjustness" of a country disinclined to recognize her value (35). I have one lofty ambition: to claim Keckley's place as the cultural critic, artist, and black feminist that she was. This ambition is best realized in examining the intertwined narratives of her life and that of the United States in the midst of transition. Indeed, one of the many gifts Keckley bequeaths us in *Behind the Scenes* is the art of writing of the self and of the nation, of their common struggles to survive enslavement, Reconstruction, and the creation of a new cultural space in which Keckley not only had a place, but had standing.

The fact that she was able to publish *Behind the Scenes* in 1868 is, in itself, a formidable accomplishment. Perhaps the answers to many of the questions that I pose here are traceable if we look at the narrative from the vantage point from which Keckley wrote it: an autobiography written by a free woman published only three years after slavery ended in the United States. Clearly, *Behind the Scenes* operates, at least in part, as a narrative of enslavement, as the opening lines of the text remind the reader. Like other formerly enslaved writers, Keckley emphasizes the hardships she endured before she bought her freedom. We know that she worked from the time she was four. Like her mother before her, Keckley was sexually assaulted during her enslavement. These scenes of slavery are familiar; however, in reading *Behind the Scenes* as a slave narrative, we must also note what is most uncommon about this telling autobiography.

Many aspects of *Behind the Scenes* make it clear that Keckley was asserting her power to write as a free woman. Unlike most narratives of enslavement, *Behind the Scenes* is not prefaced by a white patron whose purpose would have been to authenticate the text. For example, Douglass's first autobiography, *Narrative of the Life of Frederick Douglass* (1845), was authenticated by William Lloyd Garrison, who was both his friend and the architect of his early antislavery public persona. Lydia Maria Child, the white authenticator of Harriet Jacobs's *Incidents in the Life of a Slave Girl* (1861), provides the documentation necessary for the publication of Jacobs's text, validating her challenge to white patriarchy and civility that she shares in the text. Notably, Child was the second choice to authenticate and edit Jacobs's text; Jacobs had originally sought the assistance of Harriet Beecher Stowe, author of the bestselling fictionalized slave narrative, *Uncle Tom's Cabin* (1852), which had catapulted Stowe to instant fame. Stowe declined, instead suggesting that Jacobs's autobiography would be best chronicled as a part of *A Key to Uncle Tom's Cabin* (Yellin 121). In addition to suggesting that Jacobs's lived experience as an enslaved woman was—at best—a subtext to her fictionalized plantation characters, Stowe "outed" Jacobs as an escaped slave, after the Fugitive Slave Act of 1850 was passed, by writing to her employer to verify the details of Jacobs's life, a move that heightened Jacobs's precarious life as an escaped slave, even among those who had declared themselves to be abolitionists (Yellin 121).

Although Keckley decidedly refused to escape enslavement, she was in good company with other black abolitionists, both enslaved and free. As she reveals in *Behind the Scenes*, she had a lengthy correspondence with Frederick Douglass. During her life as a fugitive slave, Jacobs worked as a domestic for the family of Nathaniel P. Willis, brother of one of Mary Todd Lincoln's close friends, Fanny Fern neé Sarah Parton Willis (Sayre 278). As importantly, both Keckley and Jacobs lived in Washington, DC, at the same time. In fact, their eulogies were both delivered by Rev. Francis Grimké who described them as his personal friends. Nell Painter, author of *Sojourner Truth: A Life, a Symbol*, notes conclusively that Keckley also knew the famous abolitionist Sojourner Truth. Truth approached Keckley to gain her an audience with President Lincoln in 1864 (Painter 204). However, unlike Truth, whose escape from enslavement in 1826 preceded her rise as an advocate for women's rights and the rights of African Americans, or Jacobs, who hid in a garret for seven years before she could escape to a free state, or Douglass, whose freedom was purchased by his abolitionist friends, or even William and Ellen Craft, who escaped enslavement with Ellen disguised as her husband's master, Keckley purchased her own freedom.

As previously noted, Keckley as author is distinct from her fellow formerly enslaved peers who worked with prominent whites to validate and authenticate their narratives. Keckley writes her own preface, certainly a bold act for a woman but also exceedingly rare for a formerly enslaved woman. Publishing *Behind the Scenes* only seven years after *Incidents in the Life of a Slave Girl*, Keckley not only prefaces her own work, she does so as an advocate for Mary Todd Lincoln. Crossing the racial dividing lines of the abolitionist movement and of the slave narrative, Keckley authenticates her own right to write herself into the history of the nation and positions herself to speak on behalf of a white woman who, despite her standing as the widow of the president, proves to have no voice of her own.

Yet Keckley does have a voice as well as a presence that is discernable even from her appearance. A later portrait of Keckley, taken after her hair has turned gray and been freed from the severity of her bun, suggests that she has led an accomplished life, one that might have fallen into obscurity without the efforts to reclaim her memory by her friend and eulogist Rev. Francis Grimké, as well as by Frances Smith Foster, William Andrews, and Jennifer Fleischner, author of *Mrs. Lincoln and Mrs. Keckly*, in which she reclaims the original spelling of her name.

Elizabeth Keckley's life story would have captured the attention of American society much sooner had it not been a story about a black woman who rose to prominence as the country navigated its ravaging, political journey on its way to the Civil War. Born in Dinwiddie Court-house, Virginia, in February of 1818, she was the daughter of Agnes Hobbs, an enslaved woman who was literate, and Armistead Burwell, her white slave "master" (Fleischner 29). Keckley indicates that she was unaware that Burwell was her father until her mother told her as she lay dying in 1857. In the opening lines of the narrative, Keckley notes that she was the "child of slaves," a tribute to her mother and her mother's husband, George Hobbs, who raised her as his child until he was forced to move away when his owner relocated (Keckley 17). As importantly, we learn in these opening lines that Keckley is aware of the freedom that was conferred with her humanity. This statement gives her readers insight into her beliefs as a woman who embraced racial and gender equality, sentiments she expresses early in her autobiography in her insistence that she "... came upon the earth free in God-like thought" (18). Her beliefs are evident in the unique insights she shares in *Behind the Scenes*. Her life's story is, indeed, extraordinary even if we set aside the incredible, true story of her rise from slavery to the inner circle of the Lincoln White House.

It is, therefore, noteworthy that Keckley's life and work have been so relentlessly overlooked in both the critical and cultural canons of American literature and history. Over a century and a half before the Obamas moved into the White House as America's First Family, Keckley frequently visited and worked in the Lincoln White House as modiste and paid employee; she was likely the first person of African descent to be employed in the White House who was neither enslaved nor a house servant (Washington 225). Keckley had a personal relationship with both Abraham Lincoln and Mary Todd Lincoln. As the confidante of Todd Lincoln, she worked hard to convince the American public of Todd Lincoln's integrity after the president's assassination. In fact, her relationship with Todd Lincoln seems to be the most interesting aspect of her life, if we were to review the number of books that have been written exploring their friendship. As compelling as this aspect of her life's story is, Keckley is much more than a footnote to the history of Todd Lincoln. She traveled widely as both an enslaved woman and a free woman, living in the old slaveocracy of Virginia; then in the less radical, but soon-to-be-rebel, state of North Carolina; in the frontier state of Missouri in the city of St. Louis, a place known for its embrace of nineteenth-century Spiritualism; in Ohio—one of the destination states of the Underground Railroad; and in the highly political cities of Baltimore, Philadelphia, and Washington, DC.

Politically and socially astute, Keckley benefitted from the relationships she had with wealthy whites during her enslavement in Hillsborough, as she worked and sought her freedom in St. Louis, and in her relationships in Washington. In addition to working with the Lincolns, she was the seamstress for Jefferson and Varina Davis; Davis was wearing one of the chintz wrappers that she made for Mrs. Davis when he was captured (Keckley 74). In fact, Keckley's narrative is one of only a few extant texts that presents the cultural and visual histories of slavery, the Civil War, and African Americana immediately post-slavery.[3] The fact that *Behind the Scenes* has been so understudied as a critically important text is both ironic and implausible given the circumstances of her life.

Keckley, however, was well aware of the ironies of this system; she expressed both her understanding of it and her critique of it throughout *Behind the Scenes*. She sets the stage for this critique in the preface of her narrative, clearly articulating the reason that the question of slavery—and, by extension, enslaved people—continued to vex the American consciousness in her lifetime:[4]

> An act may be wrong, but unless the ruling power recognizes the wrong, it is useless to hope for a correction of it. Principles may be right, but they are not established within an hour. The masses are slow to reason, and each principle, to acquire moral force, must come to us from the fire of the crucible; the fire may inflict unjust punishment, but then it purifies and renders stronger the principle, not in itself, but in the eyes of those who arrogate judgment to themselves. When the war of the Revolution established the independence of the American colonies, an evil was perpetuated, slavery was more firmly established; and since the evil had been planted, it must pass through certain stages before it could be eradicated. (xiii–xiv)

Keckley lived a life of defiance in an America shaped by slavery, by nineteenth-century limits on the freedom of women, by the gendered hierarchies of power, and by racist constructions of African Americans. Simply put, Elizabeth Keckley challenged all of these concepts, even when she was legally defined as property, and created alliances with the most politically and socially powerful people of her era.

Close readers of her autobiography will note that she does not give the date of her birth. As Frederick Douglass notes in his *Narrative of the Life of Frederick Douglass* (1845), being enslaved often meant being denied the privilege of even knowing your date of birth (Douglass 1). While her date of birth is recognized as 1818, the circumstances of her birth mean that we can only estimate the actual date. Because she was enslaved, those who knew her best had some difficulty in setting her date of birth. Although, as I noted earlier, Keckley was born in 1818, Rev. Francis Grimké in his eulogy speculates that she was born in 1825 or 1827. Thus, readers shall note some temporal shifts in this volume's references to her age at specific moments in her history and Keckley's own awareness of her age. Perhaps Douglass articulates this best when he writes, "I do not remember to have ever met a slave who could tell of his birthday" (1). Like Grimké, Douglass, and millions of other enslaved people, Keckley was mixed raced; however, in the America in which she lived, the race of her father was neither legally nor socially relevant. It had, in fact, been legally irrelevant since the passage of a Virginia statute in 1662 that decreed that children would inherit the enslaved status of their mothers, a legal status that eventually applied to all slaveholding states (Hening 170). According to both law and custom, Keckley's mother's enslavement determined Keckley's own status as chattel. Within the system of slavery, Virginia was known as a breeding state, a fact that meant that it was highly profitable for white slaveholders to engage in race rape of enslaved women. Moreover, despite the popular assumptions that being of mixed race as well as being enslaved as a domestic worker offered Keckley protection, her narrative lays bare the truth that neither of these identities protected her nor the vast majority of those enslaved under similar circumstances. Keckley confirms this fact in this inclusion of an early memory of being beaten while serving in the Burwell household:

> Mrs. Burwell gave birth to a daughter, a sweet, black-eyed baby, my earliest and fondest pet. To take care of this baby was my first duty. True, I was but a child myself—only four years old—but then I had been raised in a hardy school—had been taught to rely upon myself, and to prepare myself to render assistance to others. The lesson was not a bitter one, for I was too young to indulge in philosophy, and the precepts that I then treasured and practiced I believe developed those principles of character which have enabled me to triumph over so many difficulties. Notwithstanding all the wrongs that slavery heaped upon me, I can bless it for one thing—youth's important lesson of self-reliance. The baby was named Elizabeth, and it was pleasant to me to be assigned a duty in connection with it, for the discharge of that duty transferred me from the rude cabin to the household of my master. My simple attire was a short dress and a little white apron. My old mistress encouraged me in rocking the cradle, by telling me that if I would watch over the baby well, keep the flies out of its face, and not let it cry, I should be its little maid. This was a golden promise, and I required no better inducement for the faithful performance of my task. I began to rock the cradle most industriously, when lo! out pitched little pet on the floor. I instantly cried out, "Oh! the baby is on the floor;" and, not knowing what to do, I seized the fire-shovel in my perplexity, and was trying to shovel up my tender charge, when my mistress called to me to let the child alone, and then ordered that I be taken out and lashed for my carelessness. The blows were not admin-

istered with a light hand, I assure you, and doubtless the severity of the lashing has made me remember the incident so well. This was the first time I was punished in this cruel way, but not the last. (19–21)

Notwithstanding that her mother had a child by her "master," that she was that child, that she was working in the "big house," that she was but a child herself, Keckley's remembrance sheds light on the perilous life of enslaved African Americans that had nearly been lost given the twentieth-century revisionist history that suggests that "house" servants always sympathized with their "masters."

Unfortunately for Keckley, but fortunate for the education of her readers, her memories fill the gaps of our cultural and national memories. The circumstances of her enslavement took Keckley from Virginia to Hillsborough, North Carolina, when she was eighteen, just a few years beyond the age Harriet Jacobs indicates that an enslaved girl learns "... to tremble when she hears her master's footfall" because of the sexual abuse that the enterprise of slavery depended upon to exist" (45). Her life in Hillsborough was tumultuous at best; Keckley's remembrances of that time include being asked to serve as a bride's maid for several of Hillsborough's elite young ladies and, on the other end of the spectrum, being raped and beaten. She was raped repeatedly over a four-year period when she was in the care of her then "master"—her half-brother Robert Burwell—who did nothing to stop the abuse. Since any child she bore would become the property of the Burwell family, there was little motivation for the Burwells to intercede. We might credit Burwell for refusing to sexually assault his half-sister, unlike many of the sexual predators of the system of slavery. We might also recognize—without excusing his behavior—the impact of his personal exposure to slavery in Virginia, where the dependence on breeding replaced large-scale agricultural production due to the infertility of the soil (Smithers 28). As a pastor, Burwell perhaps lacked the social clout in which to intervene in the sexual assault of Keckley by Alexander Kirkland, a member of the Hillsborough gentry. Standing 6'8", Kirkland was not a man whom Keckley could have easily defended herself against. However, Keckley refused to allow this to make her a victim. To the contrary, she gave her son his enslaved grandfather's first name, George, and acknowledged that her son later used Kirkland as his surname, an act made all the more bold because her child's father was not his "master." It is through her remembrances of Hillsborough that we learn that Keckley, unlike the female slave narrators whose stories have dominated our understanding of enslaved women, refused to apologize for being raped, thereby rejecting the blame and the nineteenth-century sensibilities that Jacobs could not avoid in *Incidents in the Life of a Slave Girl*.

In addition to refusing to accept the blame for the state-sanctioned sexual victimization that she endured, Keckley also fought back against the physical abuse that was the bedrock of the institution of slavery. In Hillsborough, Robert's wife accused her of being too proud, a quality that her slave mistress wanted beaten out of her. Subsequently, the Burwells hired a member of Robert's church, the village schoolmaster, Mr. Bingham, whom Keckley refers to as "a hard, cruel man" (32). Keckley refused to succumb willingly to the beatings he administered, fighting back, beaten and bloody, she resisted, remaining a "proud, rebellious spirit" until Bingham refused to beat her again (38). Keckley describes this experience in one of my favorite passages from *Behind the Scenes* in which she bests both Bingham and the Burwells, keeping her pride intact:

> On Friday following the Saturday on which I was so savagely beaten, Mr. Bingham again directed me come to his study. I went, but with the determination to offer resistance should he attempt to flog me again. On entering the room I found him prepared with a new rope and a new cowhide. I told him that I was ready to die, but that he could not conquer me. In struggling with him I bit his finger severely, when he seized a heavy stick and beat me with it in a shameful manner. Again I went home sore and bleeding, but with pride as strong and defiant as ever. The following Thursday Mr. Bingham again tried to conquer me, but in vain. We struggled, and he struck me many savage blows. As I stood bleeding before him, nearly exhausted with his efforts, he burst into tears, and declared that it would be a sin to beat me any more. My suffering at last subdued his hard heart; he asked my forgiveness, and afterwards was an altered man. He was never known to strike one of his servants from that day forward. Mr. Burwell, he who preached the love of Heaven, who glorified the precepts and examples of Christ, who expounded the Holy Scriptures Sabbath after Sabbath from the pulpit, when Mr. Bingham refused to whip me any more, was urged by his wife to punish me himself. One morning he went to the wood-pile, took an oak broom, cut the handle off, and with this heavy handle attempted to conquer me. I fought him,

but he proved the strongest. At the sight of my bleeding form, his wife fell upon her knees and begged him to desist. My distress even touched her cold, jealous heart. (36–38)

Keckley's willingness to fight in her own defense rejects the limits of female power that dominated the construction of womanhood in the nineteenth century. In so doing, she also utilizes a strategy that many male slave narrators used in their narratives of freedom, physically resisting slavery and the violence that was used to perpetuate it.

After the birth of her son, Keckley returned to the older Burwells' home in Virginia, leaving only when she accompanied another Burwell offspring to St. Louis, Missouri. While living in St. Louis with Anne Burwell Garland, her "mistress" and half-sister, Keckley made her living as a seamstress, hiring herself out to protect her aging mother from being leased to support the family. The Garland family struggled financially; Anne's husband, Hugh Garland, could not adequately support the family despite his work as a writer and an attorney. His most high-profile case was also at the center of the slaveocracy; he was an attorney for John F.A. Sandford, the plaintiff in the *Dred Scott* case, who was being sued by Scott and his wife, Harriet. However, the Garland family was perpetually in debt, living off the provisions of the enslaved members of the household and most particularly off the money Keckley made as a seamstress. Thus, Keckley reveals that,

> The best ladies in St. Louis were my patrons, and when my reputation was once established I never lacked for orders. With my needle I kept bread in the mouths of seventeen persons for two years and five months. While I was working so hard that others might live in comparative comfort, and move in those circles of society to which their birth gave them entrance, the thought often occurred to me whether I was really worth my salt or not; and then perhaps the lips curled with a bitter sneer. (46)

Aware of both her plight as an enslaved woman and her worth as a seamstress, Keckley managed to work enough to support herself, her son, the members of the Garland family, and the other enslaved members of their household. Her work in St. Louis, however, also provided Keckley with access to the city's elite.

Keckley's life in St. Louis provided the foundation for her life as a free, professional woman; in essence, the skills she used and connections she forged in St. Louis made it possible for her to be both free and financially secure. There, it is likely that she was acquainted with Patsy Meachum, a free woman making her living as a mantua-maker; Meachum and Keckley both appear on the 1841–1859 List of Free Negroes living in St. Louis (Frazier 78–79). She also worked with wealthy white women who could not only afford to hire her, but who also became instrumental in assisting her to become free. Thinking about her son's possibilities in life as a free person, Keckley eventually pressed Garland to set a price for her and her son's freedom, refusing to make an easy escape across the river to Illinois—a decision that was doubtless affected by the Fugitive Slave Law. After Garland died, she was allowed to purchase her freedom during the settlement of his estate. Keckley purchased her and her son's freedom in 1855 for $1,200, using money borrowed from her clients, members of the upper echelon of St. Louis society—many of whom may have been adherents of Spiritualist philosophy that was growing robustly in St. Louis. Continuing to work as a free woman, Keckley made enough money to support herself and her son and pay back her patrons in five years. Placed in context, this is certainly extraordinary: The $1,200 she paid for her freedom is the equivalent of $31,851.67 in 2015 currency. It is a sobering reminder of how much Keckley was valued while she was enslaved and an even more cogent reminder of her determination to be free.

As a free woman, Keckley relocated to Baltimore and Washington, DC, where she became the seamstress for the nation's most renowned families, members of the country's ruling elite. While there, she joined the political efforts to assist newly freed African Americans who faced racism and poverty in the North and the South. In 1862, she founded the Contraband Relief Organization, noting that,

> If the white people can give festivals to raise funds for the relief of suffering soldiers, why should not the well-to-do colored people go to work to do something for the benefit of the suffering blacks? I could not rest. The thought was ever present with me, and the next Sunday I made a suggestion in the colored church, that a society of colored people be formed to labor for the benefit of the unfortunate freedmen. The idea proved popular, and in two weeks "the Contraband Relief Association" was organized, with forty working members. (113–14)

Keckley's organization was funded by leading abolitionists, members of faith communities, and her wealthy clientele. In keeping with her ability to link her connections across racial lines, Keckley raised funds from African American religious leaders in Boston, New York—most notably Henry Highland Garnet—and Washington, DC. Leading abolitionists, including Douglass, contributed financially to the cause and raised awareness for the plight of newly free people though their lectures. Keckley also notes that she raised "... quite a sum of money among the dining-room waiters" (115). The fundraising effort was also international: Keckley received "a large quantity of stores" from England (116). Perhaps most notably, Abraham and Mary Todd Lincoln "made frequent contributions" (116).

Interestingly, it is Keckley's relationship with the former First Lady that made her narrative both sensational and doomed it to oblivion. Her friendship with Mary Todd Lincoln has captured a great deal of attention, effectively popularized by what is seen as an unlikely union. However, their relationship should not seem surprising. In America's peculiar racial history, close relationships across racial lines are often fetishized as being unusual. Given the particularly close proximity of the enslaved and the free, the abolitionists and free blacks, their relationship was not as unusual as it might seem to be in the contemporary period. Notably, Keckley was not the first formerly enslaved person to have a close personal relationship with a sitting president, nor was she the first to expose details of their private lives. In 1865, just three years before Keckley published *Behind the Scenes,* Paul Jennings, formerly enslaved in the Madison White House, published *A Colored Man's Reminiscences of James Madison*, in which he publically acknowledges the poverty of former First Lady, Dolley Madison, who had held over a hundred enslaved people in bondage when she came to the White House (Jennings 14–15). However, Keckley and Jennings, who was later purchased and freed by Daniel Webster, both had the invaluable tool of literacy that enabled them to leave a record of these relationships and their accomplishments. Here, too, is another notable fact about Keckley's life. She represents the second generation of literate enslaved people in her family. Both her mother and her enslaved father could read and write. Their letters, which she includes in *Behind the Scenes*, testify to their literacy during a time when it was illegal to teach an enslaved person how to read or write. The epistolary form is important throughout the narrative, especially in the letters Todd Lincoln wrote to Keckley which were included in *Behind the Scenes*, despite the fact that Keckley indicated that she was not aware that they would be.

Clearly, Keckley and Todd Lincoln had a great deal in common. They were born the same year. Fleischner and others have rightly argued that Todd Lincoln's history of being raised by enslaved African American women following the death of her mother likely contributed to the bond she shared with Keckley (Fleischner 6). Keckley and Todd Lincoln shared an unenviable history of having survived the deaths of their sons. Todd Lincoln had already lost one son before coming to the White House. Keckley's son, George, had left Wilberforce University and joined the Union Army as a white man near the outset of the Civil War. He was killed during the Battle of Wilson's Creek in Missouri, the second major battle of the conflict, on August 10, 1861, a few months after Keckley started to work with Todd Lincoln. It was Keckley that Todd Lincoln called to the White House as her son Willie lay dying. Keckley describes the depths of their shared grief, situating herself as a member of the Lincoln mourners in the process:

> I was worn out with watching, and was not in the room when Willie died, but was immediately sent for. I assisted in washing him and dressing him, and then laid him on the bed, when Mr. Lincoln came in. I never saw a man so bowed down with grief. He came to the bed, lifted the cover from the face of his child, gazed at it long and earnestly, murmuring, "My poor boy, he was too good for this earth. God has called him home. I know that he is much better off in heaven, but then we loved him so. It is hard, hard to have him die!" . . . I did not dream that his rugged nature could be so moved. I shall never forget those solemn moments—genius and greatness weeping over love's idol lost. There is a grandeur as well as a simplicity about the picture that will never fade. With me it is immortal—I really believe that I shall carry it with me across the dark, mysterious river of death. . . . Mrs. Lincoln was so completely overwhelmed with sorrow that she did not attend the funeral. Willie was laid to rest in the cemetery, and the White House was draped in mourning. Black crape everywhere met the eye, contrasting strangely with the gay and brilliant colors of a few days before. Party dresses were laid aside, and every one who crossed the threshold of the Presidential mansion spoke in subdued tones when they thought of the sweet boy at rest— . . . Previous to this

I had lost my son. Leaving Wilberforce, he went to the battle-field with the three months troops, and was killed in Missouri—found his grave on the battle-field where the gallant General Lyon fell. It was a sad blow to me, and the kind womanly letter that Mrs. Lincoln wrote to me when she heard of my bereavement was full of golden words of comfort. (103–05)

It is noteworthy that Keckley's own grief was almost subsumed in the Lincolns' grieving process. However, it was highly unlikely that Keckley would have had space to grieve openly. Her son had enlisted in the army as a white man. He died at a highly charged moment in the war when the backlash against blacks in both the North and the South was particularly heightened. As Keckley recounts in the words of Varina Davis, "when the war breaks out, the colored people will suffer in the North. The Northern people will look upon them as the cause of the war, and I fear, in their exasperation, will be inclined to treat you harshly" (71). Perhaps she learned an early lesson when her mother was told to stop the "nonsense" and "putting on airs" as she was grieving the permanent separation from her husband (24). Or, closer still, I imagine that she learned a great deal about protecting her own emotions during her life in Hillsborough when she truly learned what it was like to be enslaved. As a businesswoman dependent upon her relationship with prominent, politically involved women, there was little space for her to grieve publicly, even in 1868.

When she published her autobiography with a title befitting the complexities of her life—*Behind the Scenes* by Elizabeth Keckley, *Formerly a Slave, But More Recently Modiste, and Friend to Mrs. Abraham Lincoln, or, Thirty Years a Slave, and Four Years in the White House*—she reveals not only the details of her upwardly mobile life, but also the downward trajectory of Todd Lincoln's life. The backlash from this publication cost Keckley her thriving business in Washington. Keckley sold many of the items of Abraham Lincoln's clothing—a collection that she had cherished—in 1890 clearing $250, in sharp contrast to Todd Lincoln's failed attempt to sell her own clothing in 1867. Keckley was appointed to the faculty of Wilberforce University in 1892, serving as the chair of the department of Sewing and Domestic Arts, a position that enabled her to have the public platform from which to curate the 1893 fashion exhibit for the Chicago World's Fair. Keckley had had a long-standing relationship with the university. As previously mentioned, her son, George, had attended the university before joining the army in 1861. In 1868, Keckley donated some of her collection of Abraham Lincoln's clothing—given to her by Todd Lincoln—as a part of the fundraising effort to rebuild the historically black college after it burned to the ground the same night that Lincoln was killed. Over seventy years old at the time she was appointed to the position at Wilberforce, she taught there only briefly before suffering a stroke shortly after the exhibition.

In ill health, she returned to Washington, moving to the Home of the National Association of Colored Women and Children (also known as the National Home for Destitute Colored Women and Children), a charity home that was supported by the very organization she had started decades earlier to assist newly freed African Americans in their movement toward personal and financial freedom. Elizabeth Keckley died on Sunday, May 26, 1907, after having "... a most eventful and checkered career" at the home where "she was pleasantly situated, surrounded by those who tenderly cared for her," surviving her son by over forty years, her last "master" by over forty years, and all but one of the Lincolns (Grimké 7).

Yet, when she sat "toiling by day with my needle, and writing by night, in the plain little room on the fourth floor of No. 14 Carroll Place" Keckley must have been aware that she was writing something revolutionary (330). As the title suggests, Keckley takes her readers on an unlikely, but true, journey of her experiences as both an enslaved woman and insider in the Lincoln White House. Her narrative is quite unusual in its form and its function. Keckley's work is situated in both enslavement and in freedom, a freedom in which she asserts her own right to speak while escaping nineteenth-century American biopower, the social mechanism that attempted to limit outcomes of her life by virtue of her having been born a black woman in an America shaped by divides between slave and free, abolitionists and proslavery advocates, slave states and emancipated spaces. Situated at the cultural nexus of the American Dream and the realities of racism, sexism, and the Civil War, Elizabeth Keckley's body, history, and agency enable her to the "isms" that should have silenced her completely. The fact that she was able to write *Behind the Scenes* cataloging the unique circumstances of her life, simply put, suggests that Keckley nearly managed to escape American biopower and its racism and sexism as well as its religiosity, enacting her own power in ways that had not previously been seen in print.

One of the most immediate signs of Keckley's escape from biopower lies in her insistence to speak on her own behalf. As a black woman, Keckley should have been assured of having no voice. When she published *Behind the Scenes,* America was in the midst of dual racial and political crises, only two years after the Ku Klux Klan had been formed to prevent black Americans from voting. *Behind the Scenes* was also published against the backdrop of the racist political policies of President Andrew Johnson who, having survived an impeachment attempt by only one vote, was deeply embroiled in his attempt to pit African Americans and Native Americans against each other to eliminate both "problems," and at a time when the Southern states were agitating for states' rights in the aftermath of the Civil War. Johnson—whom Keckley could not have seen as a fitting successor to Abraham Lincoln—had vetoed the Civil Rights Act of 1866, the first federal law that sought to protect the rights of African Americans, though congress overrode his attempt to limit the rights of America's newly recognized free citizens. That year also marked the readmission of six Southern states, including North Carolina where Keckley had once been enslaved, back into the union. The same year, Georgia expelled all African American legislators, and Washington, Louisiana, was the scene of the Opelousas Massacre where several hundred African Americans were killed as they attempted to participate in the local Democratic Party. Clearly, these were perilous times; yet, these were also prosperous times for Elizabeth Keckley who operated her own business and who had lived a life in extremes: in the slave household and in the White House, as a business owner and a relief recipient, and as a free woman who claimed both her "white and black family" (41). Hers was not the voice that could effectively historicize this pivotal moment while the American reading public was still reeling from the vestiges of the war and still looking for a way to balance the North and the South in the "Union."

Despite all of this, Keckley focused on her own humanity in a world gone suddenly awry. Keckley's investment in her worth as a human being is due, at least in part, to her embrace of nineteenth-century Spiritualism. Both Keckley and Todd Lincoln were interested in the spiritual realm, in part to connect with their children, the greatest losses of their lives. A number of séances were held in the Lincoln White House (Fleischner 259; Lander 239). Of greater significance is the fact that Spiritualism was less a religion than it was a collective belief in the inherent worth and equality of all human beings. Spiritualists eschewed cultural notions of white supremacy, a concept that was as much a part of the "free North" as the former "slave South" in the period leading up to, during, and after the Civil War. When Keckley lived in St. Louis as a free woman, for instance, she—like all free African Americans—was legally bound to pay for a license in order to live and work legally in the city. This instance is only one of the impacts of the Black Codes, laws passed in every Southern state and many free states that limited the rights of African Americans. The laws were designed to keep free African Americans as a separate, racially marked class of citizens who could easily lose their right to exist in that space. Keckley provides a telling example of these limitations in her description of the excursion she took with the Lincolns to Richmond after the Union Army recaptured it:

> The Presidential party were all curiosity on entering Richmond. They drove about the streets of the city, and examined every object of interest. The Capitol presented a desolate appearance—desks broken, and papers scattered promiscuously in the hurried flight of the Confederate Congress. I picked up a number of papers, and, by curious coincidence, the resolution prohibiting all free colored people from entering the State of Virginia. In the Senate chamber I sat in the chair that Jefferson Davis sometimes occupied; also in the chair of the Vice-President, Alexander H. Stephens. We paid a visit to the mansion occupied by Mr. Davis and family during the war, and the ladies who were in charge of it scowled darkly upon our party as we passed through and inspected the different rooms. After a delightful visit we returned to City Point. (166–67)

In addition to revealing the extent to which state laws prohibited even the presence of free blacks, Keckley suggests that she knew—and reveled in the fact that—her presence there would be seen as racially transgressive.

Clearly, however, nineteenth-century Spiritualists embraced the transgressive. In fact, many of the leading antislavery activists, including William Lloyd Garrison, Amy Post, Harriet Beecher Stowe, Sojourner Truth, and Harriet Wilson (author of *Our Nig: or, Sketches from the Life of a Free Black*), were aligned with the Spiritualist movement (Garrison 188; Lehman 126; Koester 294; Braude, *Radical Changes*, 27, 29; Smith McKoy). It would have been impossible for Keckley to have avoided the movement during her years in St. Louis where the Spiritualist periodical, *Light from the Spirit World*, was published from 1852 to 1853 representing the large Spiritualist presence in the city (Braude, "News from the Spirit World," 422). In embedding her autobiography with references to "spirit"—which she does eleven times—Keckley signals the assertion of her human and civil rights. The Spiritualist movement also supported the rights of women, a passion that she expresses in *Behind the Scenes* as fully as she advocates for racial rights. Note that Keckley's embrace of Spiritualism does not detract from her commitment to the Fifteenth Street Presbyterian Church; African Americans regularly practiced syncretic belief systems that allowed them to recognize both spiritual rituals and the rigors of organized religion. Rather, Spiritualism provided Keckley with political support and a platform for her advocacy for the rights of black women.

*Behind the Scenes*, then, is a complex cultural, historical, and political work, one that should have enjoyed broader critical and cultural exploration. Not surprisingly, Keckley begins her narrative with a suggestion that hers is a story representative of the newly united America, noting, "My life, so full of romance, may sound like a dream to the matter-of-fact reader, nevertheless everything I have written is strictly true" (xi). Keckley's is a classic American story, a more noteworthy representation of the elusive American Dream than Horatio Alger's novel *Ragged Dick*, a bestselling rags-to-riches story in which the protagonist rises from a bootblack to a member of the middle class, published the same year as Keckley's *Behind the Scenes*. In contrast to the American public's hunger for a story about the upward mobility of Alger's Dick, a white boy raised in relentless poverty, Keckley's made-in-America story of a black girl who rose from enslavement to middle-class businesswoman was vilified. The public denunciations of Todd Lincoln's spending habits that had dominated her public image were replaced with denunciations of Keckley for daring to reveal the intimate thoughts of the former First Lady, lifted directly from the numerous letters she wrote to Keckley. According to Keckley, James Redpath, the editor of *Behind the Scenes,* used the letters without Keckley's permission despite the fact that his public work as an abolitionist should have meant that he would have respected her wishes. The Lincolns' only surviving son, Robert, who knew enough about his mother's emotional and financial hardships to have her involuntarily committed to an insane asylum in a highly publicized trial in 1875 just seven years after *Behind the Scenes* was published, convinced the publisher to have all of the copies of the book pulled (Foster 128–29). Keckley's attempt to salvage Todd Lincoln's reputation in *Behind the*

*Scenes*, in which she writes that her "intentions were good" and that "... she should be judged more kindly than she has been" seemingly failed (xiv).

Further, Keckley and her autobiography were caricatured in a satire entitled *Behind the Seams, by a Nigger Woman, Who Took in Work from Mrs. Lincoln and Mrs. Davis* with a preface signed with an *X* for Betsey Kickley (see Ottolengul). As late as 1935, David Rankin Barbee, a journalist, declared that she had not even existed. However, in keeping with his commitment to memory, Grimké responded noting that,

> No one who ever saw her, or had any contact with her, even casually would ever be likely to forget her. She was striking in appearance and of most pleasing personality.... I think of her now, as I used to see her on the sabbath mornings, in the old church edifice [on] 15$^{th}$ Street between I and K streets, as she used to come up the aisle, the very personification of grace and dignity, as she moved towards her pew. Often was heard: "Here comes Madam Keckley. All eyes were on her." (Grimké, 1935)

Long after the copies of *Behind the Scenes* were censored by the political power of Robert Lincoln, Elizabeth Keckley refuses to be forgotten. In fact, *Behind the Scenes* enjoys the distinction of having been rediscovered.

Elizabeth Keckley, simply put, resists erasure. Even her artistry lingers: One of the dresses she designed for Todd Lincoln is part of the Smithsonian's National Museum of American History Museum; the Kent State University Museum houses a quilt that she made from scraps of Todd Lincoln's dresses; the site of her enslavement in North Carolina is held as a historic site, attesting to her presence at the Burwell School, ensconced in the inseparable histories of black and white Hillsborough.

It has been my delightful task as the editor of this collection to reclaim and to resituate Keckley and her work as the true historian that she was, despite Todd Lincoln's attempt to disparage her work by dubbing her the "colored historian" (Young 143). This collection is a dedication to the unwavering strength and determination she embodied throughout her life. In *The Elizabeth Keckley Reader*, the scholars who make this volume possible remember her not as a woman who suffered the grief of losing her famous friend but rather as a woman who rose from the cultural, racial, political, and gendered chaos of American enslavement and lived a truly determined and remarkable life.

**NOTES**

1. Throughout this introduction, I have chosen to include the second "e" in the spelling of Keckley's name because her primary text was published with this spelling. As readers will note, many of the texts included in *The Elizabeth Keckley Reader, Volume One* reference her last name as Keckly in keeping with Jennifer Fleischner's research.

2. From this point in the introduction, I refer to Mary Todd Lincoln as "Todd Lincoln" in order to identify her distinctly from her husband, whom I refer to often as "Lincoln." It is useful to note that Mary Todd Lincoln, as was customary in her time, used only the last name of Lincoln in her lifetime.

3. Thanks to Aisha Francis, whose essay "Stepping Beyond the Formal Lines: Elizabeth Keckley, Gertrude Mossell and the Cost of Transgression" is included in this collection, for reminding me about the usefulness of the term, African Americana.

4. Although explorations of slavery use the word "slave" to describe those who lived in, struggled in, and survived forced servitude in America, I use the term "enslaved" to acknowledge the humanity of those held in the American system of slavery in which people of African descent were intended to be legally bound in servitude for life.

**WORKS CITED**

Alger, Horatio. *Ragged Dick* (1868). Project Gutenberg. Web. 2 July 2015. http://www.gutenberg.org/cache/epub/5348/pg5348-images.html.

Braude, Ann. "News from the Spirit World: A Checklist of American Spiritualist Periodicals, 1847–1900." Web. 28 August 2015. http://www.americanantiquarian.org/proceedings/44539462.pdf.

———. *Radical Spirits: Spiritualism and Women's Rights in Nineteenth-century America*. Bloomington: Indiana University Press, 2001. Print.

*The Bureau of Labor Statistics CPI Inflation Calculator*. Web. 2 August 2015. http://www.bls.gov/data/inflation_calculator.htm.

Craft, William and Ellen. *Running a Thousand Miles for Freedom*. Athens: University of Georgia Press, 1999.

Douglass, Frederick. *Narrative of the Life of Frederick Douglass*. Web. 15 July 2015. http://docsouth.unc.edu/neh/douglass/douglass.html.

Fleischner, Jennifer. *Mrs. Lincoln and Mrs. Keckly: The Remarkable Story of the Friendship Between a First Lady and a Former Slave*. New York: Broadway Books, 2003.

Foster, Frances Smith, Ed. Preface. *Behind the Scenes: Formerly a Slave, But More Recently Modiste, and Friend to Mrs. Lincoln; Or, Thirty Years a Slave, and Four Years in the White House*. Chicago: University of Illinois Press, 1998.

———. *Written by Herself: Literary Production by African American Women, 1746–1892.* Bloomington: Indiana University Press, 1993.
Frazier, Harriet. *Runaway and Freed Missouri Slaves and Those Who Helped Them, 1763–1865.* Jefferson, NC: McFarland Press, 2004.
Garrison, William Lloyd. *The Letters of William Lloyd Garrison.* Vol. 6. Cambridge: Harvard University Press, 1971.
Grimké, J. Francis. "Mrs. Elizabeth Keckley." Eulogy. May 28, 1907.
———. "Letter to the Editor." November 20, 1935.
Hening, William Waller. *The Statutes at Large; Being a Collection of all of the Laws of Virginia, from the First Session of the Legislature in the Year 1619.* Charlottesville: University of Virginia Press, 1969.
Jennings, Paul. *A Colored Man's Reminiscences of James Madison.* Brooklyn: George C. Beadle, 1855. Web. 6 June 2015. http://docsouth.unc.edu/neh/jennings/jennings.html.
Keckley, Elizabeth. *Behind the Scenes: Or, Thirty Years a Slave, and Four Years in the White House* (1868). Chapel Hill: University of North Carolina Press, 2011.
Koester, Nancy. *Harriet Beecher Stowe: A Spiritual Life.* Grand Rapids: William B. Eerdmans Publishing, 2014.
Lander, James. *Lincoln and Darwin: Shared Visions of Race, Science, and Religion.* Carbondale: Southern Illinois University Press, 2010.
Lehman, Amy. *Victorian Women and the Theatre of Trance: Mediums, Spiritualists, and Mesmerists in Performance.* Jefferson, NC: McFarland Press, 2009.
Miller, Rosemary E. Reed. *The Threads of Time: The Fabric of History 38 Profiles of Afro-American Designers from 1850 to the Present.* T&S Press, 2007.
Ottolengul, Daniel. *Behind the Seams, by a Nigger Woman, Who Took in Work from Mrs. Lincoln and Mrs. Davis.* New York: National News, 1868.
Painter, Nell. *Sojourner Truth: A Life, a Symbol.* New York: W.W. Norton, 1997.
Sayre, Robert F., ed. *American Lives: An Anthology of Autobiographical Writing.* Madison: University of Wisconsin Press, 1994.
Smith McKoy, Sheila. "Escaping Race: Harriet Wilson, Spiritualism and Power." Lecture, North Carolina State University, 2009.
Smithers, Gregory D. *Slave Breeding: Sex, Violence and Memory in African American History.* Gainesville: University Press of Florida, 2012.
Washington, John E. *They Knew Lincoln.* New York: E.P. Dutton, 1942.
Yellin, Jean Fagan. *Harriet Jacobs: A Life.* New York: Basic Civitas Books, 2005.
Young, Elizabeth. *Disarming the Nation: Women's Writing and the American Civil War.* Chicago: University of Chicago Press, 1999.

# VOLUME 1 | WRITING SELF, WRITING NATION

**EXISTING CRITICISM**

CHAPTER ONE

JILL JEPSON

# Disruption and Disguise in Black Feminine Entrepreneurial Identity
Mary Ellen Pleasant, Elizabeth Keckley & Eliza Potter

THE BARRIERS TO SUCCESSFUL entrepreneurship faced by black women were fundamentally and qualitatively different from those confronting white women. Black women shared with black men the barrier of entrenched racial attitudes depicting them as lazy, dishonest, childlike, impulsive, and intellectually lacking. At the same time, they faced complex gender issues that were simultaneously similar to and dramatically different from those confronting white women. Whereas white women had to create space for themselves in the public world while working to maintain their respectability, black women had a larger and more complex task. They were granted legitimacy in neither sphere and had to simultaneously build identities both as viable agents in the market place and as respectable women in the face of overwhelming racial and gender assumptions. They were denied both the benefits and freedoms of the public sphere and the protections of the private: They faced the challenging paradox of building two identities at the same time.

That the nineteenth century gave rise to a number of black women who succeeded in the marketplace is testimony to their determination and their extraordinary skill at managing public personae in the face of immensely complex and thorny barriers. Elizabeth Keckley was one of those women.

## Elizabeth Keckley

Elizabeth Keckley's girlhood, recounted in her 1868 autobiography *Behind the Scenes: Or, Thirty Years a Slave, and Four Years in the White House*, was a testament to the misery of slavery. She witnessed her father cruelly wrenched from her mother and her, never to see them again. Her mother's brother killed himself to avoid a horrible punishment for losing his master's plough lines. She saw the little boy of a friend sold "like the hogs, at so much per pound" (Keckley 28), and witnessed the boy's mother being whipped for grieving over the loss of her son because her owner "never liked to see one of his slaves wear a sorrowful face" (Keckley 29). She herself suffered cruel beatings and rape and gave birth to a son by her attacker. Yet, by the time she was a young woman she had not only bought freedom for herself and her son but had become a successful businesswoman—and ultimately would be personal dressmaker to First Lady Mary Todd Lincoln.

Keckley was born in Virginia and spent her childhood held in slavery by a family named Burwell. The earliest memory she recounts in *Behind the Scenes* is of being put to work taking care of the Burwells' new baby, although Keckley was herself only four, and of the lashing she received when she rocked the cradle so hard the baby fell to the floor. When she was eight, Keckley's father was forced to move with his master to the West, while Keckley and her mother remained in Virginia. They knew from the beginning that the separation would be complete and permanent. Her description of the occasion is heartbreaking:

> I can remember the scene as if it were but yesterday; how my father cried out against the cruel separation; his last kiss; his wild straining of my mother to his bosom; the solemn prayer to Heaven; the tears and sobs—the fearful anguish of broken hearts. The last kiss, the last goodbye; and he, my father was gone, gone forever. (Keckley 23)

At fourteen, Keckley was "lent" to the Burwells' eldest son, and four years later, was moved with them to Hillsborough, North Carolina. There, she suffered inhuman beatings and torture at the hands of both the minister and the village schoolmaster, who was a family friend. She was also raped for four years by a white man whom she refuses to name in her autobiography. This anonymous rapist was the father of her only child, her son, George.

Keckley was eventually returned to Virginia, where she lived with one of the Burwells' daughters, who had married a man named Garland. The couple was struggling financially: Garland seemed unable to make a go of it in Virginia, and eventually moved his family to St. Louis, bringing along Keckley, her mother, and their other enslaved help. But Garland's poor luck followed him and he eventually decided he could no longer keep Keckley's mother.

Keckley was devastated: "Every gray hair in her head was dear to me," she wrote, "and I could not bear the thought of her going to work for others" (44). It was at this point that Keckley first displayed her determination and inventiveness—and her entrepreneurial skill. She told Garland she would do anything she could to keep her mother with them, and he gave her permission to look for work. She was a skilled seamstress, and she set herself up in a small business, making dresses for the ladies of St. Louis. Her attempts were remarkably successful: "The best ladies in St. Louis were my patrons," she reports, "and once my reputation was established, I never lacked for orders. With my needle I kept bread in the mouths of seventeen persons for two years and five months" (Keckley 45).

It may have been this success that first made Elizabeth propose to Mr. Garland that she buy her freedom and that of her son. She had been thinking of the plan for some time before she brought it up. She had recently been proposed to by a man named James Keckley, but refused to marry him, not wanting to bring children into a world of slavery, to "add one single recruit to the millions bound in hopeless servitude" (Keckley 46). But she had also been thinking of George, questioning why he should be forced to spend his life a slave:

> The Anglo-Saxon blood as well as the African flowed in the veins; the two currents comingled—the one singing of freedom, the other silent and sullen with generations of despair. Why should not the Anglo-Saxon triumph—why should it be weighed down with the rich blood of the tropics? (Keckley 47)

Although Garland dismissed Elizabeth's suggestion that she buy her freedom and admonished her not to bring up the topic again, the seed of the idea had been sewn. When she tried a second time to discuss it with him, he offered her a coin and told her to use it to cross the Mississippi River to Illinois and freedom. To twenty-first-century sensibilities, her response is astonishing: "'No, Master, I do not wish to be free in such a manner. By the laws of the land, I am your slave—you are my master, and I will only be free by such means as the laws of the country provide" (Keckley 49). But Garland eventually reconsidered Elizabeth's request and finally agreed to sell her and her son freedom for $1,200.[1] The barrier to her liberty was still formidable—the sum enormous—but Garland's offer created a glimmer of hope. Imagining a brighter future, Elizabeth married James Keckley and tried to earn the money for her freedom. Yet, years passed and Elizabeth and her son remained in slavery.

It was with the aid of a white woman, Mrs. Le Bourgois of St. Louis, that Elizabeth purchased her freedom. Le Bourgois was one of Elizabeth's customers and, when she learned of her determination to be free, told her she would find a way to get the money: Elizabeth said she would take it only as a loan. Using her own savings and asking friends to donate, Le Bourgois soon came up with the sum. On June 27, 1855, Elizabeth Keckley and her son, George, were free.

For the next four years, Elizabeth remained in St. Louis, continuing her dressmaking enterprise, but by 1860, she was ready for a change. She had paid back Le Bourgois and her other benefactors, and she was exhausted from years of hard work. Furthermore, her eight-year marriage with James Keckley was failing. Keckley had turned out to be, in Elizabeth's words, "dissipated" as well as a liar—he'd claimed to be a free man, but was actually living in slavery.[2] He was, she said, "a burden instead of a helpmate" (Keckley 50). She informed him that she could not continue living with him unless he mended his ways. Apparently, he was unwilling or unable to do so, for she moved to Baltimore, leaving him behind. They never reunited.

In Baltimore, Elizabeth attempted to start a business teaching young black women the system of cutting and fitting dresses that she had developed. When the business failed, she left Baltimore for Washington almost completely broke. There, she found work for two and a half dollars a day, rented an apartment, and began acquiring customers. By the winter of 1860, she had gotten work from a number of Washington's elite, such as Varina Howell Davis, the wife of Jefferson Davis, who was at that time a senator from Mississippi. Davis was taken with Keckley: When the Davises prepared to go south after Mississippi seceded, she asked Keckley to go with them. Keckley refused, choosing to stay in Washington and work on her business.

It was shortly after Davis's departure that Keckley achieved the position that would mark the pinnacle of her success: She became personal dressmaker to the First Lady of the United States. Her employment at the White House was fortuitous: Mary Todd Lincoln had spilled coffee on the gown she planned to wear to the reception following her husband's inauguration, and she needed a dressmaker who could design and sew a new one immediately.

One of Lincoln's friends was a client of Keckley's and recommended her. After a brief interview and Keckley's assurances that she could complete the work in time, she made Lincoln's new gown. It was a rousing success. She was soon working as personal modiste to the First Lady. At the same time, her business was beginning to boom. She would soon be one of the most successful dressmakers in Washington, counting among her clients the wife of Attorney General Edwin McMaster and Martha Douglas, wife of Illinois Senator Stephen Douglas. Eventually, she would employ twenty seamstresses (Fleischner 104) and be in so much demand that she could scarcely keep up with the work.

The focus of Keckley's life for the next four years was her position in the White House. She described her relationship with the Lincolns as one of deep friendship. According to *Behind the Scenes,* Mary Lincoln depended on Keckley not only for fashion advice, but for personal guidance and emotional support. Mr. Lincoln called her "Madam Keckley," and chatted with her lightheartedly. At times, he shared his deeper thoughts: When Keckley congratulated him upon his re-election, he responded, "I don't know whether I should feel thankful or not. The position brings with it many trials. We do not know what we are destined to pass through. But God will be with us all. I put my trust in God" (Keckley 156-57).

Keckley also reported conversations the Lincolns carried on in front of her, even ones of a political nature, such as several arguments about the president's relationships with Secretary of State William Seward and Secretary of the Treasury Salmon P. Chase, whom Mary Lincoln did not trust. Keckley was witness as well to some of the Lincolns' most private moments, such as the death of their son, Willie, at the age of eleven.

The close relationship between Elizabeth Keckley and Mary Lincoln was particularly evident upon the death of the president. According to *Behind the Scenes,* Keckley was the only person the First Lady wished to see the morning after the assassination: It was she who bathed Mary Lincoln's head with cold water and "soothed the terrible tornado" of her grief (192).

After Mary Lincoln left the White House, Keckley traveled with her to Chicago, but she soon returned to Washington to reopen her business (258). Orders came in faster than she could fill them, she reported in her memoir. Among her clients were the daughters of President Johnson. During this period, Keckley also went south to visit her former owners, the Garlands. *Behind the Scenes* draws an extraordinary picture of this strange visit: The former slave, who had worked in the White House, was treated by her one-time owners as a celebrity.

Meanwhile, Mary Lincoln was on the verge of poverty. During her years in the White House, she had incurred enormous debts and now had no means to pay them. In March 1867, she wrote to Keckley telling her she had come up with a plan to make money by selling her gowns and other items of clothing, and called Keckley to help her. "She was the wife of Abraham Lincoln, the man who had done so much for my race, and I could refuse to do nothing for her," Keckley wrote (154). In September of that year, she closed her business and left for New York to help Lincoln in her money-making scheme. The plan was a fiasco. The public reacted to Lincoln's attempt to make money with scorn; the press was brutal; the items did not sell. Mary Lincoln made almost no money, and the ill-devised scheme came to be known as the Old Clothes Scandal.

The plan was disastrous not only for Lincoln, but for Keckley, as it left Lincoln without enough money to pay for Keckley's services. Keckley had lost money by leaving her clients, and the scandal destroyed her once-thriving Washington business. She was left in poverty, as she puts it: "toiling by day with my needle, and writing by night, in the plain little room, on the fourth floor of No. 14 Carroll Place" (Keckley 330).

In an attempt to rehabilitate her reputation—and to earn some much-needed money, Keckley wrote her memoir, *Behind the Scenes: Or, Thirty Years a Slave, and Four Years in the White House,* which was published in 1868 by G.W. Carleton and Company. It was an unusual book, a combination of slave narrative, autobiography, and exposé. Keckley devoted much of the book to Mary Lincoln, revealing her quirks, overwrought behavior, mood swings, and compulsive spending. The book that Keckley had rested her hopes upon only made her situation worse. The press savaged it. *Putnam's Magazine* said it "ought never to have been written or published" and that no "sensible person" should read it. *The New York Times* labeled it a "gross violation of confidence" and even questioned whether Keckley was actually the author. A reviewer in the *New York Citizen* called it "an atrocious invasion of [Mary Lincoln's] privacy" and an "indecent attempt to entrap the reading public into listening to the vile slanders of an angry negro servant" ("Indecent Publications"). A perniciously racist and malicious parody appeared under the title *Behind the Seams, by a Nigger Woman, Who Took in Work from Mrs. Lincoln and Mrs. Davis.*

Part of this virulent response may have been due to the way the book was published. Keckley had appended letters from which the editor, James Redpath, was supposed to omit anything of an excessively personal nature; but the publisher included them in their entirety. They also advertised the book as *Behind the Scenes—The Great Sensational Disclosure by Mrs. Keckley,* thus making Keckley's intentions appear offensive (Criniti 319). An outraged Robert Lincoln, eldest son of the president and First Lady, managed to halt printing of the book.

Keckley wrote a passionate letter to the *New York Citizen* in her own defense: "Was it because 'my skin is dark and that I was once a slave' that I am being 'denounced'?" (Criniti 322). She went on to ask again in that same letter: "As I was born to servitude, it was no fault of mine that I was a slave; and, as I honestly purchased my freedom, may I not be permitted to express, now and then, an opinion becoming a free woman?" (Criniti 323). But her attempts were of little use. She lost business clients and her once-lofty status in the black community plummeted. Some blacks who had celebrated her achievements now treated her as a disgrace. It was argued that she had made it more difficult for blacks to get positions as domestic servants (Foster, "Autobiography" 40). She also lost the friendship of Mary Lincoln, who refused to have anything to do with her again.

After removal of *Behind the Scenes* from circulation, Keckley supported herself with the few clients she could find, supplemented with a small pension she received from her son's service in the Civil War. She eventually became a respected instructor and head of the Department of Sewing and Domestic Arts at Wilberforce University, which she represented at the Chicago World's Columbian Exhibition in 1893. She returned to Washington soon after that and died nearly penniless in 1907.

ELIZABETH KECKLEY'S AUTOBIOGRAPHY displayed a self-assurance born of triumph over hardship. Although she had experienced some of the worst abuses of slavery—beatings, rape, lifelong separation from her father—rather than depicting herself as a victim of slavery, she called her life in bondage a "hardy school" to which she was grateful for "youth's important lesson of self-reliance" (Keckley 20–21). It was there, she says that she learned "those principles of character" which allowed her "to triumph over so many difficulties" (Keckley 20). As a result, Keckley's confidence in her own abilities had a bitter tinge to it: She related that, as a girl, she was repeatedly told that she would never be "worth [her] salt" (Keckley 41) and recalled that she later supported herself and seventeen others through her needlework: "While I was working so hard that others might live in comparative comfort, and move in those circles of society to which their birth gave them entrance," she wrote, "the thought often occurred to me whether I was really worth my salt or not" (Keckley 45–46).

Having supported seventeen people while still in her teens, Elizabeth Keckley was well aware of her ability to achieve through hard work and determination.[3] Her decision to buy freedom for herself and her son grew from that awareness, and her success at doing so further instilled in her a faith in her ability to accomplish what many could scarcely dream of. Like Pleasant, Keckley worked alone. When she moved to Washington to open her business, she left her entire family behind. She had already separated from her husband: She had no contact with him for the rest of her life, and never remarried. Her mother was still enslaved and remained so until her death: The fact that Keckley never worked to free her remains an enigma ("Genteel Performer" 173). Keckley was apparently close to her son, but by the time she went to Washington, he was already studying at Wilberforce University in Ohio and no longer living with her. Keckley arrived unaccompanied in Washington and went into business on her own.

Keckley had an abiding belief in the American Dream and the power of the marketplace. As Foster has pointed out, Keckley's autobiography can be seen to some extent as part of a postbellum tradition of slave narrative that depicted protagonists as the epitome of the American Dream, and their lives as quintessential "rags-to-riches" stories. Keckley had a deep belief in the ability to succeed based on hard work, thrift, ambition, and honesty. Throughout *Behind the Scenes,* she reiterated themes of industry and discipline and the ways they transformed her life. Through industry and entrepreneurial endeavor, Keckley was able first to keep her family together and later to achieve the ultimate dream of purchasing her freedom. Later, her entrepreneurial skills and hard work enabled her to become a successful businesswoman, and to attain a highly privileged position. These successes mark Keckley as a "participant in the American myth . . . one who fully enacts prophecies, takes the mythic journey and progresses from low to high" (Foster, "Romance and Scandal" 50).

Keckley's belief in the inherent value of the capitalist system was dramatically portrayed in two specific scenes in her autobiography. One was her refusal to simply escape to freedom, something her owner, Mr. Garland, sardonically suggested to her when she revealed her desire to buy her freedom. Keckley believed so firmly in the ethics of capitalism and the laws that supported them that she would sacrifice her own freedom before violating them. Ironically, it was this faith that guided her through the process of buying her own freedom and that of her son: She followed the law of the land to the letter and, when the money was offered to her as a gift, refused to consider it anything but a loan. It was only after paying back the money that purchased her liberation that she went into business on her own. At that point, she brought her faith in capitalism and her own confidence together in astonishingly lofty goals. That a former slave with no assets other than her own skill and determination could aim to work at the White House could only be considered unrealistic—if it were not for the fact that she attained that feat.

IN *BEHIND THE SCENES*, Elizabeth Keckley depicted herself as steadfastly in accordance with the standards for female behavior: She had excellent manners; selflessly nurtured others; was resolutely honest; and was kind and forgiving. During her time in Washington, she cultivated a reputation for dignity: She dressed elegantly and prided herself for being a charming conversationalist (Foster, "Autobiography" 38). According to John Washington (218), she accurately saw herself as legend in the black community, aware that people would arrive early at church to get a view of her "queenly" entrance. She also made it clear that she abided strictly by the dictates of good manners. On one occasion, she refused to send her business card to First Lady Eliza Johnson because Johnson had not sent a condolence card to Mary Todd Lincoln, a serious breach of etiquette on Johnson's part. In this way, Keckley showed that she was committed to proper comportment.

Keckley also portrayed herself as possessing the deeper qualities of a True Woman, as it was defined in her time. She was, she wrote in the preface to her book, a woman of "charitable" intentions, "prompted by the purest motive" (xiii). She was a woman of such high morality that she forgave the people at whose home she was once enslaved—and who had treated her brutally—and, when she was reunited with them years later, showed an astonishing degree of graciousness. Keckley also told numerous anecdotes of times when she nurtured others: She took care of Willie Lincoln when he was ill and comforted the First Lady after his death. When the president died, Keckley was the one person Mary Lincoln sent for: the only one, according to *Behind the Scenes,* who could comfort her. She made it clear, also, that her decency was unassailable. When a woman hoping to write a scandalous book about the Lincolns offered Keckley a bribe to recommend her for a job at the White House, Keckley was aghast. "Sooner than betray the trust of a friend, I would throw myself in the Potomac River," she told the woman. "I am not so base as that" (94). She further asserted that she was often offered bribes, every one of which she, of course, refused.

One way Keckley underscored her respectability was to offer her own behavior in comparison with that of Mary Todd Lincoln's. Lincoln's often eccentric and inappropriate actions were well known by her contemporaries. She was widely believed to be an uncouth country woman who lacked the refinement and social competence for her station. Keckley treated Mary Lincoln's behavior with some literary sleight of hand. On the one hand, she explicitly asserted that the First Lady's "intentions were good" (xiii) and that "she should be judged more kindly" (xiv) than she was. Lincoln showed "grace and composure" and was "confident and self-possessed": "No queen, accustomed to the usages of royalty all her life, could have comported herself with more calmness and dignity than did the wife of the President" (89), she wrote. But throughout *Behind the Scenes,* Keckley belies these claims with her detailed descriptions of the First Lady's coarseness and poor manners.

Among the most notable examples of Keckley's depictions of Mary Lincoln focused on the First Lady's grief over the deaths of her son and her husband. As Carolyn Sorisio (33) has pointed out, nineteenth-century standards for feminine behavior dictated that a lady grieve with restraint and self-control. At a time when care for others was the paramount task of True Womanhood, a lady set aside her own sorrow to nurture others, especially her children and husband. But Keckley portrayed Lincoln's response to the tragedies as anything but restrained: She describes "wails . . . unearthly shrieks, terrible convulsions, wild tempestuous outbursts" (Keckley 191). Lincoln's grief over Willie was so out of control—and she was so preoccupied with her own loss—that she was unable even to comfort her youngest surviving son, Tad. The First Lady also reacted to the deaths of both her son and her husband by throwing out everything that reminded her of them. Thus, Lincoln came across as vulgar, out of control, and self-centered in her grief. Even the fact that she threw out her husband's belongings is a mark against her. Contemporary standards of propriety required that she treasure keepsakes of the departed. By refusing to abide by this polite custom, she appeared not only coarse and unmannerly, but self-centered (Sorisio 34).

Keckley depicted her own grief very differently. In accordance with proper behavior, she kept her personal tragedy largely to herself: She barely mentioned her son's death in *Behind the Scenes,* and when she did discuss it, she used it to reflect on Mary Lincoln's grief over Willie. In this way, Keckley portrayed herself not only as a properly restrained mourner but as a lady who employed her private sorrow to create empathy for others. Furthermore, in contrast to Mary Lincoln's disposal of her husband's belongings, Keckley asked to be given some tokens of his, which she cherished and later donated to Wilberforce University. Thus, she acted in keeping with the genteel custom of the "sentimental keepsake" (Sorisio 33). Ironically, at the same time that Keckley was displaying her adherence to the standards of the True Woman, Mary Lincoln appeared to be acting in accordance with stereotypes of the childlike and frenzied black woman. Although Keckley never went so far as to make explicit the contrast between Mary Lincoln's behavior and her own, *Behind the Scenes* makes the comparison unavoidable.

Keckley's experience can be contrasted to that of two other women of her era. Eliza Potter was one of the leading hairdressers of Cincinnati. Mary Ellen Pleasant invested in a string of laundries and boardinghouses in post–Gold Rush California—one of her establishments housed over nine hundred boarders—and later, in silver mines. As nineteenth-century black women who achieved considerable wealth and influence through their entrepreneurial skills, Potter and Pleasant offer informative sources of comparison with Elizabeth Keckley.

Eliza Potter used a strategy similar to Keckley's to create a public image of ladylike propriety. Like Keckley, she dressed in the finest of fashion: As shown in her interactions with the railroad executives, her lovely and expensive wardrobe was a source of great pride for her. Also like Keckley, she published a revealing autobiography—a book of caustic wit exposing her white clients' foibles and vanities. Potter, however, was not derided for her depiction of white women. In fact, her exposé was lauded in the white press.

Potter used her memoir to draw attention to the fact that she invariably acted with ladylike decorum. "I defy any individual, North, South, East or West, to say I ever did or said anything but was ladylike or courteous," she wrote bluntly (201). Her tales of her travels are full of refined activities: trips to operas and the theater and garden parties. Even her training in the various skills by which she thought to make a living—flower-making, sewing, cooking, and hairdressing—she elevated to a level at which they sound appropriate for the True Woman: She refers to them not as crafts or job skills, but as "fine arts" (27). She also showed herself nurturing others. At various times, she cared for a ranting mentally ill woman, took care of an unconscious man she discovered on the street, and tended to a maid who had cholera (49).

Like Keckley, Potter used the inappropriate behavior of white women to underscore her own respectability. She excoriated vulgar people, social climbers, and hypocrites, many of whom she saw in the various social circles in whose midst she worked. *A Hairdresser's Experience* was replete with salacious tales of impropriety. She told of a foolish woman who chopped off her own hair to spite her husband; another who regularly threw tantrums so terrible her husband was nearly suicidal; another who flirted openly with married men, even in front of their wives. She related many tales of jealousy, competition, and pretense. She was especially disdainful of the "par-venu" women, who had money, but lacked the social acceptance they craved. The women she described were often rude and uncouth:

> European ladies go to parties more for the sake of meeting friends and passing an agreeable evening, than for the sake of what they eat; but I have known our ladies refuse to eat either dinner or suppers, so that they might be able to eat the more at night, or as many of them express it, that they might stuff themselves.... When the door opened there was a general rush, as though there was a fire in some part of the house from which they were endeavoring to escape, and all would be confusion to know who should seize the bouquets and anything else the table might be ornamented with ... I have known ladies take home as much as three or four dollars' worth at a time. (203)

Although white women bore the brunt of her criticism, white men fared only a little better. She told of men who were cruel to their wives, and of others who had no backbone: "At Saratoga, the gentlemen of the higher circles *dare* not make a movement outside of the charmed coterie to which they have been admitted," she wrote. "They are slaves to certain female *leaders*" (62).

Just as Keckley's depiction of Mary Todd Lincoln's inappropriate behavior helped to highlight her own respectability even without an explicit comparison between the two of them, Potter's portrayal of the foibles and vices of upper-class whites emphasized her own virtues. Moreover, the fact that both women took it upon themselves to evaluate and comment upon the behavior of white women casts them not only as upright women, but as women who understand proper behavior well enough to act as commentators—even enforcers—of respectability.

Mary Ellen Pleasant's approach to image-creation was in some ways more complex than either Keckley's or Potter's. While Potter and Keckley were both consistent in their presentation of themselves as cultured and ladylike, Pleasant was, at least in the beginning of her career, content to portray herself as a simple domestic. Pleasant's deliberate cultivation of this self-image and its role in her success will be discussed later. Suffice it to say here that, as her businesses progressed, she threw off that self-representation and worked, as Keckley and Potter did, to show herself to the world as elegant and upright. Pleasant did this less through Keckley's and Potter's chosen medium of fashion than through her opulent boardinghouses. These establishments, intended for the upper echelons of California society, did not reflect an image of simple hominess. They were places of great sophistication and style, where Pleasant could unabashedly display her refinement and good taste. Her hallmark property on Washington Street near San Francisco's central plaza, was strategically located near City Hall and the opera. It quickly became renowned for its excellent cuisine, fine wines, and lavishly furnished rooms (*Mining the Mythic Past* 60). Her own home was similarly luxurious: an opulently decorated multistory Victorian mansion she built for upwards of $100,000 *(Mining the Mythic Past* 60).

Pleasant also brought an element of elegance into her personal comportment. The placement of her house was such that she could be readily observed as she went about her various errands—some say she positioned the house deliberately for that effect. She left her home several times a week to make the rounds of shops and markets. According to Lerone Bennett Jr., she spent thousands of dollars a month for "provisions and finery" and made quite a spectacle:

She usually traveled in a carriage driven at high speed by her personal coachman, James Allen, and attended by a liveried footman. This must have been a sight to see . . . for there is not a more compelling image in the whole of American history than this image of the tall, spare, erect Black "servant" in a black dress and a large white apron being driven through the streets of San Francisco in her own specially constructed carriage, attended by a driver and footman, both in livery. (Bennett)

## Transforming Female Labor

Pleasant, Keckley, and Potter all faced an additional obstacle in their attempts to present themselves to the world as respectable women and viable entrepreneurs. A barrier to many white and virtually all black women entrepreneurs was the fact that their businesses were often based on stigmatized forms of female labor. Pleasant, Keckley, and Potter all built their businesses around traditional female service work: laundering, cooking, sewing, hairdressing, running boardinghouses. Not only were these occupations gendered as female, they fell on the downside of the great divide between manual and mental labor at a time of rigidifying class boundaries around that distinction (Blumin 121). Dealing with that stigma was a major impediment to the entrepreneurial identities of women for whom such skills were their main or only assets. While Pleasant, Keckley, and Potter worked to neutralize ingrained racial biases, they also faced a pervasive vilification of even skilled manual labor (Santamarina, "Black Labor" 170).

These women used divergent methods for dealing with that impediment. On the one hand, Potter and Keckley took an approach that involved recasting their work: transforming it from servile to professional, from wage labor to proprietorship. Pleasant employed a more complex strategy. While, later in her career, she presented herself to the world as a successful businesswoman, early on, she exploited the low status and invisibility of domestic labor, manipulating the servile representation of her work to her advantage.

Potter and Keckley worked in the growing arena of beauty and fashion, where seamstresses and hairdressers were generally seen as manual laborers who worked for white women of means, but neither woman accepted that role. Instead, they represented themselves not as laborers but as professionals and businesswomen. They emphasized the aspects of their work that would give them legitimacy in the marketplace: their high levels of skill, the entrepreneurial competence that went into the building of their businesses, and their roles as providers of expert advice to their clients.

Keckley did not refer to herself as Mary Lincoln's seamstress, but as her *modiste:* She did not merely sew dresses, but designed them and, as such, had to be conversant with the concepts behind the fashion movements of her day (Criniti 324). She depicted herself as the First Lady's consultant and guide, an authority on style and culture and an expert on the social representation inherent in dress. It was she who enabled Lincoln to present herself favorably at her first inaugural ball and who helped the unpolished Kentucky woman look, dress, and act like the First Lady of the nation (Criniti 318). Unlike an ordinary seamstress, she also created her own system for cutting dresses which she then tried to teach to others.

Keckley took this transformation of female labor one step further: She became not only a businesswoman specializing in fashion but also a social observer and commentator. Keckley describes herself not merely as a businesswoman whose primary client was the First Lady but as Mary Lincoln's personal advisor and confidante on everything from social relationships to politics. Keckley goes so far as to relate an anecdote in which Mary Lincoln asked for her opinion about the president's prospects for re-election:

> "I believe Mr. Lincoln will remain in the White House four years longer," I replied. . . . "Because he has been tried, and has proved faithful to the best interests of the country. The people of the North recognize in him an honest man, and they are willing to confide in him, at least until the war has been brought to a close. The Southern people made his election a pretext for rebellion, and now to replace him with someone else, after years of sanguinary war, would look too much like a surrender of the North. So, Mr. Lincoln is certain to be re-elected." (148)

Here, Keckley is offering not merely an opinion but a judgment supported by a knowledge of society and politics—and it is a judgment solicited by the First Lady of the United States.

For Keckley, this authority extends into an understanding of the details of the events taking place in the White House. She was the one closest to the First Lady and was well known to Mr. Lincoln. *Behind the Scenes* describes the Lincolns' private moments—such as the president weeping over his son and Mary Lincoln fretting over her debts. Most notably, she was an eyewitness to the immediate aftermath of the president's assassination—and the only witness to Mary Lincoln's grief: The First Lady "denied admittance to almost every one," she writes, "and I was her only companion, except her children, in the days of her great sorrow" (193). In *Behind the Scenes,* Keckley made it clear that she occupied a privileged position with access to knowledge unavailable to most others—even, as Fleischner puts it, as a kind of "public historian," able to record the events surrounding some of the most significant events of the era (Fleischner 103).

Potter uses similar techniques in establishing the professionalism and significance of her work. In *A Hairdresser's Experience,* she depicts herself as an authority on proper feminine behavior—so much so that she gets away with vitriolic criticism of her clients' comportment. She does this in part by foregrounding her unique background. Potter's travels put her in the position of having enjoyed experiences many of her clients would not have. Although she had traveled as a servant, she had nonetheless seen the Palace of Versailles and Covent Garden, had witnessed the great ceremonies of the baptism of the Count of Paris and the funeral of the Duke of Orleans, had visited the operas of Paris, and watched a deer hunt in England. "I saw more in France than Americans of the highest position see generally," she wrote (27).

Potter had not only traveled geographically, but socially. She had been in the homes of people of all rank, had witnessed the lives of poor and rich alike, and knew much about the way life was lived across the social strata of her day. Throughout her book, she shows herself to be a keen observer: She walks through the resort at Saratoga virtually unnoticed and absorbs details of dress, food, and conversation. On a train ride home, she pretends to be sleeping with a veil over her face and overhears a detailed conversation about women she knows. She watches, hidden, to see how others will treat a man lying unconscious in the street. All of this she not only observes, but records and comments on.

These experiences gave Potter the cachet to present herself not merely as a highly skilled worker and successful entrepreneur, but as an authority on proper behavior and morality. This sense of her own authority emerged again and again throughout *A Hairdresser's Experience.* When the white men refused to help the unconscious man, she didn't merely watch, but lectured them on what they should do. When she sees a girl dressed in bloomers—a costume feminists were trying to introduce as an alternative to restrictive feminine clothing of the time—she ordered her to "go and pull off those breeches and put a piece on your dress to let it down, and don't be disgracing all woman kind" (227). In the most dramatic example of Potter's assertion of her own authority, she told the story of a conversation she had with a group of clients:

> At last mentioning a certain lady's name, they asked if I combed her, I told them no, I did not, as I combed none but ladies. They then wanted to know what I thought constituted a lady. Laying down my work, I rose to my feet and said, "Ladies, I cannot tell you what I think constitutes a lady, and keep my seat. I must get up. I do not think all those are ladies who sit in high places, or those who drive around in fine carriages, but those only are worthy the name who can trace back their generations without stain, honest and respectable, that love and fear God, and treat all creatures as they merit, regardless of nations, stations or wealth. These are what I say constitute a lady. (279–80)

Potter went so far as to compare her work and the position it affords her to that of the physician and the minister:

> The physician writes his diary, and doubtless his means of discovering the hidden mysteries of life are great. The clergyman, whose calling inspires the deepest confidence, and into whose ear the tales of sorrow are unreservedly breathed, sends forth his diary to an eager world, and other innumerable chroniclers of fireside life have existed; but the hairdresser will yield rivalship to none in this regard. If domestic bitterness and joy, and all the heart emotions that exist, cannot be discovered by her, she defies all the rest of the world to find them out. (iii)

In this passage, Potter aligns her work with that of two of the most esteemed masculine professions of her day, identifying herself as a possessor of privileged knowledge about the "hidden mysteries of life." By claiming this special knowledge, she validates her opinions about the beauty industry, the contemporary preoccupation with social status, and the ills of a society obsessed with the superficial. She depicts the value of her profession not in terms of the services she performs for her clients, but as growing out of her role as a "social expert" and a commentator on contemporary life.

Mary Ellen Pleasant took a different, more multifaceted approach to the issue of stigmatized female labor. In contrast to Keckley and Potter, she often eschewed attempts to present a professional and entrepreneurial image, especially at the beginning of her career. She appears to have been happy to represent herself as a domestic laborer and even seemed to cultivate the image. Herbert Asbury reported in *The Barbary Coast*:

> Fewer than a score of cooks were in private service [in San Francisco], but they insisted, of course, upon being called "chefs." A notable exception to this foolery was Mammy Pleasant.... She said flatly that she was a cook, and would be called nothing else. (14)

According to Hudson, Pleasant sometimes played into racial stereotypes, allowing herself, for example, to be called "Mammy Pleasant" and donning the image of the domestic.

Another way in which Pleasant eschewed attempts to create an entrepreneurial image was in her obscuring of those aspects of her businesses that fell outside the realm of domestic labor and traditional female work. In addition to being a cook, laundress, and boardinghouse-keeper, Pleasant was also a speculator with investments in mines and real estate. These very male occupations were the sources of great monetary wealth for her. Yet, while her "female" work was clearly observable and well known, her investment dealings were largely kept under wraps. Her relationship with Thomas Bell, her investment partner and co-mortgage holder, was almost a complete mystery, and the source of her money was unknown to anyone outside a very small circle. While she forefronted her lovely boardinghouses and renowned culinary skills, she kept her talents as an investor completely private.

## Conclusion

The strategies Elizabeth Keckley employed, like those of Potter and Pleasant, enabled her to achieve a degree of extraordinary success in the face of enormous obstacles. For a woman born into slavery to transform herself into an entrepreneur and the personal friend of the First Lady of the United States is to assert the highest possibilities of achievement. Keckley clearly erred, both in becoming involved with Mary Todd Lincoln's dress-selling plan and in publishing her book exposing the First Lady's eccentricities. But the real problem for Keckley was that she had no room to err. She existed in a space strewn with gender and racial landmines. As a black woman in a white man's marketplace, her very success challenged the foundations of American social structure. She further defied social expectations by leveraging denigrated female labor to create entrepreneurial success. This undermining of white and male worldviews could not but raise deepseated fears and uncertainties. Keckley existed in an uneasy relationship with a white community who embraced her only as long as her successes were contained, silent, and within an acceptable social space. Her accomplishments created an intense tension: Her successes were posed to implode when that tension became too great. That Keckley eventually miscalculated the extent to which she could push the envelope says little about her own capabilities and much about the overwhelming odds that faced black women entrepreneurs in the nineteenth century.

### NOTES

1. $1200 was the price set by Garland to purchase freedom for Keckley and her son, George.
2. Recent sources indicate James Keckley was likely a fugitive slave.
3. See Introduction, page xvi, regarding Keckley's age.

### WORKS CITED

Asbury, Herbert. *The Barbary Coast: An Informal History of the San Francisco Underworld*. New York: Thunder's Mouth Press, 2002.

Bennett, Lerone Jr. "The Mystery of Mary Ellen Pleasant." *Ebony* 48.1, September 1993 http://findarticles.com/p/articles/mi_m1077/is_}ai_13230341.

Blumin, Stuart. *The Emergence of the Middle Class: Social Experience in the American City, 1760–1900*. New York: Cambridge University Press, 1989.

Criniti, Stephen. "Thirty Years a Slave, and Four Years a Fairy Godmother: Dressmaking as Self-Making in Elizabeth Keckley's Autobiography." *American Transcendental Quarterly* 22.1 (March 2008): 309–26.

Dean, Sharon G., Introduction. *A Hairdresser's Experience in High Life*. By Eliza Potter. New York: Oxford University Press, 1991.

Fleischner, Jennifer. *Mastering Slavery: Memory, Family, and Identity in Women's Slave Narratives*. New York: New York University Press, 1996.

Foster, Frances Smith. "Autobiography after Emancipation: The Example of Elizabeth Keckley." *Multicultural Autobiography*. Ed. James Robert Payne. Knoxville: University of Tennessee Press, 1992. 32–63.

———. "Romance and Scandal in a Postbellum Slave Narrative: Elizabeth Keckley's *Behind the Scenes.*" *Written by Herself Literary Production by African American Women 1746–1892.* Ed. Frances Smith Foster. Bloomington: Indiana University Press, 1993. 115–30.

Fraser, Isabel. "Mammy Pleasant: The Woman." *San Francisco Call,* 9 July 1901: 2.

Hudson, Lynn. "Entertaining Citizenship: Masculinity and Minstrelsy in Post Emancipation San Francisco." *Journal of African American History* 93.2 (2008): 174–97.

———. "Mining the Mythic Past: The History of Mary Ellen Pleasant." *African American Women Confront the Past, 1600-2000.* Ed. Quintard Taylor and Shirley Ann Wilson Moore. University of Oklahoma Press, 2003. 56–70.

———. "'Strong Animal Passions' in the Gilded Age: Race, Sex, and a Senator on Trial." *Journal of the History of Sexuality* 9.1–2 (January/April 2000): 62–84.

———. *The Making of Mammy Pleasant.* Urbana: University Illinois Press, 2003.

"Inaugural Ball at Washington, on the 4th of March." *Frank Leslie's Illustrated News,* XI, 23 March 1861: 278.

"Indecent Publications." *New York Citizen,* 18 April 1868.

Keckley, Elizabeth. *Behind the Scenes: Or, Thirty Years a Slave, and Four Years in the White House* (1868). Chapel Hill: University of North Carolina Press, 2011.

Pleasant, Mary Ellen. "Memoirs and Autobiography." *Pandex of the Press,* 1 January 1902: 1–6.

Potter, Eliza. *A Hairdresser's Experience in High Life.* New York: Oxford University Press, 1991.

Sorisio, Carolyn. "Unmasking the Genteel Performer: Elizabeth Keckley's *Behind the Scenes* and the Politics of Public Wrath." *African American Review* 34.1 (2000): 19–38.

Santamarina, Xiomara. "Behind the Scenes of Black Labor: Elizabeth Keckley and the Politics of Publicity," *Feminist Studies* 28.3 (2002): 514–37.

CHAPTER TWO

WILLIAM L. ANDREWS

# Reunion in the Postbellum Slave Narrative
Frederick Douglass and Elizabeth Keckley

IF, AS ROBERT STEPTO has suggested, the antebellum slave autobiography, epitomized by the *Narrative of the Life of Frederick Douglass* (1845), exemplifies in classic form the "ascent narrative" in Afro-American literature, the post–Civil War ex-slave autobiography furnishes us numerous examples of a type of descent narrative notable for its depiction of the return of a former slave to his or her Southern origins. In Stepto's formulation, the archetypal "immersion narrative" of black American fiction charts the progress of its protagonist from alienation in the North to "tribal literacy" and reintegration into the black Southern community (167–68). Although many postbellum ex-slave autobiographies might be read as prototypical "immersion narratives," it is important to note that these writers usually confine their narratives of descent to a survey of racial conditions in the South. Sometimes they pause to record the experience of recovering lost relations; it is not unusual to find them visiting their birthplaces and reflecting on the significance of the changes that time, social upheaval, and freedom have wrought.[1] In many cases, these reflections may not prove particularly arresting for the reader of today. What is striking, however, at least to this student of the history of the Afro-American slave narrative, is the incidence of emotionally charged reunions between the protagonists of postbellum slave narratives and their ex-masters or -mistresses. In these narratives the question of the ex-slave's relationship to the Southern black community may not be resolved,[2] but some sort of resolution of the ex-slave's relationship to dominant whites of his or her past consistently emerges. One may be surprised to discover how often and how easily the estrangement wrought by longstanding caste and class differences, and by time itself, is bridged in scenes in which a genuine reconciliation between black and white seems to be effected.

Typically, these Southern reunions take place under circumstances apparently advantageous to the ex-slave: The former master or mistress has become poverty-stricken since the war, while the former slave has prospered. Yet it is extremely rare to find in a postbellum slave narrative an account of a meeting in which the ex-slave's resentment of past wrongs or an ex-master's or -mistress's envy or lingering pride of caste blocks the chance for reconciliation.[3] The postbellum slave narrator seems almost determined to present these scenes of reunion as indicative of a progressive, forgiving spirit among blacks, born of their faith and hope in a God who delivers the captive and shows mercy on the sinner. "The colored people," wrote ex-slave James L. Smith, as he recalled his reunion with his former mistress in Virginia, "are ready to fulfill that passage of Scripture: 'Therefore, if thine enemy hunger, feed him; if he thirst, give him drink; for in so doing thou shalt heap coals of fire on his head'" (100). The mixture, if not conflict, of emotions that this quotation from St. Paul might ascribe to ex-slaves who are reconciled to their former masters does not become an issue, however, in most postbellum slave narratives. Men like Smith, Josiah Henson, and I.E. Lowery seem genuinely gratified to return to the open-armed embraces of the faded Southern ladies who once owned them. In part they relished the impression they made on those who once could afford to patronize them; in part they wanted to demonstrate their worth to those who, under the *ancien regime*, could never see it. The astonishment of Henson's decrepit Maryland mistress—"Why, Si, you are a gentleman!"—and the black man's witty but pointed reply—"I always was, madam"—suggest that, for Henson and others like him, reunion made possible a unique kind of recognition in the eyes of the once awe-inspiring Other. Perceiving that her former slave has become an affluent freeman, the near-destitute Mrs. Riley inquires, "What have you brought me?" Henson's reply—"Nothing. I came to see if you had anything to give me!"—is again revelatory of the psychological import of such a reunion to an ex-slave (Winks 160). The only thing this white woman *can* give him is her verbal affirmation of his long-cherished image of himself as a man of dignity, "a gentleman." To live up to this self-ideal, slaves like Henson left their masters and mistresses, took their chances in the world of freedom, and achieved success, even fame, in the course of a life of struggle in the North. Did they need their achievement endorsed by the old slavocratic order before it became fully real to them? Perhaps, but postbellum narratives of descent suggest that reunions with former enslavers were motivated by a complex of desires, some psychological, some sociopolitical, and some literary. Underlying them all, however, was what Henson calls "a strange inexpressible longing . . . to see again the home of my boyhood" (157) where an answer might finally be found to the question of what, if anything, the slave past had to give to a self-respecting, forward-looking black man or woman in the late nineteenth century.

*Life and Times of Frederick Douglass* contains what is probably the most famous scene of reconciliation in the postbellum slave narrative.[4] Given the scathing portrait of Thomas Auld that Douglass created for his 1845 *Narrative of the Life of Frederick Douglass* and reinforced in his open letter "To My Old Master, Thomas Auld" (1848), the joyful, almost sentimental, reunion with this man that Douglass recounts in his final autobiography can seem incongruous, if not downright reactionary. In the summer of 1877, Douglass returned to Talbot County hoping first and foremost, he told a correspondent for the *Baltimore Sun,* to see his former master (Preston 184). The reversal of their conditions—Auld now over eighty years old and much reduced from the man young Frederick had both hated and feared; Douglass now in the prime of his life, an international celebrity—predisposed the black man to remember only Auld's "good deeds" and to treat the old man with deference (Douglass 442). Thus when Auld greeted his former slave as "Marshall Douglass" according to his official title, Douglass insisted on the old familiar (and to some blacks no doubt demeaning) term of address—"not *Marshall*, but Frederick to you as formerly" (442). It was not long before both men were in tears; Douglass found himself so choked by his emotions that he could hardly speak. Feeling that it would be unseemly to bring words of bitterness or reproach to the ears of a man so close to death, Douglass made a special effort to make his peace with Auld. He went so far as to apologize to Auld for having attributed to him in the *Narrative* the "ungrateful and cruel treatment of my grandmother," admitting that he had been mistaken about Auld's disposition toward Betsey Bailey and assuring him that he had never wanted "to do him injustice." After all, "I regarded both of us as victims of a system" (443). The idea of the mutual victimization of Auld and himself by slavery was certainly not something Douglass had argued in his previous autobiographical accounts of slavery, although like many slave narrators in the antebellum era he was not averse to showing the harmful effects of slavery on whites as well as blacks. However, by the 1881 autobiography, Douglass was ready to declare of Auld and himself,

"Our courses had been determined for us, not by us" (441). This could easily be read as implicitly releasing the slaveholder from moral responsibility for his actions toward the slave. This suggests, in turn, at least one reason that, as Douglass admitted in *Life and Times*, "my visit to Capt. Auld has been made the subject of mirth by heartless triflers," while "serious-minded men [have] regret[ed it] as a weakening of my lifelong testimony against slavery" (442).

One of the earliest postbellum slave narratives to picture the former slave's happy return to those who once enslaved him or her is Elizabeth Keckley's widely reviewed *Behind the Scenes: or, Thirty Years a Slave, and Four Years in the White House*. Keckley recalls that in the summer of 1866 she received an invitation from the daughter of her former mistress, Anne Burwell Garland, to visit the family at Rude's Hill in the Valley of Virginia. Having often pondered the fate of Mrs. Garland and her daughters, Keckley accepted this invitation with alacrity. When she arrived, Keckley proudly notes, "I was carried to the house in triumph" (250). In the midst of the enthusiastic welcome that the white women and their ex-Confederate husbands gave to their former slave, the family's black cook interjects, "'I declar, I nebber did see people carry on so. Wonder if I should go off and stay two or three years, if all ob you wud hug and kiss me when I cum back?'" (252). Indeed Keckley's loving and respectful treatment extends beyond the Garland family. She recalls riding to a tournament, no doubt one of those celebrations of the Old South chivalric ideal, with a Colonel Gilmore, formerly a leader in the Army of Northern Virginia. The irony of being attended by such a man, especially after her lengthy association with the Lincoln family, is not lost on Keckley. But she structures her narration of the incident so as to let another ex-Confederate officer draw the conclusion that all this hospitality is "evidence of the peaceful feeling of this country; a change ... that augurs brighter days for us all" (254).

It seems unlikely that Keckley, writing in 1868, intended anything ironic by reiterating her ex-Confederate companion's prediction of "brighter days for us all." There can be little doubt that both Keckley and Douglass wrote their post–Civil War autobiographies in a mood of optimism and with a sincere desire to use their personal testimony as part of the national healing process that both hoped would follow the Civil War. In the Preface to *Behind the Scenes*, Keckley notes that, because of her "kind, true-hearted friends in the South," she would "not wound those Southern friends by sweeping condemnation, simply because I was once a slave" (xi–xii). She goes on to declare that slaveholders were less responsible for slavery than "the God of nature and the fathers who framed the Constitution" (xii). She extends this sort of generosity even to Jefferson Davis, regarded by many in the immediate post-war era as almost an arch-fiend but recalled by Keckley, who once worked for Davis's wife Varina as a dressmaker, as "a thoughtful, considerate man in the domestic circle" (69). To the former President of the Confederacy Keckley writes with an uncommon absence of malice, "I, who was once a slave . . . can say to Mr. Jefferson Davis, 'Peace! You have suffered! Go in peace'" (74).

Douglass also maintained a charitable stance toward the South in the first edition of his *Life and Times*, even though he wrote it in the immediate post-Reconstruction period, when he would have had good reason to be pessimistic about "better times for us all," especially for black Southerners. In 1881 Douglass still clung to the kind of optimism that Keckley claimed for racial prospects in post-war Dixie. Acknowledging that certain "evils" had come about as a result of black enfranchisement in the South, he nevertheless insists: "I am less amazed at these evils, than by the rapidity with which they are subsiding, and not more astonished at the facility with which the former slave has become a free man, than at the rapid adjustment of the master-class to the new situation" (381). Douglass deliberately concludes the 1881 edition of *Life and Times* with a reprinted version of a speech he gave in Elmira, New York, in 1880 in which he celebrates the advancement of the freedmen, dismisses those who speak "in a tone of despair" about black prospects, pronounces "the political situation" in the South "encouraging," and urges his people to accept, now, the responsibility of determining their own social destiny.[5]

Their optimism about the future and charity toward the past notwithstanding, neither Keckley nor Douglass soft-pedals the injustice of slavery in their postbellum autobiographies. Both, however, make a clear effort to distinguish between an unjust institution and the (white) people who ostensibly presided over and perpetuated that system. Douglass is the more explicit of the two writers in picturing blacks and whites as fellow victims of "the circumstances of birth, education, law, and custom" (441) in the slaveocracy. In this Douglass anticipates Booker T. Washington's well-known exculpation of his unknown white father in *Up from Slavery*: "He was simply another unfortunate victim of the institution which the Nation unhappily had engrafted upon it at that time" (1:216). Keckley did not have to go to these lengths to explain her former mistress's behavior as a slaveholder. Since Garland had treated her slave humanely, when compared to Auld's treatment of Douglass, Keckley did not need to go to unprecedented rhetorical lengths to rehabilitate Garland in her autobiography. Keckley, obviously, had not been forced to fight or run away from the white woman who claimed her as property. Garland allowed her to buy her freedom (and that of her son) by taking out loans from various sympathetic whites in St. Louis in 1855. More importantly, unlike Douglass, Keckley did not write a version of her slave experience before the Civil War in which she used her mistress, as Douglass had used Thomas Auld in his first two autobiographies, as "a weapon with which to assail the system of slavery" (Meyer 289). Douglass's *Narrative* had made effective rhetorical use of Thomas Auld as a foil, the personification of everything Douglass was not. Auld signified meanness and contemptibleness, Douglass magnanimity and intrinsic nobility. Douglass took a risk in blurring the sharp opposition between himself and Auld in *Life and Times*, since he could be read as having called into question not only his "lifelong testimony against slavery," but the very credibility of his first autobiography. It was Keckley's good fortune not to have been burdened by the myth of her own past in this regard. Still, her story reveals something of the same problem that Douglass had in reconciling an ex-slave's autobiography in the postbellum era with the antebellum slave narrative tradition.

As previously remarked, Keckley recalls that, while she was working as Mrs. Lincoln's modiste in Washington, DC, during the Civil War, she "wondered what had become of those who claimed my first duty and my first love" (241). Here Keckley refers unmistakably to white people, in particular the Garlands, especially the Garland women, of whom the ex-slave acknowledges she was very fond. Yet, "when I would mention their names and express interest in their welfare, my Northern friends would roll up their eyes in surprise. 'Why, Lizzie, how can you have a kind thought for those who inflicted a terrible wrong upon you by keeping you in bondage?' they would ask" (241). In reply Keckley does not wax nostalgic about the good old days in slavery; instead, she insists that to cease thinking about her experience in slavery and her relationships to whites in the South would be to deny herself access to some of her most meaningful memories. "To surrender [that] is to surrender the greatest part of my existence" (241), she maintains. Calling such self-denial a "surrender" could not have been an accident for Keckley, not on the heels of the surrender of the slaveocracy to the Union. In using the word she argues that it is not an act of weakness but of strength to hold fast to her past, despite its many painful associations. Inescapably, people like the Garlands "are associated with everything that memory holds dear," particularly Keckley's childhood, her family, and especially her mother. "It is but natural that I should sigh to see them once more," Keckley concludes. When her Northern friends, undoubtedly whites, warn Keckley that the Southern whites "are too selfish to give a single thought to you, now that you no longer are their slave," Keckley refuses to believe this: "You do not know the Southern people as I do—how warm is the attachment between master and slave" (242). To this remark, the Northerners can only observe, "You have some strange notions, Lizzie."

Keckley's white Northern friends had good reason to be put off by an exslave who told them "how warm is the attachment between master and slave." This must have sounded to them like a reprise of the rhetoric of proslavery. (It is unlikely that they knew of Keckley's having borne a son probably by the son of her master, whose passionate attraction to her, she remarks in *Behind the Scenes*, she was unable to repulse because of her enslaved status.[6] Such knowledge might have made Keckley's insistence on the "warm attachment between master and slave" sound even more ironic in her case.) Anyone who had listened attentively to the abolitionist message in the 1840s and '50s could recall the skepticism and scorn of the antislavery movement toward the patriarchal, or "positive good," justification of slavery (Rose 24–40). Moreover, one of the chief aims of the antebellum slave narrative had been to give the lie to such a sentimental image of the relationship between master and slave. Seven years before *Behind the Scenes* was published, in *Incidents in the Life of a Slave Girl*, Harriet Jacobs had spoken for dozens of slave narrators when she wrote unequivocally of black men, women, and children: "These God-breathing machines are no more, in the sight of their masters, than the cotton they plant, or the horses they tend" (8). The doubtful reception that Keckley received to her characterization of the warm attachment between master and slave is thus, at least in part, attributable to the success of the antebellum slave narrative in convincing Northern whites that Southern slaveholders really were just as cruel and selfish as Jacobs claimed they were.

When Keckley wrote *Behind the Scenes* in 1868 and Douglass his *Life and Times* in 1881, however, the political priorities of the antebellum slave narrative no longer commanded the postbellum slave narrator's exclusive allegiance. Many antebellum slave narratives, epitomized by Douglass's 1845 *Narrative*, were designed to exacerbate the sectional divisions that would eventually rend the United States into two warring camps. Abolitionist endorsement and often sponsorship of antebellum slave narratives, along with the slaveocracy's outraged response to them, both in literary and political circles, testify to the success of this tradition in driving a moral wedge between the people of the North and South so as to enlist the sympathies of white Northerners for the slave (Andrews 1–7, 97–101). But soon after the Civil War, ex-slave autobiographers, like the majority of black activists and pundits of the Reconstruction era, decided that it was no longer in the best interests of blacks, especially black Southerners, to continue to feed the sectionalism of the past.[7] The freeman and freewoman could benefit greatly from a genuine national reconciliation and from a revision of the image of the degenerate slaveholder that so many antebellum slave narratives had etched on the conscience of the nation. The antebellum slave narrator had always insisted that the slave could free him/herself from the degrading effects of slavery. For the postbellum slave narrator to argue the same thing about the slaveholder was more than morally consistent; it was politically expedient, given the progressive aims of autobiographers like Keckley and Douglass, each of whom wanted to believe that the white South could and would change, once liberated from slavery.[8]

The political significance of scenes of reconciliation, therefore, needs to be reckoned with seriously in the postbellum slave narrative. One should note, for instance, that, in the reunion scenes depicted by Keckley and Douglass, it is the former slave who takes the initiative to return to the South and reunite with the former mistress and master. By demonstrating the moral leadership in such reunions, the former slave comes before the reader of the postbellum slave narrative as an active agent in the reconstruction of the South, not as the white man's burden so often portrayed by New South politicians (Williamson 79–85). The ex-slaves' quests for reunion prove them faithful and true to the national ideal, that of a united people in the states of America. Yet these narratives are not nearly so well-known as romances like Thomas Nelson Page's *Red Rock* (1898) and Joel Chandler Harris's *Gabriel Tolliver* (1902), in which indomitable former Confederates and sympathetic Yankees re-cement the bond between North and South and point the nation toward harmony and prosperity. Of course in these romances the concern is with reconciliation between the sections, accomplished at the expense of significant reconciliation between the races. In the autobiographies of Keckley and Douglass, on the other hand, the postbellum slave narrator takes the moral as well as political lead in showing the necessity of reconciliation between the races, not just the sections, of the United States as the basis on which a true Union in freedom and opportunity had to be founded. Perhaps writers like Keckley and Douglass pictured reconciliation with the slave-owning class as too easily won; perhaps the nation was all too willing to read such scenes as indicating that black-white *rapprochement* in the South was assured and that further vigilance and activism was not needed. Regardless of how one interprets the reading that these reconciliation scenes received, their political agenda should not be undervalued or misread as merely "accommodationist," in the pejorative sense that this term has taken on in Afro-American literary criticism.

It is also worthwhile to note here two additional significances of the reconciliation scenes in postbellum slave narratives like those of Keckley and Douglass. The willingness, in fact the desire, of both Keckley and Douglass to return to their Southern roots and be reunited with their former mistress and master points up a psychological complexity in the Afro-American slave narrative tradition that can be too easily ignored. The attitude of the ex-slave toward her or his past in the South is complicated by the obvious fact that the antebellum past is the locus of much pain as well as some pleasure in recollection. The antebellum slave narrator concentrated on the painfulness of remembering the Southern past; the image of the Southern past for most slave narrators before 1865 stresses absence, deprivation, want—what was not there, what was stolen and refused by whites, what was denied by the institution of slavery. The great symbol of the Southern past for the antebellum slave narrator is the absent mother and the abandoned grandmother of Douglass's 1845 *Narrative*. Whites who pretend to a paternalistic or patriarchal relationship with their slaves are generally dismissed as, when not directly denounced for, trying to substitute something bogus for the real thing in a slave's heart.

When we encounter the defensive tone in which Keckley and especially Douglass recount their reunions with their former owners, we should realize just how effectively the antebellum slave narrators convinced whites like Keckley's "Northern friends" of what an ex-slave was *supposed* to think about his or her past, and especially about the white Southern slaveholders of that past. Keckley and Douglass acknowledge that their views of their former owners are unorthodox, maybe even heretical, but overriding the resistance that they imagine from their readers is their refusal to toe the correct political line, to conform to popular proprieties that expected ex-slaves to despise their former enslavers and purge all that ugly past from their thoughts. Keckley insists, on the contrary, that the past is not something that can or should be selectively forgotten. Everything about her Southern past, the good and the bad things, is interwoven. For instance, only by reasserting her relationship to the Garlands is Keckley able to recover valuable information about the fate of her mother's only sister. Only by returning to Thomas Auld in 1877 could Douglass gain reliable information about his birth date, which to almost his dying day he labored to fix with certainty (Preston 31). The postbellum narrator's attitude toward the slave past, in sum, is remarkably open to the proposition that something *positive*, something *sustaining*, could be gleaned from that past, even from the whites of that past, if only the ex-slave did not cling uncritically to the image of that past that antislavery writers of earlier generations had often insisted on. The scenes of reconciliation in the narratives of Keckley and Douglass, therefore, instance the Afro-American slave narrator's growing reconciliation to the idea of the Southern past as a potential resource, not necessarily or simply a curse. To fail to be reconciled to such a complex sense of the past would have seriously inhibited Afro-American autobiography's ongoing effort to keep the concept of black selfhood free from the confinements of political agendas, literary proprieties, and the expectations of readers, particularly white readers.

Slave narratives like *Behind the Scenes* and *Life and Times of Frederick Douglass* are representative of perhaps the most under-read autobiographical tradition in Afro-American literature, the tradition of the postbellum slave narrative. When critics of autobiography talk about the slave narrative, what they refer to, almost invariably, is the *antebellum* slave narratives, those published before 1865. The autobiographies that ex-slaves wrote after Emancipation have been almost entirely ignored or condescendingly dismissed from serious scholarly consideration by literary historians of black autobiography—in spite of the fact that the slave narrative continued to dominate Afro-American autobiography for seventy years, from the end of the Civil War until well into the 1920s.[9]

One of the best ways to ensure that the slave narrative tradition, as a whole, will continue to be selectively studied is to continue to treat antebellum black autobiography as a standard by which postbellum slave narrative sought to be measured. Neither Keckley nor Douglass was willing to be bound to a prior standard or tradition, even though antebellum ex-slaves had helped to build it and even though, in Douglass's case, that tradition owed much to his own previous slave narratives. When Keckley and Douglass boldly reclaimed their pasts and depicted their reunions with their enslavers, they identified themselves as revisionists intent on renewing the slave narrative as a genre that could still be relevant to the new post-slavery era. Some readers may wonder if such revisionism represents a deviation from historical truth. In a more productive reading, however, we can see that such revisionism is itself indicative of a historical truth, maybe not *the* truth (assuming there is such a thing), embedded in something believed to be past, but *a* truth emerging in something the writer faces in the present. Scenes of reconciliation in postbellum slave narratives may thus instance a principle in Afro-American literary history that we have not fully reckoned with, namely, that no literary tradition is sacrosanct, that any myth, trope, or theme from the past may undergo revisionary renewal in response to the changing demands of the present. If we can read Afro-American literature with an appreciation of this ever-renewing revisionism, we can move closer to an understanding of the dynamics of its history and import of its thematic and formal traditions.

**NOTES**

1. Representative postbellum autobiographies by former slaves in which a return to the South is featured prominently are Adams, Anderson, Brown, Bruce, Douglass, Henson, Jackson, Keckley, Lowery, and Smith.

2. In many ex-slave autobiographies that feature a descent into the South, the return is only temporary, often for little more than a visit.

3. For one such example, however, see Jackson.

4. The most extensive information available on Douglass's postbellum visits to his Maryland home may be found in Preston 159–97.

5. In 1892, when an expanded version of *Life and Times* was published, Douglass did not alter or expunge any of the hopeful language he had used in 1881 to describe black prospects in the new South. One should notice, however, that in 1892 Douglass made a point of underscoring the "reactionary tendencies of public opinion against the black man and . . . the increasing decline, since the war for the Union, in the power of resistance to the onward march of the rebel states to their former control and ascendancy in the councils of the nation" (539). In 1881 Douglass was undoubtedly a good deal more sanguine about sectional rapprochement on the basis of racial justice than he was by 1892.

6. Since this essay was published, researchers have determined that Alexander Kirkland fathered Keckley's son, George.

7. For the reconciliationist mood of black America during the Reconstruction era, see Meier 3–8 and Litwack 504–06.

8. That his optimism was widespread among black Southerners during the Reconstruction era is argued by Williamson 44–50. Though this optimism abated as the century wore on, Keckley in 1868 and Douglass in 1881 wrote when the tide of faith and hope was still relatively high.

9. Between 1865 and 1925 some seventy novel-length works of fiction were published by Afro-Americans. During the same sixty years, ninety black American autobiographers told their stories. Of this number, at least fifty were written by persons born in slavery.

**WORKS CITED**

Adams, John Quincy. *Narrative of the Life of John Quincy Adams, When in Slavery, and Now as a Freeman.* Harrisburg, PA: Sieg, 1872.

Anderson, Robert. *From Slavery to Affluence.* Hemingford: Author, 1927.

Andrews, William L. *To Tell a Free Story: The First Century of Afro-American Autobiography, 1760–1865.* Urbana: University of Illinois Press, 1986.

Brown, William Wells. *My Southern Home.* New York: A.G. Brown, 1880.

Bruce, Henry Clay. *The New Man.* York: Anstadt, 1895.

Douglass, Frederick. *Life and Times of Frederick Douglass.* 1881. London: Collier, 1962.

Henson, Josiah. *An Autobiography of the Rev. Josiah Henson ("Uncle Tom"), From 1789 to 1881.* Ed. John Lobb. London: Schuyler, Smith, 1881.

Jackson, Mattie J. *The Story of Mattie J. Jackson* (1886). *Six Women's Slave Narratives.* Introduction, William L. Andrews. New York: Oxford University Press, 1988.

Jacobs, Harriet A. *Incidents in the Life of a Slave Girl.* Ed. Jean Fagan Yellin. Cambridge: Harvard University Press, 1987.

Keckley, Elizabeth. *Behind the Scenes: Or, Thirty Years a Slave, and Four Years in the White House.* New York: G.W. Carleton, 1868.

Litwack, Leon F. *Been in the Storm So Long: The Aftermath of Slavery.* New York: Knopf, 1979.

Lowery, I.E. *Life on the Old Plantation in Ante-Bellum Days.* Columbia: State, 1911.

Meier, August. *Negro Thought in America, 1880–1915.* Ann Arbor: University of Michigan Press, 1963.

Meyer, Michael, ed. *Frederick Douglass: The Narrative and Selected Writings.* New York: Modern Library, 1984.

Preston, Dickson J. *Young Frederick Douglass: The Maryland Years.* Baltimore: Johns Hopkins University Press, 1980.

Rose, Willie Lee. "The Domestication of Domestic Slavery." *Slavery and Freedom.* Ed. William W. Freehling. New York: Oxford University Press, 1982. 24–40.

Smith, James L. *Autobiography of James L. Smith*. Norwich: Press of the Bulletin, 1881.

Stepto, Robert B. *From Behind the Veil: A Study of Afro-American Narrative*. Urbana: University of Illinois Press, 1979.

Washington, Booker T. *Up from Slavery*. Vol. 1 of *The Booker T. Washington Papers*. Ed. Louis R. Harlan. Urbana: University of Illinois Press, 1972.

Williamson, Joel. *The Crucible of Race: Black-White Relationships in the American South since Emancipation*. New York: Oxford University Press, 1984.

Winks, Robin, ed. *An Autobiography of the Rev. Josiah Henson. Four Fugitive Slave Narratives*. Reading: Addison-Wesley, 1969.

CHAPTER THREE

**FRANCES SMITH FOSTER**

# Autobiography after Emancipation
The Example of Elizabeth Keckley

THE INCREASED SCHOLARLY ATTENTION both to autobiography and to African American studies which came about in the 1970s proved to be a bonanza for African American autobiographical studies. Though the Vietnam era fostered this latest revision of the canon, the post–World War II period laid its foundation. Both Marion Starling and Charles Nichols completed dissertations in the 1940s which signaled the first serious literary study of slave narratives. Since then, studies such as my *Witnessing Slavery* (1979), *The Art of the Slave Narrative*, edited by Sekora and Turner (1982), and *The Slave's Narrative*, edited by Davis and Gates (1985), have firmly established the autobiographical works of slaves and ex-slaves as part of the American literary tradition. William Andrews's *To Tell a Free Story: The First Century of Afro-American Autobiography, 1760–1865* (1986) has broken new ground by redefining the terms of bondage and freedom with his concentration upon what he terms the "literary emancipation" of the African American narrative. Also in the late 1940s, Rebecca Chalmers Barton's *Witnesses for Freedom: Negro Americans in Autobiography* suggested ways of categorizing the many contributions since Booker T. Washington's *Up from Slavery*. Later studies of African American autobiography such as Butterfield's *Black Autobiography in America* (1974), Smith's *Where I'm Bound: Patterns of Slavery and Freedom in Black American Autobiography* (1974), and Stepto's *From Behind the Veil: A Study of Afro-American Narrative* (1979) have in their own ways responded to Barton's call. Currently, there is unprecedented attention to African American autobiographies, the genre that many modern critics recognize as the fountainhead of African American literature.

Scholarly attention, however, has concentrated upon the antebellum and the twentieth-century African American autobiographies. My intention with this essay is to suggest something of the in-between, the period immediately after the Civil War and before the turn of the century, a period wherein the genre began to expand in accordance with the changes in literary form, social environment, and African American experience. My example is Elizabeth Keckley's *Behind the Scenes: Or, Thirty Years a Slave, and Four Years in the White House*, an autobiography published in 1868. It is, in many ways, representative of the postbellum slave narratives. Analysis of its form and content reveals much about the assumptions and traditions within which African Americans of the Reconstruction period wrote and the ways in which their writings were received. Though representative, it is also a special case. The extreme controversy that its publication engendered gave this work at first unusual notoriety and then unmerited neglect.

Before focusing upon the example of Keckley's autobiography, however, it will be helpful to briefly review the origins of African American autobiography and the place of this form in literary history. Extant examples are rare, but they are frequent enough for scholars now to understand that as early as 2450 BC Assyrians, Egyptians, and Babylonians customarily inscribed prayers and personal desires upon tombs and pillars. Though male writers dominate this genre, women did participate. Princess Nj-seder-Kai's prayers are inscribed upon a tomb dated from the Fifth Dynasty, and the "Tale of Ahuri" (ca. 1570–1085 BC) is a first-person account of the life of a pharaoh's daughter (Jelinek 11–12). Autobiographical writing entered the Greco-Roman tradition several centuries before Margery Burnham Kempe wrote the earliest extant autobiography in English.[1]

Of course, the originators do not have any privileged influence upon the development or the use of that creation, and the characteristics by which autobiographies have come to be evaluated have not been determined by Africans or by British women. Colonists brought the tradition with them in such forms as criminal, travel, and religious conversion narratives to North America. Here women and men adapted those forms to the experiences that shaped their own realities. In the two most original and important forms, Indian captivity and slave narratives, women and blacks had significant impact. However, literary historians and critics, most of whom have been Anglo males, defined and deified autobiography in their own image. So pervasive has been their influence that until this day most people believe that American autobiography is a legacy from St. Augustine almost directly to Benjamin Franklin. Ignoring the African heritage of Augustine, they have established a canon which privileges the life histories of white men even as they concede that the persistent and provocative contributions of women and persons of color have made autobiography what William Dean Howells in 1909 proclaimed as the "most democratic province of the republic of letters" (798).

In the United States especially, the personal histories of lives lived or, perhaps more accurately, of lives as the authors wished to have readers believe they were lived, have captured the imaginations and offered a forum for an incredible variety of people who would otherwise not have entered the literary realms. Women and men; rich and poor; judges, criminals, and victim; inventors and embezzlers; athletes, entertainers; entrepreneurs; social reformers; and con artists have all contributed to the genre. And since, as William Andrews has reminded us, "Whatever else it is, autobiography stems more often than not from a need to explain and justify the self" (1), it is small wonder that this form would hold a particular attraction for African Americans. Today, scholars and general readers alike know about certain modern African American autobiographies such as Wright's *Black Boy*, Angelou's *I Know Why the Caged Bird Sings*, and *The Autobiography of Malcolm X*. It is important to recall, however, that African American autobiography began well before the twentieth century. From the Indian captivity narratives of Briton Hammon (1760) and John Marrant (1785) to the religious experiences of Jarena Lee (1836) and Rebecca Jackson (1830–64), from the travel narratives of Nancy Prince (1850) and William Wells Brown (1852) to the rags-to-riches sagas of Frederick Douglass (1881) and George Henry (1894), the first-person accounts of African American lives and times have entertained and informed American readers. Some, particularly the antebellum slave narratives, achieved bestseller status.

Nonetheless, William Dean Howells overstated the case when he announced that autobiography was a genre unrestricted "to any age, or sex, creed, class or color" and asserted that, despite the obscurity or humbleness of an individual, "it needs but the sincere relation of what he has been and done and felt and thought to give him a place with any other in this most democratic province of the republic of letters" (798). The American public certainly knew better. Over fifty years earlier, Ralph Waldo Emerson had complained that "men imagine that books are dice, and have no merit in their fortune; that the trade and the favor of a few critics can get one book into circulation, and defeat another" (138). As the author of many books, the editor of influential journals, and a mentor to at least two African American writers, Howells was not ignorant of the impact of extraliterary influences upon the publication, distribution, and critical reception of literary texts.

Though contemporary analyses of autobiography still tout autobiography as the "most democratic province," some critics do note the scarcity of women and people of color within this literary republic. Feminist scholars such as Paula Gunn Allen, Estelle Jelinek, Amy Ling, Sidonie Smith, and Domna Stanton have been especially diligent in examining the "female autograph." They and others acknowledge that, in the nineteenth century, racism and sexism made literacy difficult and often illegal for the white women and the people of color who together constituted then, as now, the majority of Americans. Those who were able to write or to dictate their stories generally found few publishing opportunities. And those who both wrote and published their versions of self found that the readers' expectations and prejudices required particular modifications of style and content and even then often distorted what was written.

The commentary that surrounds Elizabeth Keckley's *Behind the Scenes* presents particularly striking examples of misreadings that not only distorted her intent but, in order to justify the commentators' conclusions, consistently ignored critical elements of her text. Because of the political prominence of those with whom she interacted and the unfortunate timing of her publication, her work has suffered more radical misinterpretation and neglect than most. Not only was the book misread, condemned, and withdrawn from public circulation but its authorship was attributed to others and Elizabeth Keckley's very existence was denied.[2] Thus, another reason for using this particular work is to argue for its rightful status as an autobiography.

Things should have been different. Elizabeth Keckley's life had all the elements to delight postbellum readers. Having begun life as a poor, friendless, and abused child, she could now survey her history from a position of success achieved by her own hard work, indefatigable determination, and good character. The pattern of her life fit so exactly the prevalent formula for women's fiction that Keckley felt compelled to warn her readers that "My life, so full of romance, may sound like a dream to the matter-of-fact reader, nevertheless everything I have written is strictly true" (xi). In describing her journey from obscurity to prominence, Keckley's autobiography continued the tradition established by Benjamin Franklin and concentrated upon the incidents that molded her character—particularly those that involved political and social leaders. She was an intimate of both the Jefferson Davis household before the secession and the Abraham Lincoln household afterwards. Her narrative would undoubtedly reveal inside—maybe even titillating—information about the defeated president of the Confederacy, the martyred president of the Union, and, of course, the notorious Mary Todd Lincoln.

Nineteenth-century readers could consider Keckley's life as a fitting imitation of Lincoln's journey from rail-splitter to president or of Franklin's progress from apprentice to ambassador. Though Keckley had not obtained the status of a Franklin or a Lincoln, that was to her advantage. Her sphere was considered to be entirely different. Elizabeth Keckley was a woman, she was black, she was a former slave. According to the attitudes of that time, her progress was remarkable for one of her ilk.

Elizabeth Keckley had been a valued and loyal slave for thirty years. With her master's permission, she had purchased herself and her son, moved to Washington, DC, and established a business that employed over twenty people and catered to an elite, white clientele. Not only was Keckley a talented, responsible seamstress but she had served as a family retainer to several prominent figures. In her current position with the Lincolns, Keckley had gone from being nursemaid in a Big House to domestic servant in the Biggest House or, as she describes it and as several newspaper articles had made public, from slave to "friend and confidant" of Mary Todd Lincoln.

Elizabeth Keckley's life contained materials that could be used to delight and instruct nineteenth-century readers. And, in fact, it promised even more. In the postbellum period, when the nation wanted to turn its back on pain and divisiveness and to believe that the American Dream would survive, what better assurance could readers have desired than to be told that former slaves did not blame them for slavery and that, given the chance, they would become industrious, self-sustaining, and loyal servants? Elizabeth Keckley expressed no bitterness over slavery and exhibited no wish to change the basic order of things. She assured her readers that slaveholders were less responsible for slavery than "the God of nature and the fathers who framed the Constitution for the United States" (xii).

It was also more pleasing to her readers that Keckley was not an agitator. She was not publicly identified with the temperance, suffrage, or other reformist movements of that period. Her primary interests outside her job had been her son, who left Wilberforce University to join the Union forces; her church, Washington, DC's socially active but staid Fifteenth Street Presbyterian Church; and her friends who were among the black social elite. She worked quietly but effectively with philanthropists and abolitionists to support the Contraband Relief Association and the Freedmen's Village, two of the organizations that tried to care for the thousands of slaves and ex-slaves who migrated to Washington during and immediately after the Civil War. Though self-assured and to some a bit arrogant, Mrs. Keckley carefully observed social protocol. Small wonder that she reports many requests to write her life story. A life such as hers could be used to inspire black people, to reassure doubtful whites about the potential of the newly freed slaves, and to prove once again the vitality of the American Dream.

Elizabeth Keckley knew her life achievements were extraordinary. She cherished her reputation in the black community as a brilliant conversationalist and a generous but exacting teacher. She proudly reported that President Lincoln always addressed her as "Madam Elizabeth" (156), and she undoubtedly knew that she had become a legend who caused people to arrive early at church in order to see her "queenly" entrance each Sunday (Washington 218). Over the years she had carefully preserved memorabilia that included family letters and legal papers, scraps of fabric from garments made for her more famous clients, the glove that Lincoln wore at his second inaugural reception, and various documents from the Confederate Congress. All this, along with her strong sense of historicity, made it inevitable that she would someday write her memoirs.

Often, as Albert E. Stone reminds us, autobiography is "an act deferred, a duty often imposed by fate at the end of a long career and enjoined by family, friends, publishers, and the curious public" (28). When Mary Todd Lincoln's attempt to sell some of her clothing and jewelry became a media circus that many believed not only proved once again her social ineptitude but besmirched her martyred husband's name and embarrassed the country, Elizabeth Keckley believed that it was her duty to try to assuage the damage caused by this "Old Clothes Scandal." She felt that her testimony regarding the motivations for Mary Lincoln's actions, the actual circumstances that transpired, and, especially, Keckley's own role in these events would help squelch the pernicious rumors that threatened both Mary Lincoln's and her own reputation. This then became the occasion that caused her to accede to the "importunities of her friends" and to write her life story. But in Keckley's case, fate, friends, publishers, and the curious public turned against her.

The book she had intended as her autobiography became increasingly sensationalized. James Redpath, her editor, violated her trust by appending, with no attempt to remove the personal elements, Mary Lincoln's letters to Keckley. G.W. Carleton and Company, her publisher, first advertised the book in April 1868 as "A Remarkable Book entitled *Behind the Scenes*" that could not fail "to create a wide world of interest not alone in the book, but in its gifted and conscientious author." By May 13, the work was being promoted by the dual title: *White House Revelations or Behind the Scenes,* and by May 30, the big bold print promised *Behind the Scenes, the Great Sensational Disclosures,* by Mrs. Keckley (Washington 231–34).

The reading public took its lead from the advertisements. Rather than developing an interest in this "gifted and conscientious author," readers focused upon the book's descriptions of the private affairs of the prominent people with whom she had associated. Whereas Keckley meant to draw aside "the veil of mystery" and bring "the origin of a fact . . . to light with the naked fact itself" (xiv), her readers perceived it as uncovering scandal and publicly, as airing the Lincolns' dirty linen. Though Keckley wrote to help "stifle the voice of calumny," her work raised the volume of the voice. Mary Lincoln was mortified. Robert Lincoln was infuriated. He pressured the publishers to halt distribution, and his friends bought up the remaining copies. Though Elizabeth Keckley had intended the profits to aid Mrs. Lincoln, Mary Lincoln was so outraged that she refused to reimburse Keckley for the expenses she had incurred at Lincoln's request and thereafter pretended not to have known the woman she had formerly called her "dearest friend." Instead of easing Lincoln's financial distress, Keckley found herself facing poverty. Her business lost most of its clients. Her status in the black community declined. Some who had applauded Keckley as an example of black achievement now considered her a disgrace to the race. Because she had been accused of betraying her employers' confidence, they argued that she had imperiled the jobs of similarly employed black people.

Today *Behind the Scenes* occupies a permanent, albeit obscure, niche in Lincoln memorabilia. The letters it contains do provide invaluable information about what has come to be called "The Old Clothes Scandal," and every serious biography of Mary Todd Lincoln quotes material from Keckley's book.

According to Dorothy Porter, "Mrs. Keckley's book reveals more clearly the intimate family life of the martyred president and offers a more credible portrait of Mary Todd, than perhaps any other book about the Lincolns" (ii). *Behind the Scenes* also shows up regularly in bibliographies of slave narratives and surveys of early African American literature. Scholars acknowledge Keckley's work as a contribution to black social history; however, they tend to conclude, as did Vernon Loggins, that Mrs. Lincoln is "really the central figure" of Mrs. Keckley's book (260).

While the book is, as she intended, something more than the personal history of Elizabeth Keckley, to make Mary Lincoln the central figure of the book requires that one ignore not only a substantial portion of the work itself but the author's stated intentions and her own life history. As Loggins himself states, "Considerable comment in *Behind the Scenes* is devoted to Elizabeth Keckley's feelings toward race prejudice. She was a Negro woman proud of her color, and she lost no opportunity to push her race forward" (261). Her narrative is shaped, as was her life, by an unshakable self-confidence and a consistent self-respect. The multiple purposes of *Behind the Scenes* are unified through a structural organization based on the constant repetition of two basic themes: the preeminence of private substance over public appearance and the predestined progress for those who perceived the hidden lessons of experience and acted upon them. At times the Lincolns dominate her narrative as they were dominating her life while she was writing it, but Keckley's narrative presence and her persistent characterization of herself as an exemplar preserve her centrality. When one considers the book as a whole, noting carefully the narrator's stated goals and characterization and her narrative's structure and content, it becomes evident that *Behind the Scenes* is Elizabeth Keckley's *apologia pro vita sua*, an autobiography in the tradition of Benjamin Franklin's, and a testimony to the tenacity of the American Dream during one of the nightmares of this nation's history. As a Reconstruction autobiography, it is a pivotal work in the development of African American autobiography, adapting the form and functions of the antebellum slave narrative to the experiences and intents of the postbellum era. *Behind the Scenes* is a pivotal work, qualifying in Robert Stepto's terms as a "response" to the slave narratives' "call," that is, an "artistic act of closure performed upon a formal unit that already possesses substantial coherence" (6).

*Behind the Scenes* is similar to the antebellum slave narrative in its basic intention to provide an insider's account of slavery that would correct the myths and convince the readers of the horrible wrongness of that institution. This resemblance is most obvious in the first third of the book, which recounts Keckley's thirty years as a slave. In describing her experiences and her transformation from chattel to citizen, the author uses the pattern established for the antebellum slave narrative. She creates a protagonist who represents countless other slaves.

The title page of *Behind the Scenes* announces its author as "Elizabeth Keckley, formerly a slave...." In its immediate and prominent acknowledgment of her slave heritage, Keckley's narrative follows the tradition begun with the eighteenth-century publications of Phillis Wheatley and Briton Hammon, who were identified as "a Negro servant to Mr. John Wheatley" and "A Negro Man,—Servant to General Winslow." The authors of antebellum slave narratives rigidly adhered to these two models. Whether fugitives or legally free, authors of antebellum narratives generally emphasized their slave status, identifying themselves, for example, as "Frederick Douglass, an American Slave," "William Wells Brown, a Fugitive Slave," or "Linda Brent... a Slave Girl."[3] Keckley begins, as so many others had before her, by expressing the conundrum of being born into a life-denying environment. She says, "I was born a slave... therefore I came upon the earth free in God-like thought, but fettered in action" (17). Her early chapters chronicle a series of confrontations between her "God-like thought" and the forces that would deny her such expression. She shows the institutionalized dehumanization by concentrating upon its capricious and brutal punishments, its heartless divisions of families, and its deliberate denial of gentility and virtue to black women. As a slave she lived in Virginia, North Carolina, Mississippi, and Missouri. When she was free, she moved to Washington, DC. The pattern of her narrative follows the antebellum slave narrative's movement from South to North. Through her personal experiences and those of others she knew, Keckley presents a panoramic view of slavery. Though she assured her reader that her work would paint both the "dark" and the "bright" sides of slavery, it is apparent that the dark side is bondage and the light side is freedom.

The differences between antebellum and postbellum narratives are sometimes subtle, but they are significant. Chief among these are the changes in tone and characterization. Like antebellum narrators, the ex-slaves chronicle the atrocities and deprivations under slavery. However, they are far more likely to reinterpret their earlier hardships in light of the lessons they taught. Keckley cites her slave sufferings as the "fire of the crucible" and declares, "I was a feeble instrument in His hands, and through me and the enslaved millions of my race, one of the problems was solved that belongs to the great problems of human destiny" (xii).

As agents of cosmic truth, the slaves were more than victims. The protagonists could be portrayed in more heroic terms, as persons whose special sufferings endowed them with special attributes. For example, the four-year-old Lizzie Keckley was assigned to watch over her master's infant. Obviously this was a Herculean task for one who was still a toddler herself, and Keckley admits that she was not equal to it. When she rocked the cradle so "industriously" that the baby was tossed out, though the infant was not harmed, the young nursemaid was severely beaten. According to Keckley, this was the first of many punishments she endured. However, in recounting her first beating, she does not linger on the cruelty but emphasizes the overall benefits of her job. In retrospect, her assignment as a nursemaid was generally "pleasant" because she was transferred from the "rude cabin" to her master's household, she received a dress and an apron, and she was promised that if she performed her duties well, she could become the little girl's personal maid (20). She concludes that "notwithstanding all the wrongs that slavery heaped upon me, I can bless it for one thing—youth's important lesson of self-reliance" (19–20).

Although her perspective here might seem to be that of an extremely patient individual, Keckley's is actually more that of an ambitious and calculating hero recounting the cost of her success. Her characterization is not so much nonviolent as nonaggressive, and here again is a subtle but important difference from earlier narrators. Before the war, narrators preferred to present themselves as long-suffering and nonviolent victims of oppression. When all else failed, they resorted to guilt-provoking duplicity and elected to run rather than to fight. Frederick Douglass was one of the few antebellum narrators who confessed to having been physically defiant. In confessing this incident, Douglass emphasizes that he had suffered many inhumane beatings as part of Covey's attempt to break him "in body, soul, and spirit" (66). Finally, when Covey beat Douglass because Douglass was too ill to work and when Douglass's master refused his appeal for protection and forced him to return to Covey, Douglass resolved to defend himself from any further physical assaults. The confrontation with Covey is central to Douglass's narrative; it symbolizes his psychological transformation from chattel to human being. And yet, this passage is very ambiguous. Douglass makes it clear that Covey attacked him and that he fought only in self-defense. Douglass does not assert that he defeated Covey, only that he resisted until Covey was worn out. Moreover, Douglass suggests that, until he wrote his narrative many years later, this confrontation remained secret.

Elizabeth Keckley, on the other hand, recites several instances wherein she fought both her master and a local minister who sought to subdue her "stubborn pride" (36). Though she was not a physical match for these men, she could and did fight back so valiantly that they were exhausted with the struggle. Apparently Keckley also fought with her tongue, for she says that "These revolting scenes created a great sensation at the time, were the talk of the town and neighborhood, and I flatter myself that the actions of those who had conspired against me were not viewed in a light to reflect much credit upon them" (38). Finally, unlike Douglass, Keckley clearly triumphed because she says that each man apologized, promised never to hit her again, and kept that promise.

Given what we know about Douglass's character and his outspokenness in subsequent autobiographies, these differences in self-depictions by two people who in 1868 were friends and colleagues are not easily explained as differences in personality. Rather it is more likely that postbellum narrators were freer to admit their rebelliousness. Abolition had removed the necessity to condemn any form of physical resistance in order to discourage slave insurrections. The cultural context had changed sufficiently to allow readers to tolerate, perhaps even admire, a young girl's decision to become a fighter and not a fugitive. While postbellum readers might consider it unseemly for a black or a woman to raise a hand against a white man, such readers were also likely to appreciate the atrocity of grown men who claimed social leadership assaulting innocent girls.

The postbellum era may have been slightly more tolerant toward slave rebels, but the enormous number of newly freed slaves created considerable concern. This situation required other differences in characterization. Unlike the antebellum slave narrators, who downplayed their individual initiative and self-discipline to enhance their argument against the insidiousness of slavery as an institution, postbellum narrators needed to convince their readers that the former slaves, especially those who had passively endured their bondage, were capable of assuming the responsibilities of freedom. Keckley emphasizes her early determination to gain recognition not solely as a human being but as an individual who deserved respect and compensation for her talents and sacrifices. This emphasis upon talent and potential was partly accomplished by increasing the length of time the narratives covered. Although many narratives, such as those by Douglass, Harriet Jacobs, and J.W.C. Pennington, were written many years after the authors had escaped from slavery, most antebellum works ended soon after their writer's arrival in the North. Postbellum narratives, by contrast, normally went beyond that arrival to describe the actual or anticipated achievements of the former slave.

Keckley's narrative exemplifies this trend from its beginnings. Just as its title echoed those of antebellum narratives by its immediate and prominent identification of its author with slavery, *Behind the Scenes* also modified that form by stressing a movement up from slavery. Keckley's identification as "formerly a slave, but more recently modiste, and friend" and her juxtaposition of "Thirty Years a Slave, and Four Years in the White House" reject a static definition as "slave" or even "former slave." They suggest progressive movement, emphasizing the social distance traveled. Keckley's early ambition to leave the rude cabin foreshadowed the motivation that would propel her into the White House. It symbolized the possible strength of character of her fellow slaves who had endured the crucible and typified that of other black achievers whose autobiographical offerings would follow her model. In this way, *Behind the Scenes* is a prototype for later black success stories such as John Mercer Langston's *From the Virginia Plantation to the National Capitol*, Peter Randolph's *From Slave Cabin to the Pulpit*, and Robert Anderson's *From Slavery to Affluence*.

Finally, African American autobiographers of the Reconstruction period were free to develop other themes. Publishing as they did after the end of legal slavery, there was no need to plead the antislavery cause. As a postbellum writer Keckley could concentrate upon larger implications of the struggle between good and evil. Keckley's book downplays categories such as North and South, bondage and freedom, and slave and master. It postulates instead the interrelation of the most despised and victimized slave with the most respected and powerful slaveholder. Keckley's emphasis was in keeping with the liberal reconstructionists' goal of mending the tears in the society's fabric while reweaving the pattern in black and white. And, she was freer to enjoy the prerogatives of the autobiographical form.

Several scholars have argued persuasively that the assembly of an African American author's work—that is, its prefaces, appendices, inscriptions, and such, and the control the author asserts over that assemblage—provides critical information for anyone "who seeks an integrated vision of literary tradition and transition" (Stepto 52). Unlike most antebellum narratives, *Behind the Scenes* does not offer testimonies of authenticity, letters of recommendation, or prefaces from white people. The title page, preface, and even the copyright identify the work as that of Elizabeth Keckley only. Despite the manipulation of the volume's distribution and publicity, Keckley retained control of its narrative voice. It is, therefore, significant that the autobiographical intent evidenced in the text of the work is signaled first by these prefatory documents.

The title page identifies the work as "*Behind the Scenes* by Elizabeth Keckley, formerly a slave, but more recently a modiste, and friend to Mrs. Abraham Lincoln." The title reminds the readers that behind the public performance is unseen but influential activity. It promises a guided tour or an insider's description. The value of such information depends upon the authority of the informant and the extent to which the individual's knowledge exceeds or confirms the audience's. Consequently the role of narrator is critical, and the credentials Keckley presents imply the aspects that she thought most important to authenticate. Keckley had been "a slave," a designation that indicates a social status somewhere between three-fifths human and an article of personal, movable property. Currently she is a "modiste." Keckley is not called a dressmaker, a nurse, or a domestic servant, though in her narrative she frankly reveals that she rendered such services. As a "modiste," she is a designer, artisan, and entrepreneur of women's fashions, an authority on manners and appearances, all of which are connotations more fitting to her concept of her role in the Lincoln household and in Washington society as well. Finally, she is a friend to the former First Lady.

The subtitle, *Thirty Years a Slave, and Four Years in the White House*, defines more specifically the book's intent. The narrator offers thirty years' experience as a slave, four years as a White House retainer, and a privileged association with the widow of the former president. While the life after bondage may have been more unusual, not only are thirty years a lot longer than four but the second mention of slavery reinforces its significance to this work. The subtitle indicates the authenticity of sustained personal experience in two apparently irreconcilably separate areas. It makes clear the social distance the narrator has traveled, from chattel to confidant of the most prestigious and symbolically powerful people in our nation. The subtitle manifests what the nation had come to realize through the War Between the States, the symbiosis of these two entities. Her parenthetical identification presents the author as an exemplary answer to current questions concerning the possible roles of the newly freed slaves and gives a larger interpretation to the meaning of "Behind the Scenes." Ultimately, it reveals the coherent pattern of the book.

The opening lines of her preface reaffirm Keckley's autobiographical intentions: "I have often been asked to write my life, as those who know me know that it has been an eventful one. At last I have acceded to the importunities of my friends, and have hastily sketched some of the striking incidents that go to make up my history" (xi). Keckley refers to her life as a "romance." This does not suggest that she considers her experiences benign or ideal but rather that they exemplify her concepts of human progress. Slavery had robbed her of her dearest right, liberty. Says Keckley, "I would not have been human had I not rebelled . . . " (xii). Nonetheless, she maintained that slavery had been a necessary phase in the moral development of the United States, a phase in which she and other slaves had "aided in bringing a solemn truth to the surface as a truth" (xiii). "Bringing truth to the surface" is the plainly stated but unacknowledged key to *Behind the Scenes*. Keckley's autobiographical intentions were based upon a profound belief in the efficacy of truth.

Elizabeth Keckley's autobiography is structured in the mode of countless other American autobiographies. It establishes its narrator as an individual of insight and integrity, demonstrates the development of a superior character by the endurance of oppression and vilification, and ultimately vindicates her sufferings by the recognition of the rightness of her actions and its accompanying riches and respect. It presents a dualistic philosophy affirming the difference between public appearance and private realities as well as the ultimate revelation of the symbolic importance of real events, an approach that Roy Pascal has demonstrated is basic to autobiography as a genre.

Keckley's autobiography is divided into three parts of five chapters each. Part One describes her thirty years as a slave. Part Two relates important events during her four years as a White House intimate. Part Three focuses upon her experiences after the assassination of President Lincoln. Her seven months' involvement in the "Old Clothes Scandal" receives only one chapter. Her association with the latter incident had motivated her to publish her narrative when and as she did, but her structure plainly shows that the episode was but a part of the total story she had to tell. It was the overall story, in fact, that she believed would allow the proper perspective from which to view that particular episode. Her interest is not in summarizing each year of her life nor even in reporting her most dramatic experiences. She has omitted many "strange passages" in her history, she says, in order to confine her story to her major interest, "the most important incidents which I believe influenced the moulding of my character" (18). What is important to her is not the surface events but the attitudes and contexts that lay behind those actions.

In Chapters One through Five, she writes of her family, her childhood, her slave experiences, and her efforts to obtain her freedom. Each episode of her slave experience is used not only to portray the truth about that institution but to show how the institution affected her personality and values. Keckley authenticates her narrative with letters and other documents which offer further context for her actions. They show that the narrator considered herself an integral and dynamic part of the families with whom she interacted. For example, in a letter to her mother Keckley reminds her to "Give my love to all the family, both white and black" (41). In the first section, the narrator emerges as an ambitious, independent, but loyal individual whose industry and integrity were rewarded with freedom.

None of the many incidents reveals the depth of her character as much as her attempts to gain her freedom. Her master refused her first request to buy herself and commanded her to never again bring up that subject. But Keckley persisted. When in exasperation he offered her the fare for the ferry and told her to leave, Keckley refused, telling him that she was perfectly aware of the ease with which she could escape, but since by law she was a slave, she chose freedom only by such means as that same law provided. He named a price. Keckley transformed herself from capital to capitalist by obtaining loans from investors and purchasing herself and her son. The extended description of this episode emphasizes her strength of character and demonstrates one of the sources of Keckley's intense belief in the ultimate triumph of integrity and perseverance.

In the last chapter in Part One the narrator tells how she repaid her loans and established her business. Although she describes the discriminatory laws and practices that hindered her progress, Keckley does not campaign against them. Perhaps it was the optimism of the Reconstruction era during which she was writing, but she emphasized the role of her good reputation and her discipline in acquiring the friends she needed to establish herself as dressmaker for Washington's elite. One of the more significant relationships was with Varina Davis. Her situation in the Jefferson Davis household foreshadowed the one Keckley enjoyed with the Abraham Lincolns. Elizabeth Keckley had begun her relationship with Jefferson and Varina Davis in Washington when Varina Davis needed a dressmaker. During the period in which she was employed, Varina Davis came to have, in Keckley's words, "the greatest confidence" in her. When Varina Davis was preparing to assume the role of First Lady of the Confederacy, she urged Keckley to come south with them so they could protect her from the inevitable backlash against free blacks that the war would bring. In the chapter she titles "In the Family of Senator Jefferson Davis," Keckley tries to make it clear that it was her character and not any particular leanings of the Lincolns that gave her access to the White House.

The first part of her book is a success story designed to establish the narrator as an individual whose personal integrity and indomitable spirit resulted in remarkable achievements. The narrator is not an ex-chattel, working the emotions of a readership predominated by those who might sympathize but could never empathize. Rather she is portraying herself as a fellow participant in the American Myth—characterizing herself as what Spengemann and Lundquist call the "Hero" or one who fully enacts prophesies, takes the mythic journey and progresses from low to high, as one who in so doing has won "the right to teach and so to perpetuate a viable tradition" (509).

Keckley's four years in the White House, detailed in Chapters Six through Eleven, begin shortly after the Lincolns' arrival in Washington, DC, and end with the assassination of President Lincoln. This section of the narrative, replete with observations, experiences, and personal anecdotes concerning the Lincoln family, echoes her earlier, briefer revelations about the Davis family. In neither case does she divulge private episodes as much as she supplements what is already public knowledge with the behind-the-scenes view. Keckley describes preparations for public appearances, gives glimpses of domestic activities, and sometimes reports conversations that reveal the private intent behind the public words or actions. In essence her narrative offers to the American public verification of the humanity of those known primarily as national symbols. In doing this, however, Keckley inserts a new figure into these family portraits. She herself is an active participant. Frequently she relates conversations she had with the Lincolns or the Davises concerning well-known events. Though the personages often dominate the stage, it is always Elizabeth Keckley, the narrator, who relates and interprets their behavior.

The unifying concept in this section is the relationship between Elizabeth Keckley and Mary Todd Lincoln. Keckley reveals the First Lady as an impulsive, stubborn, and extravagant woman but one who is essentially kindhearted, often misunderstood, and occasionally maligned. Keckley is her stabilizer, her advisor, and her friend. Their relationship is similar to that between Keckley and the Garlands, described in the first section of her book. Keckley had served as nursemaid and companion to Anne Garland from infancy until she had managed to purchase her freedom. Keckley refers to Anne as "my pet" and notes that Anne, too, had been "the cause of great trouble to me" (21). When the Garland family suffered financial setbacks, Keckley had managed to rescue them also. As she reports it, when she and the family joined Mr. Garland in their new home in Missouri, "we found him so poor that he was unable to pay the dues on a letter advertised as in the post-office for him" (44). Keckley sought work as a seamstress and dressmaker and soon established such a clientele that she was able to keep "bread in the mouths of seventeen persons for two years and five months" (45). The same elements of personal integrity and self-sacrifice that she demonstrated in her relationship with the family of her slave master are prominent in her relationship with the Lincoln family. The same means by which she had enabled the family of her slave master to "move in those circles of society to which their birth gave entrance" Keckley employed on behalf of Mrs. Lincoln's attempts to do likewise (45).

In the second part of *Behind the Scenes,* the First Family is in the foreground, but Keckley presents herself as an essential participant. To Mary Lincoln, "Lizzie" Keckley may have been simply a substitute for the mammy she had left in Kentucky, but Elizabeth Keckley is the narrator and she identifies her position as that of friend and confidant. Clearly she was more than a dressmaker, for she was summoned to perform duties that ranged from combing Mary Lincoln's hair before parties to washing and laying out the body of the Lincolns' beloved son, Willie. Long before the fateful journey to New York, Elizabeth Keckley had become a regular traveling companion, accompanying Mary Lincoln on the triumphant presidential survey of war-torn Virginia and on her sorrowful relocation to widow's quarters in Chicago.

A particular incident in this section exemplifies Keckley's narrative technique. Having already established her roles as costumer and general stagehand, she says, "I had never heard Mr. Lincoln make a public speech, and, knowing the man so well, was very anxious to hear him" (174). Before describing the public appearance that she witnessed, Keckley reminds the reader of her privileged position. She recalls for us that before the speech she had observed Lincoln "looking over his notes and muttering to himself." She knew "that he was rehearsing the part that he was to play in the great drama soon to commence" (175). Later, as she relates the "great drama" of his speech, she says, "I stood a short distance from Mr. Lincoln" (177), and though she does not report the content or the occasion of that particular speech, Keckley does say that, while observing the performance, she suddenly realized the president's vulnerability and had a premonition of his assassination (178). By describing a public appearance that her readers could readily verify and claiming a "sudden thought" which she partially attributes to "remembrance of the many warnings that Mr. Lincoln had received" (178), Keckley establishes sufficient credibility to insure acceptance of her description of the private preparations for Lincoln's public appearance. In so doing, Keckley is also laying the foundation to support her other revelations of behind-the-scenes occurrences. The theme of public performance and private reality is carried out in this reminiscence. Moreover, she as witness, prophet, and narrator is the central figure in this drama.

The assassination climaxes Part Two. Again Keckley juxtaposes public knowledge and personal experience. She begins her description of this event by contrasting the jubilation of the nation which believed the war was over with its reaction to the news that its president had been shot. "A nation suddenly paused in the midst of festivity, and stood paralyzed with horror—transfixed with awe" (184). Having set the stage, Keckley places herself upon it by saying, "At 11 o'clock at night I was awakened . . . with the startling intelligence that the entire Cabinet had been assassinated, and Mr. Lincoln shot. . . . When I heard the words I felt as if the blood had been frozen in my veins" (184). The reader recalls the nation "paralyzed with horror" and can see Keckley, at this point, as part of "the nation." Her blood, like that of her fellow citizens, froze. The tableau thaws and, seeking the truth of the rumor, she goes to the White House where she joins "the outskirts of a large crowd." Like everyone else, Keckley did not know the details immediately, and her reaction is that of the general public. However, a White House emissary soon came for her and, for several days, she is behind the scenes as Mary Lincoln's "only companion, except her children, in the days of her great sorrow" (193). Their shared grief and Mary Lincoln's dependence upon her during that crisis prove their intimate friendship and establish Keckley as Mary Lincoln's mainstay, foreshadowing Keckley's later involvement in the "Old Clothes Scandal." Moreover, in demonstrating that she had been privy to specific details about earlier public occasions, Keckley reinforces her claim to special information which would cast a new light upon the situation that prompted her writing.

The third section begins with preparations for leaving the White House. The narrator carefully details these events partly to establish the position of Mary Lincoln as dependent upon an unsympathetic Congress for her sustenance and upon her "Dear Lizzie" for support. This section continues the pattern of her relationship as guardian and friend to those she served. However, Keckley emphasizes the difference between her morality and strengths and those of Mary Lincoln. For example, when they left Washington, Mary Lincoln felt herself impoverished and was often in tears. Elizabeth Keckley, on the other hand, stood at the window of the Lincolns' new home and thought ethereally about the sunbeams that reflected upon the lake. Confided Keckley, "I wondered how any one could call Hyde Park a dreary place. I had seen so much trouble in my life, that I was willing to . . . slumber anywhere" (214). Unlike Mrs. Lincoln, Mrs. Keckley had developed a greater resistance to adversity.

In an even more revealing incident, Keckley challenges those who might wish to condemn her and her race while excusing Mary Todd. According to Keckley, the Lincolns had not required their son Tad to attend school, and he was almost illiterate. After describing one of Mary Lincoln's frustrated attempts to teach Tad to read, Keckley concluded that, "had Tad been a negro boy, not the son of a President, and so difficult to instruct, he would have been called thick-skulled, and would have been held up as an example of the inferiority of race" (219). Keckley assures her audience that she was not reflecting upon the intelligence of Tad but simply upon the dual standards by which black and white people are judged. In light of the circumstances during which she was writing her book, it takes little effort to discern special significance in her statement that "I only mean to say that some incidents are about as damaging to one side of the question as to the other . . . and if a whole race is judged by a single example of apparent dullness, another race should be judged by a similar example" (220).

In the chapter preceding the "Secret History of Mrs. Lincoln's Wardrobe," Keckley takes what she identifies as "a slight retrospective glance" and describes in great detail her triumphant return as an invited guest in the home of her former owners. Here Keckley reminds us again that through her efforts the family had been able to keep up appearances even while they had no money. Juxtaposed as it is against the events of the following chapter, this is obviously a final attempt to justify her own actions in the "Old Clothes Scandal." As important as it is for characterization, however, it is also thematically significant. It serves as Keckley's vindication and testifies to the general acceptance of her life as a success story. And since she has depicted herself as an exemplar, it is also a testimony to the possibilities of Reconstruction.

In this chapter, Madame Elizabeth is the central figure. The guest of honor, she sits in state while her former owners scurry about to prepare her food and to make her comfortable and "the servants looked on in amazement" (250). She attends social functions with Confederate leaders. Keckley reports that her host, General Meems, joked about the changes in her status, saying, "Why, Lizzie, you are riding with Colonel Gilmore. Just think of the change from Lincoln to Gilmore! It sounds like a dream. But then the change is evidence of the peaceful feeling of this country; a change, I trust, that augurs brighter days for us all" (254). In one of their conversations, Keckley assures her former mistress that she harbors "but one unkind thought" about their former relationship, that she "was not given the advantages of a good education." Her mistress, now the wife of a Confederate general, apologized but asserted that Keckley had not suffered irreparable harm since she got "along better in the world than we who enjoyed every educational advantage in childhood" (257). Miss Anne had acknowledged also that her mother had been "severe with her slaves in some respects," and certainly she had been mistaken in predicting that Keckley would not be "worth her salt." Keckley's forgiveness suggests not only her own magnanimity but the possibilities that the racial animosities of the past can be overcome, that good can ultimately triumph over evil.

In the final chapter of her history, Keckley addresses the controversy that precipitated this book. Though her self-confidence and self-respect remain unshaken, the act she now relates, "The Secret History of Mrs. Lincoln's Wardrobe in New York," is still being played out. Her book is in fact an attempt to direct the final scene. Now, Keckley depicts herself as a supporting character in an unsavory drama that features Mary Lincoln before an audience whose sympathies are not yet determined. In this section, autobiography is subordinated to exposition, and characterization gives way to plot. When the appended letters are considered, the work resembles a cloak-and-dagger drama. Yet, the theme of private substance behind public appearance continues, and Keckley's faith in the efficacy of truth connects this chapter to the rest of the narrative.

The events of this chapter began in March 1867 when Mary Lincoln wrote Elizabeth Keckley that "she had struggled long enough to keep up appearances, and that the mask must be thrown aside" (267). Lincoln was so desperate for money that she had decided to sell her clothing. Keckley reluctantly agreed to help her. She spotlights the ironic reversal that made the widow of a former president petition a former slave for help by saying, "She was the wife of Abraham Lincoln, the man who had done so much for my race, and I could refuse to do nothing for her" (269).

By birth and by marriage, Mary Lincoln was expected to manifest ladylike decorum at all times. Elizabeth Keckley, on the other hand, was not. Still, Keckley reveals herself as the more refined individual. She takes pains to show that the details of Mary Lincoln's plan troubled her from the beginning. For example, Keckley says she "could not understand why Mrs. Lincoln should travel, without protection, under an assumed name" (271). Her consternation over "the strange programme" increased when she arrived in New York to discover that Mary Lincoln was, in fact, incapable of distinguishing appearance from reality. Lincoln's actions become increasingly theatrical, and Keckley acts Sancho Panza to her Quixote. Keckley establishes her superiority when she vetoes Lincoln's decision to dine in public unescorted, saying, "I realize your situation, if you do not" (283). But Keckley's superior understanding did not empower her to control this woman who "was willing to adopt any scheme which promised a good bank account to her credit" (290–91). Despite Keckley's reservations, Mary Lincoln agreed to the suggestions by the broker with whom she contracted the sale, W.H. Brady, that she obtain money from "certain politicians" by writing letters delineating her pecuniary distress and by threatening to go public with those letters if these politicians should refuse to aid their former leader's impoverished widow. So, while Mary Lincoln wrote the letters that helped scandalize her name, Keckley could only stand "at Mrs. Lincoln's elbow" and suggest "that they be couched in the mildest language possible" (294). The plan did not work. The letters became further evidence to political insiders that Mary Lincoln was emotionally unstable. Lincoln then agreed to have the letters published in the newspapers and to put her clothing on public exhibition. On the day the letters were published, Mary Lincoln returned to Chicago, leaving Keckley to deal with Brady, the wardrobe, and the political hornet's nest that Mary Lincoln's actions had stirred. Not only did Mary Lincoln compromise her reputation by this indecorous behavior but Keckley tells us that "Mrs. Lincoln's venture proved so disastrous that she was unable to reward me for my services, and I was compelled to take in sewing to pay for my daily bread" (326).

In reporting the secret history, Keckley shifts from purely first-person narration toward the objective point of view, increasingly relying upon documents to tell the story but never entirely relinquishing her voice. To prove her efforts to counter the scandalous rumors, Keckley summarizes news articles based upon her press releases. She includes letters from prominent African Americans such as Frederick Douglass and Henry Highland Garnet attesting to their willingness to help Lincoln's widow. These letters show that Keckley's loyalty was shared by other African Americans, and, by juxtaposing the eagerness of her race to support the former First Lady during her troubles with the readiness of the white population to castigate her for her failings, Keckley suggests a more ironic interpretation of the "Old Clothes Scandal."

The shift in point of view in this section does several other things. Reliance upon memoranda, letters, and news accounts distances the narrator from events and allows us to see Keckley's helplessness in this situation without diminishing her overall achievements. It allows her to authenticate her account without resorting to a posture of self-defense. Keckley does not have to criticize Mary Lincoln directly, but as she promised in her preface, she could let "the origin of a fact be brought to light with the naked fact itself" (xiv). Just as she tried to salvage a bad situation by persuading Mary Lincoln to couch her letters in the "mildest language possible," Keckley uses the language of others to exonerate herself as gracefully as possible.

Finally, Keckley reports, "As I am writing the concluding pages of this book, I have succeeded in closing up Mrs. Lincoln's imprudent business arrangement" (327). The irony becomes almost too heavy. The former slave has proven more capable of handling business and political affairs than the wife of a United States president. As she ends her narrative, Keckley is confident that she has saved Mary Lincoln from the immediate consequences of her folly and that, by writing the book, she will be able to help her even more.

In spite of the sensationalism of the last chapter and the less charitable comments that Keckley allows herself to make, the third section continues the design of the first two. After chronicling her movement from slavery to freedom and from poverty to affluence, Keckley reveals her current actions as merely another of a series of challenging situations in which she is required to play the facilitating role. In making a public proclamation of her personal experiences, she declares the illusion of appearances and the efficacy of truth. By noting such ironies as the blacks' readiness to assume what was both a civic and moral obligation while the whites bickered among themselves, Keckley echoes the Puritan idea of moral superiority achieved through adversity, a morality, in fact, that some whites had yet to achieve.

As a postbellum narrative, *Behind the Scenes* is more assertive and more critical than those published during slavery. And yet, coming as it does at a time when "The Battle Hymn of the Republic" rang in many ears and many Americans truly believed they were on the verge of a new day, it carries an optimism and faith in the American Dream that later works do not. In many ways Keckley's autobiography demonstrates a characteristic that Mary Burger has identified as central to black autobiography, "an effect of celebration in protest and affirmation in negation" (10). It anticipates those later African American autobiographers who take their tone from the blues and thereby, as Albert Murray phrases it, "affirm not only U.S. Negro life in all of its arbitrary complexities and not only life in America in all of its infinite confusions, [but] affirm life and humanity itself in the very process of confronting failures and existentialistic absurdities" (212). Keckley's autobiography is a literary riff of the kind endemic to those who play major roles behind the scenes and on center stage.

Careful attention to the total structure of *Behind the Scenes*, and especially to the characterization of its narrator, reveals a coherence and purpose heretofore eclipsed by the presence of the book's more spectacular but less important characters. The broader implications of *Behind the Scenes*, as manifested by the author's stated intentions and the repeated motifs, which work "to bring truth to the surface as a truth," reveal this work to be a contribution of singular importance to African American autobiography and thereby to American literary history.

**NOTES**

1. *The Revelations of Divine Love* written by Dame Julian (or Juliana) of Norwich sometime around 1373 predates Margery Kempe's work; however, most scholars believe as Estelle Jelinek does that *Revelations* "is more an intellectual treatise than a personal narrative." *The Book of Margery Kempe*, written between 1436 and 1438, is therefore generally acknowledged as the earliest extant autobiographical narrative in English (Jelinek 14, 15).

2. For an excellent summary of the arguments and a definitive answer to them see John E. Washington, *They Knew Lincoln*. New York: Dutton, 1942.

3. "Linda Brent" is the pseudonym used by Harriet Jacobs when *Incidents in the Life of a Slave Girl* was published.

**WORKS CITED**

Anderson, Robert. *From Slavery to Affluence: Memoirs of Robert Anderson, Ex-Slave.* Hemingford, NE: Hemingford Ledger, 1927.

Andrews, William. *To Tell a Free Story: The First Century of Afro-American Autobiography, 1760–1865*. Urbana: University of Illinois Press, 1986.

Angelou, Maya. *I Know Why the Caged Bird Sings*. New York: Random, 1970.

Barton, Rebecca Chalmers. *Witnesses for Freedom: Negro Americans in Autobiography*. New York: Harper, 1948.

Black Fashion Museum. *Modiste Elizabeth Keckley: From Slavery to the White House.* New York, n.d.

Brown, William Wells. *Narrative of William Wells Brown, a Fugitive Slave*. Boston, 1847.

———. *Three Years in Europe; or, Places I Have Seen and People I Have Met.* London, 1852.

Burger, Mary. "Black Autobiography: A Literature of Celebration." Dissertation. Washington University, 1973.

Butterfield, Stephen. *Black Autobiography in America*. Amherst: University of Massachusetts Press, 1974.

Davis, Charles T., and Henry Louis Gates Jr., eds. *The Slave's Narrative*. New York: Oxford University Press, 1985.

Douglass, Frederick. *Life and Times of Frederick Douglass,* Hartford, 1881.

———. *Narrative of the Life of Frederick Douglass, an American Slave*. Boston, 1845.

Emerson, Ralph Waldo. "Thoughts on Modern Literature." *The Dial* 1 (1840): 137–58.

Foster, Frances Smith. *Witnessing Slavery: The Development of the Ante-Bellum Slave Narrative*. Westport: Greenwood Press, 1979.

Franklin, Benjamin. *Autobiography*. Ed. Max Farrand. Berkeley: University of California Press, 1949.

Hammon, Briton. *A Narrative of the Uncommon Sufferings, and Surprising Deliverance of Briton Hammon, a Negro Man.* Boston, 1760.

Henry, George. *Life of George Henry together with a Brief History of the Colored People in America.* Providence, 1894.

Howells, William Dean. "Editor's Easy Chair." *Harper's Monthly Magazine* 119 (1909): 795–98.

Jackson, Rebecca. *Gifts of Power: The Writings of Rebecca Jackson, Black Visionary, Shaker Eldress.* Ed. Jean McMahon Humez. Amherst: University of Massachusetts Press, 1981.

Jacobs, Harriet. *Incidents in the Life of a Slave Girl.* Boston, 1861.

Jelinek, Estelle. *The Tradition of Women's Autobiography: From Antiquity to the Present.* Boston: Twayne, 1986.

Keckley, Elizabeth. *Behind the Scenes: Or, Thirty Years a Slave, and Four Years in the White House.* New York: G.W. Carleton, 1868.

Langston, James Mercer. *From the Virginia Plantation to the National Capitol; or, The First and Only Negro Representative in Congress from the Old Dominion.* Hartford, 1894.

Lee, Jarena. *The Life and Religious Experiences of Jarena Lee, a Coloured Lady.* Philadelphia, 1836.

Loggins, Vernon. *The Negro Author: His Development in America to 1900.* New York: Columbia University Press, 1931.

Malcolm X. *The Autobiography of Malcolm X.* New York: Grove Press, 1965.

Marrant, John. *A Narrative of the Lord's Wonderful Dealings with John Marrant, a Black.* London, 1785.

Murray, Albert. *The Omni-Americans.* New York: Avon, 1971.

Nichols, Charles. *Many Thousands Gone: The Ex-Slaves' Account of Their Bondage and Freedom.* Bloomington: Indiana University Press, 1969.

Pascal, Roy. *Design and Truth in Autobiography.* Cambridge: Harvard University Press, 1960.

Pennington, James W.C. *The Fugitive Blacksmith; or, Events in the History of James W.C. Pennington.* London, 1849.

Porter, Dorothy. Introduction. *Behind the Scenes.* By Elizabeth Keckley. New York: Arno, 1968.

Prince, Nancy Gardener. *A Narrative of the Life and Travels of Mrs. Nancy Prince.* Boston, 1850.

Randolph, Peter. *From Slave Cabin to the Pulpit: The Autobiography of Rev. Peter Randolph; the Southern Question Illustrated and Sketches of Slave Life.* Boston, 1893.

Sekora, John, and Darwin T. Turner, eds. *The Art of the Slave Narrative: Original Essays in Criticism and Theory.* Macomb: Western Illinois University Press, 1982.

Smith, Sidonie. *Where I'm Bound: Patterns of Slavery and Freedom in Black American Autobiography.* Westport: Greenwood Press, 1974.

Spengemann, William C., and L.R. Lundquist. "Autobiography and the American Myth." *American Quarterly* 17 (1965): 501–19.
Starling, Marion Wilson. "The Slave Narrative: Its Place in American Literary History." Dissertation. New York University, 1946.
Stepto, Robert B. *From Behind the Veil: A Study of Afro-American Narrative.* Urbana: University of Illinois Press, 1979.
Stone, Albert E. *Autobiographical Occasions and Original Acts.* Philadelphia: University of Pennsylvania Press, 1982.
Washington, Booker T. *Up from Slavery: An Autobiography.* New York: A.L. Burt, 1901.
Washington, John E. *They Knew Lincoln.* New York: Dutton, 1942.
Wheatley, Phillis. *Poems on Various Subjects, Religious and Moral.* London, 1773.
Wright, Richard. *Black Boy: A Record of Childhood and Youth.* New York: Harper, 1945.

CHAPTER FOUR

**LYNN DOMINA**

# I Was Re-Elected President
Elizabeth Keckley as Quintessential Patriot in *Behind the Scenes: Or, Thirty Years a Slave, and Four Years in the White House*

DURING THE FALL OF 1862, in response to Washington's influx of slaves assuming their freedom, Elizabeth Keckley with several anonymous others created the Contraband Relief Association, "contraband" being the designation for AWOL slaves who had made their way to Union territory. In her autobiography, *Behind the Scenes: Or, Thirty Years a Slave, and Four Years in the White House,* Keckley presents the genesis of this organization as a moment of inspiration: "If the white people can give festivals to raise funds for the relief of suffering soldiers, why should not the well-to-do colored people go to work to do something for the benefit of the suffering blacks?" (113). Her idea is greeted with enthusiasm, in an apparent moment of solidarity, both by powerful whites and by the colored residents of several major cities. Keckley concludes her description of this event with an appeal to the most powerful, the most revered, the most mythic of all: "Mrs. Lincoln made frequent contributions, as also did the President" (115). If the president contributed, her cause must have been both legitimate and unitary, for surely Abraham Lincoln would not have supported an organization whose purpose was divisive. Yet Keckley does not stop quite yet; she adds one further sentence: "In 1863 I was re-elected President of the Association, which office I continue to hold" (115). Writing in 1868, Elizabeth Keckley, a former slave who has become dressmaker to Washington's social elite, has out-Lincolned Lincoln, who had also been re-elected but who had been assassinated early in his second term.

This passage, and surrounding statements I will discuss further, reveals Keckley's complicated status in terms of her potential membership in any given community. If we accept Benedict Anderson's implied description of community as "a deep, horizontal comradeship," Keckley seems in this passage to be oddly displaced (7). In a text marketed as a slave narrative (despite the fact that Keckley's "thirty years a slave" occupy only a small section of her narrative), one might hastily assume that she would identify her community as among former slaves. Since, however, Keckley introduces class distinctions among the members of her race, identifying herself if only by association with the "well-to-do colored people" rather than with "suffering blacks," she clearly subverts any notion of undifferentiated unity among former slaves. And although her passing reference here to Mary Todd Lincoln reveals little, other points in the narrative expose the tension between them—despite Keckley's frequent assertion that she writes in part to defend Mary Todd Lincoln against their nation's unjust accusations. Keckley's (and Lincoln's) membership in a community of women is hence no less problematic than is her membership in a community of former slaves.

The Lincoln for whom Keckley demonstrates the greatest comradeship is not Mary Todd but Abraham. Throughout the text, Keckley represents herself as a mimetic example of the dead heroic president. In doing so, she claims her community as the nation and her identity neither as black nor as woman but as American. Paradoxically, such national identity erases its internal differences; in claiming her community as America, Keckley is apparently able to disregard the possibility that she belongs wholly to none of the American subcultures that comprise the nation. Indeed, acknowledging her membership in these particular communities—former slave and woman—could preclude her identity as American, for an American was implicitly if not always explicitly white and male.[1] Since "nation" is frequently assumed to consist of a community of peers "regardless of the actual inequality and exploitation that may prevail," Keckley uses her status as American to elide her lack of membership in other American communities (Anderson 7). In this case, the whole is not greater than the sum of its parts; rather, the whole remains whole only to the extent that it refuses to acknowledge its composition. To retain its power as a "symbolic force," a nation must achieve a perception of itself as an "impossible unity" (Bhabha 1). To the extent that Keckley can plausibly represent herself as an American, she need not—indeed, perhaps, must not—address the conflicted composition of such an identity. The national community, to function efficaciously as an identity, must subsume all others.

Because Keckley published her narrative in 1868, when the concern of the nation was reunification (of white citizens) rather than abolition, she could not reasonably appeal to white readers by stressing either the horrors of slavery or continuing racial inequality. To the mind of Americans still recuperating from the war, slavery had been abolished and was hence neither a problem nor an issue of continuing interest (Foster 60). Keckley, therefore, could not rely exclusively on the genre of slave narrative to create her audience. Her access, however, to the sanctum sanctorum of the Lincoln White House permitted her to individuate her life by—ironically—attaching it to the lives of the slain president and his economically stricken widow. Because Americans continued to mourn Abraham Lincoln and continued to be scandalized by Mary Todd Lincoln's apparently profligate habits, Keckley's audience would read her book in order to see what she had seen rather than to experience what she had experienced.

At times Keckley presents this synoptic possibility by virtue of her access to significant personalities rather than through her direct experience. In the court of autobiography, fortunately, hearsay is seldom stricken from the record. And although Keckley occasionally appears to be an omniscient narrator, she generally reveals the source of her information (and hence establishes her credibility). Yet in his introduction to this volume, James Olney suggests that "memoir" is the appropriate class for Keckley's narrative:

> After the first three chapters, the book could best be described as "memoir"—i.e., the sort of narrative that is grown out of personal experience but that does not focus on the personal element and describes instead external events and figures who occupy some important place in the affairs of the world. (xxxiii)

Although Olney's definition of "memoir" certainly suits Keckley's text, I will continue to use "autobiography" since I am arguing in part that Keckley's relation to the public world establishes her primary textual identity as American and her community as Americans. Lincoln occupies an important place in her world as well as in "the world"; hence to the extent that Keckley's desired self is constituted through her interactions with the nationally powerful and famous, her public role permits her both to evade and to establish revelations of a private self.

Following Lincoln's second inauguration, a "grand levee" is held; all of the invitees are white: "Many colored people were in Washington, and large numbers had desired to attend the levee, but orders were issued not to admit them" (158). Keckley's sentence structure, obviously, evades the question of the origin of those orders, though the story that follows attempts to redeem Lincoln of responsibility. Among the crowd of colored people is Frederick Douglass, until an apparently naive "gentleman, a member of Congress" spots him and asks why he isn't inside shaking Lincoln's hand (158). Douglass responds, "The best reason in the world. Strict orders have been issued not to admit people of color" (159).

This particular congressman intervenes with Lincoln, who issues an invitation to Douglass—but not to the hundreds of other individuals outside; Douglass—by virtue of his eloquence or his fame or his general exceptionalism—is apparently granted the status of honorary white. Although he is invited in because he has spoken *for* black people, slave and free, he is not invited in *as* a black man. But Lincoln is especially gracious to Douglass, and Douglass in subsequently narrating the event is "very proud of the manner in which Mr. Lincoln received him" (160). Neither Douglass nor Keckley overtly critiques the situation, though other slave narrators frequently have expressed dismay at the segregation and injustice they find in the North, especially those who write after the passage of the Fugitive Slave Law.[2] Of course, however, Keckley is not writing as a slave to would-be or could-be abolitionists but as a free American to other free Americans.

In fact, Keckley is much more likely to criticize the assumptions and behavior of recently emancipated blacks, implicitly positioning herself as, if not not-black, then at least as not-recently-freed (Keckley had purchased herself in 1855), and hence complicating any black-white dichotomy. When she speaks for these blacks, she situates herself as mediator rather than as representative:

> you [emancipated blacks] were not prepared for the new life that opened before you, and the great masses of the North learned to look upon your helplessness with indifference—learned to speak of you as an idle, dependent race. Reason should have prompted kinder thoughts. Charity is ever kind. (112)

By her choice of pronouns, Keckley reveals her uncomfortable detachment from this crowd, though earlier in the passage she acknowledges their apparent bond: "Poor dusky children of slavery, men and women of my own race—the transition from slavery to freedom was too sudden for you!" (112). Keckley is syntactically both a part of and apart from this class of people, and her vocabulary emphasizes her ambivalence. When she refers to "my own race," the others are "men and women," while earlier in the sentence these same people are "Poor dusky children." Keckley may be in the class of "free blacks," but she is determined not to be perceived as of it. Throughout this section, her narration is tentative as she attempts to offend neither the North nor the South while simultaneously arguing that a translation of "slave" into "free" will not occur simply because a geographic border has been crossed or because a document promises to acquire the status of law. The act requisite to acknowledge borders or laws seems less imaginary than the act of creating a self and subjectivity that are free. Paradoxically, to assume the responsibilities of freedom, slaves must eventually constrain their desire for freedom:

> They came with a great hope in their hearts, and with all their worldly goods on their backs. Fresh from the bonds of slavery, fresh from the benighted regions of the plantation, they came to the Capital looking for liberty, and many of them not knowing it when they found it. Many good friends reached forth kind hands, but the North is not warm and impulsive. (111)

The plantation is not evil, merely benighted; the North is not heartless or even indifferent, merely nondemonstrative; ex-slaves are not lazy or ignorant, merely too hopeful and naive. Keckley, however, is not naive, and hence not among the class white Northern citizens have termed "an idle, dependent race" (112). She can use the terminology she does to explain each group to the others because she understands herself to be a member of none; she apologizes for everyone rather than advocate anyone.

At times, however, Keckley's condescension toward other former slaves becomes more overt. In a rare and perhaps even unique statement from a former slave, Keckley declares,

> Thousands of the disappointed, huddled together in camps, fretted and pined like children for the "good old times." . . . they would crowd around me with pitiful stories of distress. Often I heard them declare that they would rather go back to slavery in the South, and be with their old masters, than to enjoy the freedom of the North. (140)

From a former slaveholder, this last statement might seem resentful or embittered; from a former slave, it is shocking, especially as Keckley otherwise herself expresses some longing for the past, as I will discuss. Since Keckley only infrequently presents conversations with other former slaves, this statement must be taken as representative of her views, at least in terms of the relationship she is constructing between her represented self and her imagined audience.

To confirm the idea that these former slaves need enlightenment first and foremost, Keckley describes the misunderstandings of an elderly woman:

> She had never ventured beyond a plantation until coming North. The change was too radical for her, and she could not exactly understand it. She thought, as many others thought, that Mr. and Mrs. Lincoln were the government, and that the President and his wife had nothing to do but to supply the extravagant wants of every one that applied to them. (141)[3]

Such an interpretation on the part of former slaves is understandable, since the law, especially subsequent to the *Dred Scott* decision, had previously equated itself and government with the slave's master, and since the master had generally been exempt from legal repercussions in his treatment of slaves. The law had previously been literally embodied in the will of the master; it would be only logical to assume that government was analogously embodied in those who governed. Keckley's greatest amusement in this situation, however, emerges not from the woman's inability to abstract "law" from the person of its symbolic representative, but from the woman's expectation that the government should fulfill her modest desires in the way of attire: "Her idea of freedom was two or more old shifts every year" (141–42). Such condescension places this woman in the realm of character and Keckley in the realm of audience; by exploiting tone to distance herself from this woman, Keckley shifts herself in the direction of her own audience—those white readers for whom this passage would serve as entertainment rather than as a call to conscience.

Although Keckley does not interrogate her own response here, she is less able to laugh when ignorance is displayed on the part of a white boy in a situation that might otherwise be analogous. Tad Lincoln is unable to read, insisting that A-P-E spells "monkey" since the word in his book is accompanied by an illustration resembling a monkey. At the time, Keckley says, "I could not longer restrain myself, and burst out laughing," but in the retelling she is much more circumspect (218). Tad Lincoln, being white, is racially unmarked and hence relieved of the responsibility of representing his race with his every act; his illiteracy makes no comment on the potential of other white boys. Tad Lincoln is ascribed a level of individuality that would have been unthinkable for a black companion, a fact Keckley recognizes:

> [H]ad Tad been a negro boy, not the son of a President, and so difficult to instruct, he would have been called thick-skulled, and would have been held up as an example of the inferiority of race. . . . If a colored boy appears dull, so does a white boy sometimes; and if a whole race is judged by a single example of apparent dulness [sic], another race should be judged by a similar example. (219–20)

If a colored boy appears dull, his dullness embraces Keckley, who has struggled throughout the text to establish her own individuality, her own ability to enflesh the great American characteristic of self-reliance.

Keckley has demonstrated herself to be particularly self-reliant through her success in purchasing herself in 1855, and in her determination to live separately from her husband after he reveals his pronounced attraction to alcohol. In stark contrast, Mary Todd Lincoln identifies herself entirely according to her relationship with her husband, having confessed that "from her girlhood up [she] had an ambition to become the wife of a President," and she is utterly unable or unwilling to function without the significant attention and good will of others (228). Although Keckley claims to have written this narrative in part to exonerate Mary Todd Lincoln from the disparagement she has suffered in newspaper articles and other sources of innuendo following Abraham's death—when Mary Todd is revealed to owe $70,000 in clothing debts—Keckley is so unsuccessful at eliciting the reader's sympathy that one cannot but notice her ambivalence. In an attempt to settle these debts, Mary Todd offers her gowns and jewels for public sale, a decision that garners her more scorn than income.

A substantial portion of Keckley's narrative consists of an explanation of this decision and the role Keckley had in its execution. To defend herself against potential accusations of impropriety in revealing the details of these events, she asserts, "Had Mrs. Lincoln's acts never become public property, I should not have published to the world the secret chapters of her life" (xv). If, as William Andrews argues in a slightly different context, "the 'lies, secrets, and silences' of women can deliver them into community or alienate them from it," Keckley inverts this process, revealing to the nation the secrets Mary Todd Lincoln has shared with her, delivering herself into the national community from which Mary Todd Lincoln has been alienated (*To Tell* 255). By declaring her information to be not secret, Keckley ironically creates the reader's desire to interpret it as secret; by revealing and hence destroying the secret, Keckley inserts herself into the community of readers who will be privy to this secret, as this same secret has initially created her communal relationship with Mary Todd Lincoln. Simultaneously, in going public with another woman's life, Keckley is able to retain proprietary control over her own private life. If autobiography in being the public revelation of private events undermines any distinction between public and private, Keckley surreptitiously reinforces that distinction, revealing the private decisions of a public figure who then functions to shield Keckley's own private life from the public gaze. Since slaves, in being private property, could not own private property, Keckley would have had no private life until 1855; having converted herself into a free woman, she is determined not to treat her own life as public property, not to invite speculation on the propriety of her own decisions.

Had Mary Todd Lincoln been a national favorite at the time of the president's death, her subsequent security might have been better ensured. She had, however, already acquired a reputation for being somewhat snobbish and even indecent. When Keckley delivers the first dress she makes for her, Mary Todd's reaction is initially petulant, then more conciliatory. By the time she actually enters the levee for which the dress has been made, she becomes actually gracious, to Keckley's surprise: "I had heard so much, in current and malicious report, of her low life, of her ignorance and vulgarity, that I expected to see her embarrassed on this occasion" (89). On her husband's arm, she is able to appear regal, though one wonders if even then her response didn't elicit disapproval—for when her dresses are eventually displayed for public sale, Keckley quotes a newspaper article: "The peculiarity of the dresses is that the most of them are cut low-necked—a taste which some ladies attribute to Mrs. Lincoln's appreciation of her own bust" (305). Keckley cannot apparently protect Mary Todd from the consequences of her own vanity.

Keckley does, however, attempt to protect Mary Todd from her impulsivity. While the two are in New York arranging for the sale of the gowns, Mary Todd travels under the pseudonym of Mrs. Clarke. When the manager of the hotel in which they stay refuses on racial grounds to serve Keckley in the dining room, Mary Todd indignantly prepares to go out to a restaurant, despite the late hour. Keckley urges her to tolerate the hotel's lack of consideration: "You came alone, and the people already suspect that everything is not right. If you go outside of the hotel tonight, they will accept the fact as evidence against you" (283).

Such poor judgment is typical of Mary Todd Lincoln as Keckley presents her in this text. At the time of Lincoln's assassination, Mary Todd has few friends in Washington, and she chooses to grieve alone until her departure, when "the wife of the President was leaving the White House, and there was scarcely a friend to tell her good-bye" (208). Mary Todd frequently claims that Keckley is her closest friend and urges her to accompany the Lincoln family back to Illinois, apparently oblivious to the fact that Keckley has no means of support outside her dressmaking business. Mary Todd's proclamations of friendship for Keckley are apparently not reciprocated, however, as she writes toward the end of her narrative:

> Mrs. Lincoln's venture proved so disastrous that she was unable to reward me for my services, and I was compelled to take in sewing to pay for my daily bread. My New York expedition has made me richer in experiences, but poorer in purse. During the entire winter I have worked early and late, and practised the closest economy. Mrs. Lincoln's business demanded much of my time, and it was a constant source of trouble to me. (326)

Presumably, some of Mary Todd's $70,000 debt is owed to Keckley. It is most ironic, of course, that thirteen years after Keckley has purchased her freedom and three years after slavery has been abolished in the United States, she is nevertheless performing significant unpaid labor for the widow of the man who had issued the Emancipation Proclamation.

Mary Todd's view is that the people of the United States owe her financial support, since they also owe "*their* remaining a nation to my husband!" (352). And as Keckley presents him, Abraham Lincoln valued nothing if not empathy and reconciliation—although Mary Todd frequently criticizes the members of his cabinet and commanders of the Union army, Abraham Lincoln speaks highly even of Confederate soldiers. Admiring a portrait of Robert E. Lee, Lincoln tells his son Robert, "I trust that the era of good feeling has returned with the war, and that henceforth we shall live in peace" (138). After the fall of Richmond, Lincoln requests the military band to play "Dixie," celebrating rather than denigrating this symbol of Southern culture, though Southern listeners might have interpreted the act less positively.

The text Keckley has written mimics this act of Lincoln's, functioning more to mute than to amplify the violence of slavery, a choice perceived as necessary if former slaves were to participate in the American Dream. If former slaves were to believe that a history of progress would continue into the future, they could only also believe that the South would progress morally (Andrews, "Reunion" 12).[4] As Lincoln speaks highly of Lee, Keckley speaks highly of Jefferson Davis: "[H]e always appeared to me as a thoughtful, considerate man in the domestic circle" (69). And for his political views, she extends forgiveness: "[E]ven I, who was once a slave, who have been punished with the cruel lash, who have experienced the heart and soul tortures of a slave's life, can say to Mr. Jefferson Davis, 'Peace! you have suffered! Go in peace'" (74).

In part because she does not devote substantial space to her life as a slave, Keckley does not emphasize the "cruel lash," though she does refer to other episodes of violence. As a four-year-old, Keckley has the responsibility of caring for an infant. When the baby falls out of its crib through Keckley's too-vigorous rocking, she is whipped for the first time, though she devotes only two comparatively neutral sentences to the experience: "The blows were not administered with a light hand, I assure you, and doubtless the severity of the lashing has made me remember the incident so well. This was the first time I was punished in this cruel way, but not the last" (21). She does devote considerably more space to a series of beatings she receives as a young woman; they are administered by a Mr. Bingham, and she is disturbed in part because of the sexual impropriety involved: "Recollect, I was eighteen years of age, was a woman fully developed, and yet this man coolly bade me take down my dress" (33). Keckley fights against these beatings, attaining and displaying a sense of self-determination in the process. The passage ends not only with her victory, but with Bingham's conversion: "[H]e asked my forgiveness, and afterwards was an altered man. He was never known to strike one of his servants from that day forward" (37). Bingham here functions as a synecdochic example of Keckley's hope for the future South.

In contrast to these passages, Keckley devotes significant space to her reunion with her former owners and to her justification for her affection for them. This reunion is apparently one event that prompts her disconcerting prefatory statement: "If I have portrayed the dark side of slavery, I also have painted the bright side" (xi). Her concern for and desire to visit her former owners are also disconcerting to her Northern acquaintances, to whom she offers an explanation:

> You forget the past is dear to every one, for to the past belongs that golden period, the days of childhood.... To surrender it is to surrender the greatest part of my existence.... These people are associated with everything that memory holds dear, and so long as memory proves faithful, it is but natural that I should sigh to see them once more. (241–42)

Perhaps the past is dear to Keckley, but to her the future is also dear, and her nation's survival depends significantly on its citizens' ability to decline vengeance. She again attempts to explain the South to the North, and the peculiar feelings of those involved in its peculiar institution: "You do not know the Southern people as well as I do—how warm is the attachment between master and slave" (242). To Northern ears, this statement would clearly echo southern paternalistic justifications for slavery, and it could tend to confirm former slaveholders' assumption that affection shared between slaves and slaveholders negated any problematic aspects of slavery (Fox-Genovese 131). As Keckley presents her reunion with her former owners, mutual affection is the predominant emotion. She is told that she is "needed to make the circle complete," and her membership in this circle is paradoxically more authentic than is her membership in the circle of former slaves, Northern women, or Northerners in general (245–46). Like many former slaveholders, her former owners' attitude toward slavery appears to have shifted dramatically. Throughout this scene, they treat Keckley as a peer, and one visitor insists that since peace has been achieved, all will soon be well: "[T]he change is an evidence of the peaceful feeling of this country; a change, I trust, that augurs brighter days for us all (254)."

Keckley's status as an American depends to some extent on the existence of an America that is one united nation. Her body with its dark skin and her legal status as a manumitted slave cannot be the site at which the nation dissolves. Slavery itself becomes an odd historical event, which in hindsight no one who participated seems to have supported: "By the end of the century, those who wrote of their lives before the war—loyal though they might be to their people and their region—were likely to present themselves as having always opposed slavery" (Fox-Genovese 346). Former slaveholders, then, claimed allegiance to their local community rather than to the economic structure under which it had defined itself. Keckley attributes the persistence of slavery not to the determination or inhumanity of slaveholders but to the law, specifically as it is situated in the Constitution of the United States:

> They [slaveholders] were not so much responsible for the curse under which I was born, as the God of nature and the fathers who framed the Constitution for the United States. The law descended to them, and it was but natural that they should recognize it, since it manifestly was their interest to do so. (xii)

That slaveholders would have acted according to their self-interest, she seems to say, is only logical.

Keckley's understanding of the power of the law is reflected in her determination, slave and free, to be obedient to it. Although she does occasionally critique laws regarding slavery, especially as they apply to mulatto children, she declines to oppose civil law to any more cosmic moral law. She obtains her freedom not by simply taking it, by becoming a new woman with a new name in the North, but by purchasing it according to the legal and economic options provided for such occasions. Addressing her master, she says, "By the laws of the land I am your slave—you are my master, and I will only be free by such means as the laws of the country provide" (49). It is the law, apparently, that grants or withholds freedom and a free subjectivity, rather than a free subjectivity that grasps freedom from a legal structure designed to prohibit it. And when she does purchase her freedom, she does not simply assert it in the text but includes the substantiating legal documents.

For Americans live under the authority of the law, and if Keckley is to define herself as an American, she cannot simultaneously present herself as an anarchist or legal relativist. When she realizes that she cannot remain in Washington as a free black without a permit, "such being the law," she does not express outrage but instead relies on the influence of sympathetic friends to see that the fee for such a permit would be suspended (65). As Keckley exhibits herself in this text, she is not merely obedient. Rather, she is the quintessential patriot whose character incorporates significant American virtues. Having purchased her freedom in part through loans provided by white acquaintances, she works first to free herself from this debt: "I went to work in earnest, and in a short time paid every cent that was so kindly advanced by my lady patrons of St. Louis" (63). So she is law-abiding, frugal, and honest—and ironically she attributes her ability to raise herself up to her experience of slavery itself: "Notwithstanding all the wrongs that slavery heaped upon me, I can bless it for one thing—youth's important lesson of self-reliance" (20). Rather than determining that she will become a member of that "idle, dependent race," slavery teaches her diligence and independence (112).

When her former owners ask whether she harbors any resentment regarding their treatment of her, Keckley cites another one-time American value: "I have but one unkind thought, and that is, that you did not give me the advantages of a good education. What I have learned has been the study of after years" (257). Presumably, more formal education would have increased her self-reliance and made her even more suited to the role of responsible businesswoman that she filled.

By establishing the Contraband Relief Association, she determines that freed slaves will become race-reliant and assumes that self-reliance will soon follow. Although her significance as an American in this text might seem to occur primarily through her association with other significant Americans—Abraham and Mary Todd Lincoln, Jefferson and Varina Howell Davis, Stephen Douglas—her significance as a public figure occurs not only through the acts she witnesses but also through the acts she performs. She establishes and raises funds for a national organization; she enlists the aid of interested others; and she finds herself re-elected president. She becomes an interesting national figure not merely because she knew Abraham Lincoln but because she mirrors him. She writes her narrative not simply because she has observed America and can tell about it, but because she demonstrates the character of the nation in the character of herself.

### NOTES

1. Although I am writing here in past tense, one could easily argue that present tense is equally appropriate. For the term "African American," for example, designates in the United States not national allegiance or membership (or dual citizenship) but race—though outside the United States the term designates both race and national citizenship; a white immigrant to the United States from an African country is generally not included in the term. To the extent that the United States remains

a racist culture wherein access to power occur through whiteness, the first half of that term, "African," could be said to confound the second half, "American," creating an oxymoron.

2. See Harriet Jacobs (375, 451, 503); Louisa Picquet (41).

3. Harriet Jacobs relates a similar incident regarding a slave woman who believed the President of the United States was himself governed by a queer (376).

4. Frances Smith Foster also addresses the attraction of the American Dream for slaves, though her discussion focuses around antebellum slaves who choose to run away in order to pursue it rather than postbellum slave narrators who urge forgiveness for the South as their only hope.

## WORKS CITED

Anderson, Benedict. *Imagined Communities: Reflections on the Origin and Spread of Nationalism.* New York: Verso, 1991.

Andrews, William L. "Reunion in the Postbellum Slave Narrative: Frederick Douglass and Elizabeth Keckley." *Black American Literature Forum* 23.1 (1989): 5–16.

———. *To Tell a Free Story: The First Century of Afro-American Autobiography, 1760–1865.* Urbana: University of Illinois Press, 1986.

Bhabha, Homi K. "Introduction: Narrating the Nation." *Nation and Narration.* Ed. Homi K. Bhabha. New York: Routledge, 1991. 1–7.

Foster, Frances Smith. *Witnessing Slavery: The Development of Ante-Bellum Slave Narratives.* 2nd ed. Madison: University of Wisconsin Press, 1994.

Fox-Genovese, Elizabeth. *Within the Plantation Household: Black and White Women of the Old South.* Chapel Hill: University of North Carolina Press, 1988.

Jacobs, Harriet. *Incidents in the Life of a Slave Girl. The Classic Slave Narratives.* Ed. Henry Louis Gates Jr. New York: Mentor, 1987.

Keckley, Elizabeth. *Behind the Scenes: Or, Thirty Years a Slave, and Four Years in the White House.* New York: Oxford University Press, 1988.

Olney, James. Introduction. *Behind the Scenes.* By Elizabeth Keckley. New York: Oxford University Press, 1988. xxvii–xxxvi.

Picquet, Louisa. *Louisa Picquet, the Octoroon: Or Inside Views of Southern Domestic Life. Collected Black Women's Narratives.* Ed. Henry Louis Gates Jr. New York: Oxford University Press, 1988.

CHAPTER FIVE

**MICHAEL BERTHOLD**

# Not "Altogether" the "History of Myself"
Autobiographical Impersonality in Elizabeth Keckley's
*Behind the Scenes: Or, Thirty Years a Slave, and Four Years in the White House*

"I AM NOT WRITING altogether the history of myself," Elizabeth Keckley proclaims almost immediately in her 1868 *Behind the Scenes: Or, Thirty Years a Slave, and Four Years in the White House* (18). Despite recounting Keckley's years as a slave and as "modiste, and friend to Mrs. Abraham Lincoln" (Title Page), *Behind the Scenes* evades generic designations such as "slave narrative" and "autobiography." It is perhaps better understood, suggests James Olney in his introduction to the Schomburg Library edition of the text, as a species of "memoirs" (xxxiii) that grows out of "personal experience" but focuses on "external events and figures who occupy some important place in the affairs of the world" (Olney xxxiii).[1] Crucial to Keckley's aesthetic is precisely her own insistence on what she is "not writing." Expressly indeterminate, the text cultivates its own discursive singularity and freedom. Individual chapters are allowed to be "rambling" (137, 236), and the story as a whole is allowed to be "imperfect" (329). Although *Behind the Scenes* may not pre-eminently be about Keckley's "self," it is still profoundly about that self, as the canny placement of the "altogether" in her proclamation intimates and as the canny arrangement of materials in her text confirms. But what the text immediately foregrounds, and subsequently and brilliantly enacts, is the selectiveness of Keckley's self-construction and her strenuous repudiation of a merely "personal" self in favor of a deliberately public one. Both the content and architectonics of *Behind the Scenes* enforce Keckley's provocative autobiographical impersonality.

More generally, this essay argues that the study of *Behind the Scenes* begins to remedy what William L. Andrews has identified as "the gap in our awareness of what was happening to black American autobiography from

1865 through the 1920s" ("Poetics" 82); in particular, Andrews notes, "The autobiographies that ex-slaves wrote after emancipation have been almost entirely ignored or condescendingly dismissed from serious scholarly consideration by literary historians" ("Poetics" 81). In its intricate staging of the relationship between autobiographical form and content and in its materialist presentation of the vocational and ontological dialectic of "author" and "modiste," of writing and dressmaking, *Behind the Scenes* is a powerful instantiation of what Andrews has labeled "free storytelling."[2] *Behind the Scenes* has received little critical attention, notable exceptions being Joanne Braxton's consideration of it in *Black Women's Autobiography* and Andrews's identification of its largely "materialist discourse" (237) in "The Changing Moral Discourse of Nineteenth-Century African American Women's Autobiography: Harriet Jacobs and Elizabeth Keckley." Braxton is particularly adept at scrutinizing the "many and varied forms" (39) that nineteenth-century black American women's autobiographical writing takes. But a good deal of her discussion of *Behind the Scenes* paraphrases the text, and she reads it as being "really two texts: a slave narrative and a confidential memoir" (43). Such statements imply a more schizoid text than Keckley in fact wrote. For all its "unpredictable shifts in the narrative action" (Braxton 43), *Behind the Scenes* still needs to be assessed as a single entity with its own formal and thematic drama, coherence, and vitality. Part of the work of recuperating a text such as *Behind the Scenes* involves determining not only what the text means, but also how it means. As Cheryl Wall has observed, African American literature has too often "been misread as mimetic representation or sociology," and "the verbal text has been treated as if it merely mirrored the social text" (9); *Behind the Scenes*, this essay insists, possesses an intrinsic aesthetic worth that is always anterior to its sociology. Formally, *Behind the Scenes* conspires to abridge and resist "romance" and its enshrinement of the "personal" and questions the validity of "romance" as generic scaffold for Keckley's autobiographical project. In her preface, Keckley notes that "My life, so full of romance, may sound like a dream to the matter-of-fact reader" (xi); in her first chapter, she remarks about reviewing her past that "Every day seems like a romance within itself, and the years grow into ponderous volumes" (18). "Romance" seems to imply for Keckley not only "dream" but "stirring incidents" (17), "a rapidly moving panorama" (17), "strange passages" (18), and a "wilderness of events" (18). She distrusts romance, apparently, not only for being fanciful or emotive, but for its root untameability. As a "wilderness," romance is a narrative thicket that Keckley cannot quite manage or tame. Tracing romance's form would lead only to the production of "ponderous volumes"; while recognizing its allure, Keckley nevertheless figures "romance" as a profligate, unreadable series of tomes. By the end of her narrative Keckley has in fact decided that her life is merely "somewhat romantic" (329), a qualification and diminution of her initial stance.

In attempting to be something other than "romantic," Keckley's text in part echoes the tropes of authenticity that characterize earlier slave narratives; "everything I have written is strictly true" (xi), Keckley maintains in her preface. If "much has been omitted" from the work, "nothing has been exaggerated" (xi). In light of this statement, romance can be understood as an informing, repressed text for Keckley's narrative. And while "omission without exaggeration" might serve as the credo that shapes the text in accordance with some principle of "truth," it also raises questions about how the text substantiates and supplements itself; Keckley's professed "omissions" seem to have as their surrogates a varied range of interpolated texts external to the romance narrative she might otherwise have written. Again, of course, the presence of such documents—family letters, letters from Mrs. Lincoln, Keckley's own emancipation documents, newspaper articles—is hardly surprising in a quasi-slave narrative concerned with its own authenticity. But Keckley's contextualizing of these documents through her self-conscious evocation of "romance" gives them their particular thrust. These ostensibly objective texts are ballasts to the potential storms and profligacy of romance, and the give-and-take between them and Keckley's first-person narration establishes the fundamental rhythm of the text. This formal dialectic is important because it enacts textually for Keckley the movement away from what Louis Renza has called "anarchic privacy" (291) toward a more publicly comprehended self.

Thus, for example, the book's third chapter, "How I Gained My Freedom," begins with Keckley's first-person account of this pivotal episode in her life but concludes with seven pages of documentary materials which become increasingly impersonal and official. Memoranda from friends who raised funds to help her purchase her freedom give way to deeds from the Missouri state commissioner, a St. Louis circuit court clerk, and a state recorder, and Keckley herself, as much amanuensis as author here, presides over this shift from a personal to extratextual account of her freedom. "The following, copied from the original papers, contain, in brief, the history of my emancipation"

(56), she writes as headnote for those papers, as if that emancipation can be secured only by rhetorically doubling it. Olney notes how the emancipation documents display a "very revealing complexity of naming" in the "transfer of ownership" (xxix). Throughout *Behind the Scenes* Keckley's "name" is in fact the most fluid of nomenclatures; at various points in the text, to give a few examples, she is "Little Lizzie" (23), "Yib" (218), "Keckley" (221), "Yiddie" (239), and "Lizzie" (248).

It is also important to emphasize how artfully Keckley structures her use of extratextual documents. She provides the narrative as a whole with an epistolary frame significant both for the equilibrium it brings to the text and its embodiment of her movement from private to public stages of action. Thus, a letter from Keckley's father, separated from the family, to her mother in the book's first chapter and a girlhood letter from Keckley to her mother that concludes the book's second chapter are effectually balanced by letters to the adult Keckley from Mrs. Lincoln (which pervade the second half of the narrative and form the bulk of the book's appendix) and several letters in the last chapter to Keckley from Frederick Douglass. The former are familial, intimate, and obvious sources of identity and strength for Keckley; the latter, implying as they do Keckley's parity with two celebrities of the era, buttress her self and her story beyond her own words. (There may also be a subtle authorial rivalry at work between Keckley and Douglass in *Behind the Scenes*; when Douglass does appear in the text, Keckley calls attention only to his oratory, never to his writing [115, 158, 316].) In the difference, moreover, between the letter of Keckley's father, which Keckley copies "literally" (25) with its abundant pathos and misspellings ("In heaven lets meet when will I am detemnid to nuver stope praying" [27]), and Keckley's own skillful prose, a larger genealogy of literacy emerges in which the daughter quite manifestly outdistances the father.

In her insertion of newspaper articles into her text Keckley also manages unassumingly yet cunningly to bespeak herself. Late in the narrative Keckley reproduces an article from the New York *Evening Express* that tells of Mrs. Lincoln's embarrassing attempt to sell her dresses for the cash necessary to resolve her debts. But Keckley immediately follows this chronicle with the statement that "So many erroneous reports were circulated" about the affair of the dresses "that I made a correct statement to one of the editors of the New York *Evening News*," and she quotes for several pages from the subsequent article "based upon the memoranda furnished by me" (306). This second newspaper text, which she generates without explicitly authoring, becomes privileged over the first article that was in no way informed by her knowledge. Ostensible self-effacement, Keckley's withdrawal from authorship in allowing her memoranda to become the basis of some newspaperman's text, in fact becomes ironically self-validating; Keckley is validated by being named within the article as Mrs. Lincoln's "bosom friend" (308) and of course by the article's overarching status as some public register of account. In the complex circulation of textual manufacturing and borrowing that characterizes *Behind the Scenes*, Keckley's memoir comes to contain, or reclaim, the "objective" newspaper article that her "subjective" memoranda made possible in the first place.

Part of the trenchancy of *Behind the Scenes* resides in Keckley's doubts, expressed in arrangements of text such as the newspaper articles, about the likelihood of creating a self through her own text, or possibly through any text for that matter. In noting how slavery taught her the "important lesson of self-reliance" (20), for example, Keckley manages to comment on her own unfolding writing project, indicating the possession of some "self" even while in slavery prior to her narrative. She does not necessarily need "text" to generate or guarantee "self," agreeing in effect with Paul John Eakin's observation that "The concept of a self-reflexive textuality wholly divorced from biography and chronicity is only a wishful fiction and nothing more" (38).

But in the frequency of her narrative passages from the personal to the extratextual, Keckley does underwrite a desire for a persona that is distinctly intellectual and social. Throughout the text, consistent with this desire, she underlines her general ratiocinative powers and specific political acumen. For example, while working for Mrs. Jefferson Davis, who tries to persuade Keckley that the South will conquer the North if civil war erupts, Keckley reasons that because the "Republican party had just emerged from a heated campaign, flushed with victory," it is unlikely "the party would quietly yield all they had gained" (72), and she casts her lot with the North. Later in the narrative she explains to Mrs. Lincoln why she believes Lincoln "is certain to be reelected" (148), and of course when "the election came off ... all of my predictions were verified" (155). As a historical commentator, Keckley in fact can be something of an iconoclast, perhaps nowhere as startlingly as in her pronouncement that slavery had its "bright side" (xi); in one of her most caustic judgments, early in the preface, she asserts that her "friends" in the South "were not so much responsible for the curse under which I was born, as the God of nature and the fathers who framed the Constitution for the United States" (xii). Keckley not only philosophizes about the difficult "transition from slavery to freedom" (112) for many ex-slaves and their "exaggerated ideas of liberty" (139) but actually organizes "a society of colored people . . . for the benefit of the unfortunate freedmen" (113) and serves as president of the association. One of the most resonant moments of her narrative, in fact, holding her acquaintances with Jefferson Davis and Abraham Lincoln in abeyance, is this realization of a "President Keckley."

Despite the misgivings she might have about textually generated identity, Keckley is still concerned with sanctioning her own authorial enterprise and her position as a black woman writer. She underscores, for example, the special knowledge that she derives from her role as Mrs. Lincoln's modiste by designating her narrative a "secret history" of her employer's "transactions" (xiii); repeating the incantational phrase "secret history" three times in the preface, along with a reference to the "secret chapters" (xv) of Mrs. Lincoln's life her book details, Keckley quite plainly calls attention to the privilege of her authorial perspective. If, in her emphasis on the secrets she possesses and discloses, Keckley seems vaguely oracular, her accompanying reiteration that she writes "history"—not "romance"—is an even more important indicator of her aspirations to pen a text that will epitomize the genre's traditional claims of objectivity and authority.

Keckley, moreover, is staunchly protective of the secrets of her text and of her position as author. Two specific portraits of other women she works into the text stabilize her own understanding of herself as a writer. In the first of these, Keckley confronts a woman who would have her "betray the secrets" (92) of the Lincoln domestic circle. After ordering a dress from Keckley, the woman expresses her own desire to "become an inmate of the White House" (93) and tries to bribe Keckley in exchange for a recommendation to Mrs. Lincoln. Keckley of course resists—"Sooner than betray the trust of a friend, I would throw myself into the Potomac River" (94)—and later learns "that this woman was an actress, and that her object was to enter the White House as a servant, learn its secrets, and then publish a scandal to the world" (95). Thwarted malevolent author, the woman epitomizes discursive fraud and, as Keckley's writing foil, underlines the latter's authorial virtues—her integrity, loyalty, and careful custody of White House "secrets." Keckley is a truth-sayer, not "actress"; she writes history, not "scandal." She will not even call her foe "a lady" (92) or give her a name, further clarifying the morality and ontology of her own writing. In a second, very different portrait Keckley introduces the figure of a "good old, simple-minded woman, fresh from a life of servitude" (140–41). This woman thinks, says Keckley "that Mr. and Mrs. Lincoln were the government, and that the President and his wife had nothing to do but supply the extravagant wants of every one that applied to them" (141). The woman herself wishes only for a new shift from Mrs. Lincoln, and Keckley cannot "restrain a laugh at the grave manner in which this good old woman entered her protest" (141). Although this vignette is essentially comic, it too contributes to Keckley's realization of herself as an author. In the obvious contrast between the old woman's ignorance of the Lincolns and her own familiarity with them and even in the disjunction between the old woman's desire for "under-garments" (142) from Mrs. Lincoln and Keckley's very creation of Mrs. Lincoln's wardrobe, Keckley gives particular expression to the uniqueness and satisfaction of being able to write as a knowing black woman. Thus, between the fraudulence of the actress and the naiveté of the old woman, Keckley can situate her own inner narrative of the White House.

Complicating any assessment of the relevance of authorship to Keckley's sense of herself is her employment as "modiste" throughout the narrative. Consistent with the text's general cultivation of an unromantic selfhood, a successful "career," as Andrews has observed, is in fact presented as Keckley's "chief goal in life" ("Changing" 235), and her dressmaking functions, in a phrase of Houston Baker's, as an "economic expressive strategy" (31); Anne Hollander notes too that "the real talent of the dress designer has been not aesthetic but commercial" (357). As a self-realized professional, Keckley even codifies a "system of cutting and fitting dresses" (64) that at one point she attempts to teach to classes of young black women. *Behind the Scenes* never obscures the primary monetary significance of dressmaking for Keckley, and her mastery of an economic discourse in fact makes possible the autobiographical occasion; having obtained some economical freedom for herself, Keckley has the luxury to consider, through her text, subjectivity's slipperiness and perils.

Keckley certainly derives considerable standing from serving as modiste for two nineteenth-century First Ladies, Mrs. Davis and Mrs. Lincoln, her ambitiousness especially evident in her confession that "Ever since arriving in Washington I had a great desire to work for the ladies of the White House" (76). Her dressmaking might in fact be understood as offering her an alternative mode of self-designation prior to and apart from writing. Or the one may anticipate the other, because for Keckley to know herself as modiste is in part to know herself as artist. The term "modiste" itself lends social stature and sophistication to Keckley, and, as Hollander has written, "The great personalities first to be associated with dress designing in nineteenth-century France were indeed artists to a degree to which earlier designers of finery did not aspire" (352). Specifically, modistes tended to deal in "imaginative trimming, accessories, and choice of fabric" and, in their concern with clothing's surfaces, were as much "stage designers" as artists (Hollander 352). The very title of Keckley's narrative suggests a stage set, and repeatedly in the text she recollects preparing Mrs. Lincoln for her entrances at some levee or soirée. Her profession not only makes intimate alignments with powerful white women a vocational reality, but, more suggestively, establishes her as a powerful director of the social scenes in which Mrs. Lincoln will perform. The services Keckley provides to Mrs. Davis and Mrs. Lincoln are less significant than her appropriations of the famous women for her own autobiographical ends.

But what is revelatory about Keckley as modiste is her almost complete disinterest in self-costuming, in fashioning herself through her own dressmaking artistry. Remarkably, she almost never tells us what she is wearing; her profession seems to have no literal reverberation for her at all. Early in her story, in a letter to her mother, Keckley does ask for a "pretty frock" (42), but, in light of the adult Keckley's lack of concern about her attire, the request seems to be presented as a youthful caprice or deliberate incongruity. As modiste, Keckley understands the relationship of her work to "the making of a self-conscious individual image" (Hollander xiv); yet she resists for herself the allure of clothing as a "self-perpetuating visual fiction" (Hollander xiv). Despite her work as a modiste, Keckley the writer mistrusts mere "image" and fictions both visual and verbal, as her repression of "romance" and decision to tell her story as "non-fiction" suggest. Essentially, the visible self is not Keckley's medium, and her own body is mostly, and strikingly, absent from the text.

Leaving her body out of the text reinforces Keckley's devotion to a fundamentally cerebral presentation of herself. Thematically, Keckley's disembodiment duplicates the characteristic formal movement in the text out from private forms of narration. This multi-inflected production of a cerebral self is in fact constitutive of Keckley's poetics of impersonality. In part, Keckley's disembodiment may be a form of protection against "cultural fictions of female passion and contaminated sexual desire" (S. Smith 55) that might discredit her narrative.[3] That she leaves her body out of her story also specifically reflects "the slave woman's sexual vulnerability" (V. Smith xxx) and slavery's conflation of "the categories of property and sexual relationships" (V. Smith xxxii). About a white man who had "base designs" (39) on her "because I was regarded as fair-looking for one of my race" (38–39), Keckley writes, "I do not care to dwell upon this subject, for it is one that is fraught with pain" (39). After four years of persecution, the man violated her and fathered her only child. Braxton has read Keckley as a type of the "outraged mother" (41), but Keckley's relative silence about the entanglement with the white man and in fact her general taciturnity about being a mother are prime markers of the calculated impersonality of *Behind the Scenes*.

Keckley's most sustained account of her body, however, revolves around memories of being whipped. Dramatizing slavery's perverse conflations of property, punishment, and sexuality, the incident significantly informs Keckley's subsequent authorial impersonality. A Mr. Bingham, the "ready tool" (32) of Keckley's mistress who is inexplicably angered with her, announces that he is going to flog Keckley and orders her to "'take down your dress this instant'" (33). Keckley, explaining that she was "eighteen years of age" and "a woman fully developed" (33), defies Bingham: "'No, Mr. Bingham, I shall not take down my dress before you. Moreover, you shall not whip me unless you prove the stronger'" (33). A struggle ensues, but Bingham tears the dress from Keckley's back and lashes her. When Bingham attempts a second and third whipping, Keckley again defies his attempts to "conquer" (36) her and even bites his finger "severely" (36). Finally, he "burst into tears, and declared that it would be a sin to beat me anymore" (37). This same scenario is then repeated with the Rev. Burwell, the husband of Keckley's mistress. Like Frederick Douglass in his battle royal with Covey, the combat wherein the slave becomes a man (297–99), Keckley, remarkably for a female slave, physically defies her tormentors to secure some autonomy for herself; furthermore, as if out-distancing Douglass, she actually effects the conversion of both of her abusers, who are afterwards steadily penitent.

In the combat with her assailants, it is the order to undress that clearly precipitates Keckley's resistance. The rest of the text works to prevent such brutal exposure of herself, and her subsequent textual disembodiment bears the traces of her first literal, proud refusals to be uncovered and violated. Her work as a dressmaker of course revolves about fitting, draping, and wrapping, and the "plot" of *Behind the Scenes* as such not only emerges from Keckley's life as a modiste but culminates in the exhibition and sale of Mrs. Lincoln's clothing. The battles with Bingham and Burwell also linger, somewhat strangely, in several of Keckley's figurations of her writing project, figurations that in a text less concerned with dressmaking and undressing, with fabric and body, might be overlooked as clichés. Thus, Keckley speaks of drawing aside the "veil of mystery" (xiv) that shrouds Mrs. Lincoln's secret history and gives special weight to the import for her text of "naked fact" (xiv). In eliding her own body from the text, Keckley not only abstracts herself as author but posits authorship as a special kind of undressing.

It is in her relationship with Mrs. Lincoln, the central relationship of *Behind the Scenes*, that Keckley's dramas of writing, dressmaking, and unromantic self-fashioning converge. As Mary G. Mason has suggested, emergent female identity "seems to acknowledge the real presence and recognition of another consciousness, and the disclosure of female self is linked to the identification of some 'other'" (22); casting Mrs. Lincoln as that chosen other, Keckley grounds her identity through her evolving relation to the First Lady. In the terms of a paradigm of Mae Gwendolyn Henderson's, Keckley enters simultaneously into a "testimonial" discourse with Mrs. Lincoln that affirms their gender identity and a "competitive" discourse that asserts their racial difference (Henderson 20). Generally, as the "black woman writer," Keckley at once "speaks familiarly" in the language of the other while remaining in "contestorial dialogue" with hegemonic discourse (Henderson 20).[4] In the constant demonstration of her intimacy with Mrs. Lincoln, Keckley makes her friendship with the famous white woman self-affirming. They unite especially in womanly sympathy and suffering when Mrs. Lincoln's son Willie dies (Keckley is "immediately sent for" [103]) and when her husband is assassinated (Keckley is Mrs. Lincoln's "only companion, except her children, in the days of her great sorrow" [193]). In a letter to Keckley, Mrs. Lincoln identifies her as "my best living friend" (301) and in conversation with her states, "'Lizabeth, you are my best and kindest friend, and I love you as my best friend'" (210). The latter example is a particularly telling use of dialogue by Keckley,[5] for in it Mrs. Lincoln is made to testify in her own voice to Keckley's depth and personhood. At moments such as these in *Behind the Scenes* the alterity of the Keckley-Lincoln relationship ripens to equality.

But as the author of *Behind the Scenes*, Keckley does assume significant ascendancy over Mrs. Lincoln, as much as she might like to minimize the contestorial implications of her narrative. The dressmaker in some fundamental way not only clothes but also anatomizes her employer: "I never in my life saw a more peculiarly constituted woman" (182). In chronicling the "secret history" of Mrs. Lincoln's transactions, Keckley commits herself to the telling of a story of "notoriety" (xiii) and, even more importantly, positions herself as Mrs. Lincoln's adjudicator, hoping that "the world" judge her "as I have judged her" (xiv). Keckley's record of Mrs. Lincoln's transgressions is a cautious expression of some desire on her part to legislate, to assume some formative role in determining public opinion and narrative, to be "Judge Keckley" as well as "President Keckley." Although the latter portion of the text is given over to Keckley's willingness "to render Mrs. Lincoln all the assistance in my power" (269), Keckley is also horrified by Lincoln's unseemly submission to the "public gaze" (289) through the exposition of her dresses. Uneasy about the way that Mrs. Lincoln "stepped beyond the formal lines which hedge about a private life" (xiii), Keckley assiduously cultivates those "formal lines" in the interest of shaping a "public gaze" for herself that might provide recognition and standing rather than shame. But the power relational between herself and Mrs. Lincoln remains volatile and unresolved. Fairly late in the text Keckley admits that she had been with Lincoln so long "that she had acquired great power over me" (209), and the actual publication of *Behind the Scenes* in fact "caused a permanent rift between the two women" (Thompson 673).

Embedded in Keckley's conflicted portrait of Mrs. Lincoln is a reverent one of the president himself, the exposé of the former perhaps allowing or necessitating the idealization of the latter. In scaling some American hegemonic chain, Keckley may have felt she could not risk a contestorial discourse with Lincoln, symbolically at least the country's most powerful white man, but only with the wife whose gendered status more closely approximates her own. As with Mrs. Lincoln, Keckley has Lincoln name her, accruing here the even greater ontological dividends of his recognition. "Mrs. Keckley has met with great success," he announces after seeing his wife in one of Keckley's designs (88); later, as their acquaintance deepens, Keckley notes that Lincoln "always called me Madam Elizabeth" (156). Although Keckley does provide intimate glimpses of Lincoln, and although her own acts of gazing upon him might seem to begin to bridge (or transgress) the hierarchical chasm between them, such moments invariably culminate in near-ritualistic celebration of the president. When, for example, Keckley sees Lincoln crying over his dead son, she looks at him "in silent, awe-stricken wonder" and allegorizes the moment as "genius and greatness weeping over love's idol lost" (103). If before a speech she observes Lincoln "looking over his notes and muttering to himself" (175), when the oration begins, he looks "more like a demi-god than a man" (177). (Keckley is of course interested here in charting the transition from private composition to public performance in Lincoln that is central to her own self-invention.) When she views the dead Lincoln, she regards "the white face of the man that I had worshipped as an idol" (190).

Through her relationship with the Lincolns, however, Keckley does take a last profound ontological step that oversees her identities as dressmaker and writer. An adumbration of this shift occurs early in the text when Keckley visits a fair in Chicago and encounters a wax figure of Jefferson Davis wearing the dress "in which it was reported that he was captured": "I worked my way to the figure, and in examining the dress made the pleasing discovery that it was one of the chintz wrappers that I had made for Mrs. Davis" (74). In finding her artistry so commemorated, Keckley experiences the museum's institutional power to preserve, honor, and publicize. With the Lincolns Keckley becomes an explicit collector. She asks Mrs. Lincoln for and receives the right-hand glove (which comes to her "soiled" [158]) that the president wears at his first reception after his second inaugural. After the assassination, she is given the president's blood-stained cloak as well as the comb and brush he used at the White House and later she acquires the president's overshoes. That so many of the garments Keckley collects are stained seems to demythologize Lincoln, to reconfigure Keckley's "worship" of him; they function as rather lurid reminders that Lincoln all too humanly sweats and bleeds. During the exposition of Mrs. Lincoln's wardrobe, visitors also remark on the worn condition and stains of many of the dresses. In terms of Anne McClintock's formulation, Keckley may even be glossing her culture's "Victorian dirt fetish" (152); dirt becomes fetishized and banished because it is "the memory trace of working class and female labor, unseemly evidence that the fundamental production of industrial and imperial wealth lay in the hands and bodies of the working class" (154). By airing the literal "dirt" of the Lincolns, Keckley begins to make visible and invert such systems of mystification; her very "collecting" is an extension and justification of her own "female labor."

As a "collector," Keckley finds a way to participate in, as James Clifford has written, a specialized "form of Western subjectivity" (Clifford 54) rooted in notions of "an ideal self as owner" (51). Collecting, Clifford argues, "has long been a strategy for the deployment of a possessive self, culture, and authenticity" (52). In assembling her collection of Lincoln memorabilia, Keckley can map out "a subjective domain that is not 'other'" (Clifford 52), and her narrative as a whole might be seen as enacting "the idea that identity is a kind of wealth"—not only of "objects," but of "knowledge, memories, experience" (Clifford 52). From this perspective her own text, a hybrid assembly of knowledge, memories, and experience, might be usefully construed itself as a "collection." Similar to her generation and assumption of an authorial identity, Keckley as "collector" reasserts the appeal of a disembodied intellectual mode of being for herself. The persona of collector ironically recalls, only to banish, the experience of being the slave who was the dehumanized possession of another; simultaneously, it posits a potentially liberating way of inhabiting some cultural space that is not even necessarily contingent on race or gender.

Furthermore, in the only letter that Keckley herself authors in the book's appendix, she extends the ramifications of her collecting to consolidate the ontological progress away from the personal that her text has charted. Writing to Bishop Payne of Wilberforce University (where her own son was educated), Keckley decides to donate her "sacred relics" (366) to the university to help in the cause of "educating the four millions of slaves liberated by our president" (367). Keckley the collector becomes Keckley the curator, whose dissemination of private treasure publicly inscribes her as privileged agent of history. As altruistic director of legend and memory, she seems to have achieved some particularly valid social self here. "Curating" for Keckley obviously denotes "educating," and her educational agenda—to instruct those "four millions of slaves"—has a decided grandeur of intent. Her own specific experience with Lincoln in fact seems to culminate as a synecdoche for the new relationship of her newly freed people to the history and government generally of the country. In that Keckley also insists on the sacredness of her relics, an assignment of value that she authors, she even gives herself a sacerdotal role to play before her text concludes.

In the course of her text Keckley radically emerges from behind the scenes to enter imaginatively into the public life of nineteenth-century America. Not only a critique of separate sphere ideology, and the specific relegation of women to the private sphere, *Behind the Scenes* clearly delineates the advantages of Keckley's paradoxical autobiographical escape from self. Within her aesthetics of impersonality Keckley locates a textual domain for herself where she is burdened neither by romance, the necessity of dramatizing her personal experience, nor representativeness, the necessity of speaking for her entire race. In developing her own preferences for more disinterested historicizing, she is able to mediate not only between black and white but also between history and myth, intervening as author-curator at that juncture where she recognizes how the story of Lincoln the man has already begun to mutate into a larger cultural allegory—of division, of emancipation, of martyrdom. In her preface, Keckley proclaims that "in all things pertaining to life I can afford to be charitable" (xii); as historian and philanthropist by the book's final pages, she thematizes charitability to render her life and storytelling as much magnanimous as free.

## NOTES

1. In that *Behind the Scenes* does not seem to constitute, in Lawrence Buell's phrase, a "developed autobiography" (47), it also lends credence to Buell's argument that autobiography "does not flower as a literary genre in America much before the time of Henry Adams" (47–48); with its "strategies of self-consciousness and self-effacement" (58), the text accords with a distinct mode of nineteenth-century American autobiographical writing.

2. In "A Poetics of Afro-American Autobiography" Andrews provides a definition of "free storytelling" taken from his book *To Tell a Free Story*: "The history of Afro-American autobiography is one of increasingly free storytelling, signaled in the ways black narratives address their readers and reconstruct personal history, ways often at variance with literary conventions and social proprieties of discourse" (89). In the essay Andrews goes on to express his belief in "the revolutionary implications of free storytelling for the evaluation of texts as well as for understanding of traditions in Afro-American autobiography" (89).

3. Andrews has noted how the "moral problems attendant to the slave woman's sexuality" tend to be not much looked at after Jacobs's account ("Changing" 227).

4. In describing the "interlocutory" (17) character of black women's writing, Henderson also postulates "an internal dialogue with the plural aspects of self" as constitutive of black female subjectivity (18). See also Smith on the multiple dilemmas of the female autobiographer of color, always "resident on the margins of discourse," negotiating "sometimes four sets of stories . . . written about her rather than by her" (51).

5. Andrews, in his "Dialogue in Antebellum Afro-American Autobiography," has written about the formal importance of dialogue to the slave narrative where it "tells us something about the negotiation of power" (91) between master and slave and stands as a crucial "liminal phase in the master-slave relationship, when neither master nor slave was in full control of the situation" (93).

**WORKS CITED**

Andrews, William L. "The Changing Moral Discourse of Nineteenth-Century African American Women's Autobiography: Harriet Jacobs and Elizabeth Keckley." *De/Colonizing the Subject: The Politics of Gender in Women's Autobiography*. Ed. Sidonie Smith and Julia Watson. Minneapolis: University of Minnesota Press, 1992. 225–41.

———. "Dialogue in Antebellum Afro-American Autobiography." *Studies in Autobiography*. Ed. James Olney. New York: Oxford University Press, 1988. 89–99.

———. *To Tell a Free Story: The First Century of Afro-American Autobiography, 1760–1865*. Urbana: University of Illinois Press, 1986.

———. "Towards a Poetics of Afro-American Autobiography." *Afro-American Literary Study in the 1990s*. Ed. Houston A. Baker Jr. and Patricia Redmond. Chicago: University of Chicago Press, 1989. 78–91.

Buell, Lawrence. "Autobiography in the American Renaissance." *American Autobiography: Retrospect and Prospect*. Ed. Paul John Eakin. Madison: University of Wisconsin Press, 1991. 47–70.

Braxton, Joanne M. *Black Women Writing Autobiography: A Tradition Within a Tradition*. Philadelphia: Temple University Press, 1989.

Broughton, T.L. "Women's Autobiography: The Self at Stake?" *Autobiography and Questions of Gender*. Ed. Shirley Neuman. London: Frank Cass, 1991. 76–95.

Clifford, James. "On Collecting Art and Culture." *The Cultural Studies Reader*. Ed. Simon During. New York: Routledge, 1994. 49–74.

Douglass, Frederick. *Narrative of the Life*. *The Classic Slave Narratives*. Ed. Henry Louis Gates Jr. New York: Mentor, 1987. 243–333.

Eakin, Paul John. "Narrative and Chronology as Structures of Reference and the New Model Autobiographer." *Studies in Autobiography*. Ed. James Olney. New York: Oxford University Press, 1988. 32–42.

Henderson, Mae Gwendolyn. "Speaking in Tongues: Dialogics, Dialectics, and the Black Woman Writer's Literary Tradition." *Changing Our Own Words: Essays on Criticism, Theory, and Writing by Black Women*. Ed. Cheryl A. Wall. New Brunswick: Rutgers University Press, 1989. 16–37.

Hollander, Anne. *Seeing Through Clothes*. Berkeley: University of California Press, 1993.

Keckley, Elizabeth. *Behind the Scenes: Or, Thirty Years a Slave, and Four Years in the White House.* New York: Oxford University Press, 1988.

Mason, Mary G. "The Other Voice: Autobiographies of Women Writers." *Life/Lines: Theorizing Women's Autobiography.* Ed. Bella Brodzki and Celeste Schenck. Ithaca: Cornell University Press, 1988.

McClintock, Anne. *Imperial Leather: Race, Gender and Sexuality in the Colonial Contest.* New York: Routledge, 1995.

Neuman, Shirley. "Autobiography and Questions of Gender: An Introduction." *Autobiography and Questions of Gender.* London: Frank Cass, 1991. 1–12.

Olney, James. Introduction. *Behind the Scenes.* By Elizabeth Keckley. xxvii–xxxvi.

Renza, Louis A. "The Veto of the Imagination: A Theory of Autobiography." *Autobiography: Essays Theoretical and Critical.* Ed. James Olney. Princeton: Princeton University Press, 1980. 268–96.

Smith, Sidonie. *A Poetics of Women's Autobiography: Marginality and the Fictions of Self-Representation.* Bloomington: Indiana University Press, 1987.

Smith, Valerie. Introduction. *Incidents in the Life of a Slave Girl.* By Harriet Jacobs. New York: Oxford University Press, 1987. xxvii–xl.

Thompson, Kathleen. "Keckley, Elizabeth (1818–1907)." *Black Women in America: An Historical Encyclopedia.* Ed. Darlene Clark Hine. Brooklyn: Carlson, 1993. 672–73.

Wall, Cheryl A. "Introduction: Taking Positions and Changing Words." *Changing Our Own Words: Essays on Criticism, Theory, and Writing by Black Women* Ed. Cheryl A. Wall. New Brunswick: Rutgers University Press, 1989. 1–16.

CHAPTER SIX

**JANET NEARY**

# Behind the Scenes and Inside Out
Elizabeth Keckly's Revision of the Slave-Narrative Form

IN SEPTEMBER 1862, WHEN Abraham Lincoln read a draft of what became the Emancipation Proclamation, declaring that all slaves in Confederate states would be legally free on January 1, 1863, around 400 recently escaped slaves were living homeless in Washington, DC. By the end of the war, that number had risen to 40,000 (Reef 58). Elizabeth Keckly,[1] a former slave living in the capital, sympathized with the newly freed men and women who arrived daily in the city with little more than the clothes on their backs. Since purchasing her own freedom in St. Louis, Keckly had established herself as a modiste to elite families in Washington, doing well enough to open her own shop and sustain a number of employees. It is from this vantage that, in the summer of 1862, after observing fundraising campaigns organized for wounded white soldiers, she determined to make a similar appeal to the black community on behalf of newly emancipated slaves. Her narrative *Behind the Scenes: Or, Thirty Years a Slave, and Four Years in the White House* (1868) describes the moment at which she was struck by the idea: "If the white people can give festivals to raise funds for the relief of suffering soldiers, why should not the well-to-do colored people go to work to do something for the benefit of the suffering blacks?" (113). Within weeks, Keckly had organized and was serving as the president of the Contraband Relief Association, which provided material support to newly freed men and women establishing themselves in the North.

Keckly's intimate awareness of the precarious situation of emancipated slaves and her advocacy on their behalf provides a striking contrast to her discussion of Mary Todd Lincoln's financial difficulties in her narrative. Although she explicitly sympathizes with Mrs. Lincoln, and in fact states that her primary motive in writing the narrative is to clear Lincoln's name—"To defend myself I must defend the lady that I have served" (xiv)—the representation of

Mary Lincoln as a privileged woman forced to sell her couture dresses and live in modestly appointed guest rooms takes on an ironic cast when held up against Keckly's advocacy for free men and women settling in makeshift encampments and struggling to acquire basic necessities. As the Lincolns' personal tailor and a trusted confidante of Mary, Keckly had a unique perspective on the First Lady's rise and fall in the eyes of public opinion, and her narrative thus offers to lay bare the "secret history of [Mrs. Lincoln's] transactions" (xiv). After Abraham Lincoln's assassination, when Mary's soaring debts came to light, she turned to Keckly for both emotional support and help in selling her wardrobe to raise funds in a clandestine private auction; the scheme failed miserably and became the public debacle known as the Old Clothes Scandal. Newspapers of the time note that while the public was curious about Lincoln's private life and financial predicament, people had very little sympathy for her circumstances. According to Keckly, however, this was not the case within the black community. In the wake of the scandal Keckly marshaled her considerable contacts to raise money on Lincoln's behalf, noting that "[t]he colored people were surprised to hear of Mrs. Lincoln's poverty, and the news of her distress called forth strong sympathy from their warm, generous hearts. Rev. H.H. Garnet, of New York City, and Mr. Frederick Douglass, of Rochester, N.Y., proposed to lecture in behalf of the widow of the lamented President, and schemes were on foot to raise a large sum of money by contribution" (313–14). This disclosure, like many in the narrative, may surprise readers of the text. In 1867, when one might expect representatives of the government to be providing support and relief to newly emancipated slaves, many of the formerly enslaved were taking up a collection for Mary Lincoln.[2]

    This striking historical coincidence is emblematic of the structure of *Behind the Scenes* as a whole, which repeatedly confounds narrative expectations and reverses what Robert Stepto calls the "race rituals" which structure the classic slave narrative (229). Although Keckly inscribes her text within the slave-narrative tradition through her subtitle and the reproduction of key narrative tropes of slave experience—family separation, the female slave's vulnerability to sexual abuse, brutal beatings at the hands of white slaveholders—most of the narrative concentrates not on Keckly's experiences as a slave but rather on those of the Lincolns' in the White House, observed from Keckly's perspective as their personal tailor. Because of this emphasis critics have identified the work as a departure from the slave-narrative tradition, an assessment that along with its postbellum publication has kept it from receiving the widespread attention of other women's slave narratives, in particular Harriet Jacobs's *Incidents in the Life of a Slave Girl* (1861), which many take to be *the* representative account of a female experience of slavery.[3] Readers versed in the conventions of slave narratives expect the primary subject of the narrative to be Keckly's experience of enslavement, an expectation that is both acknowledged and refused through the narrative's language of revelation. For example, recalling Lydia Maria Child's rhetoric in her Preface to *Incidents,* in which she takes responsibility for presenting the "monstrous features" of slavery with the "veil withdrawn" (8), Keckly's self-penned Preface states that "[t]he veil of mystery must be drawn aside; the origin of a fact must be brought to light with the naked fact itself" (xiv).[4] However, the language of revelation and exposure is applied to Mary Lincoln's motivations in selling her old clothes, rather than to Keckly's experience of enslavement or the sexual vulnerability of black women to white men under the slave regime.[5] In light of Keckly's activism on behalf of newly emancipated slaves, this reversal is likely a stratagem designed to call attention to the ways in which traditional slave narration—with its attendant conventions of authentication—leaves certain racial assumptions intact.[6] Keckly's narrative, while seeming to avoid the black subject—causing Rafia Zafar to call the text "a black autobiography without African Americans" (152)—actually dismantles the apparatus of racial authenticity, presenting a significant challenge to the persistence of a black/white racial binary in the postbellum period and drawing particular attention to the persistence of the visual logic of this binary that continued to operate forcefully after Emancipation.[7]

Essential to this reading is an understanding of the slave narrative as more than a version of autobiography in which the perspective of a single subject is paramount, but rather as a form of racial negotiation that takes shape in response to the contradictions within Western discourse that challenge the very notion of black subjectivity.[8] Although she moves quickly through the events of her life in slavery, Keckly's narrative reflects the formal requirements of slave narration throughout, responding to and revising the elements that constitute the slave narrative's conventions of authentication: the variety of tropes, documents, and guarantees that confirm and cosign the black literary voice. *Behind the Scenes* includes a justificatory Preface, documentary evidence, and a scene of literacy, but the racial protocols underlying those narrative gestures—white authority legitimating black experience—are reversed.

In *Behind the Scenes* Keckly's authority underwrites the status and actions of the white figures in her text: Her letters authenticate Mary Lincoln's version of events, she includes Tad Lincoln's reading lesson in place of her own, and the narrative gaze fixes primarily on the white bodies within the text as they take shape in her vocation, dressmaking. The authenticating documents integrated into *Behind the Scenes,* such as her emancipation papers and the letters between Keckly and Lincoln, are superseded by the dominance of Keckly's own editorial voice; Keckly offers or withholds information as *she* sees fit.[9] Because the conventions of slave narratives were so well known by 1868, Keckly's inversion of black and white figures within otherwise traditional authenticating elements casts attention on the racial expectations that motivate slave-narrative construction, literally revising the notion of racial authenticity.

The novelty of my argument lies in its formal reading of *Behind the Scenes* as unified by its revision of slave-narrative conventions, which makes it possible to understand the text as a powerful rebuke of the racial logic extending from slavery into the postbellum period. Where other critics have understood the narrative as fundamentally ambivalent, riven by class divisions and Keckly's alternation of seemingly contradictory condemnatory and conciliatory stances regarding the role of slavery in both her own life and the life of the nation, attention to the narrative's formal elements reveals a sustained critique of white racism.[10] For example, a focus on these structural elements of the narrative belies the reading that Keckly exhibits a strong desire "to prove herself" (Andrews, "Changing" 234); Keckly's inversion of black and white figures within the slave narrative's structures of authentication suggests not only that she feels she has nothing to prove, but also that she finds the requirement that she provide proof of the truth of her experience absurd.[11] Similarly, the explicit class divisions revealed in the text, such as the rhetorical distance Keckly adopts in her discussion of the mass of newly emancipated slaves arriving daily in Washington, ultimately inform a rhetorical strategy Keckly uses to draw attention to the lack of care the newly reunited nation provided for its most vulnerable citizens.

Among those critics who have discussed *Behind the Scenes* within the slave-narrative tradition, many see Keckly as overly optimistic about the status of her freedom. Xiomara Santamarina, following Zafar and Frances Smith Foster, reads the narrative as Keckly's miscalculation that the working loyalty between black and white women would extend to the confidence and loyalty of a white readership, who roundly rejected the book: "[Keckley fails] to recognize how her subordinate status as a servant meant that her work-related attributes could only be narrated by her employer, not by herself" (Santamarina 159).[12] While not going so far as to declare the narrative failed in this way, Jennifer Fleischner provides a psychological account of the narrative's apparent inconsistencies, calling them "strategies of unconscious repression or deliberate suppression, substitutions, splitting, and inversions that seem intended to mask some of the anger and sorrow associated with her experiences of racism and slavery" (99).

By contrast, I read *Behind the Scenes* as a successful activist text that eschews seeking the approval of her white audience and challenges the persistence of racial binaries.[13] Reading Keckly's narrative as unified by its revision of slave-narrative conventions allows for an alternate understanding of the text not as a *mis*calculation of interracial sentimental female affiliation forged through work or an attempt to manage personal feelings of loss and rage in the wake of slavery, but as a calculated reversal designed to undermine the persistence of a pernicious racial divide.[14] The success of Keckly's sharp-eyed critique might be measured by the vitriol exhibited by the narrative's failed reception, which lays bare the ideological assumptions about blackness her text targets through its revision of the slave-narrative form. Correctly perceiving *Behind the Scenes* as an attack on the racial status quo, contemporary reviewers painted Keckly as a servant "who has forgotten her place" (Fleischner 95). The narrative even engendered a particularly virulent racist parody entitled *Behind the Seams,* which inadvertently confirms Keckly's own analysis of racial ideology in so-called free society through the caricature of Keckly as an illiterate, immodest, ignorant slave named "Betsey Kickley" who must sign her name with an "X."[15] Reading Keckly's narrative as unified by its revision of slave-narrative conventions claims a political unity of purpose for the text and sheds new light on her interventions into literary and visual representations of African Americans in the postwar period.

In addition to recalibrating our understanding of *Behind the Scenes* as a major contribution to (rather than departure from) the slave-narrative tradition, recognizing Keckly's appropriation of the genre's authenticating strategies exposes her sophisticated textual intervention into a visual culture that was quickly becoming the nineteenth century's dominant "mode of social perception" (Manuel 27).[16] In overturning the race rituals performed by the conventions of authentication, which rely on fixed notions of "black" and "white," Keckly undermines the ideological presumptions that link blackness with enslavement and whiteness with literacy and truth. Moreover, through her vocation as a dressmaker, Keckly is well positioned to highlight the constructedness of what may appear to be finished products. While other critics—particularly Elizabeth Young and Carme Manuel—have identified *Behind the Scenes* as an intervention into national iconography, I argue that Keckly's deployment of visual tropes and metaphors represents a fundamental refiguring of how we understand the visual world.[17]

Manuel argues that "Keckley rewrites popular visual representations of blacks and restores their visibility in order to construct a new politics of historical truth" (28); I argue that Keckly goes farther than simply expanding the range of images admitted into the national archive by interrogating the values that construct that archive. African Americans' experience of visual objectification gave them good reason to be skeptical of the equation of visual evidence and truth. Just as Keckly challenges the notion that her narrative requires authentication because of her racial status, so, too, does she challenge the idea that race is self-evident. Her strategy of inversion and juxtaposition pits textual and visual conventions of representation against one another to erode the aura of "truth" and challenge the notion that we "know something when we see it." During the scene depicting her whipping at the hands of a white man, for example, Keckly likens herself to a statue, invoking conventions of visual art to highlight the spectacular character of black suffering in traditional slave narration. Later, an image in Tad Lincoln's primer impedes his reading lesson and becomes an occasion for Keckly to remark on the double standard for black and white illiteracy. These scenes, along with her substitution of Abraham Lincoln's spectacular vulnerability in place of the enslaved's and her use of clothing as a narrative device—which both metonymically represents white flesh and highlights her role at the center of events of national importance—represent a profound challenge to the visual culture of her time. In *Behind the Scenes* visual details or metaphors intrude upon each of the expected slave-narrative tropes and become the organizing principle of the text: Conventions of authority and self-determination mapped onto black and white subjects are overturned in *Behind the Scenes*, subverting the racial logic expressed in the slave narrative's conventions of authentication. Despite writing her narrative with abolitionist editor James Redpath (who has no textual presence in the narrative), Keckly rejects the racial protocols of conventional slave narration, radicalizing the form.[18] In so doing, she establishes the slave narrative as a mode of cultural critique that exceeds the political mandates of abolition as well as the historical moment of the antebellum, and intervenes in an epistemological conflict over race.

## "A black autobiography without African Americans"

The rare appearance of Keckly's own body in her narrative and the corresponding focus on white bodies represents a significant departure from the presentation of the suffering black body in classic slave narratives.[19] Keckly includes one scene describing her own abuse, but it functions as a critique of what Saidiya Hartman calls the "inaugural moment in the formation of the enslaved" (3); her correlative shift in narrative focus to vulnerable white bodies—and specifically Abraham Lincoln's body—illustrates the unequal propositions of black and white materiality wherein blackness is construed as base materiality in opposition to the inherent meaningfulness or referentiality of whiteness.[20] Carol Henderson argues that the presentation of damaged black flesh was a representational strategy designed to make black humanity visible to readers: "the alliance between abolition and political action rested not only on *seeing* the body in pain but also on *being* the body in pain because it is this rhetorical use of pain that marks the slave body and makes it visible" (39; original emphasis). Hartman identifies the cost of this route to empathy: "if the scene of beating readily lends itself to an identification with the enslaved, it does so at the risk of fixing and naturalizing this condition of pained embodiment and . . . increases the difficulty of beholding black suffering since the endeavor to bring pain close exploits the spectacle of the body in pain and oddly confirms the spectral character of suffering and the inability to witness the captive's pain" (20).

Central to both Henderson's and Hartman's analyses is the re-inscription of a dominant visual paradigm. In Henderson, black flesh must be scarred to cross the threshold from invisibility to visibility; Hartman recognizes this mode of visibility as spectacle antithetical to empathy: "the elusiveness of black suffering can be attributed to a racist optics in which black flesh is itself identified as the source of opacity, the denial of black humanity, and the effacement of sentience integral to the wanton use of the captive body" (20).

The presentation of the suffering black body is an ambivalent mechanism of self-authorization, potentially bolstering the invisibility/opacity of a fixed notion of blackness.[21] Keckly's narrative addresses this convention, implicated in a "denial of black humanity," by first acknowledging the spectacular character of the black body in pain, and then shifting the narrative gaze to the spectacle of white physical vulnerability on a national scale—in the form of President Lincoln's assassination. By showcasing white vulnerability while she maintains a disembodied, editorial distance, Keckly implicitly critiques the association of blackness with embodiment, reversing what Hartman calls "racist optics."

In the early part of her narrative Keckly, like Harriet Jacobs, demonstrates the link between physical vulnerability and sexual violation to which female slaves are susceptible. Although whipping appears under the guise of correction, Keckly emphasizes the sexual motivation often animating the abuse of female slaves. The beating Keckly describes in the finest detail—a whipping she endures after she had grown into "strong, healthy womanhood"—reveals both sexual jealously (on the part of the mistress) and sexual desire (on the part of the master or master's proxy). At the time of the incident, Keckly was living with a relatively poor family, the Burwells, who were in charge of a small church in Hillsborough, North Carolina. Mrs. Burwell, whom Keckly describes as "morbidly sensitive" (31), constantly punished Keckly for unnamed offenses, a pattern that culminated in allowing a local schoolmaster, Mr. Bingham, to act as her proxy in punishing Keckly: "She whom I called mistress seemed to be desirous to wreak vengeance on me for something, and Bingham became her ready tool" (32). Sexual jealously is implied as the vague "something" of which Keckly is guilty, and Mrs. Burwell's suppressed jealously translates into the overtly sexual nature of the beating she receives from Mr. Bingham:

> It was Saturday evening, and while I was bending over the bed, watching the baby that I had just hushed into slumber, Mr. Bingham came to the door and asked me to go with him to his study. Wondering what he meant by this strange request, I followed him, and when we had entered the study he closed the door, and in his blunt way remarked: "Lizzie, I am going to flog you." I was thunderstruck, and tried to think if I had been remiss in anything. I could not recollect of doing anything to deserve punishment, and with surprise exclaimed: "Whip me, Mr. Bingham! what for?"

> "No matter," he replied, "I am going to whip you, so take down your dress this instant."
>
> Recollect, I was eighteen years of age, was a woman fully developed, and yet this man coolly bade me take down my dress. (32–33)

Although Keckly refuses, Bingham tears her dress from her back and repeatedly wields the whip over her "quivering flesh." Rather than suppressing what Hartman calls "the spectacular character of black suffering" (3), Keckly emphasizes it by refusing to make any noise, likening herself to a statue. She prompts the reader to become a more immediate witness to the scene when she writes,

> Oh God! I can feel the torture now—the terrible, excruciating agony of those moments. I did not scream; I was too proud to let my tormentor know what I was suffering. I closed my lips firmly, that not even a groan might escape from them, and I stood like a statue while the keen lash cut deep into my flesh. (34)

Keckly's subjectivity is contained in her silence, her refusal to acknowledge pain that she knows would provide satisfaction to her tormentor.[22] But interestingly, rather than narrating her experience of the abuse in that moment, she shifts her perspective to the time of writing—"I can feel the torture now"—creating conspicuous rhetorical distance and aligning herself with reader/witnesses. She states that "the rawhide descended upon *the* quivering flesh" (34; emphasis added), foregoing the use of the possessive pronoun "my" and enhancing the scenic quality of her description. In so doing, she calls our attention to the familiarity of the scene of whipping and the anonymity of the figure at the center. Although she exerts her individuality by refusing to make a sound, her flesh could be *any* black flesh in this canonical scene within slave narration. By highlighting the iconic (and routine) nature of the scene of abuse, a convention anticipated by the reader, Keckly refuses to conflate her subjectivity with pain.

After this scene, Keckly's body rarely appears in her narrative. Instead, her narrative is organized around a spectacular instance of violence against a white body: the assassination of President Lincoln. Written after his death, the narrative constantly foreshadows Lincoln's assassination. Although he is described in supernatural terms—"more like a demi-god than a man"—

Lincoln is betrayed by his body, "crowned with the fleeting days of mortality" (177). After remarking on the bold and stately tableau made by Lincoln and Tad during one of Lincoln's addresses, the idea of his vulnerability intrudes on Keckly: "[A] sudden thought struck me, and I whispered to the friend at my side: 'What an easy matter would it be to kill the President, as he stands there! He could be shot down from the crowd, and no one be able to tell who fired the shot'" (178). The striking accuracy of Keckly's premonition transforms the tableau from an icon of national pride into a *memento mori*.

The substitution of violence against a white figure, the head of state, for the routinized violence against black bodies reverses the conventional representational strategy of slave narratives and serves to illustrate the differing symbolic functions of black and white flesh within the nation and within the genre. As Lindon Barrett argues, "[w]hereas the black body is understood in the redundant terms of its own materiality, the white body is understood as referential, in other words as significant and meaningful" ("African-American" 437). Keckly's reversal emphasizes the materiality of white flesh, but also reveals its social significance: The white body is never understood in terms of its base materiality, even at its most inert and inanimate state—in death.

News of Lincoln's assassination comes during the Northern celebration of the fall of Fort Sumter. Keckly describes the whole of the nation as "transfixed" by the news: "[S]carcely had the fireworks ceased to play, and the lights been taken down from the windows, when the lightning flashed the most appalling news over the magnetic wires. 'The President has been murdered!' spoke the swift-winged messenger, and the loud huzza died upon the lips. A nation suddenly paused in the midst of festivity, and stood paralyzed with horror—transfixed with awe" (184). Unlike the spectacle of the suffering black slave, whose ability to inspire empathy rests on "fixing and naturalizing this condition of pained embodiment" (Hartman 20), the national spectacle of Lincoln's assassination arrests the bodies of the people in the crowd. By substituting Lincoln's physical vulnerability for the rehearsal of black suffering, Keckly exploits "the inherent meaningfulness of white bodies ... their legibility, their ability [to] stand in for terms and narratives that do not inhere in their physical presence" (Barrett, "Hand-Writing" 325), throwing into relief the unequal propositions of black and white embodiment. Whereas black figures have to prove their humanity through a variety of symbolic gestures, white figures are significant even in death. The representation of damaged black flesh is both what Douglass calls "the blood-stained gate, the entrance to the hell of slavery" (6), and the mechanism by which readers of slave narratives come to recognize the humanity of the slave; by contrast, the spectacle of Lincoln's assassination registers as a singular tragedy unable to be exchanged in a representational market.

## "Facts which float upon the surface"

While Lincoln's assassination is the most dramatic example, Keckly's focus on the physicality of the white body—not under the lash, but as it takes shape under her needle—provides the most sustained critique of the race rituals governing slave narratives.[23] Characterized by weakness and fragility in contradistinction to her own disembodied presence as seamstress/editor/narrator, the measurements, outline, irrational emotional reactions, and even secretions of white bodies take center stage in *Behind the Scenes*. It is white flesh—often metonymically represented through clothing—which is on display, and whose signification Keckly manages in her everyday work as a seamstress. As Barrett argues, the treatment of "the vexed African American body" is the "central textual dilemma for ex-slave narrators" ("Hand-Writing" 315) and its management is a key strategy of authentication:

> In order to authenticate themselves as African Americans, [ex-slave] narrators must highlight the primary terms by which African American identity is construed—the body and the life of the body. Nevertheless, because the claims these narrators are making on the government and culture of the United States are based on denunciations of an enforced and spurious confinement to a life merely of the body ... these narrators must not only recover their bodies within their narratives but also, more importantly, remove their bodies from these narratives. ("Hand-Writing" 315)

Keckly uses clothing as a narrative device, allowing her to emphasize her presence—as the clothing's fabricator—while removing her own body from view. Moreover, by focusing on the literal "dirty laundry" of white figures in the text, Keckly continues to press her strategy of reversal, accentuating the materiality of white figures that would seem larger than life and overturning the cultural logic of race in the United States.

Keckly's treatment of the auction at the center of the Old Clothes Scandal illustrates this nicely. When put up for sale to raise money after Lincoln's assassination, Mary Lincoln's dresses become objects of curiosity and disgust, engendering public outrage and symbolizing the indecorous behavior of a former First Lady. One newspaper account included by Keckly notes,

> The feeling of the majority of visitors is adverse to the course Mrs. Lincoln has thought proper to pursue, and the criticisms are as severe as the cavillings are persistent at the quality of some of the dresses.... Some of them, if not worn long, have been worn much; they are jagged under the arms and at the bottom of the skirt, stains are on the lining, and other objections present themselves to those who oscillate between the dresses and dollars, "notwithstanding they have been worn by Madam Lincoln," as a lady who looked from behind a pair of gold spectacles remarked. (303–04)

This last "notwithstanding" provides the prurient slant: the spectacle of Mary Lincoln's physical body on display through her used clothing, underscored by the gold spectacles from behind which a lady gazes. Instead of presenting the exposed black body on the slave auction block, Keckly presents the white body on public display in the form of Mrs. Lincoln's clothing auction. This reversal of the racial gaze interrupts the readerly expectation of the slave narrative, but also illustrates the differential treatment of black and white embodiment. While exposure of the black body is considered a necessary route to empathy and recognition in slave narration, exposure of the white body is considered unseemly.

Keckly's use of clothing to stand in for white bodies is central to her critique of postbellum racism: The history of emancipation and the history of clothing are often registered in a single garment. On the occasion of President Lincoln's second inauguration, Keckly asks Mary Lincoln for the president's right-hand glove worn to the first public reception of his new term. To explain this strange request, Keckly tells Lincoln, "I shall cherish it as a precious memento of the second inauguration of the man who has done so much for my race. He has been a Jehovah to my people—has lifted them out of bondage, and directed their footsteps from darkness to light. I shall keep the glove, and hand it down to posterity." Mary Lincoln finds this request rather distasteful: "You shall have it in welcome. It will be so filthy when he pulls it off, I shall be tempted to take the tongs and put it in the fire. I cannot imagine, Lizabeth, what you want with such a glove" (154). But Keckly's interest in the glove—a symbol of racial uplift—is directly tied to its filthiness as an index of white materiality. The day after the reception Keckly is delighted to pick up the soiled glove "bearing the marks of the thousands of hands that grasped the honest hand of Mr. Lincoln on that eventful night" (154–55). Keckly specifically asks for the "right-hand glove," because it registers the "thousands of hands" that shook Lincoln's own. More than a congratulatory gesture, the handshake is a contract, a form of recognition between equals. Keckly's request for the right-hand glove simultaneously emphasizes the materiality of white bodies and the symbolic entrance of black people into the national body.

Keckly's request for the soiled right-hand glove also demonstrates her awareness that material is never just that: Imbued with meaning, clothing and bodies serve as constructions steeped in power and consequence. Clothing represents the malleability of appearances and she presents it as both a foil and an analogue for racial identity. In her preface, Keckly refers to writing her narrative as "bringing a solemn truth to the surface *as a truth*" (xiii; emphasis in original). The unusual emphasis seems to indicate that truth can be distorted in its journey to the surface, or, at the very least, that surfaces and truth do not always correspond. It is in the conjunction between appearance (as constructed through clothing) and racial identity (as conferred by skin color) that Keckly locates her critique of postbellum racism. By showing how changing clothes changes white figures' reception in society, Keckly forwards the notion that appearance is a matter of interpretation. As a seamstress Keckly acts at the center of meaning-making; her work is vital to establishing the status of the figures she clothes.

Although Keckly uses clothing to reverse the propositions of black and white embodiment, ultimately she wants to critique the way a certain kind of racial vision remained the same following emancipation. In her preface, she explains that her motivation for writing was to exonerate Mrs. Lincoln's part in the Old Clothes Scandal. She writes, "The world have [sic] judged Mrs. Lincoln by the *facts which float upon the surface,* and through her have partially judged me, and the only way to convince them that wrong was not meditated is to explain the motives that actuated us" (xiv; emphasis added). Although she claims the authority to remake the meaning of "facts which float upon the surface," she is all too aware of the ways in which surfaces are made to represent deeply entrenched ideological positions. This is nowhere more evident than in a curious passage in which an ex-slave making her way in the North confuses the United States government for the plantation. In her relief work with newly freed slaves Keckly encounters an older woman who is shocked that the government fails to provide two undergarments a year, her allotment as a slave in the South:

> "Why, Missus Keckley," said she to me one day, "I is been here eight months, and Missus Lingom an't even give me one shife. Bliss God, childen, if I had ar know dat de Government, and Mister and Missus Government, was going to do dat ar way, I neber would 'ave comed here in God's wurld. My old missus us't gib me two shifes eber year."
>
> I could not restrain a laugh at the grave manner in which this good old woman entered her protest. Her idea of freedom was two or more old shifts every year. Northern readers may not fully recognize the pith of the joke. On the Southern plantation, the mistress, according to established custom, every year made a present of certain under-garments to her slaves, which articles were always anxiously looked forward to, and thankfully received. The old woman had been in the habit of receiving annually two shifts from her mistress, and she thought the wife of the President of the United States very mean for overlooking this established custom of the plantation. (141–42)

Within the context of the narrative reversals and inversions Keckly undertakes, this "joke" operates as an ironic moment of instruction. The older woman's observations are included less to have a laugh at her expense than to show how easily race relations of the postbellum North could be confused with those in the antebellum South.

Despite the chapter title, "Old Friends," attention to clothing also reveals a dark undercurrent in the scene of her reunion with her former masters in the South, undercutting readings of the narrative which may overstate Keckly's positive disposition toward reconciliation.[24] As Keckly sits and talks with Mrs. Garland, her former mistress, Mrs. Garland remarks on "the peaceful feeling of this country." While Keckly declines to include her response to Mrs. Garland's musings, the next paragraph suggests the continuing solipsism of white Southerners even in this new "peaceful" climate. Keckly writes, "I had many long talks with Mrs. Garland, in one of which I asked what had become of the only sister of my mother, formerly maid to Mrs. G.'s mother" (254). Garland responds bluntly: "She is dead, Lizzie. Has been dead for some years" (255), and then launches into a memory of her mother's relationship with her "maid," intending to show their closeness, but revealing, instead, the inequalities that structured their relationship:

> My mother was severe with her slaves in some respects, but then her heart was full of kindness. She had your aunt punished one day, and not liking her sorrowful look, she made two extravagant promises in order to effect a reconciliation, both of which were accepted. On condition that her maid would look cheerful, and be good and friendly with her, the mistress told her she might go to church the following Sunday, and that she would give her a silk dress to wear on the occasion. Now my mother had but one silk dress in the world, silk not being so plenty in those days as it is now, and yet she gave this dress to her maid to make friends with her. Two weeks afterward mother was sent for to spend the day at a neighbor's house, and on inspecting her wardrobe, discovered that she had no dress fit to wear in company. She had but one alternative, and that was to appeal to the generosity of your aunt Charlotte. Charlotte was summoned, and enlightened in regard to the situation; the maid proffered to loan the silk dress to her mistress for the occasion, and the mistress was only too glad to accept. She made her appearance at the social gathering, duly arrayed in the silk that her maid had worn to church on the preceding Sunday. (255–56)

Mrs. Garland's memory of this moment of "reconciliation," which she understands as great kindness on her mother's part, reverberates into the narrative present, suggesting that the moment of "reconciliation" between Keckly and the Garlands may be more superficial than Mrs. Garland can guess. If we read this scene as a parable of Reconstruction, as I think we are meant to, those in power make certain provisions for former slaves on the condition that they "look cheerful, and be good and friendly." Yet the provisions are quickly and easily revoked, much like the dress, at the whim of those in power. Once again the appearance of things does not always represent the structures of power operating behind the scenes.

Rather than painting a picture of sunny reconciliation, Keckly's portrait of reunion in "Old Friends" suggests the continuities rather than the distinctions between antebellum and postbellum race relations, a fact Keckly elegantly captures by linking metaphors of clothing with metaphors of enslavement. This symbolic linkage comes to a head in the scene of reunion when, describing what she understands as the warm feelings between a mistress and her "maid," Mrs. Garland exclaims: "Ah! love is too strong to be blown away like gossamer threads. The chain is strong enough to bind life even to the world beyond the grave" (257). Garland's freighted word choice unconsciously discloses the elements of coercion and force couched in the sentimental language of affection and devotion. Using clothing as a narrative device, Keckly recasts and controls the meaning of the white bodies within her realm of influence, but she is well aware that the social and political structures of power that fix the meaning of black bodies have outlived slavery.

## "Don't I know a monkey when I see it?"

Keckly's most powerful revision of the conventions of authentication is her substitution of Tad Lincoln's reading lesson for her own. From early slave narratives featuring the trope of the talking book to Douglass's depiction of his first, aborted reading lesson, literacy has operated as a symbolic boundary within the slave narrative. Before the abolition of slavery, literacy is represented as a prohibition or exclusion connected to systems of white power, but also as an entry-point into abstract thought, a sign of freedom from embodiment.[25] In his 1845 *Narrative*, for example, Douglass calls literacy the "pathway from slavery to freedom" (33) and represents his transition from object to subject within his narrative as a transformation from bodily existence to symbolic presence affected by his acquisition of literacy. As Valerie Smith has argued, however, literacy is an ambivalent mechanism of self-authorization in African American narrative, which "pay[s] homage to the structures of discourse that so often contributed to the writers' oppression" (6). On the one hand, rehearsing the scene of literacy grants the narrators "significance and figurative power over their superordinates, [and by] their manipulation of received literary conventions they also engage with and challenge the dominant ideology" (2). On the other, the stress placed on the scene of literacy as the key to freedom has the counter-effect of suggesting that "without letters, slaves fail to understand the full meaning of their domination" (3). Smith reads the resolution of this dilemma in an expansion of our understanding of literacy to include oral culture, "the consciousness of the uses and problems of language, whether spoken or written.... In this view the unlettered person who can manipulate the meanings and nuances of the spoken word might also be considered literate" (4). However, the expansion of our critical understanding of literacy to include oral prowess leaves the structure and function of literacy as prohibition/arrival intact; by contrast, Keckly's revision of the scene of literacy with a white protagonist challenges the symbolic boundary between black and white that literacy represents. More than simply inverting the racial conventions governing the scene of literacy established in the slave-narrative genre, the content of Tad Lincoln's reading lesson, which features an apparent discrepancy between an image and text, uses a visual icon to interrupt the authority of literacy. In *Behind the Scenes* literacy operates not as a neutral sign of reason that can be appropriated by white and black alike, but rather as a highly subjective discursive formation whose significance is shaped by the visual logic of race.

Shortly after Lincoln's assassination, Keckly accompanied Mary Lincoln and her surviving sons, Robert and Tad, to Hyde Park where Lincoln attempted to create a new domestic routine. Tad, who had "never been made to go to school" (217), was encouraged to begin daily lessons with his mother. As Lincoln opens the literacy primer to the first page, we are presented with a reading lesson that differs markedly from both Frederick Douglass's aborted lesson with Mrs. Auld and his "stolen" lessons from the street. Unlike Douglass, who hungers for literacy, Tad must be coaxed into his lesson. This reversal of racial position—white privileged protagonist in place of enslaved black protagonist—rewrites the stakes of literacy; literacy serves here not as a "pathway to freedom," which the protagonist already possesses, but as an unstable foundation for establishing human authenticity. In fact, race interrupts the analogy between Douglass and Tad Lincoln. Tad's illiteracy is drawn as a function of his privilege: "Tad had always been much humored by his parents, especially by his father" (216), who had overlooked a speech impediment and never made him go to school. His illiteracy has no effect on his social standing. He is considered "a bright boy, a son that will do honor to the genius and greatness of his father" (220). Tad Lincoln is socially legible through his familial relations—his whiteness is referential, significant. His individuality and social status exist in stark contrast to the anonymous, illiterate black boy Keckly invokes later in the scene as Tad's foil, denied individual subjectivity and reduced to a symbol of the inferiority of his race.

Significantly, Keckly's critique begins with the non-correspondence between an image and a word. In the scene of the reading lesson, the first word in the primer is "Ape." Although Tad reads the letters correctly, when his mother asks him what "a-p-e" spells his immediate reply is "Monkey!" Instead of reading the word, or even "the sounds of the different letters," Tad "reads" the accompanying illustration: "The word was illustrated by a small wood-cut of an ape, which looked to Tad's eyes very much like a monkey; and his pronunciation was guided by the picture, and not by the sounds of the different letters" (217). The illustration, intended as a reading aid, supplants the word itself. Furthermore, it does so incorrectly. Tad interprets the picture of an ape as a picture of a monkey. His insistence that "A-p-e" spells monkey is based on his belief that he can accurately identify what he sees: "An ape!" he cries incredulously, "'taint an ape. Don't I know a monkey when I see it?" (218). As Mary Lincoln corrects him, the reading lesson devolves into a discussion of scientific empiricism and species differentiation: "Tad, listen to me. An ape is a species of the monkey. It looks like a monkey, but it is not a monkey" (218). The potential discrepancy between an image of an ape and the letters "a-p-e" interrupts the pedagogic strategy of Tad's primer and suggests the damaging racial implications of a seemingly innocent misunderstanding. Tad's minor hysteria over the notion that something can be different from what it looks like encapsulates mid-nineteenth-century racial anxiety, dominated by debates over what constitutes racial difference, species differentiation, and the rights of man.[26]

In her analysis of "[t]he uncertain status of the body in slavery discourse," Shirley Samuels examines cultural objects such as the "topsy-turvy doll" which physically perform the racial reversal Keckly figuratively performs in *Behind the Scenes*: "Held one way, the doll appears as a white woman with long skirts. Flipping over her skirts does not reveal her legs, but rather exposes another racial identity: the head of a black woman, whose long skirts now cover the head of the white woman" (Samuels 157). Like the topsy-turvy doll, which "can be only one color at a time," Keckly's racial reversal in *Behind the Scenes* makes a "double gesture [that] at once present[s] and refus[es] a reversibility of identity" (157).[27] Samuels identifies the "problem of identity," on display in toys like the topsy-turvy doll, as a problem of "recognition" (158). In her subsequent analysis of pro- and antislavery rhetoric she identifies a shared rhetorical strategy in both: "the stark physicality of seeing conceived of as engraving impressions on the mind" (163). Although Tad is working with a literacy primer in the scene—not a political primer, such as the pro- and antislavery primers that Samuels discusses which circulated in the years leading up to the Civil War—Keckly demonstrates how this "neutral" text becomes a flashpoint for the racial significance attributed to literacy via the presentation of a visual image.

Samuels juxtaposes the pedagogical strategy of abolitionist primers against the backlash registered in a prominent proslavery tract, *The Devil in America* (1859), to show that mid-nineteenth-century anxieties over the location of identity became lodged in a powerful desire to make internal characteristics visible—for both abolitionists and defenders of slavery. While not collapsing the antithetical rhetorical aims of *The Slave's Friend* and *The Devil in America*, Samuels's essay addresses the collapse in both between the "logic of miscegenation and the logic of sentimentality," both of which "involve the impression of, and mixing of, external and physical states in the interior state of the heart" (159). *The Devil in America* argues that the threat of abolition is its promotion of the unholy breakdown of all kinds of "natural" boundaries: "The Demon of Atheism, for instance, has been sent to use 'Philosophers' and 'sons of science' to 'prove that men and monkeys are the same'" (quoted in Samuels 158–59). As both Thomas Gossett and Winthrop Jordan have pointed out, early nineteenth-century scientific theories of polygenesis and species differentiation that labored to link African-derived people to apes and monkeys depended on interpretations of external characteristics taken as indications of inherent inferiority.[28] By rewriting the scene of literacy with a figure central to national domestic life, a president's son and former resident of the White House, Keckly interrupts the symbolic association of whiteness with reason and blackness with materiality. Tad's mistake, and his irrational attachment to it, raises the dehumanization of people of African descent considered by many defenders of slavery to be the evolutionary link between humans and apes; it also reveals this link to be an error of willful misrecognition.

Keckly asserts that her aim in including Tad's reading lesson is not to reflect on his intellect, but, rather, "to say that some incidents are about as damaging to one side of the question as to the other. If a colored boy appears dull, so does a white boy sometimes; and if a whole race is judged by a single example of apparent dulness [*sic*], another race should be judged by a similar example" (220). Race, which Keckly obliquely refers to as "the question," is literally thrown into question by the discrepancy between what Tad believes he sees (a monkey) and what is written ("a-p-e"). In Tad's mind the word's meaning defers to the image, which in turn defers to the minstrel-like performance of a monkey playing the organ that Tad has seen in the street. The racial valences of the example, which Keckly uses to undermine scientific debates about the place of African-derived people in the Chain of Being, are perversely confirmed by *Behind the Seams,* the parody of Keckly's narrative, in which the author depicts Tad Lincoln's confusion over the illustration as explicitly racial. In the racist parody, Tad Lincoln proclaims, "Tain't an ape . . . its [*sic*] either a large monkey or a small nigger, I can't tell exactly, because one is so much like both, I can't tell tother from which" (17). The word and the image, presented as seamless in the primer, actually reveal the discontinuity between image, word, and body (in this case the body of the monkey in the street). The non-correspondence of image and text signifies beyond the singularity of Tad's illiteracy and implies the non-scientific, highly subjective nature of both written and visual discourse.

By casting doubt on the self-evident nature of visible signs in the form of letters, words, and images, Keckly casts doubt in turn on systems of racial classification based on physical or visible signs such as blackness or whiteness. Keckly concludes the scene by commenting on the racial significance of literacy, revealing the scene itself to be an example of the non-correspondence of a visible sign (Tad's white skin) and its meaning: "Whenever I think of this incident I am tempted to laugh; and then it occurs to me that had Tad been a negro boy, not the son of a President, and so difficult to instruct, he would have been called thick-skulled, and would have been held up as an example of the inferiority of race" (219). Keckly reveals not only that literacy is false evidence of white superiority, but also that literacy itself is discursively produced. The misunderstanding that would be fodder for a joke is sobering when considered in the context of the real effects of the misrecognition of visible signs made into racial signifiers.

Keckly's inversion of black and white figures within the scene of the reading lesson presents a challenge to specifically visual presumptions about racial designation. Tad's rhetorical question—"Don't I know a monkey when I see it?"—must be answered with a resounding "No." Yet Keckly's inversion of black and white figures does not invert the social significance of black and white as racial categories productive of racial conditions. Despite his illiteracy Tad remains privileged and significant as an individual, whereas an illiterate black boy would be seen as a symbol of the inferiority of the race.[29] The inversion therefore demonstrates that racial difference itself is discursively produced in the same way a word's meaning takes on significance. In his discussion of writing as a graphic representation of language, Ferdinand de Saussure contends that a written word's meaning is not self-evident, but rather "[t]he pronunciation of a word is determined, not by its spelling, but by its history" (31). In Tad Lincoln's reading lesson we see that the meaning of a word is produced through its difference from or likeness to other words or images, which is ultimately a social determination. In the example of the reading lesson the conflict between the word's likeness to an image and its difference from other letters—"M-o-n-k-e-y"—is a conflict magnified by the difference in interpretation between Tad and the other adults in the room.

Keckly's revision thus offers the primer as another ironic tool of instruction: Intended to instruct the student in literacy by providing mnemonic words and images corresponding to each letter, the primer instead instructs readers of *Behind the Scenes* in the possibilities of misunderstanding and misremembering. The distance between seeing and knowing is filled with the vagaries of perception. Keckly stages the discrepant engagement of the written word and the visual image to highlight the discursive production of race.

## "Why should I not be permitted to speak?"

Although her individual perspective was some years removed from slavery, Keckly's narrative captures a nation only very recently post-emancipation, and the national historical proximity to slavery directs her narrative throughout: Details of her own life parallel events of national significance and she narrates national milestones from her perspective as an intimate laborer inside the White House. Written during a period of optimism among African American writers regarding the possibility of positive race relations in the newly reunited nation, the convergence of Keckly's perspective in the narrative with that of the nation nevertheless marks an inconclusive liberation: Slavery is no longer legal, but as her narrative shows, the ideological propositions underlying racial hierarchies remain intact; as Keckly observes, black citizens were turned away from the second inaugural levee, a supposedly "open" reception at the White House to celebrate President Lincoln's re-election in 1865 (158).[30]

The unevenness of the narrative, what James Olney calls the "mixed production" of *Behind the Scenes* (xxvii), reflects these contradictions within the nation; yet *Behind the Scenes* is unified by its strategic response to the persistence of a black/white binary in post-emancipation America. In her role as a dressmaker, narrator, and editor, Keckly redeploys visual tropes to critique the generic proposition within the slave narrative that white authority legitimates black experience. The formal reading I offer here presents an alternative way of looking at Keckly's discursive choices. Ripping the slave narrative apart at the seams and refashioning it, Keckly's literary and material labors reconstruct how we see the scenes she puts before us. By calling attention to the racial expectations of narrative structure, coded in the slave narrative's conventions of authentication, Keckly forces the reader to recognize the discursive production of race in place of the icon of the black body.

The problem Keckly addresses affects all ex-slave narrators: Blackness, which has been violently produced as a visual sign of enslavement, must be wrested from this sociopolitical association and redeployed in new terms. While Keckly is not the first to challenge the stability of racial categories in the context of the slave narrative—one thinks here of the Crafts' narrative of passing in *Running a Thousand Miles for Freedom* or Solomon Northup's narrative of kidnapping in *Twelve Years a Slave*—she is the first to completely invert the racial paradigm of the formal properties of the slave narrative. In so doing, she highlights the discursive production of racial categories rather than simply asserting a positive "black" image or expanding the national archive to include images of black people at the center of the nation. *Behind the Scenes* produces strategic moments of dissonance between multiple discourses of authenticity to undermine the very notion of racial or literary authenticity, thus advancing the rhetorical strategies of resistance employed by earlier ex-slave narrators who remained bound by the political exigencies of abolition.

While the classic slave narrative is rhetorically calibrated toward abolition, the calibration of Keckly's narrative reveals how focusing on abolition left damaging racial binaries intact. Rather than departing from classic slave-narrative conventions, Keckly depends upon her readership's anticipation of those conventions to create an ironic postbellum commentary on race relations in "free" society. Her canny revision of the racial protocols of the slave narrative reveals how the form itself has been organized in response to the visual logic of racial slavery. Thus, the rhetorical question she asks in her preface, "why should I not be permitted to [speak]?" inaugurates her confrontation with the racial propositions her narrative overturns, radically addressing both those readers who doubt Keckly's role placing "Mrs. Lincoln in a better light before the world" (xv, xiv) and those who require that the black voice be contained in what John Sekora calls a "white envelope." Her 1868 conjugation of the slave-narrative form illustrates the continuation of a particular kind of racial vision in the postbellum period and challenges that vision by skewering the authenticity protocols of the genre.

NOTES

1. I have chosen to spell Keckly's name as she herself did, rather than the way her name is spelled in her published narrative. I would like to thank Jennifer Fleischner for this historical restoration. In researching her book *Mrs. Lincoln and Mrs. Keckly,* Fleischner discovered Keckly's original signatures in her own hand on her application for a war pension after her son's death in the Civil War. I have kept the spelling "Keckley" in quotations from other scholars. See Fleischner, *Mrs. Lincoln and Mrs. Keckly: The Remarkable Story of the Friendship between a First Lady and a Former Slave* (New York: Broadway, 2003), 7.

2. Domina argues that Keckly's discussion of her leadership of the Contraband Relief Association situates her as a figure parallel to Lincoln, with both being "re-elected President"—Keckly of the CRA and Lincoln of the country: "Writing in 1868, Elizabeth Keckley, a former slave who has become dressmaker to Washington's social elite, has out-Lincolned Lincoln, who had also been reelected but who had been assassinated early in his second term" (139). Young also notes that, "[s]yntactically and thematically," certain passages in the narrative "align[] Keckley with Lincoln, as parallel figures equally pulled to important locations by the needs of service" (121). As I will show in this essay, rather than "out-Lincolning" Lincoln, as Domina argues, I understand Keckly to be using a series of parallels, racial reversals, and inversions to show the disparity between black and white access to social power and the fixity of antebellum racial logic in the postbellum social landscape.

3. Andrews cites *Behind the Scenes* as an exception to the general rule that "the narratives of former slaves published after 1865 have attracted relatively few readers" (*Slave Narratives* viii). Despite its relative popularity, however, it has received only a fraction of the critical attention directed toward such antebellum narratives as *Incidents*. I suggest, here, that one reason for this is its formal idiosyncrasy. While early critics of the narrative, namely Foster and Andrews, identify *Behind the Scenes* as a slave narrative and take up direct comparisons of *Incidents* and *Behind the Scenes*—with Foster alternatively calling *Behind the Scenes* "autobiography after emancipation" (Foster, "Autobiography") and "postbellum slave narrati[on]" (Foster,

*Written* 117) and Andrews calling it a "postbellum slave narrative" (Andrews, "Reunion")—more recent critics understand the narrative as a departure. In his introduction to the Schomburg edition of the text, Olney writes that "*Behind the Scenes* both is and is not what we might understand by the term *slave narrative*. Even when it rather briefly is in that mode, its perspective, from after four years in the White House, determines a very different story from one told by someone who has very recently escaped from slavery" (xxx; original emphasis). Similarly, in her book *Mastering Slavery,* Fleischner cites the narrative's focus on Mary Lincoln as the prime reason for its "unsuitability as a representative text" (93). Like Fleischner's, Domina's reading of the narrative rests on the signal reversal Keckly's text enacts, "revealing to the nation the secrets Mary Todd Lincoln has shared with her" (145), rather than her own secrets; Domina argues that "[b]ecause Keckley published her narrative in 1868, when the concern of the nation was reunification (of white citizens) rather than abolition, she could not reasonably appeal to white readers by stressing either the horrors of slavery or continuing racial inequality. . . . Keckley, therefore, could not rely exclusively on the genre of slave narrative to create her audience" (140–41). In her discussion of Keckly's use of documentary materials in her narrative, Manuel argues that Keckly's deliberate omission of a biographical sketch of her written by white journalist Mary Clemmer Ames is a direct result of her desire to distinguish the political project of her narrative from the slave narrative, noting that Ames's article "mimics the dynamics of a dictated slave narrative" (38). The most comprehensive critical treatment of the narrative, Young's "Black Woman, White House," notes that "[t]he text has traditionally been discussed primarily for its biographical information about Abraham and Mary Todd Lincoln" and that it "conforms to no one genre, moving among war memoir, presidential biography, domestic novel, and slave narrative" (118, 125). While Young highlights highly circumscribed conditions of production of the text identical to those faced by ex-slave narrators—"a racist culture that denied not only civility but literary voice to African-Americans except under the most mediated of terms" (111) —she understands *Behind the Scenes* to be first and foremost a Civil War narrative "on a continuum with other black women's texts of the Civil War era" (118), including Mattie Jackson and Frances Rollin: "The Civil War frames internal conflicts in their texts, while the fracture of national identity creates an avenue of entry into national discourses that would otherwise exclude them" (111). By contrast, as this essay will show, I understand *Behind the Scenes* to be a text unified by its sustained reversal of the race rituals structuring the classic slave narrative, thus staking the narrative as less ambiguous and more activist in its antiracist position than earlier critical frameworks have acknowledged.

    4. Andrews argues, compellingly, regarding the likelihood that Keckly read *Incidents*:

> The narratives of Jacobs and Keckley were published only seven years apart by women who lived and worked in the Washington, D.C., area from 1862 to 1865, both of them active participants in relief efforts for the "contrabands" from the

South. The chances of their meeting each other or knowing about each other were more than slight. But even if the two women never met, it seems unlikely that Keckley would never have heard or taken notice of *Incidents*, given the publicity it received in the early 1860s, the public presence of its activist author in Keckley's hometown for three years, and, perhaps most important, the striking parallels between what Jacobs revealed about her slave past and what Keckley knew to be true about her own. ("Changing" 228)

Young, drawing on Fleischner, cites this literary echo as a moment of usurpation and narrative inversion: "Adapting the language of the slave narrative, Keckley turns it against Mary Todd Lincoln. As Jennifer Fleischner argues [in *Mastering Slavery*], in Keckley's descriptions of the First Lady, a "narrative inversion takes place, in which the 'mistress' comes to be cast in the role of the black slave as 'Other'" (136).

5. Fleischner notes that, "With a title-page describing Mrs. Keckley as 'formerly a slave, but more recently modiste, and friend to Mrs. Lincoln,' *Behind the Scenes* takes as its subject 'the secret history' of Mrs. Lincoln's ill-fated 'old-clothes' sale of 1867, not the secret history of slavery" (93).

6. As one of the anonymous readers for this journal notes, narratives of passing or narratives that "directly challenge racial constructions of bodily difference" do not at first seem to fit into this paradigm. However, my argument here is that ex-slave narrators had to work against the formal requirements of the slave narrative—namely the race rituals performed in the conventions of authentication—which codify racial difference in what Sekora has called the "Black Message/White Envelope" structure of slave narratives. Thus, even a text that concentrates on escape rather than enslavement or passing as a way of undermining notions of racial difference—such as *Running a Thousand Miles for Freedom*—has to contend with the specifically visual assumptions of race upon which traditional conventions of authentication rely. William Craft handles this by producing the incongruent image of the master speaking as the fugitive slave, illustrating (as I will show Keckly does) that phenotypical characteristics such as complexion are not facts with fixed meanings, but are constantly shifting social symbols that can be manipulated to various ends. Thus, *Behind the Scenes* represents an advancement of the challenges ex-slave narrators presented to the structures of racial difference codified in the negotiated form of the slave narrative, rather than a radical break from the genre.

7. While Keckly's narrative may present an extreme case, Young reminds us that her strategy of absenting her body fits into a pattern of black women's life writing during this period: "Overembodied in racist white culture, black women writers entered into national discourse from a position of rhetorical disembodiment. In contrast to the two-fisted Douglass, the hand of the black woman writer in the Civil War era was positioned as yet another phantom limb" (111).

8. As Olney establishes in both his introduction to Keckly's narrative and his foundational essay, "I Was Born," the conventions of authentication that structure the

slave's narrative work to authenticate not only the veracity of the slave's account, in doubt because of the racial status of the author/narrator, but work to authenticate the very existence of the black subject at their center. That is, the ex-slave narrator must prove not only the truth of her experience of enslavement, but also the truth of the humanity of black subjects to white readers. Insofar as the slave narrative addresses the exclusion of blacks from subjectivity, the literary narrative itself functions as evidence of humanity where blackness is a putative void. Ironically, an assessment of blackness is both a precursor and an obstacle to establishing the veracity of the slave's narrative.

9. Although some commentators debate whether or not Keckly intended to include Mary Lincoln's letters in the narrative, the way she presents the letters signals Keckly's editorial control to her readership: "Mrs. Lincoln wrote me the incidents of the journey, and the letter describes the story more graphically than I could hope to do. I suppress many passages, as they are of too confidential a nature to be given to the public" (296). In *Behind the Scenes,* Keckly provides the authenticating voice and it is Mrs. Lincoln's character which is at stake: "If I have betrayed confidence in anything I have published, it has been to place Mrs. Lincoln in a better light before the world" (xiv).

10. Andrews marks the "many tensions and apparent contradictions in *Behind the Scenes*" as the aspect of the narrative that "make it one of the most intriguing and provocative personal narratives in nineteenth-century African American literature" (*Slave Narratives* 8). Young's analysis takes the reading of *Behind the Scenes* as a divided text the furthest, arguing that "we can also see Keckley's oscillation between condemnation and apology—and the psychic 'splittings' that characterize her narrative as a whole—as a literary version of the Civil War 'border state'" (124).

11. For readings of *Behind the Scenes* as Keckly's attempt to authorize herself, see Andrews, "Changing"; Michele Birnbaum, *Race, Work and Desire in American Literature, 1860–1930* (Cambridge: Cambridge University Press, 2003); Domina; and Young. My argument differs from these readings in that I read Keckly as not only usurping the role of authenticator, but also challenging the requirement of authentication through her racial inversion.

12. Andrews also argues that Keckley "banked on her reader's respect by recounting her career as a female entrepreneur dedicated not only to her own economic independence but to the advancement of her people" (*Slave Narratives* 7).

13. While I argue that the text presents a successful challenge to racialist thinking, I am not arguing that the text was "successful" in terms of positive recognition or monetary compensation for Keckly. Andrews argues that although the narrative was widely noticed and reviewed in the white press . . . Keckley came to regret the attention, most of it negative, some of it scurrilous, that *Behind the Scenes* received. Feeling betrayed by her white editor, the antislavery journalist James Redpath, and convinced that the Lincoln family had turned on her without justification, the au-

thor of the most important African American autobiography of the Reconstruction era watched her book fade from view within a few months of its sensational appearance. For the remainder of her thirty-nine years Keckly retreated from the public eye, becoming increasingly reclusive in her later years, partly because of ill health and poverty. She never again wrote for publication. She died in 1907, a resident of the National Home for Destitute Colored Women and Children in Washington, DC, (*Slave Narratives* 4).

14. In addition to the formal reading I forward in this essay, Keckly's membership in prominent and politically active black churches in Washington and her leadership in vigilance societies, which culminated in her founding the Contraband Relief Association in 1862, provide historical evidence to suggest Keckly's political beliefs would not allow her to mistake her individual friendships for more broadly defined social equality.

15. Appearing six months after the publication of *Behind the Scenes, Behind the Seams* was published anonymously but written by Southern apologist Daniel Ottolengul (sometimes printed as "Ottolengui"). Young also argues that the parody reveals the success of Keckly's critique, noting generally that the mimicry involved in the narrative strategies of parody "ironically intersect[s] with Keckley's own," and more specifically that "while the parody aims to nullify Keckley's text, it ultimately confirms the techniques of *Behind the Scenes*" (144).

16. In her analysis of the narrative's intervention into national iconography Manuel notes that "Daguerreotypes, photographs and cartoons were related to the emergence of new practices of observation and national identity formation" (27).

17. Manuel calls *Behind the Scenes* "an act of black textual signifying on the visual world as created by white America" (27); Young writes that "[f]or black women writers excluded from national discourse by virtue of both race and gender, 'civil wars' involve battling not only the dominant national culture but also *alternative iconographies*—including those constructed by white women and African-American men—that would exclude them as well" (111; emphasis added).

18. To be clear, as I have been arguing, this is not to suggest *Behind the Scenes* as a radical break from the slave-narrative tradition, but rather as an extension or advancement of earlier narrators' strategies of resistance, calling attention to the way white racism is coded into the negotiated form of the slave narrative.

19. See Barrett, Henderson, Hartman, Wiegman, and DeLombard.

20. On the unequal propositions of black and white embodiment, see Barrett, who, quoting Elaine Scarry, argues that "[t]he body, within the ideologies of the dominant American community, holds the ultimate terms of identity for African Americans. As the dominant community would have it, the identity of African Americans is bound up primarily, if not exclusively, with 'the most contracted of spaces, the small circle of living matter'" ("African-American" 419).

21. For example, DeLombard argues that Douglass's violent opening must be read in the context of a narrative trajectory in which he represents his transitions from the "embodied subject[] . . . [of] an 'American slave'" to the "more universal [subject position] of American citizen." Thus, Douglass's early accounts of witnessing violence to the slave body (Hester, Demby) are set against the acts of "testifying, physical autonomy, and Northern freedom" at the narrative's conclusion (DeLombard 253).

22. On silence as a strategy of black female slaves' resistance, see Young 113, 142. It should be noted that, while the strategic silences discussed by Young represent one important strategy of resistance, Mullen claims "talking back" and a vibrant oral tradition form the core of a black female radical tradition extending from nineteenth-century black women's narratives including those by Harriet Jacobs and Harriet Wilson (Mullen). Although Keckly remains silent *during* her abuse, she is not silent *about* the abuse; furthermore, her narrative can and has been interpreted as a "tell-all." As noted above, Keckly's contemporary critics criticized her most harshly for speaking out on something about which she was expected to remain silent.

23. On the significance of sewing and clothing in *Behind the Scenes,* see also Young, who argues that Keckly "conjoins needle and pen . . . in a militarized mode of political critique" (135) and Manuel, who argues that "Keckley did not want to be considered a simple dressmaker (*i.e.,* skillful in her ability to control the mechanics of sewing), but rather a *modiste* (an artist who emphasized her special way of cutting, who could be an arbiter of tastes, etc.)" (29–30). Young notes that "[i]n postwar America, it is the slaveholder, not the slave, whose state of undress brings humiliation" and that "the sartorial circuitry of *Behind the Scenes* allows Elizabeth Keckley both to dress down her enemies and dress up herself" (134, 135). I agree with this analysis, but read this reversal as part of the larger strategy of reversal Keckly pursues in her inversion of the race rituals of slave-narrative conventions of authentication; as I have shown, representations of black embodiment constituted a key convention of slave narration which Keckly overturns. Moreover, I understand Keckly's representation of clothing and her role as modiste not simply as a way of establishing her authority as a tastemaker, but also as a way of highlighting the constructedness of visual icons.

24. On African American perspectives on reunion and reunification, see Andrews, "Reunion."

25. On literacy and embodiment in the slave narrative, see Barrett, "African-American."

26. On this anxiety and its visual stakes see Samuels's discussion of pro- and anti-slavery discourse in "The Identity of Slavery" and Halttunen on the antebellum world of "appearance." On Tad Lincoln's reading lesson as a kind of visual illiteracy or "white sight," see Sarah Blackwood, "Making Good Use of Our Eyes: Nineteenth-Century African Americans Write Visual Culture," in *Visual Culture and Race,* spec. issue of *MELUS* 39.2 (2014): 42–65.

27. Young also discusses *Behind the Scenes* as "a world turned upside down" (133).

28. It is important to note that these pseudo-scientific theories were anything but marginal to the national conversation about citizenship, freedom, and natural rights. In his *Observations upon Jefferson's Notes on Virginia,* Clement Clark Moore summarizes both the justification and implications of the placement of the African American in the Chain of Being as occupying a mediating position between humans (further differentiated by Jefferson into the Man of "rights of Man") and animals:

> [T]he intellectual faculties of man were found to set him at such an immense distance from all other animals, that it was absolutely necessary to devise some scheme for filling up the chasm. The resemblance of the bodily structure of the orang-outang to that of the human species, and the consequent similarity in many of its actions to those of men, were not overlooked; but every art was employed to prove that it was endued with reason, and that it ought to be reckoned a lower order of man. But as there was still a long jump from an ape to a man, some happy geniuses bethought them of setting the Africans as a step which would make the transition perfectly easy. So that in the same proportion as the ape was raised above its proper sphere, the inoffensive negro was pulled down from his just rank in the creation. (quoted in Jordan 504)

29. The revised reading lesson highlights what Barrett calls the "spurious homology" between literacy/whiteness and illiteracy/blackness ("African-American" 415), expressed in Keckly's assertion that an illiterate black boy is understood as a symbol of the intellectual deficit of the whole race, whereas an illiterate white boy is understood in the specificity of his social and familial connections. Tad Lincoln is represented as an individual with social power despite his illiteracy, a circumstance Keckly parodies by addressing Tad as "Master Tad" to highlight the paradox of an illiterate white boy's status as her social superior. Although Tad is not her master, Keckly pointedly placates Tad with mock racial deference. Her address is ironic, but Tad responds in earnest, bowing his head to Keckly "in a patronizing way" (219).

30. As Keckly notes, Frederick Douglass was the exception eventually made to this rule barring black people from the reception (158). On 1868 as a period of optimism in African American writing, see Andrews, "Reunion," in which he writes, "[t]here can be little doubt that both Keckley and Douglass wrote their post–Civil War autobiographies in a mood of optimism and with a sincere desire to use their personal testimony as part of the national healing process that both hoped would follow the Civil War" (8). The argument I have presented here suggests that Andrews overstates Keckly's optimism, despite her representation of an *apparently* rosy reunion with her former owners. On postbellum slave narratives more generally, see Andrews, *Slave Narratives.*

## WORKS CITED

Andrews, William L. "The Changing Moral Discourse of Nineteenth-Century African American Women's Autobiography: Harriet Jacobs and Elizabeth Keckley." *De/Colonizing the Subject: The Politics of Gender in Women's Autobiography.* Ed. Sidonie Smith and Julia Watson. Minneapolis: University of Minnesota Press, 1992. 225–41.

———. "The Representation of Slavery and Afro-American Literary Realism." *African American Autobiography: A Collection of Critical Essays.* Ed. William L. Andrews. Englewood Cliffs: Prentice Hall, 1993. 77–89.

———. "Reunion in the Postbellum Slave Narrative: Frederick Douglass and Elizabeth Keckley." *Black American Literature Forum* 23.1 (1989): 5–16.

———, ed. *Slave Narratives after Slavery.* New York: Oxford University Press, 2011.

Barrett, Lindon. "African-American Slave Narratives: Literacy, the Body, Authority." *Imagining a National Culture.* Spec. issue of *American Literary History* 7.3 (1995): 415–42.

———. "Hand-Writing: Legibility and the White Body in *Running a Thousand Miles for Freedom*." *American Literature* 69.2 (1997): 314–36.

DeLombard, Jeannine. "'Eye-Witness to the Cruelty: Southern Violence and Northern Testimony in Frederick Douglass's 1845 *Narrative*." *American Literature* 73.2 (2001): 245–75.

Domina, Lynn. "I Was Re-Elected President: Elizabeth Keckley as Quintessential Patriot in *Behind the Scenes: Or, Thirty Years a Slave and Four Years in the White House*." *Women's Life-Writing: Finding Voice/Building Community.* Ed. Linda Coleman. Bowling Green: Bowling Green State University Popular Press, 1997. 139–51.

Douglass, Frederick. *Narrative of the Life of Frederick Douglass, an American Slave, Written by Himself.* 1845. Documenting the American South. Web. 1 January 2014.

Fleischner, Jennifer. *Mastering Slavery: Memory, Family, and Identity in Women's Slave Narratives.* New York: New York University Press, 1996.

Foster, Frances Smith. "Autobiography after Emancipation: The Example of Elizabeth Keckley." *Multicultural Autobiography: American Lives.* Ed. James R. Payne. Knoxville: University of Tennessee Press, 1992. 32–63.

———. *Written by Herself: Literary Production by African American Women, 1746–1892.* Bloomington: Indiana University Press, 1993.

Fredrickson, George M. *The Black Image in the White Mind: The Debate on Afro-American Character and Destiny, 1817–1914.* New York: Harper and Row, 1971.

Gates, Henry Louis Jr. *The Signifying Monkey: A Theory of African-American Literary Criticism.* New York: Oxford University Press, 1988.

Gossett, Thomas. *Race: The History of an Idea in America.* Dallas: Southern Methodist University Press, 1963.

Halttunen, Karen. *Confidence Men and Painted Women: A Study of Middle-Class Culture in America, 1830–1870.* New Haven: Yale University Press, 1982.

Hartman, Saidiya. *Scenes of Subjection: Terror, Slavery, and Self-Making in Nineteenth-Century America.* New York: Oxford University Press, 1997.

Henderson, Carol E. *Scarring the Black Body: Race and Representation in African American Literature.* Columbia: University of Missouri Press, 2002.

Jordan, Winthrop D. *White over Black: American Attitudes toward the Negro, 1550–1812.* Chapel Hill: University of North Carolina Press, 1968.

Keckley, Elizabeth. *Behind the Scenes: Or, Thirty Years a Slave, and Four Years in the White House.* 1868. New York: Oxford University Press, 1988.

Kickley, Betsey (pseud.). *Behind the Seams, by a Nigger Woman, Who Took in Work from Mrs. Lincoln and Mrs. Davis.* 1868. New York: National News, 1945.

Manuel, Carme. "Elizabeth Keckley's *Behind the Scenes*; or, the 'Colored Historian's' Resistance to the Technologies of Power in Postwar America." *African American Review* 44.1–2 (2011): 25–48.

McCaskill, Barbara. "William and Ellen Craft in Transatlantic Literature and Life." *Running a Thousand Miles for Freedom: The Escape of William and Ellen Craft from Slavery.* Athens: University of Georgia Press, 1999. vii–xxv.

Mullen, Harryette. "Runaway Tongue: Resistant Orality in *Uncle Tom's Cabin, Our Nig, Incidents in the Life of a Slave Girl,* and *Beloved.*" *The Culture of Sentiment.* Ed. Shirley Samuels. New York: Oxford University Press, 1992. 244–64.

Olney, James. Introduction. Keckley xxvii–xxxvi.

Reef, Catherine. *Poverty in America.* New York: Infobase, 2007.

Samuels, Shirley. "The Identity of Slavery." *The Culture of Sentiment.* 157–71.

———, ed. *The Culture of Sentiment: Race, Gender, and Sentimentality in 19th-Century America.* New York: Oxford University Press, 1992.

Santamarina, Xiomara. *Belabored Professions: Narratives of African American Working Womanhood.* Chapel Hill: University of North Carolina Press, 2005.

de Saussure, Ferdinand. *Course in General Linguistics.* New York: McGraw-Hill, 1966.

Sekora, John. "Black Message/White Envelope: Genre, Authenticity, and Authority in Antebellum Slave Narrative." *Callaloo* 32 (Summer 1987): 482–515.

Silber, Nina. *The Romance of Reunion: Northerners and the South, 1865–1900.* Chapel Hill: University of North Carolina Press, 1993.

Smith, Valerie. *Self-Discovery and Authority in Afro-American Narrative.* Cambridge: Harvard University Press, 1991.

Stepto, Robert Burns. "I Rose and Found My Voice: Narration, Authentication, and Authorial Control in Four Slave Narratives." *The Slave's Narrative.* Ed. Charles T. Davis and Henry Louis Gates Jr. New York: Oxford University Press, 1985. 225–41.

Wiegman, Robyn. *American Anatomies: Theorizing Race and Gender.* Durham: Duke University Press, 1995.

Young, Elizabeth. "Black Woman, White House: Race and Redress in Elizabeth Keckley's *Behind the Scenes*." *Disarming the Nation: Women's Writing and the American Civil War.* Chicago: University of Chicago Press, 1999. 109–48.

Zafar, Rafia. *We Wear the Mask: African Americans Write American Literature, 1760–1870.* New York: Columbia University Press, 1997.

VOLUME 1: WRITING SELF, WRITING NATION

**NEW CRITICISM**

CHAPTER SEVEN

REGIS M. FOX

# Behind the Scenes of American Liberalism

WITH FEW EXCEPTIONS, BLACK women appear sparingly in Steven Spielberg's 2012 award-winning motion picture *Lincoln*. On occasion, glimpses of a black female servant's hands (or alternate appendage) populate the screen, her visage cropped from view. Women also figure among the number of black slaves in the daguerreotypes scoured by an inquisitive, young Tad Lincoln in the opening scenes, as they do in the audience of sundry public orations dispensed by the title character, and in the gallery of the House of Representatives during the January 1865 vote on the Thirteenth Amendment, the film's ostensible climax. One brief exemption to this peripheralization is Lydia Smith (played by S. Epatha Merkerson), black housekeeper and lover to Radical Republican leader Thaddeus Stevens (played by Tommy Lee Jones). She, as the film's logic would have it, partially motivates Stevens's decades-long crusade for the abolition of slavery: He brings home the original copy of the constitutional provision, in the immediate wake of its passage, as a "gift" to her. The other arguable exception to the ornamental status of black women, if one still restricted in representational scope, is black author, activist, and seamstress for the Lincoln White House, Elizabeth Keckly (played by Gloria Reuben).[1] By the end of *Lincoln,* its namesake emerges as paragon of governance due to a shrewd capacity to disarm Democratic opposition, convincing them to "see the here and now" in the context of heated congressional deliberation. Notably, a conversation with Keckly on the White House steps precipitates Lincoln's pivotal tactical adjustment, securing his enduring sociocultural and diplomatic legacy.

 Tethering Keckly's identity so narrowly to the storied ascent of white masculine prowess, however, eclipses a meaningful accounting for her foundational pedagogy, entrepreneurship, and community organizing. Evidently pensive and aware in the film, Keckly nevertheless lacks the complex characterization readily attending her white counterparts (stifled ambition *à la* Robert Lincoln, raging grief *à la* Mary Todd Lincoln, etc.). Tentative smiles and incipient tears, in turn, project an air of fragility, while exceedingly close physical proximity to employer, Mary Todd Lincoln, connotes seeming dependence. In response to Keckly's pressing question to the president in her very first appearance, Lincoln deigns not reply, further absenting any sense of tangible authority on her part. Subsequent ambiguity only amplifies a persistent omission of black female interiority. In the end, Spielberg reduces her—like Lydia Smith—to little more than a plot point.

Alternate scholarly and popular cultural representations of Keckly are equally unsettling, as contemporary critics across disciplines have misread, and thereby minimized, her literary and political significance. For instance, Jennifer Fleischner, author of the only full-length history of the relationship between Mary Todd Lincoln and Keckly, writes that "Lizzy's presence in [Abraham Lincoln's] family circle also likely contributed to his evolving comprehension of black life in America" (263). She particularly invokes Keckly's "quiet relationship with the President," noting that "while combing his hair or sewing in the sitting room when he happened to enter, they sometimes fell into conversation" (ibid.). While such interactions certainly leave open possibilities for a measure of influence on the part of the seamstress, Fleischner typically casts such contact as altogether constructive, namely as a vehicle for Lincoln's enhanced civility and ethics, while retreating from a fuller interrogation of Keckly's silence in this necessarily uneven power dynamic. Here, as elsewhere, the Lincolns' integrity is inflated in inverse relation to Keckly's humanity.

What's more, in the oft-cited *Mary Todd Lincoln: A Biography*, Jean H. Baker positions Keckly's book *Behind the Scenes* as a "ghostwritten exposé" whose "testimony is suspicious," inexplicably claiming its initial circulation as a "novel" (212–13). Further, Baker emphasizes the orientation of the memoir as fundamentally vengeful, retaliatory, and aggressive (280). Samuel A. Schreiner Jr. resuscitates the Baker school of thought almost ten years later by attributing her work to "two enterprising New York newspapermen," despite multiple authoritative studies linking the project to Keckly and the editorship of James Redpath (69). Both Baker's and Schreiner's nearly seamless integration of Keckly's insights in *Behind the Scenes* into their modern historical accounts as fact—at times without acknowledgment—only compounds the offense.

This constitutes an elision of Keckly's subjectivity, ultimately covering over her literary expression of self-definition and critical consciousness.

Instead of contributing to an intensifying re-mythologization of Lincoln-as-Great-Emancipator, this essay adopts an alternate perspective on Elizabeth Keckly's life and writing. Theorizing both the overt and covert ways in which she makes visible the constraints of American liberalism as political economy and affective performance, I undercut gestures of de-authorization within present-day scholarship in which Keckly's presence is enlisted exclusively in the service of verifying Mary and/or Abraham Lincoln's humanist impulses. Of all Keckly's purported motives for penning her autobiographical piece—clearing Mary Lincoln's name regarding the "Old Clothes Scandal," alleviating her own poverty, even procuring revenge—I argue that her interrogation of precisely how liberal ideology informs juridical practice, processes of citizenship, and bodily rituals of duty, remain especially undertheorized.[2] To do so, I concentrate pointedly on Keckly's performances of counter-memory and of non-normative intimacy.

## Anti-Pastoral Reach

Keckly, formerly Elizabeth Hobbs, was born in Dinwiddie County, Virginia, in February 1818 to a bondswoman named Agnes Hobbs. "Mammy Aggy," as she was often referenced on the plantation, served as nurse and seamstress in the household of Armistead and Mary Burwell. Despite Colonel Burwell's status as Elizabeth's biological father, a slave named George Hobbs at a neighboring plantation who was married to Agnes dutifully performed the roles of husband and father until the family's permanent dispersal during Elizabeth's childhood. As a slave, Elizabeth dispensed with her labor primarily within the inner sanctums of relatively well-to-do families such as the Burwells. Fleischner speculates that Agnes imparted the skills of stitching, spinning, and weaving to Elizabeth at the age of three, during occasional reprieves from their respective charges (39). After using proceeds from her sewing skills to purchase freedom for herself and her son in 1855, Keckly separated from an intemperate husband and moved from St. Louis to Baltimore, and eventually to Washington, DC, where she crafted elegant apparel for the likes of Varina Davis, the soon-to-be First Lady of the Confederacy, and eventually Mary Todd Lincoln. Keckly's memoir, *Behind the Scenes: Or, Thirty Years a Slave, and Four*

*Years in the White House*, follows Keckly from the nadir of enslavement to the pinnacle of Western affairs of state.

Usefully, Fleischner specifically locates memory as a mode of survival passed down to Elizabeth from her mother Agnes, and to her from earlier generations of Burwell slaves from both the West African coast and the Niger Delta (32). Indeed, as scholars such as Frances Smith Foster, Saidiya Hartman, and William Andrews suggest, bondsmen and -women, as well as recently emancipated slaves, often asserted insurgent nostalgia despite the agonies of captivity.[3] Relatedly, I maintain that Keckly engages in subversive performances of cultural memory called anti-pastoral reach throughout *Behind the Scenes* in ways that problematize conventionally archivable, state-sanctioned systems of knowledge production. In particular, Keckly confronts pastoral processes of memorialization, activating a keen sense of personal belonging and place in her memoir. These recollections, even when coincident with dominant transcripts, cannot finally be reduced to the instrumental designs of the slaveholding regime.[4]

For instance, in response to Northern suspicion of her curiosity regarding her former owners in the wake of the Civil War, Keckly replies, "You forget the past is dear to everyone, for the past belongs [to] that golden period, the days of childhood. The past is a mirror that reflects the chief incidents of my life" (241). Continuing on, she writes, "To surrender it is to surrender the greatest part of my existence—early impressions, friends, and the graves of my father, my mother, and my son. These people are associated with everything that memory holds dear, and so long as memory holds dear, and so long as memory proves faithful, it is but natural that I should sigh to see them once more" (241–42). Memory, in Keckly's formulation, exceeds the Western domain of rational retrieval. Instead, her incarnate reminiscences move in the realm of faith. In a distinct shift to first person, she selectively recalls "the chief incidents of my life" as a means to forge her own worldview, while never finally submitting the full details of "the greatest part of my existence" for public consumption. Hence, to take into account those directly culpable for her enslavement marks not a concession to the conditions of subjection, but registers an attempt to create meaning and purpose apart from violent circumstances. Such a gesture resonates with Keckly's commentary in the Preface that Southerners "were not so much responsible for the curse under which I was born, as the God of nature and the fathers who framed the Constitution of the United States" (xii). That is, Keckly refuses to privatize racism, seeking instead to expose its juridical sanction and naturalization as law. For her, anti-black terror functions institutionally, rather than on the level of the individual. Anti-pastoral reach allows retention that fortifies, without traumatizing.

However, just as Keckly foregrounds anti-pastoral reach as a vehicle through which to access her own truths, she also does so specifically to launch a broad-based critique of liberal sentimentality. Therefore, readings that associate the significance of Keckly's July 1866 reunion with the Garlands, the family of a former master, in Rude's Hill, Virginia, with a capacity to bolster Keckly's self-esteem affirm her humanity, or to more generally assuage white fears of black resentment, yet and still, curtail Keckly's insight into the underside of liberal affective economies.[5]

An example of precisely how such analyses fall short relates to Keckly's literary depiction of the aforementioned postwar visit to the home of her former charges, at least one of whom concludes a letter to Keckly about her impending visit with the conspicuous imperative, "Come; I will not take no for an answer" (246). After an elated chorus of "It is Lizzie! It is Lizzie!" at the sight of their former slave, the Garlands "carr[y her] to the house in triumph" (250). Yet, amidst the euphoric fanfare, the voice of the Garlands' nameless black cook notably intervenes: "I declar, I nebber did see people carry on so. Wonder if I should go off and stay two or three years, if all ob you wud hug and kiss me so when I cum back?" (252) Aside from the notable shift into dialect, the passage produces a crucial slippage. Indeed, the cook's testimony—"I nebber did see people carry on so"—positions the celebratory response as far from common practice in this household. Though both are ostensibly free women at the point of this exchange, Keckly and the anonymous cook garner starkly divergent treatment. I argue that this critical difference, the gap between placation and servitude, renders the Garlands' sycophancy as a thinly veiled expression of a liberal discourse of exception, or a species of individualism, whereby singular ascent supersedes collective justice. By remembering the words of the cook in this way, via anti-pastoral reach, Keckly authors a performance in which the "faithful slave returned to the homestead" cannot be severed from the postbellum "faithful servant." Put differently, it is precisely the exploitation of the unidentified laborer that makes the excessive praise of Keckly possible in the first place; they constitute flip sides of the same dehumanizing coin.

Keckly also deploys anti-pastoral reach to make visible the coerciveness of liberal affect as she and Mrs. Garland muse over the exploits of a perhaps less celebrated, though no less important antebellum aunt than Frederick Douglass's Aunt Hester, Agnes's sister, Charlotte. "A maid in the old time meant something different from what we understand by a maid at the present day," observes the Southern matriarch, nostalgically (255). "My mother was severe with her slaves in some respects, but then her heart was full of kindness," she adds, reinforcing the by-now-stagnant trope of the "feeling plantation slave mistress." I reproduce Mrs. Garland's story at length below:

> [My mother] had your aunt punished one day, and not liking her sorrowful look, she made two extravagant promises in order to effect a reconciliation, both of which were accepted. On condition that her maid would look cheerful, and be good and friendly with her, the mistress told her she might go to church the following Sunday, and that she would give her a silk dress to wear on the occasion. Now my mother had but one silk dress in the world [...] and yet she gave this dress to her maid to make friends with her. Two weeks afterward mother was sent for to spend the day at a neighbor's house, and on inspecting her wardrobe, discovered that she had no dress fit to wear in company. She had but one alternative, and that was to appeal to the generosity of your aunt Charlotte. Charlotte was summoned, and enlightened in regard to the situation; the maid proffered to loan the silk dress to her mistress for the occasion, and the mistress was only too glad to accept. She made her appearance at the social gathering, duly arrayed in the silk that her maid had worn to church on the proceeding Sunday. (255–56)

Though the two women proceed to laugh together, and even to chide those doubting their loyalty to one another, the sincerity of these acts is undercut by the arresting anti-pastoral reach toward Aunt Charlotte. Just as the dominant transcript seeks to recuperate Charlotte's body as testament to white female compassion and generosity, Keckly subversively recalls what Lori Merish characterizes as "a familiar ritual of domestic seduction" in which "the mistress gives Charlotte the dress in exchange for the slave's evident pleasure in serving her" (248). Notably, Charlotte is voiceless in this recollection: Accordingly, "the narrative's silence [...] underscores that the sympathetic exchanges envisioned here are dictated by the mistress's desire, and constitute a species of narcissism" (Merish 249). Given the scene's strategic placement in the memoir—on a continuum with Keckly's depiction of her own silencing by past owners and patrons—I contend that Keckly memorializes Charlotte by elucidating a liberal production of compulsory black acquiescence.

In fact, when the former mistress poses the final query, "Do you always feel kindly towards me, Lizzie?" Keckly declines to give the emphatically affirmative answer Mrs. Garland craves. "What Ann Garland wants here is Keckley's sentimental consent," Merish confirms, "a performance of sympathy that would legitimate Garland's identity as a 'good mistress,' and she stages a ritual in which Keckley refuses to participate" (250). Though Joanne Braxton claims that "the bond between freedom and literacy" constitutes "a theme noticeably absent from Keckley's *Behind the Scenes*," in this moment, Keckly rejects the posture of docility expected of her, forgoing complicity, specifically by challenging the Garlands' suppression of her access to formal education (Braxton 44). "To tell you candidly, Miss Ann, I have but one unkind thought, and that is, that you did not give me the advantages of a good education. What I have learned has been the study of after years," Keckly admits, if euphemistically. Demonstrating precisely the unintended irony by which Mrs. Garland purports that "a maid in the old time meant something different from what we understand by a maid at the present day," Keckly goes off script in a way that Charlotte most likely could not. Mrs. Garland's desire to recapitulate and renew her mother's liberal generosity subsequently rings hollow, as Keckly calls up anti-pastoral reach to denaturalize interracial dynamics of domination and control.

## Privilege and Pretense

A second preoccupation of *Behind the Scenes* is the at-once ritualized and invisibilized performance of white privilege. Keckly's literary representation of interracial patron-client relationships in the mid-nineteenth-century North exposes especially insidious modes of compulsion in this regard, including maternalism. Often striking in its instrumentality, the maternal relation deploys fictive kinship ties, amongst other less explicit filial logics, to extract docility and submission.

Keckly dramatizes precisely such a dynamic when detailing an exchange with Mrs. General McClean, the daughter of General Sumner, upon Keckly's initial arrival to Washington, DC. Indirectly referring to Mrs. McClean's ensuing conduct as her "emphatic way," Keckly depicts the influential customer's urgent demand for a new frock. "I have just purchased material, and you must commence work on it right away," commands McClean. To Keckly's response vis-à-vis the unfeasibility of such a project on such short notice, McClean retorts, "Pshaw! Nothing is impossible! I must have the dress made by Sunday." Not surprisingly, Keckly's subsequent attempts to reiterate her position, as well as to apologize, are met with irritation. "Now don't say no again. I tell you that you must make the dress," McClean interjects imperatively (79).

McClean thereafter propositions Keckly by offering to help her gain employment at the White House—as long as her dress is complete in time for Sunday's soirée. In the end, Keckly depletes significant resources to meet the looming deadline. Yet, despite the narrative's characterization of this final incentive as "the best [inducement] that could have been offered," it is arguably McClean's preliminary invocation of privilege that secures Keckly's consent (80). Under the belated guise of potential liaison between Keckly and Mary Lincoln, McClean first forcefully asserts her race and class advantage over and above her black counterpart. As the script of white supremacy—even when cloaked in a liberal spirit of commercial collaboration—stipulates Keckly's categorical assent, McClean wrests the requisite response from her interlocutor. Brusquely, if smilingly silencing the one whose services she so desperately desires, McClean infantilizes Keckly by deauthorizing her speech. As author, Keckly rhetorically stages an acquisition of fidelity rooted in strictly hierarchized terms of order, an all-too-familiar and violent scenario of dominance.

A related instance features Keckly's interaction with one of her white patrons in St. Louis, a woman aptly named Mrs. Le Bourgois, prior to the former's emancipation from slavery. Following Mr. Farrow's disclosure of his belief that Keckly would likely fall prey to abolitionists' schemes during her trip up North, Le Bourgois arrives unannounced at Keckly's door. "Lizzie, I hear that you are going to New York to beg for money to buy your freedom," she declares. "I have been thinking over the matter, and told Ma it would be a shame to allow you to go North to *beg* for what we should *give* you. You have many friends in St. Louis, and I am going to raise the twelve hundred dollars required among them" (54). In the wake of Le Bourgois's pronouncement, "the flowers no longer were withered, drooping" (55). "Again, they seemed to bud and grow in fragrance and beauty," observes a third-person narrator (ibid.).

Notably, tropes of brightness and sweetness scaffold the entire conversation between the two women: "Like a ray of sunshine [Mrs. Le Bourgois] came, and like a ray of sunshine she went away," relays Keckly (55). The overt logic of the passage, then, christens Le Bourgois as Keckly's savior. Seemingly impervious to the rigorously policed constructions of the social to which her surname alludes, Le Bourgois accumulates redemptive capital in the eyes of readers by relieving Keckly and her son of the "bitter heart-struggle" of slavery (ibid.). However, given Keckly's ambivalent theorization of suicide as a possible "bright side of slavery" earlier in her volume, I maintain that the effects of light as a framing device exceed the affective register of unconditional gratitude and praise. As evidenced in Frederick Douglass's *Narrative*, "sunniness" indexes a black opacity at odds with liberal, Enlightenment-refined injunctions toward rationality and comprehensibility.[6] Indeed, many nineteenth-century black women thinkers manipulated obscurity to subversive ends in their texts. "Alas! the sunny face of the slave is not always an indication of sunshine in the heart," confirms Keckly in the memoir's opening pages (29). Embedded with political meaning and experience, Keckly's sunbeams and blossoms, in fact, subtly conjure the saccharinity, posture, and pretense of liberal racial sentimentality.

Thus, proposes Dana Luciano, "Le Bourgois's offer reads alternately as expressing the 'human' kinship of sympathy, responding generously to another's display of grief, or, less sentimentally, as expressing a kind of genteel feminine modesty on behalf of Southern custom" (255). And yet, Le Bourgois's unsolicited appearance at Keckly's residence, not to mention her ability to casually mull over "the matter" of Keckly's basic survival at her leisure, belies the sympathetic orientation of her pitch. Le Bourgois remains principally, if not exclusively, concerned with safeguarding the status of the local white community. The narrative act of "saving face," choreographed so carefully by Keckly in this instance, positions white etiquette as little more than an expression of privilege meant to instate a relation of longstanding indebtedness. Moreover, Keckly's performance illuminates the ease with which whites' saving face often comes at the expense of any substantive engagement with black life.

Similarly, privilege surfaces in *Behind the Scenes* through the projection of a staple of the white liberal imaginary: interracial intimacy. Modern historical scholarship and commercial publications alike constantly reproduce this falsehood when addressing Keckly's legacy, interring Keckly and Mary Todd Lincoln's dynamic in pastoral, wistful longing. Presumably mistaking physical proximity or a shared employment landscape for mutually sustaining emotional ties, biographers routinely spotlight Keckly and Lincoln's special acquaintance, their "genuine friendship."[7] According to Fleischner, "It is easy to see why well-dressed women considered themselves almost intimates with their dressmakers," for "[t]he laborious dressmaking techniques of the day made close relationships between women and their dressmakers largely impossible to avoid" (133). Interestingly, despite Fleischner's initial suspicion in her monograph of a "too easy use of the word" friendship with respect to Keckly and Lincoln's entwined histories, she finally retreats from the asymmetry inherent in the relation, granting a unique "warmth, understanding, and intimacy" between the two given the nature and duration of their business together (5–6).

But, as Lauren Berlant argues, intimacy constitutes a kind of affective artifice. At once ideologically and materially violent, intimacy as normative institution fails to acknowledge its own intrinsic idealism and ambivalence, if not its virtual impossibility. "[I]ntimacy . . . involves an aspiration for a narrative about something shared, a story about both oneself and others that will turn out in a particular way" (281), corroborates Berlant in a twentieth-century, though not unrelated context: It "builds worlds; it creates spaces and usurps places meant for other kinds of relation. Its potential failure to stabilize closeness always haunts its persistent activity" (282). Further, as Berlant theorizes, the intimate remains tethered to the performative, trafficking in hollow iconography and gestures of deep feeling. Deemed natural, rites of intimacy imported across divergent terrain, in fact, cover over the acuteness and specificity of uneven contexts of subjection.

The artificiality of interracial intimacy emerges on multiple occasions in the memoir, especially in scenes in which Keckly is cast as a "mammy" figure. Though Keckly's relationship with the Garland daughters most readily prompts such a reading,[8] I contend that Keckly's association with Mrs. Lincoln likewise invokes the increasingly stale "mammy" image, a trope Patricia Hill Collins refers to as the quintessential "asexual woman, a surrogate mother in blackface" (80–1). Katherine Helm, niece of Mary Lincoln and author of *The True Story of Mary: Wife of Lincoln,* too, invites such an assessment, claiming that her aunt often "reverted to the impulse of her childhood, which had been to seek the love and help she had unfailingly found in her black mammy. In the faithful, sympathetic colored woman, Elizabeth Keckley [. . .] Mary saw the only available substitute, and to her she turned blindly for sympathy and advice" (266). In Helm's configuration, Lincoln collapses Sally, a black bondswoman employed by the Todd family during Mary's childhood, with Elizabeth, a free black entrepreneur in postbellum Washington, DC. For Lincoln, "mammy" represents an anonymous, yet ever-present reserve of black sustenance, while Helm, in her uncritical reproduction of the term *mammy* as an expression of endearment, renders Sally nameless, thereby extending her foremother's legacy.

In this vein, pictures of exploited labor—conceived by the dominant group in a matrix of motherly affection, autonomy, and consent—abound in *Behind the Scenes*. Indeed, as the extensive array of services for which Keckly is responsible in the Lincoln household increases, the institutionalized character of white privilege enables this escalation to circulate as intensified care and nurturing shared between employer and employee. As Sau-Ling C. Wong argues, "[. . .] by conceding a certain amount of spiritual or even physical dependence on people of color—as helpers, healers, guardians, mediators, educators, or advisors—without ceding actual structural privilege, the care-receiver preserves the illusion of equality and reciprocity with the caregiver" (69). Following Wong, the fantasy of "Keckly-as-mammy" presumes black volition while precluding any significant access to power or authority. According to the prevailing political rationality of liberalism, Keckly's progressively more intensive, if diversified meniality indexes not obligation or duress, but mutuality and shared investments in buttressing "the biopower of white comfort."[9]

Importantly, mythologies of superhuman black female strength remain central to the traction of the dehumanizing "mammy" stereotype and to the liberal production of interracial intimacy. Hence, Helm cites the ostensibly "unfailing" quality of Sally's support for Mary Lincoln. Likewise, in *The Spy, the Lady, the Captain, and the Colonel,* an illustrated biography for young adults featuring a section on Keckly, the historical tendency to de-emphasize black women's subjectivity in order to accentuate their physical potency asserts itself. While the text arguably offers complex perspectives on Keckly's ambivalent relationship to Emancipation, as well as on her spiritual grounding and commitment to political activism, it appears unable to relinquish the worn trope of black women's unyielding fortitude. "She was the rock of strength on which Mary Lincoln leaned," notes the narrator in one prominent example (58). In this case, Keckly's resilience coincides with little more than her apparent stamina in staving off Lincoln's mental and emotional collapse in the wake of her husband's assassination.

Usefully, bell hooks locates at least one of the problems inherent in such a move. As she traces continuities between the nineteenth- and twentieth-century Women's Movements in *Ain't I a Woman: Black women and feminism*, hooks maintains, "When feminists acknowledge in one breath that black women are victimized and in the same breath emphasize their strength, they imply that though black women are oppressed they manage to circumvent the damaging impact of oppression by being strong—and that is simply not the case" (6). As hooks clarifies, black endurance does not yield panacean social transformation. Instead, liberal stereotypes of extraordinary black female strength—relics of antebellum conditions of containment—facilitate a mode of white self-exoneration whereby accountability for structural domination is elided.

Finally, alongside the "mammy" caricature, Keckly turns up quite often as the First Lady's dearest companion. Given their mutual status as grieving mothers and as ostensible outsider figures in midcentury DC polite society, the two are quick to be labeled comrades. Keckly is even identified as Mary Lincoln's "trusted friend and confidante" on Keckly's tombstone.[10] As interraciality alone does not prohibit alliance, it is necessary to acknowledge the feelings of interest, community, comfort, and pride likely vested in their ongoing connection. Nevertheless, liberalism, in its erasure of particularity, posits the effects of the affiliation as proportional, if not identical, for each woman. Instead, I argue, a nuanced spectrum of aggression characterizes patron-client interactions, including that of Mary Lincoln and Elizabeth Keckly, throughout much of the era.

As in many of the previous scenarios, acts of interracial respect and regard—of friendship—frequently obscure rigid power dynamics. For example, just prior to the president's assassination, Keckly requests permission from her "friend" to attend what would become Lincoln's final public speech. "Certainly, Lizabeth; if you take any interest in political speeches, come and listen in welcome," Mary replies. "Thank you, Mrs. Lincoln. May I trespass further on your kindness by asking permission to bring a friend with me?" continues Keckly. "Yes, bring your friend also," answers Lincoln, adding immediately thereafter, "By the way, come in time to dress me before the speaking commences" (175). Though hallmarks of intimate familiarity adorn the scene, from the use of a pet name to a general aura of hospitality, I suggest that competing rhetorical elements are simultaneously at play.

That is, Keckly strategically situates interracial friendship as a rapport rooted in tolerance, for Lincoln does not actually "welcome" Keckly to witness the lecture. Rather, she allows her to do so with the caveat that she must first dispense with her requisite domestic tasks. Of the consequence of such tolerance, David Theo Goldberg observes, "[. . .] liberals are moved to overcome the racial differences they tolerate and have been so instrumental in fabricating by diluting them, by bleaching them out through assimilation or integration. The liberal would assume away the difference in otherness, maintaining thereby the dominance of presumed sameness, the universally imposed similarity in identity" (7). Despite an ethos of seeming congeniality, Keckly cannot acknowledge Lincoln's informality with equivalent signs of acquaintance. Indeed, she cannot refer to her employer by her first name, apply the term *friend* to their patron-client relationship in her employer's presence, or exceed her careful, deferent stance very much at all. Therefore, Lincoln, in fact, only reconstitutes the terms of forced intimacy inflicted by Keckly's past owners/patrons from Mrs. Garland; to Mrs. McClean; to Mrs. Jefferson Davis, First Lady of the Confederacy.

Another moment in the memoir, involving the Lincoln family's move to Chicago following President Johnson's inauguration, especially resonates with these previous experiences with white privilege, but manifests itself through the trope of friendship, in particular. According to Keckly, "When Mrs. Lincoln first suggested her plan [to take Keckly with her to Chicago], I strongly objected; but I had been with her so long, that she had acquired great power over me" (209). While the ambiguity of the passage leads some critics to attribute Keckly's hesitancy to a deep "emotional bond" between the two women,[11] the episode as readily provokes a reading of Keckly's muted critique of the coerciveness of interracial intimacy. Thus, as Keckly attempts to explain to her employer that she cannot possibly desert her own business and philanthropic pursuits in Washington to travel to Illinois, Lincoln sternly interrupts: "Now don't say another word about it, if you do not wish to distress me. I have determined that you shall go to Chicago with me, and you must go" (209–10). In an all too common gesture of silencing, construed by the figure of authority as an articulation of fondness and devotion, Lincoln compels Keckly's compliance.

It is on the first night in transit to Chicago, though, that Lincoln explicitly invokes the notion of friendship. As Keckly attends to the former First Lady's latest ailment, Lincoln announces, "Lizabeth, you are my best and kindest friend. I wish it were in my power to make you comfortable for the balance of your days. If Congress provides for me, depend upon it, I will provide for you" (210). In another, off-script moment, however, Keckly supplies quite the telling response to Lincoln's declaration: silence. Countering Lincoln's routine suppression, both her allocation of erratic hours and wages and the continued stifling of Keckly's voice, with an abrupt, self-imposed quietness on her own terms, Keckly retreats from her employer's performance of intimacy. "The trip was devoid of interest," resumes the narrator unemphatically. "We arrived in Chicago without accident or delay" (ibid.). In place of the affirmation, gratitude, or approval prescribed by the hegemonic racial order, Keckly offers a resounding calm. Her refusal to speak back to Lincoln's assertion forces readers to linger, to borrow from Berlant again, with Lincoln's haunting "failure to stabilize closeness." Keckly enacts a rhetorical disjunction that at once exposes the racialized rites and rituals—as well as the slippages—at the heart of the project of liberalism.

## Intimacy: Restyled

In closing, however, it is important to signal the ways in which Keckly contrasts the intimacy driven by dominant ideological and fetishistic impulses with that motivated by nonrational forces. Of the latter, Berlant asserts, "in practice the drive toward [intimacy] is a kind of wild thing that is not necessarily organized [in a conventional] way, or any way" (284). Keckly's relationship with her son, to take just one example, epitomizes precisely such a dynamic. The apparently peripheral mention of George's life and death throughout the course of the memoir, not unlike details around her sexuality or her mother's continued residence at the South after Keckly's move North, confounds many critics. Yet, the ostensibly tangential affiliation with her son not only concretizes her reduction to the status of "mammy," a role in which—by definition—her own family's needs must be overlooked, but reconceptualizes black maternal affection. In fact, in admitting that "God knows that she did not wish to give him life," Keckly conveys a fierce connection to her offspring (39). She expresses an unruly closeness to her child, a love profound enough to encompass her labor for his freedom and formal education and her ambivalence and pain over the violent circumstances of his birth.[12] Keckly's passion for her son, then, is not effortless or inborn. It is not a space of privilege, but a site of struggle.

In this regard, Keckly's contestation of circumscribed understandings of family, motherhood, and intimacy coincides with broader critiques of liberalism evident in her memoir. Indeed, *Behind the Scenes* problematizes prevailing discourses on sovereignty, progress, and individualism. Keckly likewise challenges entrenched ethics of tolerance and exceptionalism, privilege and decorum, universality and self-possession. By deploying practices of anti-pastoral reach and non-normative intimacy, in particular, Keckly literally stages an intervention into the dominant political rationality of the day. Though conventional wisdom contains the significance of Keckly's life and writings, fixing her alternately as Mary Lincoln's arch nemesis or best friend, a closer reading reveals her insights into the inner workings of liberalism as political, economic, and affective machine. Typically cast beyond the pale of legitimate black resistance, Keckly plumbs theories of power, authority, and value in a manner of enduring consequence today.

## NOTES

1. According to James Emerson in *The Madness of Mary Lincoln*, "Historians have been misspelling Elizabeth Keckly's surname as *Keckley* since 1868. Jennifer Fleischner recently found her actual signatures and revealed the true spelling in her book *Mrs. Lincoln and Mrs. Keckly* (193). I have chosen to retain the correct usage, rather than the spelling used in the copyright, in my own references to Keckly, though I do not edit her name when referencing works of secondary criticism.

2. The "Old Clothes Scandal" refers to Mary Lincoln's infamous attempts to auction off her extravagant wardrobe in the wake of her husband's assassination in order to alleviate her debt.

3. See Andrews's "Reunion in the Postbellum Slave Narrative" (14), Foster's *Written by Herself* (127), and Hartman's *Scenes of Subjection* (72).

4. See Hartman on the pastoral: "In the social landscape of the pastoral, slavery is depicted as an 'organic relationship' so totalizing that neither master nor slave could express 'the simplest human feelings without reference to the other.' Thus the master and the slave are seen as, if not peacefully coexisting, at the very least enjoying a relationship of paternalistic dependency and reciprocity. In this instance, paternalism minimizes the extremity of domination with assertions about the mutually recognized humanity of master and slave" (52).

5. For example, see Fleischner's *Mrs. Lincoln and Mrs. Keckly* (298) and Andrews's "Reunion in the Postbellum Slave Narrative" (12).

6. Of "apparently incoherent [slave] songs," Douglass observes in his *Narrative*, "They would sing, as a chorus, words which to many would seem unmeaning jargon, but which, nevertheless, were full of meaning to themselves. I have sometimes thought that the mere hearing of those songs would do more to impress some minds with the horrible character of slavery, than the reading of whole volumes of philosophy on the subject could do" (27).

7. See Richard Stiller's *The Spy, the Lady, the Captain, and the Colonel* (51) and Jerrold Packard's *The Lincolns in the White House* (29, 120).

8. Of Nannie Garland, Keckly writes, "She slept in my bed, and I watched over her as if she had been my own child" (239).

9. See Vorris Nunley's *Keepin' It Hushed*, on the "biopower of white comfort" (16).

10. See the author's note in Jennifer Chiaverini's *Mrs. Lincoln's Dressmaker* (352), among other sources, regarding the tombstone.

11. See Fleischner's *Mrs. Lincoln and Mrs. Keckly* (293–94).

12. Keckly is raped by a white man named Alexander Kirkland, rival of the "pious" slave-breaker, Mr. Bingham, depicted in the memoir.

## WORKS CITED

Andrews, William L. "Reunion in the Postbellum Slave Narrative: Frederick Douglass and Elizabeth Keckley." *Black American Literature Forum* 23 (1989): 5–16. Web. 15 June 2012.

Baker, Jean H. *Mary Todd Lincoln: A Biography.* New York: W.W. Norton, 1987.

Berlant, Lauren. "Intimacy: A Special Issue." *Critical Inquiry* 24 (1998): 281–8. Web. 30 June 2012.

Braxton, Joanne M. *Black Women Writing Autobiography: A Tradition within a Tradition.* Philadelphia: Temple University Press, 1989.

Chiaverini, Jennifer. *Mrs. Lincoln's Dressmaker: A Novel.* New York: Plume, 2013.

Collins, Patricia Hill. *Black Feminist Thought: Knowledge, Consciousness, and the Politics of Empowerment*, Revised Tenth Anniversary Edition. New York: Routledge, 2000.

Douglass, Frederick, and Harriet Jacobs. *Narrative of the Life of Frederick Douglass, an American Slave & Incidents in the Life of a Slave Girl.* New York: Modern Library, 2004.

Emerson, James. *The Madness of Mary Lincoln.* Carbondale: Southern Illinois University Press, 2007.

Fleischner, Jennifer. *Mrs. Lincoln and Mrs. Keckly: The Remarkable Story of the Friendship Between a First Lady and a Former Slave.* New York: Broadway Books, 2003.

Foster, Frances Smith. *Written by Herself: Literary Production by African American Women, 1746–1892.* Bloomington: Indiana University Press, 1993.

Goldberg, David Theo. *Racist Culture: Philosophy and the Culture of Meaning.* Oxford: Blackwell Publishers, 1993.

Hartman, Saidiya. *Scenes of Subjection: Terror, Slavery, and Self-Making in Nineteenth-Century America.* New York: Oxford University Press, 1997.

Helm, Katherine. *The True Story of Mary, Wife of Lincoln: Containing the Recollections of Mary Lincoln's Sister Emilie (Mrs. Ben Hardin Helm), Extracts from her War-Time Diary, Numerous Letters and Other Documents now First Published.* New York: Harper & Brothers, 1928.

hooks, bell. *Ain't I a Woman: Black Women and Feminism.* Boston: South End Press, 1981.

Keckly, Elizabeth. *Behind the Scenes: Or, Thirty Years a Slave, and Four Years in the White House.* New York: Oxford University Press, 1988.

*Lincoln.* Dir. Steven Spielberg. Perf. Daniel Day-Lewis, Sally Field, and David Strathairn. DreamWorks Pictures and Participant Media, 2012. Film.

Luciano, Dana. *Arranging Grief: Sacred Time and the Body in Nineteenth-Century America.* New York: New York University Press, 2007.

Merish, Lori. *Sentimental Materialism: Gender, Commodity Culture, and Nineteenth-Century American Literature.* Durham: Duke University Press, 2000.

Nunley, Vorris L. *Keepin' It Hushed: The Barbershop and African American Hush Harbor Rhetoric.* Detroit: Wayne State University Press, 2011.

Packard, Jerrold M. *The Lincolns in the White House: Four Years that Shattered a Family.* New York: St. Martin's Press, 2005.

Schreiner Jr., Samuel A. *The Trials of Mrs. Lincoln.* Lincoln: University of Nebraska Press, 2005.

Stiller, Richard. *The Spy, the Lady, the Captain, and the Colonel.* New York: Scholastic Books, 1970.

Wong, Sau-Ling. "Diverted Mothering: Representations of Caregivers of Color in the Age of 'Multiculturalism.'" *Mothering: Ideology, Experience, and Agency.* Ed. Evelyn Nakano Glenn, Grace Chang, and Linda Rennie Forcey. New York: Routledge, 1994. 67–91.

CHAPTER EIGHT

AISHA FRANCIS

# Stepping Beyond the Formal Lines
Elizabeth Keckley, Gertrude Mossell, and the Cost of Transgression

It may be charged that I have written too freely on some questions, especially in regard to Mrs. Lincoln. I do not think so. . . . She stepped beyond the formal lines which hedge about a private life, and invited public criticism.
—Elizabeth Keckley, *Behind the Scenes:*
  *Or, Thirty Years a Slave, and Four Years in the White House,* 1868

[B]ut on the whole, according to their means, their opportunities for remaining at home, the irritating circumstances that surround them (and of our women especially), tempted by two races, they do well. After due deliberation and advisedly I repeat that they (remembering the past dreadful environment of slavery) do well.
—Mrs. N.F. Mossell, *The Work of the Afro-American Woman,* 1894

CONDUCT, MORALITY, AND VIRTUE have long been recognized as important themes of African American writing and storytelling. Throughout the nineteenth century, these motifs particularly elucidate black people's expectations of themselves regarding the conduct of life and upward mobility. While much that can be said about these themes extends to the race as a whole, this article focuses on black women's voices, and will examine black women's cultural production as a frame of reference. I argue that Elizabeth Keckley's *Behind the Scenes: Or, Thirty Years a Slave, and Four Years in the White House* (1868) and N.F. (Gertrude Bustill) Mossell's *The Work of the Afro-American Woman* (1894) represent a continuum of writing that reveal important perspectives about black women's efforts to exert agency through the written word—even at the risk of breaking some of the very social rules that their texts are reinforcing. This ironic and purposeful transgression offers lessons about persistence, self-determination, and the power of the pen to wield truth despite dogged attempts to silence and repress black women's point of view. Their rich textual legacy uncovers how nineteenth-century black women positioned themselves as credible witnesses in an era when black people in this nation were just beginning to experience de jure citizenship. In this sense, one can and should claim Keckley and Mossell as cultural foremothers of today's explosion of black women journalists, activists, academics, and bloggers who are seeking their own versions of twenty-first–century truth while taking this history into account.

The impact of black journalistic publications of the nineteenth century has been well documented. Through this cultural production, African American women sought to influence the actions and interactions of elite and working-class black audiences, and to sway public opinion among all manner of white readers with varying opinions about the moral and mental capacity of blacks. The insistence on constructing the parameters of proper behavior and deportment, and educating the public to interrogate the paradoxes of living as a woman of color in the United States are significant components of the black conduct literature these women produced. Their voices are central to the continued effort to develop a richer understanding of the African American struggle for freedom and equity. This article positions the rhetoric of Elizabeth Keckley and Gertrude Mossell (who used the pen name, Mrs. N.F. Mossell) as examples of black conduct literature, and demonstrates that their writing was an exercise in active citizenship and social reform. Too often, the opinions of black women from this era are viewed through the lens of assimilation, which is unproductive and demonstrates a lack of appreciation for the social constraints of the era in which these early writers labored. Ahistorical comparisons of protest methodologies negate nineteenth-century black women's success at attempting to shift the terms of debate about their own condition, while claiming the prestige of womanhood previously denied them. To be sure, black women were not the only groups of people struggling to be heard in this era.[1] However, understanding the motives of black women writers and analyzing their practices in a proper historical context uncover their productivity that lies beneath the surface.

As early as the eighteenth century, black women were compelled to write and speak publicly to articulate their opinions regarding the perceptions of themselves vis-à-vis race. Most notably, Phillis Wheatley and Maria Stewart urged audiences to re-evaluate black Americans' potential and ability to serve as leaders, influencers, and respected citizens in their communities—and to some extent in the public sphere at large. This plea emanated from unconventional black women who illumined the hypocrisy of national ideologies that upheld the tradition of moral exceptionalism amidst the institution of slavery. Still, such messages were intermittent and diffuse in the face of an insurmountable tide of pejorative public opinion and customs. As a result, any seditious intent in Wheatley's published verse remained veiled and suggestive. Similarly, though Stewart's speeches issued a bold call for white and black audiences alike to recommit to the ideals of Christian morality, she remained an isolated, itinerant lecturer. Ultimately, both women experienced short-lived public careers.[2]

Later, the Reconstruction era gave rise to a critical mass of black women publishing and lecturing on themes of reform and retribution.[3] The cultural production of these writers was published in an atmosphere that increasingly valued social conformity to Victorianism and religious conformity to Protestantism.[4] Through the written word, these black women were espousing their proficiency with rhetoric and creating sophisticated ways to demarcate rather than disguise their acumen and ambition. Examples of this phenomenon can be gleaned in Anna Julia Cooper's *A Voice from the South* (1892), Mossell's *The Work of the Afro-American Woman* (1894)—which will be considered later in this article—and Fannie Barrier Williams's speech "The Present Status and Intellectual Progress of Colored Women" (1893), to name a few. In many respects, slave narratives formed an important bridge spanning the divide between the extant publications of a few exceedingly rare antebellum black women who experienced public recognition and the wave of Progressive Era black women's writing that followed. Among these narratives, Elizabeth Keckley's *Behind the Scenes: Or, Thirty Years a Slave, and Four Years in the White House* is a fascinating surviving example.[5]

So glacial was the pace of social progress, that decades after Keckley published *Behind the Scenes* Victorian morays remained entrenched in middle-class American culture such that many women writers of the late nineteenth century (black and white) published under their husbands' initials or used pseudonyms to pacify those among their audience who were likely to be offended by their indiscrete decision to publish. Assuming an androgynous pen name, or the protective covering of the title "Mrs.," was a manner of acquiescing to public expectations of women's modesty. In this tradition, Mossell chose to employ this conservative strategy by using her husband's (Nathan Francis Mossell) initials as her pen name. However, Keckley chose to write as herself in a time when most women of social standing made concerted efforts not to share their opinions publicly. This decision may reveal as much about her business sensibilities as it does about an overt stance she was taking on women's independence. The sole proprietor of a high-end dressmaking shop, Keckley thrived on word-of-mouth referrals. Her writing and the frank way that she approached this project had as much to do with her intention of using the publication to brand herself and her business as it did with her professed purpose of reclaiming the reputation of her preeminent client, Mary Todd Lincoln.

Regardless of how they chose to attribute authorship, black American women putting pen to paper in the nineteenth century were most often resolute in their intention to use text as a tool through which to frame a depiction of black Americans based on self-determination and pride, rather than subscribing to derogatory designations of blackness perpetuated by white American culture. As Frances Smith Foster stresses, "Much of the African American print culture with which we are most familiar was written and published for an interracial audience. Racial etiquette, common sense, and untranslatable language influenced what, how, and how much was written" (115). As I have argued, this cultural production exhibits enough congruent features to be considered a subgenre that I coined as black conduct literature.[6] Through the Keckley and Mossell texts, readers can trace the intended outcomes of black conduct literature, which are to force readers to contend with recognizing black people's humanity through their participation in the public sphere. Their personhood being established, authors of black conduct literature seek to promote access to education and economic opportunity as birthrights of full citizenship. Finally, beyond making a persuasive and exculpatory argument regarding the affirmative constitution and character of black Americans, black conduct literature acknowledges and specifically references the historical legacy of slavery, while praising black Americans for the strides they made in spite of their disadvantages. Whenever possible, the authors of these texts include anecdotal evidence and empirical data to delineate the dire effects of undue discrimination. After establishing the framework for their argument and supporting their case with verification, the authors present to the reader tangible forms of activism that will render significant improvements in the condition of black womanhood in particular and the black race in general. The utility of black conduct literature lies in its conveyance of the power of the word as a resistance strategy used to combat a national climate antagonistic toward blackness.

Through black conduct literature, black women present the performance of proper etiquette and uphold the politics of respectability as a compelling strategy for discrediting unjust assumptions about their subject position. Because conventional wisdom positions etiquette texts as a non-confrontational and marginal method of producing change, this forum may seem like an unconventional approach to gaining racial equality. However, in the context of black women's cultural and historical legacy, the wholesale adoption of a strict moral code was a plausible—if impotent—approach to solving the oppressive race problem. Employing the "politics of respectability" is a strategy defined by black women's trials concomitant with their indefatigable quest for political influence, which they hoped to leverage to gain honorable consideration in the public sphere. Historian Evelyn Brooks Higginbotham first interrogated this concept in her seminal text, *Righteous Discontent*, and a generation of scholars has since employed its tenets to decode black women's process of exercising agency. Writing as self-identified black women, Keckley and Mossell tested the nation's claim of freedom of the press even while they also challenged the efficacy of public expectations of black women's conduct. They did so by shrewdly pushing the boundaries on the impotent freedom that black people were afforded in nineteenth-century America.

As someone ahead of her time, Keckley's legacy is worth due consideration in this contemporary moment. Keckley—the ultimate informant, truth-teller, and exposé artist before her time—serves as an unwitting journalistic foremother to Mossell. Ultimately, Keckley paid a hefty price for her boldness, but not before leaving her imprint on the world and ushering into existence a new model of authority and agency for black women. Notions of respectable white womanhood of the time assumed a hierarchical and spherical construction of culture. Meanwhile, through transgressing into the public sphere, Keckley demonstrates an atypical willingness to try to bend the rules in her favor and claim the public sphere of (white) womanhood as her own. She had a story to tell, and she told it, despite the fact that telling her story ended her most notable friendship and her career. To allow her narrative to exist uncontested would have been to validate a black woman's voice at a time when doing so was an aberration. Everything she stood for—entrepreneurship, education, philanthropy, and networked participation in organized efforts to settle waves of newly freed former bondsmen—are still viewed today as noble and necessary pursuits.

However, *Behind the Scenes* did not catapult Keckley into the public sphere. She was already there by virtue of her position in Washington, DC, circles. Elizabeth Keckley was a well-known member of the most public of spheres in the mid-nineteenth century—the White House. Prior to securing Mary Todd Lincoln as a client, she worked for the family of Jefferson Davis, who would later become president of the Confederacy. She was, it seems, destined to count a presidential family among her clientele one way or the other. Driven and ambitious, Keckley had designs on enhancing the wardrobes of the capital's inner circle from the time she relocated to the District from St. Louis with the purpose of setting up her sewing business. As part of an elite black community, Keckley was well connected, and she leveraged her network for many purposes. Gauging from her epistolary relationship with Frederick Douglass, whom she knew from the antislavery circuit, and Henry Highland Garnet, who was her minister at the elite Fifteenth Street Presbyterian Church in Washington, DC, Keckley was a known quantity among the constellation of remarkable men and women who worked to advance the antislavery cause.

From the beginning of her narrative it is clear that while Keckley is a member of elite society, she is not always compelled to play by the rules of her societal strata. Undoubtedly, she was intimately acquainted with proper decorum in order to navigate the condition of slavery and emerge with her life intact. In order to establish a business as a clothes-maker in an era when the cut of a dress and its embellishments were highly scrutinized, Keckley had to know the social implications of her designs. Yet, several transgressive acts are recounted in her interactions with the white community both when she was enslaved and later as free woman. In one example, a wealthy client summons Keckley to her home with urgency. After receiving the message, Keckley decides to visit the lady the following day, much to her client's chagrin. When the client demands to know why she had failed to come as instructed,

Keckley responds, "You did not say what you wanted with me yesterday, so I judged that this morning would do as well" (Keckley 36). What is wonderful about this exchange is that Keckley demonstrates her agency and freedom to make judgment calls that would not have been afforded to people inside the confines of the system of chattel slavery.

What accounts for Keckley's brave self-possession exemplified in this exchange? One possibility is that her status as an unmarried woman and a business owner provided her with an unusual level of independence. Unfortunate circumstances—Keckley's decision to separate from an alcoholic husband who misrepresented himself as a freedman to win her affections, and the fact that she lost her son during the Civil War—provided her with autonomy from the expectations of society that were heaped upon wives and mothers whose relations would typically bear the fall out of any transgressions. On the other hand, being without male protection or immediate familial bonds also left her vulnerable to poverty and abandonment. Still, this combination of circumstances may have attributed to the gamble she was willing to take in penning *Behind the Scenes*.

Another consideration is that Keckley's carriage was a birthright inherited from her mother and stepfather, two clearly proud individuals who showered young Keckley with as much affection as they could muster in the environment of chattel slavery. History demonstrates that Keckley's genealogy includes two generations of women who experienced sexual exploitation. Both she and her mother were subjected to racialized sexual violence that resulted in children conceived by white masters. The forced silences of Elizabeth Keckley and her mother, Agnes Hobbs, give rise to the fact that we can never know whether there was anything mutual about the nature of these relationships. However, because of the master/slave power dynamic, it is highly unlikely that the unions producing Elizabeth Keckley and later, Keckley's own son, George, were consensual. In black writing of the Civil War and post-war eras, allusions to painful experiences like rape and other forms of abuse often papered over a slew of injuries to black women especially with regard to sexual violence. In the main, Keckley hews to this tradition of omission when it comes to relaying the sordid details of her own past. She writes, "The savage efforts to subdue my pride were not the only things that brought me suffering and deep mortification. . . . Suffice it to say, that he persecuted me for four years, and I—I—became a mother (16)." Using the rhetorical strategies of subtlety and inference, Keckley refers to the sexual violation she experienced during slavery. The effect of her choice is to reveal the racist hypocrisy of those who perversely portrayed their crimes against her as a response to wanton, sullen, or proud behavior.

On the other hand, one of her tactics to accomplish the mammoth task of establishing credibility is to prove the degree to which she—and by extension other black Americans—defied the supposed negative social and moral consequences of blackness. In one instance, she chooses to confound the rhetorical tradition of modesty and euphemism to detail a series of brutal beatings at the hands of a master who claimed to be a clergyman. The graphic recollection reveals the hypocrisy of her master, Rev. Robert Burwell. Burwell contracted with another man to whip Keckley on a weekly basis to quell what he called her "stubborn pride" (Keckley 13–16). Keckley fought back, though unlike Frederick Douglass, she was not able to physically overtake the torturer. After several weeks of these encounters, she shares that her tormentor suddenly repented of his actions in a shower of tears, shame, and seeming embarrassment. He vowed never to strike her again. Ultimately it was Keckley who "broke" this stand-in for an overseer instead of the other way around.

Interestingly, the most daring rhetorical strategy her narrative incorporates is the publication of numerous letters between Mary Todd Lincoln and her. It further trampled the static idea of what a black woman's position should be. This contravention in and of itself coupled with the fact that it was being carried out by a black woman are the twin causes of the swift and severe backlash against *Behind the Scenes*. Mary Todd Lincoln's estranged son, Robert, used his position to successfully lobby the publisher to withdraw every copy of the Keckley exposé from circulation (Fleischner 318). Mary Lincoln had been subject to the national gossip mills for years, yet there is no evidence that other authors of indiscreet accounts about her were as effectively silenced as Keckley was. It would have been particularly galling and embarrassing to have a black woman who she formerly employed commit this offense. Whether the inclusion of these letters was a purposeful choice that Keckley made, or she was double-crossed by a disingenuous book editor, is not so much the point. The fact is that as a civic-minded, well-traveled, and highly connected African American woman, Keckley should have been versed in the traditions of the exposé writings of her era and their aftereffect. In addition, she knew the risk of willingly allowing such personal correspondence to be borrowed and transcribed by a third party. Frances Smith Foster aptly illustrates this point, writing, "Our ancestral scribes knew, maybe better than many emailers do today, that discretion is the best part of valor. Printed material can fall into the wrong hands or can be used for purposes for which it was not intended" (115). While Keckley was conscious of the risk she was taking by sharing private letters, it is likely she did not anticipate the vitriol to which she was subjected after publishing *Behind the Scenes*. Still, her choice was to shield painful parts of her own background from public consumption, while shining a spotlight on the raw internal life of Mary Todd Lincoln, as revealed through their correspondence. Keckley had to have been aware of the possibility that sharing this collection of private letters could end badly; yet she made a calculation that the risk was worth the potential reward of rehabilitating the reputation of her friend Mrs. Lincoln by allowing the public to know the former First Lady through the primary sources she was sharing. For the author, the harsh backlash was a difficult lesson in the limitations of her status as a privileged and independent black woman in the Reconstruction era.

## A Black Woman's Work

To ascertain how and why Keckley found herself in such a tenuous situation after the publication of *Behind the Scenes,* it is critical to see her work in relationship to black conduct literature. Notwithstanding various forms of oppression that existed, racial progress in this era was often subjectively measured by the degree to which one could mimic the accepted standards of morality. Although it is difficult to determine what precise measures defined "success" during such precarious times as the antebellum era, progress could objectively be characterized by access to education, the attainment of professional employment, or self-employment, and ownership of material goods—all of which presumably signified, or led to, increased economic stability. As Keckley relates in the opening pages of her manuscript: "a wrong was inflicted upon me; a cruel custom deprived me of my liberty. . . ." (3). Yet, she persevered to attain access and status. Keckley and others like her were operating against a large body of contrary evidence that arose from the slave era and the period of colonization. So then, it is interesting that Keckley states that her first motivation for taking up the pen as a sword is not to enhance the welfare of her people, or even to promote herself. Rather, she professes that her purpose is to come to the defense of the former First Lady of the United States of America. Keckley contends that her welfare is so inextricably bound with that of Mary Todd Lincoln's that "To defend myself I must defend the lady I have served" (5). It is a bold move to presume that her own word could sway the court of public opinion to support the reputation of a white woman whose stature eclipsed her own at a time when black people had not yet been deemed citizens of the United States. This assumption that the combination of her word and work ethic could protect the reputation of a former First Lady and insulate Keckley's own life from volatility is one of several counts of transgression of racial place she exemplifies.

Black women's conduct literature exists amid prevailing nineteenth-century ideas that devalued and even derided women's work, preferring to confine their societal role to the domestic sphere. Following the Victorian model of separate spheres, the United States Congress defined women's work as a distinct type of enterprise that did not merit monetary compensation (Deegan xxix). Therefore, white society women's labor outside the home was generally undertaken as unpaid volunteerism. In this manner, the idea that women should freely offer their skills to civic or religious organizations that sought to improve the social conditions of the community was not unique to black communities or to black conduct literature. However, Keckley bucked this trend from an early age. She also demonstrated remarkable negotiation skills by managing to earn a salary for the type of essential household work that white women found beneath them.

While she was enslaved, Keckley not only earned enough to support an entire family of "her owners" in St. Louis, but she leveraged her earning power and strong community relationships to buy her freedom and that of her son. Unlike white women of the upper class where the prospect of working would have upended social mores, black women were no strangers to the necessity of work and understood the economic necessity of their earning capacity regardless of class stratifications. Poor, middle class, or wealthy—most black women worked. While many viewed their work as drudgery—and for some it undoubtedly was such—we know from writings like *Behind the Scenes* that others appreciated the agency that employment afforded them, despite the difficulty that working posed in certain circumstances.[7] Keckley used her work in the service of not just her immediate family but for collective improvement. She was a job creator, employing several apprentices in her dressmaking shop and design studio (Fleischner 323). Furthermore, she encouraged by example other black women to build wealth and to pursue entrepreneurship, which made her all the more unusual for the period. The very existence of her business demonstrated how black women could increase their capital gains through sole proprietorships and industrious pursuits. Her living example was a blueprint for how black women could translate their skills into an economic enterprise that benefited the extended black community instead of the former slaveholding community.

In practice, the "black middle class" of the nineteenth century often consisted of women and men like Keckley who were employed in various kinds of domestic service including dress- and lace-making, tailoring, and portering which seem blue collar by today's standards. In many white communities, individuals with similar service positions would have been discounted. However, within black communities, status was determined by a complex constellation of markers including literacy, higher education, political clout in the Republican Party, religious affiliation with the conservative Episcopalian and Presbyterian denominations, an association with successful and highly public community leaders, and membership in exclusive literary salons, giving circles, and civic organizations that looked to shore up black culture. By these measures, Elizabeth Keckley was an extraordinary success. However, that success could not fully insulate her from the impact of discrimination and sexism.

These twin evils affected the amount of time and monetary resources that reformers like Keckley could devote to their causes. Keckley was chosen as Lincoln's dressmaker as much for her talent as for the bargain that her lower-than-market-rate pricing presented for the penny-pinching president's wife (38). Even with an A-list clientele, Keckley struggled to keep her business afloat after Lincoln's assassination. This vulnerability might help explain why she was willing to close her shop indefinitely and relocate to New York City to help her famous—but financially ruined—client, Mary Todd Lincoln. When the business venture Lincoln hatched failed, Keckley sought to improve her chances of financial solvency through publication. In making this decision, Keckley stepped well outside of the racial confines of place. One can surmise that this resilience and persistence resulted from a dogged belief that true freedom remained elusive unless one claimed access to the fullness of citizenship including by giving voice to ideas in the public sphere.

Life circumstances afforded Keckley with access to an informal education;

however, she was an avid proponent of formal instruction as the clearest pathway to uplift for newly emancipated black Americans. While Keckley approaches the labor of writing with dignity and pride, her private letters from Frederick Douglass indicate self-consciousness about her lack of a complete education. She again mentions this sore spot to her former slave masters who note with regret that they did not invest in helping Keckley develop her reading and writing skills, though history would have made this outcome exceedingly unlikely and even illegal in some areas of the United States. While lamenting her own educational gaps, Keckley turned her focus on securing a formalized instructional pathway for her son. Although he could pass for white—and did so to enter the Union Army—it is a telling show of racial pride that he aligned with an educational institution, Wilberforce University, established to provide an education for people of color. Then, as now, middle-class blacks had educational choices however circumscribed by race and financial capacity. This group gave tremendous thought to how they educated themselves and who educated their children. Wilberforce was a prominent institution of choice for many mixed-race blacks whether recently emancipated or from that small set of people who had been freedmen prior to the Civil War. Sending her son there was a clear signal of their status in black society and how important this status was to Keckley (Fleischner 323).[8]

In addition to the work of owning a business and the self-conscious struggle to shore up her own knowledge, Keckley devoted considerable time to the work of community organizing. As a philanthropist, she formed the Contraband Relief Association, a self-help group funded by blacks and white allies to help meet the basic needs of recently enslaved people newly settled in contraband camps throughout the capital. These masses of people represented the first of the nation's several great migrations of black people from the South to the North. Despite her good intentions and efforts to support the less fortunate among her race, Keckley reveals in *Behind the Scenes* the complex class dynamics at play in the Reconstruction era. Keckley relates the story of her encounter with one aged former slave who is finding it difficult to adjust to the seismic shift that Emancipation wrought. The author uses an unflattering form of Southern dialect that displays remarkably little empathy for the woman's circumstances. In this way, Keckley depicts the wide gulf between the black establishment—which she represents—and the unseemly newcomers who the relief fund is assisting. Of this latter group she laments "[p]oor dusky children of slavery, men, and women of my own race—the transition from slavery to freedom was too sudden for you! The bright dreams were too rudely dispelled" (50). Through her story, the camp's inhabitants are viewed as woefully unprepared for new-found independence, and dazed by dislocation from peonage.

Perhaps Keckley was pandering to a white audience, or maybe she did not realize the derogatory slippage in her recounting. Regardless, her tone indicates that while she clearly believed in racial unity of purpose, Keckley also embodied an approach to life that aligned with the classist underside of respectability politics often at work in black conduct literature. Like other authors of black conduct literature, Keckley takes pains to demonstrate that her personal moral character is far above reproach, even if others of her hue struggle to effectively navigate proper comportment. She subscribes to this code of conduct even when it might not be in her best interest. For example, Keckley recounts that when appealing to the prominent white community of customers and acquaintances in her network for loans with which to buy her freedom, her moral code was tested in a dramatic exchange with a potential patron who was skeptical of investing in her dream of freedom, remarking that she would surely leave St. Louis permanently as soon as her liberty was granted. At his admission Keckley reports that she grew, "sick at heart, for I could not accept the signature of this man when he had no faith in my pledges. No; slavery, eternal slavery, rather than be regarding with distrust by those whose respect I esteemed" (23). The reader is asked to believe that Keckley would rather remain a slave than be deemed untrustworthy by an upstanding member of white society. Holding herself to this extremely high standard of virtue situates Keckley in a long lineage of African Americana literature that trades on an exaggerated performance of purity and moral fortitude with the intention of outperforming the supposed moral purity of their white contemporaries. Almost always overpowered by systemic racism, they find that the effectiveness of their efforts becomes less a marker of success than does the mere existence of writing as a form of resistance and transgression. Even if the rhetoric did not yield its intended effect at the time of publication, scholars have long recognized how worthy of celebration this era of black women's writing is for its powerful attempt to redefine and expand Americanization.

## Mrs. N.F. Mossell: Balancing Decorum and Political Desire

A generation later, the hopes of Keckley's text are realized in the self-efficacy of one of the most important bio-bibliographies of it time, *The Work of the Afro-American Woman*, by Mrs. N.F. Mossell. If Keckley's black conduct text is a cautionary tale of the dangers that publication entails, Mossell's approach is certainly more proscribed. In producing a tome that is part sociological study, investigative report, and advice book, Mossell, who conservatively published under her husband's initials as a form of modesty, succeeds in documenting the late nineteenth-century impact of African American women's participation in the political, social, and economic life of the United States.[9] It includes a wide array of resources, from a detailed account of black women's role in the Chicago World's Fair, which Keckley participated in, to a directory of businesses owned by black women. *The Work* is an early articulation of a prototypical black feminist aesthetic that relishes the accomplishments of black women and advocates democratized citizenship, equal opportunities for women's education, and community activism. Because one purpose of Mossell's text was to celebrate the achievements of her contemporaries, it is a highly intertextual of the primary sources in much the same way that *Behind the Scenes* serves as a resource for those looking for inside information on the Lincoln White House.

Despite her conservative edges, Gertrude E.H. Bustill Mossell was quite an independent woman. While raising two daughters, she worked in various professions throughout her long life and was an unflagging civic leader. In addition to being a journalist, clubwoman, educator, and public speaker, she was a consummate society woman. Each of her publications, which included children's books and news columns, is a testament to the value of black women's work and a reminder of the important social work they had yet to do. Born in Philadelphia, she received a top-notch education thanks to the liberal beliefs and financial security of her prominent black Quaker family. Her ancestors had been free for three generations before her birth, and her parents instilled their progeny with a respect for their heritage and a duty to use their education, talents, and any concomitant privileges to serve black Americans who had not benefited from such auspicious beginnings. It is plausible that her family lessons included instruction in the language of social and moral redemption and recuperation that pervaded the late nineteenth century.

Codified behavioral codes and black Americans' embodiment of these tenets are intertwined with a painful collective experience of loss in reference to black women's ability to maintain control of their personhood, standards of living, and sexual encounters in a time when self-possession was violently threatened as a matter of course. As W.E.B. Du Bois avers, the character of black womanhood was suffering from the effects of over two centuries "of systematic legal defilement of Negro women . . . [which] had meant not only the loss of ancient African chastity, but also the hereditary weight of a mass of corruption from white adulterers, threatening almost the obliteration of the Negro home" (Du Bois 50). Akin to the relationship Elizabeth Keckley had established with Frederick Douglass and Henry Highland Garnet, Gertrude Mossell could point to a number of race men like Du Bois to whom she could appeal for allegiance with her cause. Like their black female counterparts, these black male intellectuals, such as Reverend Alexander Crummell, W.E.B. Du Bois, Booker T. Washington, Charles Chesnutt, and Martin Delaney, also published work on the subject of virtue and conduct. Their work has been consistently acknowledged as a cornerstone of black intellectual thought on morality and the conduct of life. Late nineteenth-century conduct texts penned by black men often denote the black woman as the pillar of cultural importance and communal integrity, which indicates the significance of gendered behavioral codes and the necessity of evaluating these codes through a female lens. In fact, Felipe Smith surmises that the "discourse of utopian black ladyhood emerged as forcefully from the struggles of black men over territorial rights to the 'previously colonized' bodies of black women as from the women's club movement, whose agitation for feminist causes put them at odds with the proprietary claims" of black patriarchy (Smith 115). While acknowledging their brother allies, the work of black conduct literature written by black women focuses on women's own efforts to redress black female virtue. Thus, prescriptive cultural production by black women deserves to be analyzed in the context of extensive discourse on black women and morality of which Keckley is certainly a foremother.

Rather than reflecting an atmosphere of pompous class-stratification and exceptionalism, the bio-encyclopedia or bio-bibliography was intended to be a source of pride and hope for black Americans of various means. The popularity of the genre is an indication of this fact. Literally, hundreds of bio-encyclopedia collections were published between the 1880s and 1930s. These comprehensive texts substantiate the results of a few decades of freedom and demonstrate that access to educational and business opportunities had indeed led many African Americans to achieve monetary and social success. Because terms such as progress, advancement, and uplift were all measured through educational and professional achievements, the bio-bibliography was positioned as an important sociological tool to substantiate the achievements and potential of black Americans to themselves and to those outside the race.

    The pastiche format of *The Work* contributes to its value as a unique form of black cultural production. It functions as both a prescriptive text and an anthology of African American essays, poetry, and journalism. Mossell describes the black woman's place in American history and notes the relevance of improvements in race and gender discrimination that were made toward the end of the nineteenth century. In addition, she presents an argument that introduces a proposal for reclaiming the value of the black woman while simultaneously uplifting the race. Her project equates "race pride" with "national feeling," which evokes the connection between uplift and patriotism, or more specifically between blackness and citizenship (9). She concludes her lengthy summary of the history of Africans in America with a call for blacks to be increasingly involved in significant reform campaigns of the late nineteenth century. One of her purposes is to outline the characteristics of a "race woman" and to provide some advice on how to successfully negotiate this role while maintaining a thriving household (Mossell xxv).[10] Her aim is to provide a road map and record book of the many ways that black women were extending their influence in the domestic sphere and in political agency and community activism.

    In addition to filling her conduct book with practical details for improving her readers' quality of life, Mossell melds her experiences as an educator and a journalist to make the text accessible and practical by dealing primarily with what she regards as "popular questions" (9). The tenor of Mossell's text considers both a highly educated audience, and those community members who are less formally educated. She consistently uses a personal and intimate tone and takes care to relate her ideas to a broad African American public. She does this so much so that she solicits the reader's feedback in anticipation of updating her advice book. She says, "the author would be grateful to her readers if, by personal communication, they would make any correction or suggestion looking toward a more extended and revised edition of this work in the near future" (5). Although a revised publication of *The Work* never appeared, the text concludes with an appendix that lists the names of seven more notable black women whose names were received after her printing deadline in the bio-bibliographic section of her book. In addition to these seven individuals, Mossell includes a collective congratulatory note to "a number of young women [who] have graduated as trained nurses from the Provident Hospital, Chicago" and to twenty-four African American women graduates from Johns Hopkins University (177). Mossell bookends her text with connections to the growing community of African American women who have aspirations to improve their lives by attaining an education, working outside the home as businesswomen and professionals, and by promoting themselves and each other. Importantly, Mossell's solicitation and promotion of black professional women in *The Work* is a successful attempt at self-actualization. In this way, Keckley is a foremother of Mossell, and the former exemplifies the latter's ideal of how enterprising black women should conduct themselves. Both Keckley and Mossell demonstrate that they take themselves and their work seriously enough to assert their expertise to a broad audience. Serving as a living example to those within one's immediate circle of influence is one thing, but extending that value to others through writing is a critical leap that few nineteenth-century black women leaders took.

Mossell bookends her text with the chronicles of black women—like Keckley—who aspired to improve their lives by attaining an education, working outside the home as businesswomen and professionals, and promoting themselves and each other. While those of her time considered Keckley's self-promotion vulgar, one can wager that Mossell would have understood and empathized with her attempts to publicize her business. Indeed, Keckley's trade is the sort that would have merited inclusion in Mossell's directory, had her storefront remained open by the late 1800s. As it stands, Keckley's grand experiment with publicity as a form of self-preservation did not produce the desired outcome. Instead, she forfeited her strained, but valuable, friendship with Mary Lincoln, and lost several white customers due to the dust-up. However, for all that she sacrificed by venturing into this early version of direct marketing that traded on her products and her point of view, she maintained her pride of authorship and self-possession. When placed in historical context, her textual demonstration of black behavior and white reaction to it lay bare the complicated notion of speaking for oneself in an era when black women were not said to have the ability to form coherent logic, let alone be seen as offering their testimony as part of petition to help someone as powerful as a former First Lady. Nevertheless, Keckley deemed it necessary to utilize the written word as a weapon against the misrepresentations of her friend and by extension her own self.

By example of her successful entrepreneurship, Keckley dared to encourage women to access their earning power through ingenuity. But when she stepped outside the confines of a traditional role for a woman of her era, Keckley's bravery backfired and she was a victim of unsparing retaliation. One can only imagine that Keckley's reputation might have been assisted by Mossell had they been contemporaries. In *The Work,* Mossell praises the industry and economic prowess of black women "who have built up businesses for themselves that net thousands of dollars" (24). She notes that independence and financial security are important components of a society conducive to the development of educated and noble black women. In her estimation, black women needed more supporters who had established their foundations so securely that they could help each other without worry of destabilizing their own standing. Additionally, Mossell recognizes class distinctions in the black community with a more nuanced approach than Keckley afforded. Mossell charges that women who have sufficient resources must utilize their time, finances, and intellect to promote the advancement of black women. In this sense, both of these black conduct texts include a through line of racial uplift—that self-help ideology that describes one prevalent response of educated black Americans to legal segregation.[11] Through conduct texts, blacks sought to counter the racist notion that they were inferior by incorporating racial identity into ostensibly universal categories of Western progress and civilization. It is important to note that the desire to establish security through education opportunity and meaningful work stemmed from the appeal of full citizenship and equal rights to the economic benefits of American society, not from a pathological aspiration to become white.

Through the Keckley and Mossell texts, readers can trace the two-fold intended outcome of black conduct literature unmerited arguments that barred black Americans from exercising the privileges of full citizenship in the United States. One purpose is to promote the positive impact of access to education and economic opportunity. The other outcome is that the genre forces readers to contend with black women's recognition through their participation in the public sphere. Many challenges faced black women who claimed and publicized their knowledge of accepted "American" social and economic practices. However, one of the most damaging misreadings of black women's writing in this era is that it suffers from a preoccupation with gaining acceptance from majority culture—and that is not the line of thought being invoked here. Keckley and Mossell did not seek to imitate knowledge of the values of dominant culture because they had an inferiority complex. Rather, they aptly inculcated the values of majority culture because their livelihoods depended on being able to interpret and influence the style, tastes, and predilections of the majority. It is telling how much these same themes resonate today. As nineteenth-century literary black women struggled to create space for themselves and their ideas in the context of a societal fabric hell-bent on solidifying their erasure and inferiority, so too do black women journalists, scholars, entrepreneurs, and essayists in today's knowledge and creative economies struggle to achieve representation and recognition on their merits. Fortunately, these early examples of black conduct literature provide an entrée into a lineage of hope and resilience to which the current generation can refer for inspiration and encouragement in the midst of ongoing struggle.

### NOTES

1. For instance, Ann Gere's *Intimate Lives* argues that Jewish, Mormons, and other marginalized women groups employed the similar lobbying tactics, which now seem comparatively conservative.

2. Wheatley's private letters do reveal her pointed political opinions. But, of course, they were not published during Wheatley's lifetime.

3. Maria Stewart's short lecturing career in the 1830s stands at the forefront of a history of black feminist activism. Other speakers and writers who followed by the 1880s include Mary Ann Shadd Cary, Frances E.W. Harper, Julia A.J. Foote, Mary Church Terrell, Ida Wells-Barnett, and many other active participants of the black women's club movement.

4. Scholars have increasingly delved into the effective and inventive ways that nineteenth-century African Americans navigated, participated in, and challenged the systems and tenets of Victorianism and Protestantism. Frances Smith Foster's *'Til Death or Distance Do Us Part* (2010) and Tera Hunter's *To 'Joy My Freedom* (1997) are particularly cogent examples of this line of research.

5. Keckley has commanded varying degrees of public interest in the twenty-first century leading to a stage play of her story and her inclusion as a historical figure in Steven Spielberg's *Lincoln* (2012). In terms of scholarship, Xiomara Santamarina's

*Belabored Professions* (2005) and Carolyn Sorisio's essay "Unmasking the Genteel Performer" in *African American Review* contain wonderfully nuanced readings of Keckley's autobiography.

6. In previous research, I expound on a more detailed argument of how discussions of behavior, dress, and public comportment permeate much of African American literature from 1880 to the contemporary moment such that they constitute a codified generic tradition, termed black conduct literature (Francis).

7. See Xiomara Santamarina's *Belabored Professions* for an extended reading of *Behind the Scenes* in this context.

8. Her association with Wilberforce lasted several decades. In the late nineteenth century Keckley was a sewing instructor there.

9. Mossell's husband, Nathan Francis Mossell, was a noted surgeon and the first black graduate of University of Pennsylvania School of Medicine.

10. In the African American tradition, a "race woman" is one who dedicates herself and her life's work to uplifting the social, economic, and psychological conditions of African Americans. This designation fell out of favor after the Harlem Renaissance, largely because the definition required black women to foreground racial identity as opposed to their gender.

11. By 1890 "educated" black Americans numbered about 2 percent of the black population (Gaines, xiv). Gaines does not define what level of training or skills that constitutes "educated" in this context.

## WORKS CITED

Danky, J.P., & Hady, M., eds. *African American Newspapers and Periodicals: A National Bibliography.* Cambridge: Harvard University Press, 1999.

Du Bois, W.E.B. *Souls of Black Folk.* Edited and Introduction by David W. Blight and Robert Gooding-Williams. New York: St. Martin's Press, 1998.

Fleischner, Jennifer. *Mrs. Lincoln and Mrs. Keckly: The Remarkable Story of the Friendship Between a First Lady and a Former Slave.* New York: Broadway Books, 2003.

Foster, Frances Smith. *'Til Death or Distance Do Us Part: Love and Marriage in African America.* New York: Oxford University Press, 2010.

Francis, A.X. "Hometraining and How to Be: Black Conduct Literature and the Politics of Identity in United States Culture, 1880–2000." Dissertation. Vanderbilt University, 2004.

Gere, A.R. *Intimate Practices: Literacy and Cultural Work in U.S. Women's Clubs, 1880–1920.* Champaign: University of Illinois Press, 1999.

Higginbotham, E.B. *Righteous Discontent: The Women's Movement in the Black Baptist Church, 1880-1920.* Cambridge: Harvard University Press, 1994.

Hunter, T.W. *To 'Joy My Freedom: Southern Black Women's Lives and Labors After the Civil War.* Cambridge: Harvard University Press, 1997.

Keckley, Elizabeth. *Behind the Scenes: Or, Thirty Years a Slave, and Four Years in the White House.* New York: Penguin Books, 2005.

Santamarina, Xiomara. *Belabored Professions: Narratives of African American Working Womanhood.* Chapel Hill: University of North Carolina Press, 2005.

Sorisio, Carolyn. "Unmasking the Genteel Performer: Elizabeth Keckley's *Behind the Scenes* and the Politics of Public Wrath." *African American Review* 34.1 (2000).

———. "Unmasking the Genteel Performer: Elizabeth Keckley's *Behind the Scenes* and the Politics of Public Wrath." *African American Review* (Spring 2000). Accessed 17 December 2015 via www.questia.com.

CHAPTER NINE

**NANETTE MORTON**

# Private Spaces, Public Meanings

IN HIS STUDY OF plantation architecture, John Michael Vlach writes that the ordering of slaveholders' large farms and larger plantations, still discernable in photographs taken more than half a century later, reflects the slaveowners' desire to "mark their dominance over nature and other men" through spaces designed to establish, reinforce, and maintain "a strict, hierarchical order" (1–5). Slaves lived and worked in spaces which emphasized their inferior status and permitted their owners to scrutinize and control them. Faced with such spatial organization, slaves "simply appropriated, as marginalized people often do, the environments to which they were assigned" (16).

Slave narratives most commonly represent the narrators' escape from the confining and defining slave space of the South, to the free and subjectivity-granting space of Canada or the Northern states. In escaping from Maryland to New York, for example, Frederick Douglass achieved a fundamental change in status—from chattel to man, from bond to free. In *Narrative of the Life of Frederick Douglass*, Douglass de-emphasizes the racial prejudice of the North, while triumphantly emphasizing his own ability to earn money as a free man in a free space: "there was no Master Hugh standing ready, the moment I earned the money, to rob me of it" (325).

But the free space of the North, like the slave space of the South, is lacking in that it too fails to provide the emotional value of *place*. While geographer Yi-Fu Tuan defines space as an area that gives one "the sense of being free," he describes place as "centers of felt value where biological needs are met" (2–4). Far from being free, slave space is the instrument of the slave's confinement. For this reason, place becomes particularly important, as bell hooks notes in her definition of what she refers to as *homeplace*:

Historically, African American people believed that the construction of a homeplace, however fragile and tenuous (the slave hut, the wooden shack), had a radical political dimension. Despite the brutal reality of racial apartheid, of domination, one's homeplace was the one site where one could freely confront the issue of humanization, where one could resist. (42)

Homeplace's value derives from the slaves' determination to recognize each other's humanity even as the inhabitants also occupy Southern slave space, where they are defined as objects. During both the post- and antebellum eras, homeplace serves as "a safe place where black people could affirm one another and by so doing heal many of the wounds inflicted by racist domination" (42). In *My Bondage and My Freedom,* Frederick Douglass eulogizes his grandmother's cabin, the early homeplace he barely mentions in his first narrative. A fisherwoman and farmer of some skill, Douglass's grandmother "was . . . more provident than most of her neighbors"(36). Douglass depicts her homeplace as the site of fertility, nurturance, and plenty. In *Incidents in the Life of a Slave Girl,* Harriet Jacobs takes refuge in the homeplace of her free grandmother, who is "the mistress of a snug little home, surrounded by the necessaries of life" (17).

In slave space, however, the boundaries of homeplace are always permeable and liable to disruption. Douglass is removed from his grandmother's homeplace to the Lloyd plantation by the age of seven. Jacobs, too, is removed from her parents' home to the domestic slave space of her owner. Jacobs underlines the nature of the master's domestic space (which is simultaneously slave space) by writing of her married aunt, who sleeps on the mistress's bedroom floor, rather than with her husband (148). Jacobs herself is denied the right to marry and is sexually pursued by her master. The only way she can escape this "cage of obscene birds" is by hiding in her grandmother's attic, a limbo that is neither slave nor free (52).

Because Douglass is a man, his descriptions of post-slavery life concentrate not on the ability to establish a homeplace whose boundaries cannot be breached by slavery (an ability imperiled by the Fugitive Slave Act), but on the public spaces that represent the public sphere in Northern free space. In *My Bondage and My Freedom,* properly recognized subjectivity is achieved with the occupation of public space, and the recognition of one's rights as a citizen. Public conveyances, therefore, become Douglass's battle sites, as Douglass is forcibly dragged from the first-class carriage of one railway car, and shunned when he occupies others (400–03). In Douglass's *Narrative*, the abolitionist speaker's platform is the ultimate free space, since it betokens the free man's participation in the political life of the nation. In *My Bondage and My Freedom*, however, the stage is yet another site of discrimination, as Douglass's white abolitionist colleagues censor the contents of his speeches and disapprove of his plans to start a newspaper. "'A woodsawyer' offering himself to the public as an editor! A slave brought up in the depths of ignorance, assuming to instruct the highly civilized people of the North in the principles of liberty, justice and humanity! The thing looked absurd" (393–94). In *My Bondage and My Freedom* the British Isles, where Douglass goes on an extensive lecture tour, replace the Northern states as truly free space.

For Douglass, access to public space and the public sphere is the ultimate proof of freedom and subjectivity. For Harriet Jacobs, however, the space in which her subjectivity is to be recognized is in keeping with the nineteenth-century ideal, and as such, it is private rather than public. Similarly, Jacobs champions the enslaved woman's right to occupy a domestic space unthreatened by the economic and sexual depredations of slavery. In *Incidents in the Life of a Slave Girl*, therefore, she depicts the slave-owner's domestic space as a slave space which perverts the nineteenth-century's domestic ideal of nurturance and chastity. Jacobs writes that her mistress "would station herself in the kitchen, and wait till [dinner] was dished and then spit in all the kettles and pans that had been used for cooking. She did this to prevent the cook and her children from eking out their meager fare with the remains of the gravy and other scrapings" (12). The master, in turn, "pays no regard to his marriage vows" and sexually assaults Jacobs, whispering "foul words in my ear" and peopling "my young mind with unclean images" (36–37).

Jacobs must argue for her right to access a domestic space of her own, not only because she has been a slave, but because the loss of her chastity and her apparent lack of fragility, emphatically exclude her from the nineteenth-century's ideal of True Womanhood, which demands whiteness, fragility, and sexual purity of the wives and mothers who are the center of the family's domestic space (Accardo and Portelli 84). While Jacobs expresses remorse for her "fall" (she eventually bears the children of a freely chosen white lover), she also sharply criticizes the value system which systematically denies the right to unthreatened domestic space to enslaved African-Americans even as it valorizes the sanctity of the home (Jacobs 54). Jacobs declares her right to occupy her own domestic space with her children. Nonetheless, when she ends her narrative, economic necessity in the free space of the North prevents her from establishing a home of her own (201).

Standing in sharp contrast to the narratives of Jacobs and Douglass, Elizabeth Keckley's narrative *Behind the Scenes: Or, Thirty Years a Slave, and Four Years in the White House* (1868) draws together the African American's right to access both an undisturbed, private, domestic homeplace and the public sphere in free postbellum space. Published seven years after *Incidents*, only three of the book's eighteen chapters deal with Keckley's life as a slave. Instead, Keckley focuses on her later achievements; already a notable dressmaker, she was able to climb to the pinnacle of her profession within a few years after her manumission. It is her connection with people of prominence—particularly with Abraham and Mary Lincoln—that makes up the bulk of the narrative. More important to Keckley than the perils of slavery is her access to the White House as a *modiste,* nurse, and confidante, roles indicative of her social and economic success. As Frances Smith Foster notes, the very title page of Keckley's *Behind the Scenes* stresses "a movement up from slavery . . . emphasizing the social distance traveled" (Foster, "Autobiography after Emancipation" 45).

How different, then, is Keckley's triumphant social progress from that of her antebellum counterpart Harriet Jacobs, who, in the words of Valerie Smith, "escapes overwhelming persecutions only by choosing her own space of confinement" (Smith, "Loopholes of Retreat" 213). As William Andrews notes, the action of Jacobs's employer, who buys the fugitive slave's freedom without her consent, "inevitably circumscribes the freedom that it bestows; to obtain one sort of freedom, Jacobs must submit to another form of powerlessness" (Andrews, "Changing Moral Discourse" 231). Jacobs's personal sense of gratitude, coupled with her economic circumstances, binds her to her employer (Jacobs 201). "Jacobs seems to be saying that power, the ability to act on and *realize* freedom, stems, in the North as well as the South, not from principle but from property, from that which can be claimed like a home or a hearthstone as 'my own'" (Andrews, "Changing Moral Discourse" 231). Even though Jacobs can legally claim her own body, this claim does not automatically provide access to a personal domestic space equal to that occupied by the married, middle-class white women to whom her narrative is addressed.

While Jacobs champions her right to her own domestic space by establishing another standard of virtue for herself, Keckley sidesteps the century's image of an ideal woman altogether. In her narrative, hard work and perseverance take the place of a chastity that is not hers, as a slave, to maintain. In spite of the limitations of her role, it is Keckley's ability to occupy and form affective ties within the White House, as much as her possession of a private space, which indicates her subjectivity has been publicly recognized.

The White House was (and is) the most public and private of spaces. The site of the country's governance, it is public space and the center of a public sphere exclusively dominated by white males. As the president's official residence, however, the White House is, simultaneously, a private, domestic space. Keckley's role as seamstress places her squarely in the private sphere and the domestic space to which it is confined. At the same time, Keckley is a public figure in her own right; a successful businesswoman, she is also a recognized leader in the African American community and an organizer of charitable events and institutions. Even though Keckley is not officially attached to the White House's areas of governance, it may be argued that her position as free woman and increasingly influential and indispensable factotum within this space, coupled with her relative prominence outside of it, is emblematic of African Americans' new role as free participants within the newly reconstituted republic and the spaces that are the sites of its public sphere. Once a symbol of Keckley's slave status and the site of her oppression, her occupation of another's domestic space becomes a mark of her freedom and her participation in matters of national importance.

Only after the publication of her book, when she is cast off by the surviving Lincolns and reviled by the press, does Keckley recognize that such an interpretation was a misstep: An employee and an African American in a world where social boundaries, despite dramatic changes wrought by emancipation, are still rigidly defined, she is an "inferior" who has presumed to talk out of turn. Keckley has assumed that her occupation of the domestic space of the White House and her role within it accord her the public recognition of her subjectivity that would allow her to comment on that space within the public sphere. It does not. The harshness that characterized her narrative's critical reception is apparently prompted by a desire to put Keckley "in her place," a desire that presages the repressive inequality that will characterize postbellum race relations.

Like Douglass and Jacobs, Keckley documents the early disruption of the family homeplace. Keckley's father is forced to leave his wife and daughter to go west with his master. When Keckley's mother mourns her husband's absence, her impatient mistress tells her to stop "putting on airs . . . there are plenty more men about here, and if you want a husband so badly, stop your crying and go find another" (Keckley 25). When the fourteen-year-old Keckley is separated from her mother and sent to live in the household of her master's eldest son, she does not protest: She has already learned that grief is impermissible.

Characteristically, Elizabeth Keckley reminds the reader of her economic value. "From the very first I did the work of three servants, and yet I was scolded and regarded with distrust," she reports (32). Beaten into submission, she also experiences sexual abuse. Unlike Jacobs, however, Keckley does not express guilt: She is not at fault and she refuses to shoulder blame, writing, after she gives birth to a son, "If my poor boy ever suffered any humiliating pangs on account of birth, he could not blame his mother, for God knows that she did not wish to give him life, he must blame the edicts of that society which deemed it no crime to undermine the virtue of girls in my then position" she writes (39). As William Andrews notes, Keckley's lack of sexual purity "is basically irrelevant to the image Keckley intends to create for herself in the postbellum social order" ("Changing Moral Discourse" 232). The enslaved woman's economic worth is tied to reproduction; the white middle class woman's worth is tied to her chastity. In detailing earning power, Keckley thoroughly separates her sexuality from any discussion of worth.

Her worth, however, is proven with her craft; she states clearly that "With my needle I kept bread in the mouths of seventeen persons for two years and five months" (45). By doing so, Keckley prevents her impecunious master (now Hugh Garland, husband of Anne Burwell) from sending Keckley's mother—the family's "Mammy"—out to work for strangers. The master's proposal to hire out "Mammy" violates the very emotional dependence that he has fostered for the family's own benefit. In Keckley's words, the master has "proposed to destroy each tendril of affection, to cloud the sunshine of her existence when the day was drawing to a close" (45). The pseudo-familial tie between Keckley's mother and the Garland family does not supersede the fundamental tie of ownership and economic exploitation. Referred to as a member of the family, Keckley's mother is, nonetheless, in danger of being expelled in the interests of maintaining a domestic space that she herself has been denied. In spite of the stereotype, which designates Mammy as the woman in charge of the household, this example illustrates that she was not free of the master, who could sell her body, her labor, and her children at will.

Although the tie of ownership produces an unspoken but barely concealed ambivalence, Keckley does not downplay the emotional bond between herself and her owners. In one letter, she bids her mother to "[give] my love to all the family, both white and black" (41). Keckley later devotes one chapter of the latter part of the narrative to a kindly description of a postbellum visit, an indication that her emotional attachment is real. At the same time, she never forgets that any affective tie between master and slave is superseded by the tie of ownership. Buying herself is the only way in which she can legally sever that tie and leave the Garlands' domestic space in order to create a homeplace that will not be disrupted by master's will.

Through self-purchase Keckley also confirms her ability to take her place in the capitalist market as a free woman. In order to buy herself and her son, she must find six white businessmen to act as guarantors. One of her potential signatories expresses his doubts, saying, "When you reach New York the abolitionists will tell you what savages we are, and they will prevail on you to stay there, and we shall never see you again" (52). The man's doubts plunge Keckley into despair. "I was beginning to feel sick at heart," she writes, "for I could not accept the signature of this man when he had no faith in my pledges" (52). Her description of the grief brought on by the white man's doubt is far more explicit than any of her reactions to other, personal losses. As William Andrews notes,

> No one, least of all Keckley herself, is concerned about this slave woman's sexual respectability; at issue is something much more important—her financial reputation. Whether or not having a spotless business reputation in the antebellum South mattered all that much to Keckley, we may be sure that she wanted her *postbellum* audience to know of her unswerving fealty to the ethics of the market place. A self-supporting businesswoman like Keckley could hardly afford to do otherwise. ("Changing Moral Discourse" 233)

Finally, the money is raised by a group of Keckley's customers, including, appropriately enough, a woman named Mrs. Le Bourgois. Proud of her enterprising spirit and the hard-won trust it engendered, Keckley reprints the complex paperwork surrounding her emancipation. It takes her five years to repay her sponsors. After doing so, she departs to Washington, DC, where she rents "apartments in a good locality, and soon had a good run of custom" (Keckley 65).

When Keckley was a slave, she occupied and was defined by slave space, an area that overlapped the master's domestic space. Although she now rents rooms to conduct her business, she often works in the domestic space of her employers. But while her occupation of the domestic spaces of others was once a mark of slave status, it now marks her economic success and public recognition of her status as a free businesswoman. Having built a reputation for reliability and talent, Keckley is soon recommended to Varina Davis, the wife of Jefferson Davis, the man who would later become the president of the Confederacy. Keckley writes that she " . . . was employed by [Mrs. Davis] on the recommendation of one of my patrons and her intimate friend, Mrs. Captain Hetsill" (66). On the eve of the Civil War, Varina Davis offers to take Keckley South, predicting that "when the war breaks out, the colored people will suffer in the North. The northern people will look upon them as the cause of the war, and I fear, in their exasperation, will be inclined to treat you harshly" (71). Keckley rejects Varina Davis's offer of protection, concluding that "the people [of the North] would fight for the flag they pretended to venerate so highly" (72).

Varina Davis appeals to Keckley's instinct for self-preservation. She also appeals to the dressmaker's ambition: When the South wins, Varina reasons, Jefferson Davis will become president and Keckley will work at the White House. While Keckley's loyalties will not permit her to support a proslavery regime, her ambition is hardly in abeyance. In a matter of weeks, General McClean's wife provides Keckley with a recommendation that secures her an introduction to the White House. After an interview and some haggling (during which Keckley drops Varina Davis's name and acquiesces to Mary Lincoln's request that she "work cheap"), Keckley agrees to make Mary Lincoln's gown for President Lincoln's first formal reception at the White House, for which Keckley notes that she " . . . dressed [Mrs. Lincoln's] hair, and arranged the dress on her. It fitted nicely, and [Mrs. Lincoln] was pleased"(88). The president tells his wife that she looks "charming" and, in words of praise that the *modiste* undoubtedly savors, says that "Mrs. Keckley has met with great success" (88). And indeed she has: By her own estimation, Keckley completes some fifteen or sixteen dresses for the president's wife in one season alone.

Although Lincoln biographer Strozier suggests that Mary Todd Lincoln "attached herself to Lincoln with all the intensity resulting from those unfulfilled childhood longings," she also attaches herself to Elizabeth Keckley, replicating the most important relationship of her childhood (Strozier 73). Lincoln is the daughter of Robert Todd, a successful lawyer, businessman, politician, and slave-owner from Lexington, Kentucky. Mary's mother died when she was seven, and Mary and her six siblings were primarily cared for by slaves "Mammy Sally" and Judy, a nursemaid. In his psychological analysis of the Lincolns, Charles Strozier writes that Mary, "seemingly cried out for support, love, and nurturing from her father, her missing mother, and anyone else who might help her" (Strozier 73).

If Keckley's relationship with Mary Lincoln lacks the violent compulsion that was her experience as a slave, it is still characterized by both the economic inequality and the emotional interdependence of the relationship between Keckley's mother and her owners, the Garlands. Elizabeth Keckley's willingness to accept her position as the First Lady's pseudo-mammy suggests that in spite of the fact that she has established a space of her own in the workrooms she so proudly maintains, this space is not a homeplace. Keckley dissolved her marriage and sent her son away to Wilberforce University in Ohio. Her space, therefore, lacks the emotional bonds that would make it a homeplace. It is perhaps for this reason that she is susceptible to Mary Todd Lincoln's affection, dependence, and apparent recognition of her as a subject. She is, as Mrs. Lincoln writes plaintively at one point, the First Lady's "best living friend" (Keckley 301). Beset as it is by social and economic inequities, the friendship draws Keckley into the Lincoln domestic space.

Perhaps the best example of Keckley's sense of inclusion is her description of a speech President Lincoln delivers from the White House shortly before his assassination. Arriving at the White House, Keckley sees Lincoln "looking over his notes and muttering to himself" (177). At the appointed time, the president "advanced to the centre window over the door to make his address" (176). While Lincoln faces the lawn in order to address the public, he remains inside one of the upper rooms and within sight of his private preparations, a position that highlights the public/private nature of the White House. Significantly,

Keckley is *inside* with the Lincolns, rather than outside, with the majority of the audience. With Keckley and Mary Todd Lincoln are "a number of distinguished gentlemen, as well as ladies" (177). Keckley interprets her presence as a symbol of the acceptance of African Americans into the public space in which the public sphere is conducted.

At the same time, we know that Keckley is present in a domestic capacity; when she asks if she can attend, Mary Todd Lincoln readily acquiesces, adding, "By the way, come in time to dress me before the speaking commences" (175). With this in mind, the symbolism suggested by Keckley's presence changes. Does her position as the First Family's hireling suggest that African Americans, in spite of emancipation, will still be "hewers of wood and drawers of water?" Keckley forestalls such an interpretation, however; although she notes the class differences between herself and the president's wife on other occasions, she de-emphasizes her inferior social status here, portraying herself as a reliable witness and thus, in some sense, a participant in public events once barred to the former slave.

While Mary Lincoln begins by consulting with "Lizabeth" about her wardrobe, Elizabeth Keckley soon begins to fill other roles. Called to the White House to nurse gravely ill eleven-year-old Willie Lincoln, Keckley comforts both the child and his desperate parents. When he dies, she prepares the child's body for burial. Her description of the Lincolns' grief includes a lengthy eulogy written by Nathaniel P. Willis—the "Mr. Bruce" of Harriet Jacobs's narrative. The death of Keckley's own son on a Civil War battlefield is almost an afterthought, mentioned only in order to record Keckley's grateful reception of the First Lady's "golden words of comfort." Fulsome in describing the Lincolns' grief, Keckley is economical when it comes to her own; she does not even mention the name of the son whose death is "a sad blow to me" (105).

Jennifer Fleischner suggests that this description of Willie Lincoln's death holds profound psychological importance for Keckley, who, forbidden to mourn her losses in childhood, substitutes the Lincolns' grief for her own. Slavery had also encouraged Keckley to expend her emotional resources on the white slave-owner's family instead of her own, a psychological process she repeats in freedom. This is compounded by the likelihood that Keckley's son never lived in Washington. The description of Willie Lincoln's death in his parents' domestic space and his funeral in the East Room of the White House, therefore, substitutes for this lack in Keckley's life, while her supportive presence strengthens the emotional ties between herself and Mrs. Lincoln.

Even as Keckley's identification with the Lincolns becomes stronger, she maintains an independent role outside of the Lincoln household. While Keckley's occupation of a space within the White House symbolizes the position that African Americans will potentially take in the public sphere of a newly reconstituted republic, her position as the founder and president of the Contraband Relief Association is a concrete realization of this potential. In 1862, African American refugees begin to flock to Washington "fresh from the benighted regions of the plantation" (111). The newly freed slaves had hoped to find an Edenic free space; instead, they find that "mute appeals for help too often were answered by cold neglect" (112). Impoverished and accustomed to the dependence that paternalism had encouraged and enforced, blacks are spoken of as "an idle, dependent race" (112). Keckley, industrious and independent, has an idea: "If the white people can give festivals to raise funds for the relief of suffering soldiers, why should not the well-to-do colored people go to work to do something for the benefit of the suffering blacks … [T]he next Sunday I made a suggestion in the colored church, that a society of colored people be formed to labor for the benefit of the unfortunate freedmen" (113). Frederick Douglass matches Mrs. Lincoln's contribution of $200 and waives his customary lecture fee for fundraisers, while other prominent African Americans, such as the pastor and antislavery activist Henry Highland Garnet, also contribute to the cause.

Keckley's economic distance from refugees' desperation, coupled with her ability to organize efforts to relieve it, is proof, in this narrative, that African Americans are worthy of taking part in the public sphere of the newly reconstituted republic. To cement this impression, Keckley describes both Frederick Douglass's admission into the official celebration of Abraham Lincoln's second inauguration and her own inclusion in Lincoln's tour of the defeated South.

The first event, Keckley writes, "was one of the largest receptions ever held in Washington" (Keckley 158). African Americans, however, were explicitly denied entrance. After learning Douglass had been denied entry, a white congressman asks Lincoln himself if he would like to be introduced to Douglass. Lincoln obliges by shaking hands, expressing his admiration, and telling Douglass that he "[values Douglass's] opinions highly." Douglass proudly recounts the president's remarks for the benefit of Keckley and others at "a friend's house where a[n undoubtedly more inclusive] reception was being held"(160). Neither Douglass nor Keckley protest the exclusion of the rest of Washington's African American citizens that evening.

This sense that African Americans—or, more accurately, a select few—are finally being admitted into the country's public sphere is cemented by Keckley's account of her own inclusion in the Lincolns' circle. When the Confederate capital of Richmond falls in 1865, Mrs. Lincoln asks Mrs. Keckley to accompany her as she joins Lincoln on a victorious foray into the defeated South. Presumably, Keckley is Mary Todd Lincoln's paid companion. Keckley says nothing of this inequitable relationship. Instead, she revels in her ability to occupy what has so newly become a free space.

Along with the rest of the presidential party, Keckley enters the now-deserted Confederate Capitol building in Richmond. The building still shows signs of a rapid and desperate evacuation: "desks [were] broken, and papers scattered promiscuously in the hurried flight of the Confederate Congress. I picked up a number of papers, and, by curious coincidence, the resolution prohibiting all free coloured people from entering the state of Virginia" (Keckley 166). Keckley's entry into the state, and into the Capitol building itself, represents the triumphant breaching of such boundaries. As a symbolic gesture, the once-proscribed freewoman "sat in the chair that Jefferson Davis sometimes occupied; also in the chair of the Vice-President, Alexander H. Stephens" (166). Her subjectivity officially recognized by the Emancipation Proclamation, Keckley is free to occupy the newly designated free space.

This new ability to be recognized as a subject in what was formerly slave space is paralleled by Keckley's acceptance into the domestic space of her former owners—an event characterized not by triumph but by a careful and healing reconciliation. Keckley's reconciliation does not excuse the brutality of slavery. Rather, as William Andrews has noted, the visit and subsequent autobiography expresses "a mood of optimism" and "a sincere desire to use... personal testimony as part of the national healing process that [Keckley]... hoped would follow the Civil War" (Andrews, "Reunion" 8).

Keckley's emotional ties to the South lead her "home" to the people who once deprived her family of its homeplace. Because Keckley, unlike her antebellum counterparts, is not attempting to gain support for the abolitionist cause, she is free to recognize two seemingly irreconcilable elements: Formerly exploited, she nonetheless loves, and is loved by, her former exploiter. During her visit to "Nannie" Garland Meem's household in Virginia, Keckley is greeted as a part of the family, and "carried into the house in triumph" by Nannie Garland Meem (whom Keckley describes as her foster child), Maggie Garland, and Anne Garland, Nannie and Maggie's mother and Keckley's former mistress. When they find that their visitor has not eaten, Nannie and Maggie immediately "rushed to the kitchen and brought me a nice hot breakfast" (252).

In other antebellum narratives, the Southern kitchen is most emphatically slave space. Michael Vlach writes that the kitchen was a structure separated from the rest of the house in many upper-class Southern homes. While this was ostensibly done for practical considerations, the arrangement also separated the servers from the served (Vlach 43). The gospel-hungry slaves of Jacobs's narrative are relegated to the kitchen; in Douglass's *Narrative* punishment is meted out in it. In Keckley's narrative, however, the kitchen is reintegrated into the Southern home's domestic space as the women who were once served enter the kitchen to serve the woman who once waited on them (251).

By documenting both the Garlands' affections and shared space, Keckley quietly affirms her equality with her former owners. Interestingly, however, she insists on spatial separation between herself and Mary Lincoln, who comes "to my apartments to consult me in relation to a dress" (152). Here, segregation is self-imposed: "I never approved of ladies, attached to the Presidential household, coming to my rooms," Keckley writes decidedly.

> I always thought that it would be more consistent with their dignity to send for me, and let me come to them, instead of their coming to me. I may have peculiar notions about some things, and this may be regarded as one of them. No matter, I have recorded my opinion. I cannot forget the associations of my early life. (152–53)

Deference was a necessary part of the stock-in-trade of any successful African American in an environment in which pride in one's success could all too readily be deemed insolent. Indeed, Keckley's stated reason for enforcing boundaries resembles what seems to have been a traditional method of protecting the spaces that black women made their own. And yet, although this demarcation of boundaries may be taken as a subtle expression of power, Keckley, without irony, supports the status quo even as she simultaneously asserts her own independence and equality. Eventually, however, Keckley finds that independence threatened by her relationship with Mary Lincoln.

After President Lincoln's assassination, Keckley becomes an even more important part of the Lincolns' private circle. Locked in the private space of the White House, "Mrs. Lincoln never left her room, and while the body of her husband was being borne in solemn state from the Atlantic to the broad prairies of the West, she was weeping with her fatherless children in her private chamber. She denied admittance to almost every one, and [Mrs. Keckley] was her only companion, except her children, in the days of her great sorrow" (193).

Keckley's movement from the space of public mourning to the Lincolns' private rooms suggests that her relationship with Mrs. Lincoln has become more personal as she takes on the role of comforter. At the same time, however, Keckley remains Mary Lincoln's employee; among the bills for President Lincoln's funeral (paid by the Commissioner of Public Buildings) is an itemized account of the services of "Elizabeth Kickley," which includes six weeks of "Services as first Class Nurse & attendant . . . at $35.00 per week" (J. Washington 225). Although the two women increasingly share a private, domestic space in which Mary Lincoln repeatedly declares her friendship, Elizabeth Keckley's economic dependence threatens the hard-won work space/domestic space Keckley calls her own.

Keckley is wary of this loss of independence. When Mary Lincoln leaves for Chicago, Keckley initially refuses to accompany her. "You forget my business, Mrs. Lincoln," Keckley reminds the president's wife. "I cannot leave it. Just now I have the spring trousseau to make for Mrs. Douglas and I have promised to have it done in less than a week" (209). In spite of her pecuniary embarrassments, the former First Lady presses Keckley, promising her that she will be "well rewarded" for this neglect of business—"if Congress makes an appropriation for my benefit" (209). When Keckley hesitates, the former president's wife is insistent: "I cannot do without you . . . I have determined that you shall go to Chicago with me and you *must* go'" (209–10). On the way to Chicago, Mary Lincoln repeats her mantra of dependence: "'Lizabeth, you are my best and kindest friend, and I love you as my best friend" (210). This friendship, much like the relationship between a "mammy" and her charge, demands that Mary Lincoln be the center of Keckley's attentions. At the same time, she urges Keckley into a position of economic dependence. Adrift from the moorings of her own space, Keckley is increasingly susceptible to being drawn into the role she once rejected.

When the promised congressional appropriation does not materialize,

Keckley returns to Washington to reopen her business. The next year, Mary Lincoln, unable to maintain a house in Chicago, once again requests Keckley's assistance. Declaring herself "unable to live on $1,700 a year," Mary Lincoln asks Elizabeth Keckley to meet her in New York "to assist me in disposing of a portion of my wardrobe" (267–68). Keckley abandons her own space once again and arranges to meet Mary Lincoln in New York.

Yet, why does Keckley consistently jeopardize the independence—and the space—she has worked so hard to maintain? The trip to New York must have been taken at great economic cost; that June, Keckley reports, "[o]rders came in more rapidly than I could fill them" (222). Although Mary Lincoln continually assures Keckley that these trips will be economically advantageous, it is clear that it is an emotional rather than an economic imperative that drives Keckley to remain in Mary Lincoln's employ. Of the earlier trip to Chicago, Keckley writes, "I strongly objected; but I had been with [Mary Lincoln] so long, that she had acquired great power over me" (209). Although Keckley's combined work/domestic space is intermittently filled by employees who undoubtedly recognize Keckley's status as a subject, the ties Keckley forms with these women are not the same as those that make a domestic space a homeplace. Indeed, Keckley always speaks of her "work-girls" as an undifferentiated group who reply to her in a "chorus" (223). Without independent domestic ties, Keckley is peculiarly susceptible to Mary Lincoln's emotionally extortive nature. Keckley's own explanation for her actions is just as emotionally compelling: "[Mary Lincoln] was the wife of Abraham Lincoln, the man who had done so much for my race, and I could refuse to do nothing for her, calculated to advance her interests" (269).

In New York, Mary Lincoln proves unable to navigate the city's public spaces. The president's widow advises Keckley to "secure rooms for her at the St. Denis Hotel in the name of Mrs. Clarke, as her visit was to be *incog*" (271). Keckley is dubious: "I had never heard of the St. Denis, and therefore presumed that it could not be a first-class house. And I could not understand why Mrs. Lincoln should travel, without protection, under an assumed name. I knew that it would be impossible for me to engage rooms at a strange hotel for a person whom the proprietors knew nothing about" (271). Mrs. Keckley realizes, in a way that Mrs. Lincoln does not, that space defines one's status. Away from the domestic space that would normally demarcate her respectability, Mrs. Lincoln has entered a promiscuous public space unprotected by either the shield of a suitable companion or a recognizable name—both of which would be guarantors of her respectability.

Mary Lincoln's response to the hotel's racial segregation further endangers her and situates Keckley further away from a secure homespace. Accustomed to domestic spaces shared by people of different social status, Mary Lincoln attempts to apply those rules to unknown public space. When she attempts to secure an adjoining room for Mrs. Keckley, the clerk makes the "pointed rejoinder" that he has no room for Mrs. Keckley on the same floor, "[f]riend of yours or not" (275). Without a clear indication of her social superiority, Mary Lincoln's desire to share a space with a black woman puts her own position in question. When the hotel rents Keckley a room on the fifth floor, Mary Lincoln imperiously demands to be moved there as well, declaring, "What is good enough for [Keckley] is good enough for me" (275–76). The former First Lady pays dearly for her impetuous social defiance; "I never expected to see the widow of President Lincoln in such dingy, humble quarters," Keckley writes (276).

When Keckley is turned away from the dining room, the former president's wife proposes to dine elsewhere. Keckley, however, stands firm: "No, Mrs. Lincoln, I shall not go outside of the hotel to-night, for I realize your situation, if you do not. Mrs. Lincoln has no reason to care what these people may say about her as Mrs. Lincoln, but she should be prudent, and give them no opportunity to say anything about her as Mrs. Clarke" (213). Going out into the streets at night unaccompanied would only confirm the hotel clerk's suspicions that the mysterious guest is a woman of questionable morals. Convincing Mrs. Lincoln of this, however, proves difficult: "she was so frank and impulsive that she never once thought that her actions might be misconstrued" (283).

Even as Keckley's narrative celebrates the progress that has allowed her to enter the White House as a free and independent businesswoman, Keckley is subjected to the segregation that undoubtedly characterized her antebellum existence. Her recognition of her progress on one hand and her undoubted awareness of her continuing sociospatial realities on the other create a curious contradiction in her text; while she insists upon recognizing the social superiority of the First Lady, she also places herself on an equal footing with her employer. It is clear that in undertaking the delicate business of selling the First Lady's clothing, the two women act together.

Mrs. Lincoln is unable to command the price she desires for her clothing from secondhand clothes dealers. Two "commission brokers," named Brady and Keyes, are soon apprised of her true identity. "I regret to say," Keckley writes, "[that] she was guided by their counsel" (288). This "counsel" includes instructions to compose a series of letters, which "are then shown by Brady to "certain [Republican] politicians," who are told that they will be published "if [Brady's monetary] demands, as Mrs. Lincoln's agent were not complied with" (294). When political blackmail proves to be unsuccessful, Mrs. Lincoln puts her wardrobe on exhibition for public sale and goes to Chicago, leaving Keckley to look after the business by acting as business manager, press agent and fundraiser. Keckley's loyalty costs her her own business: "Mrs. Lincoln's venture proved so disastrous that she was unable to reward me for my services, and I was compelled to take in sewing to pay for my daily bread," Keckley writes (327).

Although Keckley's account of her occupation of the White House's domestic space seems to symbolize African Americans' newly won claim to public space, site of the public sphere, Keckley is, in the end, unable to translate her domestic role as dressmaker, nurse, and confidante into the public one of commentator. Attempting to defend both herself and her employer in print, she trusts that her readers will grant her a fair hearing when she publishes *Behind the Scenes*. As Frances Smith Foster notes, Keckley is a victim of her own success: "She allowed her faith in the efficacy of truth, or her belief in her own specialness, to blind her to the clear evidence that Anglo-Americans routinely resented and resisted any African American volunteering any opinion on any matter that did not focus upon slavery or racial discrimination" (*Written by Herself* 121). Still, the book may not have had such damaging consequences had Keckley herself not been betrayed.

Although only her name appears on the title page, it is known that Keckley depended upon her editor, James Redpath, for advice. An abolitionist and advisor to Lincoln, Redpath had published works by the African American writer William Wells Brown and written a biography of radical abolitionist John Brown. Keckley entrusted Redpath with the letters she received from Mary Lincoln with the understanding that Redpath would select pertinent quotations for the text. Instead, without Keckley's consent, he published the letters verbatim at the end of *Behind the Scenes* (Washington 238–39). In the letters, Mary Lincoln bemoans her fate and vituperatively criticizes Republican politicians who refuse to help her in her hour of need.

Initially, *Behind the Scenes* was advertised in *The American Literary Gazette & Publisher's Circular* as a book "crowded with incidents of a most romantic as well as tragic interest, covering a period of forty years" (J. Washington 231). Soon, however, it became "A LITERARY THUNDERBOLT" (232–34). One New York newspaper called Keckley's book "grossly and shamelessly indecent" (quoted in Foster's *Written by Herself* 128). Its publication was a crime akin to "the listening at keyholes, or the mean system of espionage which unearths family secrets with a view to blackmailing the unfortunate victims" (quoted in Foster's *Written by Herself* 128). Jennifer Fleischner writes that "[t]hough variously motivated, the offended all seem to have been antagonized by Keckley's trespass across the racially defined social, class, and behavioral barriers that legalized slavery had reinforced" (95). Elizabeth Keckley never saw Mary Lincoln again.

Curiously, Mary Todd Lincoln—like Keckley—died without a domestic space of her own. Although Mary Lincoln was in debt after her husband's assassination, she was awarded $22,000 in 1865—the rest of President Lincoln's salary. A congressional decision to award her $3,000 a year for life never assuaged her fear of poverty. A compulsive spender, Mary Lincoln's mania for buying and hoarding grew, and she became increasingly paranoid, so much so that in 1875, her only surviving son, Robert, had her committed to an asylum for a time. Although Mary Todd Lincoln was able to retreat to the home of her sister, she never lost the fear of poverty and homelessness which drove her to make use of, and then discard, Elizabeth Keckley's friendship: When she died in her sister's house in 1882, $3,000 in gold was found in the top drawer of her dresser.

Without a homeplace of her own, Elizabeth Keckley spent her last years in a room in Washington, DC, at the Home for Destitute Colored Women and Children, an institution that she herself had helped to found in the 1860s. John Washington describes the room as "a little dingy one in the basement with one window facing the setting sun. Over the dresser was a picture of Mrs. Lincoln" (222). Although historian John Washington asserts that Mrs. Keckley "continued to sew for the best families in Washington," the scandal did great damage to Keckley's business (240). Despite the fact that she later taught sewing at Wilberforce University, Keckley was forced to depend on the monthly pension she received from the government—compensation she received for the loss of her only son. Although she was not a pauper—she paid a small sum for her room—Mrs. Keckley occupied a space that reflected a profound loss of status.

The loss of the ties she had formed with Mrs. Lincoln seem to have produced a psychological upheaval; Washington reports that, "[l]ike Mrs. Lincoln, [Mrs. Keckley] suffered greatly from headaches and crying spells nearly all the time. She would never tell anyone what she grieved about" (240–41). When her bills, including one for her own grave and headstone, were paid, Keckley's estate of $179.11 went to the National Association for the Relief of Destitute Colored Women and Children. While the Home can be seen as a homeplace (it was, after all, a place where destitute African Americans could recognize each other's humanity in a dehumanizing world), it is not clear that Keckley, who was seemingly without close ties, saw it as such. Still, generous to the last, she supported the organization founded to secure some semblance of a homeplace for African American women and children in an America where they would continue to need such a site of recognition of their humanity and resistance to American racism.

## WORKS CITED

Accardo, Annalucia, and Alessandro Portelli. "A Spy in the Enemy's Country: Domestic Slaves as Internal Foes." *The Black Columbiad: Defining Moments in African American Literature and Culture*. Eds. Werner Sollors and Maria Diedrich. Cambridge: Harvard University Press, 1994. 77–87.

Andrews, William L. "The Changing Moral Discourse of Nineteenth-Century African American Women's Autobiography: Harriet Jacobs and Elizabeth Keckley." *De/Colonizing the Subject: The Politics of Gender in Women's Autobiography*. Eds. Sidonie Smith and Julia Watson. Minneapolis: University of Minnesota Press, 1992. 225–41.

———. "Reunion in the Postbellum Slave Narrative: Frederick Douglass and Elizabeth Keckley." *Black American Literature Forum* 23.1 (1989): 5–16.

———. *To Tell a Free Story: The First Century of Afro-American Autobiography, 1760–1865*. Urbana: University of Illinois Press, 1988.

Domina, Lynn. "I Was Re-Elected President: Elizabeth Keckley as Quintessential Patriot in *Behind the Scenes; Or, Thirty Years a Slave, and Four Years in the White House*." *Women's Life Writing: Finding your Voice/Building Community*. Ed. Linda S. Coleman. Bowling Green: Bowling Green State University Popular Press, 1997. 139–51.

Douglass, Frederick. *My Bondage and My Freedom*. 1855. New York: Dover Publications, 1969.

———. *Narrative of the Life of Frederick Douglass, an American Slave*. 1845. *Classic Slave Narratives*. Ed. Henry Louis Gates Jr. New York: Mentor-Penguin Books, 1987. 243–331.

Fleischner, Jennifer. *Mastering Slavery: Memory, Family and Identity in Women's Slave Narratives.* New York: New York University Press, 1996.
Foster, Frances Smith. "Autobiography after Emancipation: The Example of Elizabeth Keckley." *Multicultural Autobiography: American Lives.* Ed. James Robert Payne. Knoxville: University of Tennessee Press, 1992. 32–63.
———. *Witnessing Slavery: The Development of Ante-bellum Slave Narratives.* Westport: Greenwood Press, 1979.
———. *Written by Herself: Literary Production by African American Women, 1746–1892.* Bloomington: Indiana University Press, 1993.
Gwin, Minrose C. *Black and White Women of the Old South: The Peculiar Sisterhood in American Literature.* Knoxville: University of Tennessee Press, 1985.
Helm, Katherine. *Mary, Wife of Lincoln.* New York: Harper & Brothers, 1928.
hooks, bell. *Yearning: Race, Gender and Cultural Politics.* Boston: South End Press, 1990.
Jacobs, Harriet. *Incidents in the Life of a Slave Girl.* 1861. Cambridge: Harvard University Press, 1987.
Keckley, Elizabeth. *Behind the Scenes: Or, Thirty Years a Slave, and Four Years in the White House.* 1868. New York: Oxford University Press, 1988.
Litwack, Leon F. *Been in the Storm So Long: The Aftermath of Slavery.* New York: Vintage-Random House, 1980.
———. *North of Slavery.* Chicago: University of Chicago Press, 1961.
Olney, James. "'I Was Born:' Slave Narratives, Their Status as Autobiography and as Literature." *The Slave's Narrative.* Eds. Charles T. Davis and Henry Louis Gates Jr. New York: Oxford University Press, 1985. 148–75.
Rawick, George. *The American Slave: A Composite Autobiography.* Vol. I. Westport: Greenwood Press, 1972.
Smith, Valerie. "'Loopholes of Retreat': Architecture and Ideology in Harriet Jacobs's *Incidents in the Life of a Slave Girl.*" *Reading Black Feminist: A Critical Anthology.* Ed. Henry Louis Gates Jr. New York: Penguin Books, 1990. 212–26.
Strozier, Charles. *Lincoln's Quest for Union: Public and Private Meanings.* New York: Basic Books, 1982.
Tuan, Yi-Fu. *Space and Place: The Perspective of Experience.* Minneapolis: University of Minnesota Press, 1977.
Vlach, John Michael. *Back of the Big House: The Architecture of Plantation Slavery.* Chapel Hill: University of North Carolina Press, 1993.
Washington, Booker T. *Up from Slavery.* 1901. New York: Magnum-Lancer Books, 1969.
Washington, John E. *They Knew Lincoln.* New York: E.P. Dutton, 1942.
Weiner, Marli. *Mistresses and Slaves: Plantation Women in South Carolina, 1830–80.* Urbana: University of Illinois Press, 1998.
White, Deborah Gray. *Ar'n't I a Woman? Female Slaves in the Plantation South.* New York: W.W. Norton, 1985.

CHAPTER TEN

**JANAKA LEWIS**

# Elizabeth Keckley and Lessons of Freedom

IN 1901, W.E.B. DU BOIS reflected on the problems with the Freedmen's Bureau's government-prescribed Reconstruction in an article published in the *Atlantic Monthly*:

> What shall be done with slaves? Peremptory military commands, this way and that, could not answer the query; the Emancipation Proclamation seemed but to broaden and intensify the difficulties; and so at last there arose in the South a government of men called the Freedmen's Bureau, which lasted, legally, from 1865 to 1872, but in a sense from 1861 to 1876, and which sought to settle the Negro problems in the United States of America. (Du Bois 354)

Du Bois studies this seemingly ambitious "government of men" in his essay, focusing on "the occasion of its rise, the character of its work, and its final success and failure ... as one of the most singular and interesting of the attempts made by a great nation to grapple with vast problems of race and social condition" (354). He makes it clear early on, however, that his study is not an optimistic one.

Du Bois initially paints a picture of the fugitive slaves that penetrated Northern army lines as "old men, and thin ... women with frightened eyes, dragging whimpering, hungry children; men and girls, stalwart and gaunt"—hardly the picture of the triumphant and free family unit. Those arriving in 1861, when slaves of Missouri rebels were declared free, came as self-declared freedmen deserted and captured populations (354). This, Du Bois argues, is the beginning of the Freedmen's Bureau as these men, women, and children had to be provided for; they "welcomed" the "contrabands" as military laborers, a group whose number grew as time went on, until Lincoln officially emancipated the slaves of rebels in January 1863. Du Bois states that the need to answer the officers' questions of "What must be done with slaves arriving almost daily?" led [Edward] Pierce of Boston to establish the ground for the bureau (355). Pierce founded the Port Royal Experiment, an economic, educational, and healthcare program in Civil War–era South Carolina to benefit newly freed slaves. It was also known as the Sea Island Experiment. Charlotte Forten was the first black teacher to join this effort.

Narratives of Reconstruction (in both its historical and metaphorical senses) witnessed and written by the very people undergoing significant transformation reveal much about individual and national history. When stories by and about black women are incorporated into the history of Reconstruction, we are able to see that some of the strongest efforts, especially through education, were made by them. In *Righteous Propagation* Michele Mitchell discusses reforms that came from and during Reconstruction as African Americans shared interests as "sociopolitical body" (7). She writes, "Organizing freedom was arduous work that entailed individual initiative as well as collective endeavor, but for all of its challenges Reconstruction presented novel opportunities for black mobilization" (7).

In this vein, the tradition of narratives of mobilization were highlighted during the decade in which Elizabeth Keckley's narrative of her personal journey from slavery to the White House is published. Keckley's *Behind the Scenes: Or, Thirty Years a Slave, and Four Years in the White House* (1868) appears in print within a decade after William and Ellen Craft publish the details of their journey of escape with Ellen disguised as a white man and her husband as her slave (1860), and Charlotte Forten circulates her story of instructing African American students in the Sea Islands (the aforementioned Port Royal Experiment) in the media ("Life on the Sea Islands," *Atlantic Monthly,* 1864). In past and present representations, the story of Elizabeth Keckley has often been shadowed by the memory of Mary Todd Lincoln, wife of the sixteenth United States President, Abraham Lincoln, who Keckley represents as part of her text but not the complete narrative. As such, the texts that do discuss Keckley predominantly describe her relationship to Mary Lincoln. As slaves were defined by more than their enforced servitude, however, Elizabeth Keckley (who, after buying her freedom, had free administration over her labor as a seamstress) was defined by more than even her work for her most famous clients. Keckley's *Thirty Years a Slave* (calculated more precisely as twenty-three years by some historians) is as much a part of the way she positions herself as American historian and firsthand witness as are her references to a well-known national address. As narrator, Keckley locates her own story and that of the freedmen and freedwomen that come after her within a familiar historical context. This strategy not only helps bring African American histories to light but also fills in gaps in national accounts of prominent figures and events during the Civil War period.

Keckley's freedom is the freedom to contract and control her labor, to command authority as a woman on her own terms instead of those of a spouse, and to help improve the lives of freedmen and freedwomen. With the end of her enslavement comes the ability to write freely of her experiences with her master's family as well as with her later employers. She weaves the histories of free African Americans into national narratives of the presidency and wartime history. Most significantly, she uses her freedom to speak and to write as a position from which to illustrate her own humanity—her character, her life's labors, and her ability to use her testimony to ensure that stories of other freedmen and freedwomen are told. Mary Todd Lincoln is not used to offer recommendation or credibility to Keckley's story; in fact, Keckley asserts that she provides this service for Lincoln. References to the Lincolns are instead part of Keckley's strategy to fill in the gaps of American history of African Americans freed before, during, and after the Civil War.

Keckley acknowledges from the beginning of her narrative that she is connected to many different spaces and the histories they hold. Although this is her story, she cannot separate it from details such as the poverty of the Garland family, the daughter and son-in-law of her master Burwell to whom she is loaned and whom she supports with her sewing. She cannot leave out her sewing efforts for future Confederate First Lady Varina Davis (who asked her to accompany herself and husband Jefferson Davis when they moved South at the start of the Civil War).

Keckley also cannot omit firsthand details of Abraham Lincoln's life and death during her tenure as dressmaker for Mary Todd Lincoln. As significant to Keckley's narrative are accounts of refugees, then freedmen coming to Washington, and her work to secure their safety and livelihood during a critical historical juncture. Thus, this text is not solely *about* any of these other parties; it is a means of establishing Keckley's authority and credibility on a variety of subjects.

By writing and publishing a narrative that uses her life as a slave and as a

White House employee as a frame within which she relates to her public all that she does and sees, Keckley seizes the position of authority from those who might try to tell who she is. Even the documents written by others that attest to her freedom become part of her narrative—she positions them where she desires in her story. Keckley commands discourse with an audience that could potentially be very diverse and uses her experience as a lens to comment on national events.

In his introduction to *Behind the Scenes,* William Andrews asserts that Harriet Jacobs's *Incidents in the Life of a Slave Girl* and Keckley's narrative "serve as bookends of the Civil War" and thus focus on different aspects of black women's experiences (Andrews, xviii–xix). Their methods are similar, however, as they both use the narrative form to reclaim their agency from oppression of slavery and servitude. This is not to say that Keckley consciously emulates Jacobs's work, although it is possible that she had read it. Instead, it is significant that both women, at the beginning and end of the turbulent decade of the 1860s, use personal narratives to assert their humanity. Keckley, like Jacobs, emphasizes her right to freedom throughout the text, and it is from this platform that she positions herself to tell the story of America during her lifetime.

## Telling Her Story

The first two chapters of Keckley's autobiography focus on her life as the slave of the Burwell family of Virginia (where she was born) and, later, North Carolina. Her literary effort is then dedicated to describing her efforts toward a free life, but she must tell the circumstances from which she came in order to express the value of her liberation. She writes, "My master, Col. A. Burwell, was somewhat unsettled in his business affairs, and while I was an infant he made several removals" (7). Yet, through residence in many locations at the will of her master, Keckley still considers herself free. "I came to earth free in God-like thought, but fettered in action," (7) she asserts. The mission of her life, then, as expressed in her narrative, is to gain the latter aspect of this freedom.

Keckley's first tours "behind the scenes" are those of her own life in her master's household. Through a series of scenes, Keckley crafts her history as the center of the Burwells'. She is, indeed, free in thought and even uses instances in which she is in another's control to her benefit. Her descriptions of scenes become a metaphor for her ability to see, to tell, and to craft a history that establishes her as a credible witness. As a free woman, she is in a position to shape her narrative toward her own end, and as she does so, she realizes the significance of her past on her present state:

> I am now on the shady side of forty, and as I sit alone in my room the brain is busy, and a rapidly moving panorama brings scene after scene before me, some pleasant and others sad; and when I thus greet old familiar faces, I often find myself wondering if I am not living the past over again.... Hour after hour I sit while the scenes are being shifted; and as I gaze upon the past, I realize how crowded with incidents my life has been. (6)

Part of the privilege of freedom for Keckley is being able to sit alone in her room with a "busy brain" and reflect specifically on her life, through both good and bad scenes. The ones she represents are specifically of her choosing as a narrator who has embraced her opportunity to write. Rather than randomly accounting for events, Keckley's narrative chronicles what motivated her to seek freedom, how she did so, and what she did from a position of liberation.

The first stage, like narratives of enslavement written by Frederick Douglass and Harriet Jacobs, shows Keckley's awareness of her restricted state. As a four-year-old, Keckley was charged with the care of a baby and was lashed severely the first time she allowed the baby to fall. Yet her emphasis is not on her punishment as she simply states, "this was the first time I was punished in this cruel way, but not the last" (9). Keckley describes the false promise of family, as the man she calls her "father" is brought to the household before being taken by his own master to the West. Keckley recalls the misery of having her family broken apart, noting, "I can remember the scene as if it were but yesterday" (9). Through these moments, Keckley only hopes for a better future even if it comes in the afterlife: "We who are crushed to earth with heavy chains, who travel a weary, rugged, thorny road, groping through midnight darkness on earth, earn our right to enjoy the sunshine in the great hereafter" (10). In each moment of pain, Keckley is ever looking forward even when she cannot see what will come next.

Other scenes of violence in her early years take place in Hillsborough, North Carolina, where she moves after being loaned to Burwell's son Robert and his family. She writes of being flogged by Mr. Bingham, a local schoolmaster, whose abuse she challenges, saying, "Nobody has a right to whip me but my own master, and nobody shall do so if I can prevent it" (14). When he does so nonetheless, cutting into her flesh with a rawhide, she immediately demands an explanation from her master, who assaults her as well. Her response is significant, as she perceives the philosophical injustice as well as the physical harm. She states that her spirit rebelled at the unjust way in which she was treated, and it was then impossible to subdue her anger and forgive (15). In Keckley's reflection, this is the turning point as her spirit drives her toward freedom. She will struggle again with Bingham before he is finally subdued by his conscience, then must fight with Robert Burwell again before he reverts to peace as well.

These, Keckley's "revolting scenes," do not even compose the worst moment of her narrative. Like other enslaved women who wrote before her, Keckley writes about her appearance being the source of abuse as she is sexually assaulted. She notes,

> I was regarded as fair-looking for one of my race, and for four years a white man—I spare the world his name—had base designs upon me. I do not care to dwell upon this subject, for it is one that is fraught with pain. Suffice it to say, that he persecuted me for four years, and I—I—became a mother.... If my poor boy ever suffered any humiliating pangs on account of birth, he could not blame his mother, for God knows that she did not wish to give him life; he must blame the edicts of that society which deemed it no crime to undermine the virtue of girls in my then position. (15)

Like Jacobs, Keckley feels a sense of honesty toward her readers, and although rape and pregnancy have significant effects on her life, she chooses not to dwell on them. Keckley reveals these details in efforts to tell the truth. In the same statement, Keckley attempts to excuse her son from a less-than-noble birth for which she has no responsibility. Keckley makes clear the power dynamic to which she is subject, and the means by which she and her son are victimized.

As soon as she makes this revelation about social immorality, however, Keckley adds to her narrative of life in Hillsborough where she is ironically asked to sew dresses and serve as attendant to several brides. Although she is happy to be included, Keckley is saddened that her expectations of full inclusion and of her own occasion are limited. She writes,

Janaka Lewis | 189

There have been six weddings since October; the most respectable one was about a fortnight ago; I was asked to be the first attendant, but, as usual with all my expectations, I was disappointed, for on the wedding-day I felt more like being locked up in a three-cornered box than attending a wedding. (17)

Perhaps these "failed expectations" are a result of her inability to participate in these weddings as the honoree. Keckley can only associate with this plateau of womanhood through her work. When she leaves Hillsborough and is given to Burwell's sister, Anne Burwell Garland, she and her son move with the Garland family to St. Louis. There she is made to support the Garlands by sewing for "the best ladies in St. Louis" (20). Keckley initially offers her services as a community dressmaker in order to prevent her aging mother from being leased out by the Garlands. Keckley fears the work will wear on her mother. With this labor, however, even as an enslaved woman, Keckley gains a reputation as a seamstress and dressmaker. She details her clients and several of the orders she fills in St. Louis, which foreshadow the demand for her work from an even more well-known clientele in Washington, DC. Keckley understands that although she does not own her body, she possesses her labor, and it is that credit that she represents throughout the text.

Keckley knows that she is not the primary beneficiary of her work, as she embarks upon this "career," because she has to help her master's family. She understands, however, that she commands her craft. Her artistry contributes to her standing in the community, which shows that Keckley considers herself as more than a means of forced labor. Additionally, Keckley understands the economic value of her labor, as she calculates the practical evidence of her success: As not only a detail of her life, but as a way to illustrate the success of her work, she states that she supported the Garland household "of seventeen persons for two years and five months" (21). She is able to do, by her own hand, what her master cannot do with his own labor—support a family for an extended period of time. Keckley illustrates that her masters and their social networks depend on her labor to the extent that they literally could not live without her. This understanding of the economic power of the slave, articulated by Frederick Douglass in 1845, becomes the cornerstone of her text. Keckley ultimately illustrates what it means for an enslaved woman to understand both her economic impact and how she can take control of her status, and the motif of craft comes to shape and permeate Keckley's narrative. If she can sew a bridesmaid's dress and sell her dressmaking services to support others, she can sew for her own financial benefit. This is ultimately the turning point that motivates her to secure her freedom and serves as a reflection on the transition from being physically owned to representing her freedom within society and on the page.

Keckley's narration of events in her life that lead up to the Civil War fills in details that historical accounts of the same time omit. Du Bois accounts for "men [who] were enlisted as soldiers or hired as laborers, as women and children were guarded in camps," but does not include a description of the women who labored independently outside of war efforts (357). This is, perhaps, because the focus of the Freedmen's Bureau was on the men who headed families. As the bureau developed, efforts were taken to provide land on which the men could live and work. Congress attempted to establish a "Bureau for Freedmen" in the War Department in 1864 to allow for "general superintendence of all freedmen"—establishing regulations, leasing lands, adjusting wages, and representing them in civil and military courts. This bill was defeated in the Senate and replaced in 1865 as a "Bureau of Refugees, Freedmen, and Abandoned Lands" (357). It was to extend one year past the "War of Rebellion," in which time the Secretary of War could issue "rations, clothing, and fuel" and sell and lease land to ex-slaves in forty-acre parcels. This bill, Du Bois argues, allowed the government to "assume charge of the emancipated Negro as the ward of the nation," but instead left black men "emasculated by a peculiarly complete system of slavery" and now forced to work amidst the "stricken, embittered population of their former masters" (357). If the men were emasculated, one might ask, what happened to the women who also lost aspects of self in the transition from plantations to contraband camps? One can only speculate, as their plights remained absent from national narratives.

Du Bois discusses the final form of the Freedmen's Bureau through the act of 1866, which extended its existence to July 1868, authorized additional commissioners, sold forfeited lands to freedmen and Confederate public property for Negro schools (357). The freed slave, however, was still described by Du Bois as "crouched," "bewildered between friend and foe" (360). The black man, he argues, had emerged from slavery which "classed [him] and the ox together" after which the cleft between whites and blacks grew. The figures who remain, however, in Du Bois's analysis are "a gray-haired gentleman . . .

who stood at last, in the evening of life, a blighted, ruined form, with hate in his eyes" and "a form hovering dark and mother-like, her awful face black with the mists of centuries, [who] had aforetime bent in love over her white master's cradle, rocked his sons and daughters to sleep . . . ay, too, had laid herself low to his lust and borne a tawny man child to the world, only to see her dark boy's limbs scattered to the winds. . . ." (360).

Elizabeth Keckley illustrates Du Bois's commentary with details that she actually experienced. She accounts for the mother who has lost her "tawny man child," in her case her own son to war efforts, but it also revises the form of the "dark and mother-like" woman. Although the opposition to Negro education was great in the South, Du Bois states that successful Reconstruction efforts were credited to hard work, the "aid of philanthropists and the eager striving of black men" (363). The work of black women, both inside and outside of traditional family structures, is also evidence of success.

Mary Helen Washington asserts that these women were activists *and* intellectuals, "more committed to the idea of uplift than to their own personal advancement, partly because they could not isolate themselves from the problems of poor black women" (l). Elizabeth Keckley, Anna Julia Cooper, and other women who worked in conjunction with groups and larger institutions for the purpose of helping black Americans realize their freedom also contributes to a model of black feminist thought that extends beyond their individual networks.

## Lessons of Freedom

It is easy to read Keckley's narrative as one of ascension by her own right through her work. Rather than seeing herself only as part of the Lincoln story, however (although she quotes deliberately the moments in which Mrs. Lincoln refers to her as her "best" or "dearest" friend), Keckley uses that story as a layer of her narrative experience. It becomes part of the foundation on which she builds her discussion of the turmoil in America during the Civil War with specific references to the plights of black refugees, then freedmen and freedwomen. Like Jacobs's descriptions of the Nat Turner revolt and its aftermath in her own household, Keckley issues her own versions of then-current events but writes them specifically from her perspective; she is part of, not removed from, these histories. She is at once former slave who can see the struggles of those trying to realize freedom and a self-made member of the black middle class whose network includes such figures as Frederick Douglass and Henry Highland Garnet.

Keckley's focus on Mary Lincoln's dependence on her through Lincoln's tenure in the White House and his death seems to be her way of demonstrating, as in her masters' households, how a family she serves cannot do without her. As the author of her own narrative, Keckley escapes subordinate status in the story that is told—yes, she is charged with "insubordination" and breaking codes of private confidence, but this is the result of having assumed her prerogative as a writer (a direct effect of her freedom). Keckley departs from the reliance on others to vouch for her in order to vouch for her own authority and credibility. To this end, perhaps being considered a "gossip" was not the worst thing that Keckley could have endured, as famous figures become part of Keckley's story rather than imprisoning her in theirs. Ultimately, Keckley's ability to use the White House as a location in which her own freedom is displayed and the freedoms of others are realized is the primary success of her text. As in her handiwork, she crafts these stories deliberately, and her own life story becomes symbolic of the visibility she tries to give to other freedom stories.

Keckley's awareness of her personal freedom transcends promotion of national freedom. In the accounts of those who condemn her work, Keckley is the metaphorical "slave" of the Lincolns who overstepped her boundaries by telling their secrets, but Keckley has already written herself out of the confines of subservience to her later employees. She illustrates, first in her years as a slave and then in her years as a free woman, her negotiations of her own freedom. In the end, she orchestrates her own mobility in both circumstances and illustrates what it means to live as a person who is both legally and inherently free. The union of these stories into a singular narrative positions Keckley as an authority on both slavery and freedom. Freedom for Elizabeth Keckley is not just freedom of her physical being. It is freedom to profit from the circulation of her work and freedom to move through any space she pleases.

Finally, Keckley's freedom is accompanied by the ability to relate what she sees and act when she can for the benefit of others. Once she has secured her own freedom, she wants to help others to experience the same state of security. In the moment that Keckley dedicates her time and resources to aid "suffering blacks," Keckley has not only asserted her freedom but also asserted a higher position on the social hierarchy; she includes herself in the class of the "well-to-do colored people" (51). Her assertion of her status here is also representative of the point in the narrative from which she speaks. She is upwardly mobile but ever mindful of the position from which she has come. Freedom is represented in this text by Keckley's ability to seize the power of representation from others. When she ceases to be known by the name of her master or solely by the families that employ her, she gains and establishes significant means of authority.

Keckley offers a different mission for texts published after the Civil War. By composing her own narrative of freedom, Keckley ensures that she transcends the margins of the history she records. With her model, formerly enslaved black women become central figures in their own narratives. Although she has been reduced in some criticism to merely another domestic figure in a famous household, as long as Keckley's words remain, she is an authority on presidential and Civil War history as well as personal and collective freedom from the institution of slavery.

As Du Bois signals the key to Reconstruction as the figures and voices that lead African Americans into the next stage, I argue that Keckley is not only a voice for her time or the text that signals the *end* of a critical period in America's history. She serves as a precursor to the Women's Era writing of the late nineteenth century that calls for women to represent their experiences in writing. Although her own freedom is no longer at stake once she makes the journey toward Washington, her narrative suggests that true liberation depends on the freedom of African American women in general. Washington, DC, becomes a site where Keckley's freedom is realized along with those of other black men and women, including Anna Julia Cooper, who becomes a key figure in Washington's educational scene later in the century.

In "Our Raison D'Etre," the opening to her 1892 collection *A Voice from the South,* Anna Julia Cooper argues strongly for the representation of African American women by themselves. She writes, "The 'other side' has not been represented by one who 'lives there.' And not many can more sensibly realize and more accurately tell the weight and the fret of the 'long dull pain' than the open-eyed but hitherto voiceless Black Woman of America" (ii). With the phrase "open-eyed," Cooper offers an insightful metaphor in her description of the black woman. As Keckley witnesses the events within the Lincoln household, witnessing things others would never have been able to, as Ellen Craft watches the white men around her with enough detail that she can imitate their every gesture, Cooper suggests that black women both experience and see the concerns and issues of America in a way that those of other races and gender do not.

Cooper does not go as far to accuse others of misrepresentation; she states, "As our Caucasian barristers are not to blame if they cannot quite put themselves in the dark man's place, neither should the dark man be wholly expected fully and adequately to reproduce the exact Voice of the Black Woman"; instead, her argument acknowledges the absence in accuracy without black women's input (iii). Cooper raises her own voice to make this acknowledgement. As she establishes her voice, she also brings light to areas that were left unseen.

Cooper offers what she calls "broken utterances" with the hope that they can "in any way help to a clearer vision and a truer pulse-beat in studying our Nation's Problem" (assumedly race relations) (iii). Her essays, however, are both eloquent and well supported. The first, "Womanhood a Vital Element in the Regeneration and Progress of a Race," is a case study of women's involvement in historical moments. It initially reads as a course on civilization, beginning: "The two sources from which, perhaps, modern civilization has derived its noble and ennobling ideal of woman are Christianity and the Feudal System" (9). Cooper establishes the history of women's capability to a time as early as her audience can possibly remember, thus suggesting that before any of them lived women played an essential role.

Cooper continues, "Our satisfaction in American institutions rests not on the fruition we now enjoy, but springs rather from the possibilities and promise that are inherent in the system, though as yet, perhaps, far in the future" (12). She marks an interesting dichotomy that connects the past with the future and leaves the present as a time to be moved past. Thus, she suggests that there is current dissatisfaction with American institutions but that the "inherent possibility" of the past could be recreated. She suggests something important about how we might consider Keckley's narrative when she writes, "We have not yet reached our ideal in American civilization.... But there can be no doubt that here in America is the arena in which the next triumph of civilization is to be won; and here too we find promise abundant and possibilities infinite" (12). By setting America as the stage in her text for the "next triumph of civilization," Cooper both creates excitement about what the country could be and establishes herself as an authority for how such promise can be realized. From its very beginning, therefore, Cooper becomes a consultant on civilization and a guide to its improvement.

Before specifically mentioning women of color, Cooper argues that the "hope for our country primarily and fundamentally rests" on "the homelife and on the influence of good women in those homes" and even quotes Ralph Waldo Emerson that "a sufficient measure of civilization is the influence of good women" (12–13). To return to the title of her essay, it is obvious that she is arguing for the recognition of womanhood in rebuilding and moving "a race" forward, but in her initial examples she makes women's visibility an issue for the human race in general. Cooper supports this argument with evidence of regard for women in European civilization and also with the Gospel of Jesus Christ, which preaches "reverence for woman as woman regardless of rank, wealth, or culture" (13).

Cooper then presents a lesson plan for evaluating women through the perspective of the Gospel. She argues that "Throughout his life and in his death [Christ] has given to men a rule and guide for the estimation of woman as an equal, and a helper, as a friend, and as a sacred charge to be sheltered and cared for with a brother's love and sympathy . . ." which defines women as a gift from God for a purpose and charges men with care and kindness. She then emphasizes that women develop the history of the church through their Christian influence (19). Finally, Cooper summarizes that "the position of woman in society determines the vital elements of its regeneration and progress . . . not because woman is better or stronger or wiser than man, but from the nature of the case, because it is she who must first form the man by directing the earliest impulses of his character" (21). Thus, this essay becomes a lesson in Christianity, civilization, and human character that places woman at the center of each. As a teacher, Cooper provides evidence needed to make these cases, and it would be difficult to argue against her most effective case studies—history and religion.

Although she instructs her readers on past practices, Cooper does not let the past serve as the sole voice of reason. After establishing the means necessary to improve "a race," she charges women with using their God-given responsibilities to do so. She writes, "Woman, Mother—your responsibility is one that might make angels tremble and fear to take hold! To trifle with it, to ignore or misuse it, is to treat lightly the most sacred and solemn trust ever confided by God to human kind" (22). She does not leave the men completely responsible for not recognizing women's gifts and talents; women must make their influence known. Thus, Cooper's lessons are addressed to a diverse audience—to all men who have not realized the influence of women in the history of the country's most powerful institutions and to women who have not asserted themselves in improving humankind.

Cooper makes the critical move to issues of progress within the African American race at this juncture by adding her argument to that of Dr. Alexander Crummell, a son of an enslaved father and free mother who became a priest, missionary, and nationalist. Cooper writes, "I would beg [however, with the Doctor (Crummell's) permission] to add my plea for the Colored Girls of the South; that large, bright, promising fatally beautiful class that stand shivering like a delicate plantlet before the fury of tempestuous elements, so full of promise and possibilities, yet so sure of destruction… Oh, save them, help them, shield, train, develop, teach, inspire them!… There is material in them well worth your while, the hope in germ of a staunch, helpful, regenerating womanhood on which, primarily, rests the foundation stones of our future as a race" (22).

As Cooper reflects on the past of American civilization in order to prove the necessity of women's work, she then reflects on the progress of African Americans since slavery. "The race is just twenty-one years removed from the conception and experience of a chattel, just at the age of ruddy manhood. It is well enough to pause a moment for retrospection, introspection, and prospection" (26). The processes of retrospection and introspection that Cooper advises most certainly make Keckley's work relevant decades later. Specifically, the timeframe to which she refers is that in which Keckley writes and publishes. Retrospection, then, involves looking back on Emancipation and Reconstruction-era writing and reflecting on how African Americans can continue to make progress.

Cooper also argues that reflection should not be the dominant mode of planning; the race must actively move forward:

> But this survey of the failures or achievements of the past, the difficulties and embarrassments of the present, and the mingled hopes and fears for the future, must not degenerate into mere dreaming nor consume the time which belongs to the practical and the effective handling of the crucial questions of the hour; and there can be no issue more vital and momentous than this of the womanhood of the race. (27)

Without hesitation, Cooper asserts that the most important issue in making progress is allowing women to take their place in actively creating a brighter future for black men, women, and children. Cooper suggests that black Americans cannot help the past that they inherited, one that is rife with "degradation," but that they can recreate and regenerate their race. This ability to change, she argues, cannot be carried out but for the black woman: "Now the fundamental agency under God in the regeneration, the re-training of the race, as well as the ground work and starting point of its progress upward, must be the black woman" (27). In line with the argument about the burdens of motherhood made by her contemporaries (namely Lucy Craft Laney in her 1899 address to the Hampton Negro Conference), Cooper says black women must retrain the race to make greater strides toward overall progress.

The physical work once linked to men is no longer solely their responsibility. Cooper writes, "with all the wrongs and neglects of her past, with all the weakness, the debasement, the moral thralldom of her present, the black woman of to-day stands mute and wondering at the Herculean task devolving upon her. But the cycles wait for her. No other hand can move the lever. She must be loosed from her bands and set to work" (28). At this point, the physical work of lifting the race is now the responsibility of woman. But *others* must "loose," or permit her to do the task that is hers alone.

The essay ends with making concrete the need for women's efforts. Cooper argues, "Our meager and superficial results from past efforts prove their futility; and every attempt to elevate the Negro . . . cannot but prove abortive unless so directed as to utilize the indispensable agency of an elevated and trained womanhood" (29). Returning to her internal revolution, she states, "A race cannot be purified from without. . . . We must go to the root and see that that is sound and healthy and vigorous; and not deceive ourselves with waxen flowers and painted leaves of mock chlorophyll" (29). It is not enough that others can see the accomplishments of African Americans from the surface (the "mock chlorophyll"); the race has to be healed and made healthy from its very root.

Cooper concludes that the work to be done is not based on individual efforts but on the improvement in the "parts" of the race that have been underrepresented and underused: "We too often mistake individuals' honor for race development and so are ready to substitute pretty accomplishments for sound sense and earnest purpose" (29). She states, "A race is but a total of families.

The nation is the aggregate of its homes. As the whole is sum of all its parts, so the character of the parts will determine the characteristics of the whole" (29). This is the time, she offers, in which women will have their chance to work in the classroom and in the home to improve the nation.

In Cooper's analysis, reconstruction means the rebuilding of communities with the woman given the opportunity to lead. It extends beyond the legal reconstitution of the South and looks into the future in a way that that plan did not. By incorporating the black woman's role, she offers, the silence that has been inflicted on her can be broken. This includes the silence of mistreatment and abuse in slavery and the silence of being omitted from public discourse after slavery. In her opening, written at Tawawa Chimney Corner, Cooper writes,

> One muffled strain in the Silent South, a jarring chord and a vague and uncomprehended cadenza has been and still is the Negro. And of that muffled chord, the one mute and voiceless note has been the sadly expectant Black Woman,
> An infant crying in the night,
> An infant crying for the light;
> And with no language—but a cry. (i)

Cooper likens the Black Woman to an infant—making her desires heard but still with room to develop in her means of expression. In her demands for women's inclusion in the rebuilding of the African American race after slavery, Cooper gives words to the cry she defines. Thus, the chords of progress can be heard more clearly through the earlier narratives of Elizabeth Keckley and other women writing freedom before, during, and after the Civil War.

African American women's narratives of freedom and reconstruction tell us the ways in which they promote their own versions of progress in addition to the ways they were connected in this endeavor. Elizabeth Keckley and her contemporaries who were teachers inside and outside of the classroom make it their purpose to establish legacies of freedom on many levels. They are concerned with reconstructing African American children's and women's lives within the classroom, improving the lives of their families, the circumstances in their homes. More than teaching one particular text, these women create and circulate curricula for living free lives. Documented in print, their lived experiences become history that is circulated to others as they emerge from institutional and metaphorical bondage.

## WORKS CITED

Andrews, William L. Introduction. *Behind the Scenes: Or, Thirty Years a Slave, and Four Years in the White House.* 1868. New York: Penguin Books, 2005. vii–xxii.

Cooper, Anna Julia. *A Voice from the South.* 1892. New York: Oxford University Press, 1988.

Craft, William and Ellen. *Running a Thousand Miles for Freedom: The Escape of William and Ellen Craft from Slavery.* Baton Rouge: Louisiana State University Press, 1999.

Du Bois, W.E.B. *Black Reconstruction.* New York: Atheneum, 1962.

——— "The Freedmen's Bureau." *Atlantic Monthly* 87 (1901): 354–65.

Faulkner, Carol. *Women's Radical Reconstruction: the Freedmen's Aid Movement.* Philadelphia: University of Pennsylvania Press, 2004.

Fleischner, Jennifer. *Mrs. Lincoln and Mrs. Keckly: The Remarkable Story of the Friendship between a First Lady and a Former Slave.* New York: Broadway Books, 2003.

Foner, Eric. *Forever Free.* New York: Knopf, 2005.

———. *Short History of Reconstruction.* New York: Harper and Row, 1990.

Forten, Charlotte. "Life on the Sea Islands." 1864. *Two Black Teachers during the Civil War.* New York: Arno Press, New York Times, 1969.

———. *The Journals of Charlotte Forten Grimké.* New York: Oxford University Press, 1988.

Jacobs, Harriet [as Linda Brent]. *Incidents in the Life of a Slave Girl: Written by Herself.* 1861. Orlando: Harcourt Brace, 1973.

Keckley, Elizabeth. *Behind the Scenes: Or, Thirty years a Slave, and Four Years in the White House.* 1868. New York: Penguin Books, 2005.

Laney, Lucy Craft. "Burden of the Educated Colored Woman." Report of the Hampton Negro Conference No. 111 (July 1899), 37 42. Web: 11 November 2015.

Mitchell, Angelyn. *Freedom to Remember.* New Brunswick: Rutgers University Press, 2002.

Mitchell, Michele. *Righteous Propagation: African Americans and the Politics of Racial Destiny after Reconstruction.* Chapel Hill: University of North Carolina Press, 2004.

Rutberg, Becky. *Mary Lincoln's Dressmaker: Elizabeth Keckley's Remarkable Rise from Slave to White House Confidante.* New York: Walker, 1995.

Santamarina, Xiomara. *Belabored Professions: Narratives of African American Working Womanhood.* Chapel Hill: University of North Carolina Press, 2005.

Washington, Mary Helen. *Invented Lives: Narratives of Black Women, 1860–1960.* Garden City: Doubleday, 1987.

## EXISTING CRITICISM CONTINUED

CHAPTER ELEVEN

# Splitting the "I"
(Re)reading the Traumatic Narrative of Black Womanhood
in the Autobiographies of Harriet Jacobs and Elizabeth Keckley

**CLARENCE W. TWEEDY**

Until the legacy of remembered and re-enacted trauma is taken seriously, black America cannot heal....When we examine our history we see African-American antiracist resistance move from being rooted in a love ethic and a moral philosophy centered on peace and reconciliation to a rhetoric and practice of violence.
—bell hooks, *Rock My Soul*

AFRICAN AMERICAN WRITERS, SUCH as Harriet Jacobs and Elizabeth Keckley, used their autobiographies to subvert the boundaries of race and gender. Through their collective writing, they redefined and re-imagined racial/gender identity by portraying African American women not as objects but as human subjects. In nineteenth-century women's slave narratives, depictions of personal trauma and racialized violence operate with distinct sociopolitical agendas that attempt to re-narrate both personal as well as collective racial identity. And, what becomes clear are that scenes of trauma, in Jacobs's *Incidents in the Life of a Slave Girl* (1861) and Keckley's *Behind the Scenes* (1868), are not about the recuperation of the reality of the event; rather, the reality of the traumatic event is lost or subsumed under the narrator's/author's desire for self-agency as well as bodily and racial autonomy. In their texts, race is severed from biological connotations in favor of race as a sociopolitical construct, challenging the racialized and gender boundaries imposed upon black women in American society. Thus, the modification of personal traumatic experiences operates to precisely control memories of trauma, creating narrative as well as fictional resolutions to their violent experiences.

Historically, acts of violence against African Americans were used to maintain a system of white supremacy that defined black people as second-class citizens. More importantly, Jacobs and Keckley struggled against and resisted a continual system of violent racism in the United States, ranging from the physical and sexual assaults of slavery to internalized psychological effects of trauma that fused notions of submission and domination into representations of the black body. However, at the same time, sadomasochistic representations of the black body were used by African American writers to subvert signs of powerlessness, while asserting and redefining the black experience. Hence, traumatic experiences are re-inscribed in order to psychologically cope with the negative effects of traumatic experiences. Jacobs and Keckley do not reproduce realities of traumatic events, but, rather, they modify traumatic memories to precisely control and invest textual scenes of violence with their desires for self-mastery as well as bodily autonomy. For Jacobs and Keckley, representations of sadomasochistic violence function as reproductions that, on the one hand, challenge the social definitions and limitations of black identity while, on the other hand, creating a means through which authors lay claim to their subjectivity.

Jacobs's and Keckley's depictions of violence reveal traumatic narratives engaged in public debates about social injustice, immorality, and the humanity of black women. Traumatic narratives are demonstrative of a subconscious revelation; and the fictive recuperation of trauma occurs for the individual to cope psychologically with past traumatic events (Tate 96). Their traumatic narratives serve as intersections of personal experiences and sociopolitical desires. What the audience witnesses are not scenes of victimization but, rather, moments of psychological mastery over personal trauma and heroic resistance to exploitation. According to Diana Miles, the victim's traumatic testimony is an attempt to both "revisit and revise the lost moment, thereby integrating it into the consciousness" (1). For trauma survivors, the silence that often surrounds violent experiences is partially due to their inability to comprehend what has happened to them, and their failure to translate into language an experience that initially was too psychologically overwhelming. Miles also contends:

It is important to note that testimony has an address, and when the testimony appears in the form of a published text, it is addressed to the world.... All testimony requires an audience of ethical listeners who will not only receive the narrative but will also act upon the ethical demand behind the testimony, which is to ensure that the traumatic event will not occur again. (5)

What is most critical about Miles's approach to trauma is that it provides a blueprint on how writers use traumatic experiences to urge audiences toward taking actions to change the social and racial status quo.

Through revising their individual traumatic experiences, Jacobs and Keckley fought against white definitions of black passivity, subordination, and racial inferiority. Instead of the black body being simply ritualistically displayed as a victim, they used traumatic experiences to construct autobiographical sites of resistance. With regard to resisting trauma, David Aberbach argues, "Creativity, the affirmation of the wholly individual ability to imagine, may act as a vital part of survival, of re-emergence of the whole and unique human being" (3). Through the very act of writing, Jacobs and Keckley not only survived and mastered traumatic experiences but also worked to redefine their individual identities and the collective humanity of black women. According to Jacob Arlow, victims of trauma re-create and modify violent experiences to regain control over the powerlessness of their bodies (42). In Jacobs's and Keckley's narratives, scenes of violence are used to re-assert psychological control over traumatic memories, experiences, bodies, and self-identity.

Contemporary critics, such as Kelly Oliver, Gwen Bergner, and Claudia Tate, have argued for the application of psychoanalytical models to the analysis of race and trauma in African American literature. Kelly Oliver insists that the development of a psychoanalytical theory that addresses how oppression operates between the psyche and racialized concepts of alienation and shame is critical to transforming psychoanalysis into a useful means of analyzing racial oppression (iv). Furthermore, Bergner and Tate each have formulated psychoanalytical theories that address the development of individuality and subjectivity within a social context. To this end, psychoanalysis has been critical in understanding notions of shame and affect that operate between the individual psyche and the social construction of race. In *Taboo Subjects,* Bergner argues that "psychoanalysis provides a critical vocabulary for theorizing racialization, as it intersects with sex and gender, for both black and white Americans" (xix). The connection between race and society is more readily understood through what Bergner terms the racially symbolic: a pattern of organizing human difference through comparisons against the privileged signifier of whiteness (xxvi). The symbolism of race determines who is vested with the signs of power and who is powerless. While Tate, in *Psychoanalysis and Black Novels*, uses Freudian and post-Freudian theories to demonstrate how African American texts negotiate "the tension between public, collective protocols of race and private individual desire, thereby forming an enigmatic surplus" or what she refers to as a "textual enigma" (13). Tate's notion of textual enigma reveals that African American rhetorical performances generate arguments that are external to their racial/social arguments (13). By looking at the textual enigmas of African American texts, Tate develops a conceptual framework that investigates the authors' inscription of personal traumatic experience, pain, and pleasure in their writing. Thus, understanding the motivations of the narrator versus the role of protagonist is crucial to understanding the functions of various racial dilemmas as well as depictions of trauma that occur in African American texts (Tate 17).

In this sense, the repetition of traumatic experiences signals possible means for resolving psychic conflicts. Therefore, Jacobs's and Keckley's acts of telling or giving testimony, especially through the written word, bring an end to their silence and reveal truth through traumatic narratives that confront external as well as internal effects of racism. Jacobs's and Keckley's descriptions of traumatic experiences create representations of black women that produce two competing identities within their narratives. These seemingly conflicting identities are generated through their depictions and incorporation of traumatic memories in their autobiographies. Suzette A. Henke argues that the incorporation and the repetition/mastery of trauma in autobiographies create three points of self-referentiality or subject positions: (1) authorial consciousness, (2) a fragmented version of the self, and (3) a coherent subject of utterance created through the process of narrative disclosure (xv). Both Jacobs and Keckley create discursive bodily and rhetorical identities in order to remake themselves into coherent and self-made subjects.

First, the discursive body is a traumatic representation of the victimized body through which the author masters traumatic experience through textually re-creating the event, while second, the rhetorical body/identity is a representation of desired social and public personas created by modifying traumatic experiences into moments of heroic resistance through assertions of womanhood and morality. Thus, the author's identity is psychically split in an attempt to cope with painful and internalized experiences of racial trauma. Primarily, Freud developed notions of "splitting" in "Fetishism" and "Splitting the ego in the Process of Defence" (Laplanche and Pontalis 428). Freud argued that victims of psychoses, based in traumatic events, demonstrate psychical attitudes toward external reality (Laplanche and Pontalis 429). Some victims take reality into consideration, while others disavow reality as a means of self-protection. For Jacobs and Keckley, their psychological and narrative acts of splitting manifest defenses against unwanted traumatic affects caused by violent encounters with their slave masters, displacing unwanted affects into discursive and textual identities, while creating self-agency through the emergence of their authorial voices. The psychical splitting between objectified bodies within the text and their public identities outside of the text ends their feelings of alienation from the social domains of true womanhood and citizenship.

## Reconstructing Harriet

From the outset of *Incidents in the Life of a Slave Girl*, Jacobs's shame and anxiety in regard to sexual violations of her person suffered at the hands of Mr. Flint are obvious, even to the point that she asserts that slave women cannot be judged by the same standard of morality espoused by the cult of true womanhood. According to Gwendolyn Etter-Lewis, the slave woman was confronted by a "crippling double bind [that] made it difficult if not impossible for these women to freely speak or write about their lives in any form but especially in autobiography" (159). Certainly, Jacobs used writing as means of speaking freely about her life, while condemning those who were responsible for her suffering. Through writing, she escapes the crippling double bind of silence by being silent and not revealing some of the key details of her story. Jacobs contends: "But, O, ye happy women, whose purity has been sheltered from childhood, who have been free to choose the objects of your affection, whose homes are protected by law, do not judge the poor desolate slave girl too severely" (64). It is at this moment, as well as in her prologue, that unwanted affects of shame and humiliation intrude into the sociopolitical intent of her autobiography. And, in order to mitigate the psychological impact of these painful memories, aspects of her traumatic experiences are concealed within the narrative. William Andrews asserts: "Harriet Jacobs was confronted with probably the most difficult rhetorical problems of any slave narrator in the antebellum era. She wanted to indict the southern patriarchy for its sexual tyranny over black women like herself, yet she could not do so without confessing with 'sorrow and shame' to her willing participation in a miscegenetic liaison that produced two illegitimate children" (240). Jacobs engages in a rhetorical strategy of disclosure and concealment, reflecting the historically disparate treatment of black women at the whims of white society.

To this end, Jacobs employs sentimental tropes as a means of demonstrating resistance to Mr. Flint's authority over her body. Valerie Smith argues: "By pointing up the similarities between her own story and those plots with which her readers would have been familiar, Jacobs could thus expect her readers to identify with her suffering. Moreover, this technique would enable them to appreciate the ways in which slavery converts into liabilities the very qualities of virtue and beauty that women were taught to cultivate" (37). Jacobs creates a subversive discourse through which she mitigates and minimizes psychological trauma, while shaping and precisely controlling self- as well as public identity. Her cultivation of womanhood through the garnering of sympathy serves as a mask through which she hides the effects of physical and psychological abuse, re-narrating self-identity from being an objectified slave into a self-made subject.

Furthermore, she psychically splits into two distinct identities: Harriet Jacobs, as the narrator, versus Linda Brent: the protagonist invested with unwanted affect, stemming from past moments of physical and sexual violation. For her, sexuality is problematic in the sense that it is deeply intertwined with psychological, racial, and physical trauma. Thus, she deals with sexual trauma by affixing the blame, not to black women's desires, but to the immoral desires of white men. In effect, the revelation of Jacobs being sexually harassed and possibly molested operates as a means through which she re-imagines black women's sexual agency and cultural identity as continually resisting hegemonic constructions of black womanhood. In this scheme, she concurrently occupies two positions in the narrative: object and subject. For Jacobs, splitting underlies a psychological defense against traumatic memories, which intermingles the author's life with that of the protagonist, creating a "safe means of telling one's own life story through several layers of camouflage" (Etter-Lewis 163). Jacobs, as a survivor of childhood abuse, implements metaphors and other kinds of indirect language to "disguise/buffer the remembered pain" (Etter-Lewis 160). According to Dori Laub, traumatic events "become more and more distorted in their silent retention and pervasively invade and contaminate the survivor's daily life. The longer the story remains untold, the more distorted it becomes in the survivor's conception of it. . . ." (79). Although Laub's argument specifically addresses holocaust survivors, the caveat of her analysis can be extended to Jacobs's narrative. If reread closely, there is a persistent intrusion of her adult voice, overwriting/re-narrating childhood trauma. Literally, traumatic memories become concealed, distorted, and even erased in an attempt to find psychological resolution for her suffering.

First, for Jacobs, the possibility of rape by her master is a continual threat that she faced daily as a child. She writes: "Soon she will learn to tremble when she hears her master's footfall. She will be compelled to realize that she is no longer a child. . . . That which commands admiration in the white woman only hastens the degradation of the female slave" (Jacobs 46). The scene of her master's sexual stalking conceals the reality of traumatic events. It is left up to the readers' imagination as to why she must fear the master's "footfall." Thus, any possible, or actual, sexual assaults by Mr. Flint, unwanted touching, or even physical violations, et cetera, remain hidden within the narrative. The fear that she individually felt is narrated in the third person rather than first-person narration. Thus, she displaces her fear into a collective fear of all slave women. This projection of fear into a collective identity of black women announces the intrusion of her narrative voice which is no longer bound to the painful memories of abuse. Similar to other victims of abuse, Jacobs as narrator severs herself from the harsh realities of her experience by psychically splitting into two distinct identities. Her ego is split between outside text versus inside text, public persona versus a discursive textual identity (Brent), buffering her against painful, traumatic memories. In effect, Jacobs's feelings of terror and shame are cast out of the narrator and placed into the pseudonym of Linda Brent.

Furthermore, the seduction theme of Jacobs's narrative is traumatic reenactment of sexual abuse and powerlessness that she re-creates into a site of resistance and self-empowerment. Mr. Flint's unwanted pursuit and harassment of Jacobs functions as a primary staple of her sentimental plot of seduction. Valerie Smith argues:

> As it is true with popular literature generally, this paradigm affirms the dominant ideology . . . the power of patriarchy . . . the seduction plot typically represents pursuit or harassment as love, allowing the protagonist and reader alike to interpret the male's abusiveness as a sign of his inability to express his profound love for the heroine. (41)

Jacobs/Brent re-interprets Mr. Flint's sexual desire for what it truly was, a display of power over her body and sexual agency. And she reframes the discussion from being about black women's sexuality into a discourse about violent, white male desire (85). She resists his rapacious desire by using the sentimental seduction plot from her position as narrator, revealing notions of the paternalistic slave-master to be nothing more than a disguise for and justification of white male sexual desire and violence. Thus, the shame of Brent's loss of innocence is displaced and transformed into a pronouncement of the master's guilt, leading to her decision to sleep with Mr. Sands. Jacobs provides a second-person-plural narration that justifies her choice as being necessary in order to avoid further degradation. Jacobs writes:

> It seems less degrading to give oneself, than to submit to compulsion. There is something akin to freedom in having a lover who has no control over you, except that which he gains by kindness and attachment. A master may treat you as rudely as he pleases, and you dare not speak; moreover, the wrong does not seem so great with an unmarried man, as with one who has a wife to be made unhappy. There may be sophistry in all this; but the condition of a slave confuses all principles of morality, and, in fact, renders the practice of them impossible. (84–85)

Once again, Jacobs as the narrator is outside the text divested from the emotional trauma of the scene. And, what remains is Jacobs's wording of "has no control over you," "may treat you as rudely as he pleases," and "you dare not speak": a collective "you" that conjoins the experiences of both black and white women. This collectivized "you" helps to establish a sympathetic connection between her audience and Brent's condition of servitude that makes the adherence to moral principals all but impossible.

Second, Jacobs's sexual economy represents a significant challenge to white hegemony over her reproduction and sexuality. She manipulates the sentimental seduction plot as a means of outlining a strategy of resistance to

Flint's desire and as justification of her miscegenistic liaisons with Mr. Sands as being a result of victimization. She argues that although her choice of giving herself to and having children with Sands out of wedlock may seem immoral to her readers it represents an accurate reflection of how slavery induces black women to make immoral choices in order to maintain some semblance of virtue and agency (Jacobs 64). Houston Baker Jr. argues: "This new code of ethics emphasizes a woman's prerogative to control her own sexuality—to govern the integrity of her body" (Baker 52–53). Although Jacobs's decision to control her sexuality challenges Mr. Flint's authority over her sexual autonomy, her decision ultimately fails to permanently disrupt the economics of the slave plantation. The children produced from her relationship with Sands remain the property of her master. His wealth increases from Jacobs's acts of reproduction: a fact made painfully evident with Mr. Sands having to deceitfully purchase their children above "fair" market value (Jacobs 118–19). In this regard, Jacobs, outside of the text, embodies the desires of black womanhood to resist victimization: a psychological split between authorial desires and the limitations of slave women's self-agency.

For her, the only means of negating Flint's power over her and gaining self-agency is to escape. Yet again, Jacobs and Brent psychically split into the literate negotiator, whose sexuality is repressed in favor of the embodiment of motherhood, and the victim of sexual assaults, whose choice to have a sexual relationship with Sands demonstrates a passive aggressive attack against Flint's continual abuse. According to Houston Baker Jr., Jacobs's narrative seeks, joins, and creates a "community of women [that] controls its own sexuality, successfully negotiates (in explicitly commercial terms) its liberation from a crude patriarchy, and achieves expressive fullness through the literate voice of the black, female author" (Baker 55). Counter to Baker's argument that control of her sexuality leads to liberation from patriarchy, Jacobs uses her autobiography as a means of psychologically divorcing herself from sexuality and memories of subordination. Thus, her hiding place operates as a space through which the pain she endures becomes a projection of the maternal ideal: a woman whose motherly love grants the strength to endure hardship. Jacobs's identity resurfaces in the repression of sexual trauma and the emergence of maternal ideals of womanhood. She writes: "To this hole I was conveyed as soon as I entered the house. The air was stifling; the darkness total.... I suffered for air even more than for light....Yet I would have chosen this, rather than my lot as a slave...." (Jacobs 127). In this moment, Jacobs endures the bodily suffering caused by the crawl space because she hears the laughter of her children. At this point in the autobiography, Jacobs, as the narrator, is emotionally reinvested back into the text. She no longer uses a third-person or second-person-plural narration to emotionally detach from a reconstruction of painful memories. Instead, Jacobs returns to the use of the first person. The "I" of the passage is representative of her as narrator, the mother, and not the collective "you" of Linda Brent's trauma.

Jacobs's use of "I" represents the emotional return of her self-made public identity of womanhood into the narrative. Her audience is no longer held at bay from intense emotions or bodily pain. Jacobs's hiding spot becomes not only a symbol of a womb—a womb to which she returns in order to escape her lot in life, but, more importantly, a point through which Jacobs introjects into the autobiography desired, positive affects of hope and joy. She writes:

> For the last time I went up to my nook. Its desolate appearance no longer chilled me, for the light of hope had risen in my soul. Yet, even with the blessed prospect of freedom before me, I felt very sad at leaving that old homestead, where I had been sheltered so long by the dear old grandmother. (Jacobs 171)

She presents readers with a maternal lineage of black womanhood and bodily agency through suffering that challenges white patriarchal authority over black women's physical and psychological autonomy. And it is from out of this desolate place that Jacobs is transformed by the prospect of her impending freedom. Through her bodily suffering and recovery, she announces a new identity of black women as mothers, gaining access to the virtues of republican womanhood.

### The Skin, the Flesh

Similar to Jacobs, Keckley uses rhetorical power of sympathy to negotiate the conflict between traumatic memories and her public persona. Thus, her intent in writing an autobiography lies beyond a story of escape from and condemnation of the institution of slavery. Rather, she provides an autobiographical claim to the fundamental principles of American citizenship: bodily autonomy and self-hood. Or to put it another way, what Keckley's text "immediately foregrounds, and subsequently and brilliantly enacts, is the selectiveness of [her] self-construction and [a] strenuous repudiation of a merely 'personal' self in favor of a deliberately public one" (Berthold 107). At the beginning of her narrative, Keckley employs the notion of suffering womanhood that is commonplace in sentimental fiction to establish her public persona as a free black woman. In her autobiography, the slave narrative and sentimental fiction are interdeterminative of each other, both bound up with the social conventions of the time (Olney xxxiii). As Elizabeth Barnes reminds us, in "the sentimental scheme of sympathy, others are made real and thus cared for—to the extent that they can be shown in relation to the reader.... Sympathy thus proves a mediated experience in which selves come to be constituted in relation to—or by relating to other imagined selves, while those selves are simultaneously created through the projection of one's own sentiments" (4–5). Keckley uses her narrative to define her subjectivity by projecting unwanted affects into the discursive body of the text.

Keckley produces an oscillating drama through which she occupies at different, as well as concurrent points, the positions of both sadist and masochist. Her identity shifts back and forth between memories of physical disempowerment and a strategy of rhetorical self-empowerment as well as violated object versus self-made subject. Keckley's retelling of traumatic experiences divests the physical and psychological pain of slavery into an objectified body in the narrative, while as author she operates as a disembodied voice, creating an authorial identity that projects a public image of self-determination and agency. Moreover, she employs two primary tropes of sentimental fiction: suffering womanhood and spiritual conversion in order to exert control over her private as well as public identity. According to Elizabeth Barnes, "[i]n typical sentimental fashion, seduction fiction puts sociopolitical anxieties concerning the nature of authority into personal context, where private interpersonal relations intersect with public concerns" (Barnes 9). Keckley's public and private concerns intersect with the scenes of physical violation and the psychological splitting between voice and body. Her autobiography constitutes a construction of an "other-self," carving out a mediated space for the emergence of an autonomous black womanhood. For Keckley, splitting underlies a psychological defense against the physical and emotional abuses of her childhood.

Thus, Keckley's story creates a heroic narrative that seeks to eliminate her victim status in exchange for a status of self-reliant womanhood. Jerry H. Bryant contends that African American texts deal with racial violence by representing the author's search for self-esteem which cannot be gained by being seen as the victim (3). Keckley's key moments of self-agency are derived through the modification of her violent encounters with Mr. Bingham. These conflicts lead to the return of her narrative "I" to the text by defying Mr. Bingham's authority over her through acts of physical and verbal resistance. Hence, in the first chapters of the text, Keckley uses an authorial voice that returns the power of self-expression to her traumatized body, transforming feelings of pain into acts of self-expression and defiance, mitigating, as well as re-inscribing, trauma not as an adolescent but from her perspective as an adult. As Elaine Scarry contends,

> It is intense pain that destroys a person's self and world, destruction experienced spatially as either the contraction of the universe down to the immediate vicinity of the body or as the body swelling to fill the entire universe. Intense pain is also language-destroying: as the content of one's world disintegrates, so the content of one's language disintegrates; as the self disintegrates, so the content of one's language disintegrates, so that which would express and project the self is robbed of its source and its subject. (35)

Keckley uses the cognitive distance created by splitting to re-create herself as a subject. This cognitive distance forms a boundary between self and body, rewriting painful memories into sites of self-empowerment. Pain becomes bound to the re-narrated body resisting domination, while demonstrating mastery over the past. Critics such as Lori Merish contend that these moments of violence endow Keckley "with a kind of charismatic authority, a Christ-like power to convert those who would oppress her," while acutely conveying her "vulnerability, especially [the] sexual vulnerability, of the black female body under slavery" (245). Although Keckley uses the trope of spiritual conversion through depictions of bodily suffering, her rhetorical strategy is not directed toward a passive construction of religious conversion but an active realignment of power through a narrative expression of self-agency. Keckley's realignment of power brings to an end feelings of alienation that have consistently denied her any form of self or cultural expression. Thus, the tropes of suffering womanhood and spiritual conversion present a double bind that affirms her human status and, at the same time, denies her the ability to exercise agency and bodily autonomy. Keckley's solution to this crisis of self is the development of a unique rhetorical strategy through which, on the one hand, self-expression is severed from the body and, on the other hand, re-invested into a self-made identity in her final moments of resistance to Bingham. Her depictions of trauma reproduce the body as a slave-object and an object of spiritual conversion that effectively severed her from her authorial voice. Thus, her voice is the product of re-inscribed traumatic memories.

For example, at the age of fourteen, Keckley is sent to live with her master's eldest son, Mr. Burwell, a Presbyterian minister, with a convalescent wife (Keckley 31). Once there, she is immediately treated with distrust and scorn by the Burwells. Finally, when Keckley turns eighteen the conflict between her and the Burwells, using local schoolmaster, Mr. Bingham, as their proxy, erupts into two key moments of violence. The first conflict begins with Bingham's declaration: "Lizzie, I am going to flog you," to which she replies, "what for?" (Keckley 33). Her question of "what for" creates two sites of contest: ownership over her body and Bingham's authority over her self-hood. She writes:

> "No matter," he replied, "I am going to whip you, so take down your dress this instant"... Recollect, I was eighteen years of age, was a woman fully developed, and yet this man coolly bade me take down my dress. I drew myself up proudly, firmly, and said: "No, Mr. Bingham, I shall not take down my dress before you. Moreover, you shall not whip me unless you prove the stronger. Nobody has a right to whip me but my own master, and nobody shall do so if I can prevent it."... It cut the skin, raised great welts, and the warm blood trickled down my back. Oh God! I can feel the torture now—the terrible, excruciating agony of those moments. I did not scream; I was too proud to let my tormentor know what I was suffering. (Keckley 33–34)

Keckley's refusal to undress challenges the master/slave dichotomy which demands willing submission to Bingham's desire to punish her. Through these depictions of violence, she asserts control over her body and self-identity. Her refusal to scream out in pain, while using language to maintain her sense of self-identity begins the process of breaking the shackles of Bingham's authority. Keckley refuses to submit to his demand that she remove her clothes before he begins to beat her. According to Lori Merish "... clothes take on a crucial gendered significance: in particular, the clothed body is placed in opposition to exposed, and sexually vulnerable, female flesh" (245). However, clothes mean more than protection of her flesh; rather, Keckley's refusal to undress is about power over her body versus powerlessness. Keckley's clothes offer little or no protection for the flesh as it shreds under the extension of her master's power: the whip.

Furthermore, by keeping her clothes on she subverts negative sexual stereotypes of black women. Instead, of the scene becoming sexually charged by Keckley's willing compliance to Bingham's desire, she invests her narrative self with modesty as well as authority over her body, while the master's desire remains unfulfilled and exposed to public critique. For Keckley, clothing symbolizes the beginning of a psychological defense against shame and humiliation. Thus, her narrative re-creation of trauma functions as a mode of play that provides her with "mastery of [the] traumatic situation through repetition" and a remodified "version of the experience" (Arlow 42). She remodifies traumatic experiences by re-narrating both her conscious and subconscious verbal resistance: refusing to scream, making utterances of defiance against Bingham's will. Her retelling of the story denies "the reality of what was originally traumatic" in favor of maintaining her self-respect through a "precisely control[led]" reproduction of traumatic event(s) (Arlow 42). Through the act of writing, she dislocates Bingham's power and agency over her physically, morally, and psychologically. Keckley's textual revelations establish her as the sole agent over her body and identity, solidifying her subject position as a free woman.

More importantly, Keckley uses first-person narration to sever her authorial identity from both traumatic memories and her objectification as a slave. Repeatedly, her first-person narration acts to re-affirm her self-agency. There are two identities invested in moments of bodily anguish: Keckley the narrative "I" and the memory of her objectified body. It is easy to surmise that in the actual moment of torture that survival was foremost on her mind and not making statements of pride as well as resistance. Pain acts to obliterate language not to empower it (Scarry 35). For example, her phrases of "*the* quivering flesh" and "it cut *the* skin" demonstrate her psychological disconnection from the event. In effect, it is not Keckley who is being hurt; rather, it is a displaced or dispossessed body that is being punished, the representative "it" of her body is severed from the discursive "I" of the narrator. Thus, in her recalled memory, the trickling warm blood and "great welts" are projected onto the objectified body of the text, while affects of pride and resistance are introjected into Keckley as author.

Bingham's final attempt to punish Keckley also ends in failure. At this point in the narrative, Keckley reverses the power dynamics of the master/servant relationship between her and Bingham. Different from the first beating, Keckley describes this scene as though it were a moment that exists in the present. The splitting of her ego is no longer manifested; rather, her personality and body are reunited. Repeatedly, the author's self-expressive voice is introjected back into the objectified body through her use of such phrases as "I stood bleeding," "my suffering," "my distress"—no longer are flesh and voice separate (Keckley 37–38); but, they are fused in a defiant and discursively empowered identity of emerging black womanhood. She is no longer Keckley the objectified body, but Keckley a self-made subject.

## Conclusion: The Self-made Subject

Through the revelation of their individual traumatic experiences, Jacobs and Keckley historicize black women's resistance to slavery in an attempt to cope with violent experiences by creating a new and discursive identity of black womanhood. For Jacobs, black womanhood is based in the sentimental trope of suffering womanhood, exposing the evils within the domestic spaces of slavery. Moreover, her psychical splitting shows a conscious need to control the traumatic memories of sexual abuse. Finally, Keckley's post-antebellum narrative de-centers the focus of the slave narrative genre from bodily abuses of slavery to values of self-reliance, rejecting the suffering model of black womanhood in favor of a black womanhood firmly rooted in notions of bodily autonomy. Through their use of autobiography and sentimentalism, Jacobs and Keckley created a mediated space from which their authorial voices challenged myths about black women's hyper-sexuality, while promoting Victorian morality and dismantling the negative perceptions of African American women.

## WORKS CITED

Aberbach, David. *Surviving Trauma: Loss, Literature and Psychoanalysis.* New Haven: Yale University Press, 1989.

Andrews, William. "The Changing Moral Discourse in Nineteenth-Century American Women's Autobiography: Harriet Jacobs and Elizabeth Keckley." *De/Colonizing the Subject: The Politics of Gender in Women's Autobiography.* Eds. Sidonie Smith and Julia Watson. Minneapolis: University of Minnesota Press, 1992. 225–41.

Arlow, Jacob A. "Trauma, Play, and Perversion." *Psychoanalytic Study of the Child,* 42.1 (1987): 31–44.

Baker, Houston Jr. *Blues, Ideology, and Afro-American Literature: A Vernacular Theory.* Chicago: University of Chicago Press, 1984.

Barnes, Elizabeth. *States of Sympathy.* New York: Columbia University Press, 1997.

Bartky, Sandra Lee. *Femininity and Domination: Studies in the Phenomenology of Oppression.* New York: Routledge, 1990.

Bergner, Gwen. *Taboo Subjects: Race, Sex, and Psychoanalysis.* Minneapolis: University of Minnesota Press, 2005.

Berthold, Michael. "Not 'Altogether' the 'History of Myself': Autobiographical Impersonality in Elizabeth Keckley's *Behind the Scenes.*" *American Transcendental Quarterly* 13.2 (1999): 105–20.

Bryant, Jerry. *Victims and Heroes: Racial Violence in the African American Novel.* Amherst: University of Massachusetts Press, 1997.

Etter-Lewis, Gwendolyn. *My Soul Is My Own: Oral Narratives of African American Women in the Professions.* New York: Routledge, 1993.

Henke, Suzette A. *Shattered Subjects: Trauma and Testimony in Women's Life-Writing.* New York: St. Martin's, 1998.

hooks, bell. *Rock My Soul.* New York: Atria Books, 2003.

Jacobs, Harriet. *Incidents in the Life of a Slave Girl.* New York: Library of America, 2000.

Keckley, Elizabeth. *Behind the Scenes: Or, Thirty Years a Slave, and Four Years in the White House.* New York: Oxford University Press, 1988.

Lane, Christopher, ed. *The Psychoanalysis of Race.* New York: Columbia University Press, 1998.

Laplanche J. and J.B. Pontalis. *The Language of Psychoanalysis.* Trans. Donald Nicholson-Smith. New York: The Hogarth Press, 1973.

Laub, Dori. *Testimony: Crisis of Witnessing in Literature, Psychoanalysis, and History.* New York: Routledge, 1992.

Merish, Lori. *Sentimental Materialism: Gender, Commodity Culture, and Nineteenth-Century American Literature.* Durham: Duke University Press, 2000.

Miles, Diana. *Women, Violence, & Testimony in the Works of Zora Neale Hurston.* New York: Peter Lang, 2003.

Oliver, Kelly. *The Colonization of Psychic Space: A Psychoanalytic Social Theory of Oppression*. Minneapolis: University of Minnesota Press, 2004.
Olney, James. Introduction. *Behind the Scenes*. By Elizabeth Keckley. New York: Oxford University Press, 1998. 3-42.
Scarry, Elaine. *The Body in Pain*. New York: Oxford University Press, 1985.
Smith, Valerie. *Self-Discovery and Authority in Afro-American Narrative*. Cambridge: Harvard University Press, 1987.
———. "Loopholes of Retreat: Architecture and Ideology in Harriet Jacobs's *Incidents in the Life of a Slave Girl*." *Reading Black, Reading Feminist*. Ed. Henry Louis Gates Jr. New York: Meridian-Penguin, 1990. 212–27
Tate, Claudia. *Psychoanalysis and Black Novels: Desire and the Protocols of Race*. New York: Oxford University Press, 1998.

CHAPTER TWELVE

## Dressing down the First Lady
Elizabeth Keckley's *Behind the Scenes:
Or, Thirty Years a Slave, and Four Years in the White House*

**MICHELE ELAM**

Lizabeth, you are my best and kindest friend, and I love you as my best friend.
—Mary Todd Lincoln to Keckley, *Behind the Scenes*[1]

My association with Mrs. Lincoln ... clothed me with romantic interest.
—Elizabeth Keckley, *Behind the Scenes*

"I HAVE BEEN HER confidante, and if evil charges are laid at her door, they also must be laid at mine. To defend myself, I must defend the lady that I have served. The world have judged Mrs. Lincoln ... and through her have partially judged me, and the only way to convince them that wrong was not meditated is to explain the motives that actuated us" (xiv). With her remarkable, brief invocation of "us" in the Preface to *Behind the Scenes* (1868), seamstress Elizabeth Keckley (1824–1907) unites her reputation with that of the president's wife in order to stage their narrative separation. More interested in defending her own honor rather than her "imprudent" (xiii) lady's, Keckley must at once claim identification with Mary Todd Lincoln to establish her prestigious place in the White House-hold as modiste and intimate, yet distance herself from the widow's fall from social grace. When Mrs. Lincoln sold her presidential finery and clothes in 1867 in order to pay off her notorious debt of $70,000 to seamstresses, milliners, and shopkeepers, Keckley—as her dressmaker—risked appearing vicariously responsible for the scandal. Readers of Keckley's exposé, it turned out, did not hold her responsible for her patron's weaknesses; nevertheless, her narrative had a unanimously hostile reception on all political sides. Attempting to explain why both erstwhile abolitionists and secessionists alike condemned her, James Olney has limned the complex rhetorical angling involved in "writing within, and simultaneously against"[2] the literary tradition of Southern apologism in the postbellum era. William Andrews and Frances Smith Foster persuasively situate *Behind the Scenes*, particularly the first third of the work that recounts her enslavement by the Burwells in Virginia and then by the Garlands, in the tradition of the slave narrative, and to some extent explain her rise and fall as a function of generic constraint.[3]

Yet, given Keckley's tempered representation of slavery, the public anger suggests *Behind the Scenes* was provocative not simply for discussing her "thirty years a slave" but for exposing the last "four." The genre of the exposé engages the realist impulse to uncover truths, implicitly enjoining criteria of authority and validity; the attacks on Keckley's claim to represent what "really" happened engage these criteria, suggesting what she breached is not literary form but the shape of social reality. The *National News* in New York, for instance, quickly published a coarse parody entitled *Behind the Seams, By a Nigger Woman, Who Took in Work from Mrs. Lincoln and Mrs. Davis*, with a preface signed with an *x* (her mark) by "Betsy Kickley."[4] In its insistence that the "mulatto" author's close relationship with these famous women warrants her no more than an epithet, that her employment as seamstress deserves no name beyond ad hoc "work" "took in," the dismissive title betrays a frustrated recognition of the latent power of "nigger" women. Similarly, the *National News* and the other condemnatory reviews of Keckley's account focus less on her accounts of mistreatment as a slave and almost exclusively on her revelations about the Jefferson Davis and Lincoln families, in whose service she was serially employed after moving from St. Louis to Washington, DC, in 1860.

Clearly, many felt Keckley had "taken in" those whose work she had taken up, and which by its nature had allowed her into the inner sanctum of their households. The *New York Citizen* charge is representative, accusing Keckley of being "grossly and shamelessly indecent," and the book "an offence of the same grade as the opening of other people's letters, the listening at keyholes, or the mean espionage which unearths family secrets with a view to blackmailing the unfortunate victims."[5] The book's publisher, G.W. Carleton, finally recalled *Behind the Scenes* under pressure by Robert Lincoln, the Lincolns' oldest son. As the *Citizen*'s pique suggests, indignation at (and fear of) what was perceived as Keckley's near-criminal indiscretions is tied most specifically to her betrayal as a trusted employee, for clearly the writer of the article had in mind a grade of offenses associated with domestic servants, those putatively most in a position to open letters, peer through keyholes, or unearth family secrets—were they to bother. Keckley's apostasy lay not simply in pointing to white precedents of exposé, although she insists that "[i]f these ladies [in the Washington circle] could say everything bad of the wife of the President, why should I not be permitted to lay her secret history bare" (xv). Nor was the furor simply over violations of caste, over "a slave girl who has forgotten her place... [and trespassed] across the racially defined social, class, and behavioral barrier that legalized slavery had reinforced."[6]

Keckley, after all, had purchased herself in 1855; she was no longer a slave when employed by Mrs. Davis or Mrs. Lincoln. Her relatively novel status before national emancipation as self-employed ex-slave becomes a crisis, apparently, only after the war. The book's publication—and with that, Keckley's capitalization on her past employment for her own ends—marks a shift from enslaved to "free" labor, from commodity to producer. The supposedly simple prepositional character of what are, in fact, profound transitions ("from" enslaved and "to" wage laborer) does not occur at the moment Keckley buys herself in 1855 but rather when, in 1868, she writes a book for others to buy. That is, her move from object to agent does not occur by *fiat* at the moment of her purchase with borrowed funds, nor even when she pays back her white sponsors years later. And the exercise of her sovereignty is not damned simply because she is somehow a "free agent," "master" of oneself, as Frederick Douglass puts it in *Narrative of the Life of Frederick Douglass* (1845) when he purchases himself. Indeed, the supposedly radical language of self-possession appears less provocative when one considers that the right to possess "selves" made slavery possible—one reason why Harriet Jacobs, if not Douglass and Keckley, rejects the transaction altogether when, in *Incidents in the Life of a Slave Girl* (1861), her Northern benefactor first offers to buy her freedom. Rather, the problem for reviewers appears less Keckley's position as her own person, editorial peer, and "white observer" (Foster, *Written by Herself* 121) than that this "self-reliance" (Keckley, *Behind the Scenes* 20)[7] interrupts the social and economic reliance between black and white women institutionalized by slavery before, and now threatened by, the war's aftermath. Keckley's *Be-*

*hind the Scenes* is seen as victimizing her employers not because she is acting as an independent but because she tries to profit from white dependency on black "help." In that sense Keckley's narrative is less a refusal of the continued commodification of her body and labor after emancipation as an attempt to make *white people's lives* the desirable commodity to be circulated and sold in this new free market.

## Fickle Dames and Angry Servants

Keckley can lay claim to her employers' lives in part through the imbricated rhetorics of family and work imported from slavery to a postwar domestic service industry. If Southerners had long invoked domestic metaphors to sanction slavery (master as *pater,* mistress as mother, slaves as extended family—children, "uncles" or "mammies"), similar terms of obligation and affiliation underwrote postbellum domestic service. As Mary Todd Lincoln's biographers confirm, and Keckley makes clear in her Preface, she was one of Mrs. Lincoln's best friends, her "confidante," and "intimately associated with that lady in the most eventful periods of her life" (xiv).[8] Yet Keckley also insists that she is certainly not the "special champion of the widow of our lamented President" (xv), that Mrs. Lincoln is a woman of "jealous freaks" (124) and "the most peculiarly constituted woman" (182) she has ever met. By the end of the narrative, financially ruined by Mrs. Lincoln's broken promises of support and the widow's depleted means after her husband's death, Keckley complains that "fortune, fickle dame, has not smiled upon me" (330). No dame is more fickle in Keckley's narrative than Mrs. Lincoln, but Keckley insists the book was "not written in the spirit of 'the angry negro servant.'"[9] Her defense, however, no doubt incited critics' worst fears, for her comments imply there already exists a type (suggested by the quotation marks bracketing "the angry negro servant") and a genre ("written in the spirit" of that type) which she confirms through her very disavowal. In fact, Keckley herself is one of the first writers, if not the inaugural one, in the tradition to which she refers—a tradition of "negro" servants writing ("angrily" or not), a tradition of "servant narratives" emerging from the slave narrative.[10]

Coined "women's work," domestic service is most typically and specifically a "female-female relationship,"[11] and the most common arrangement in the late nineteenth and early twentieth centuries between white women and those of another class and race. With the standardization of domestic service (which included cooking, housekeeping, sewing, governess duties, and sometimes wet-nursing) in the 1850s came the rise of "housewives' manuals, training schools for domestics, and regular articles on the subject in popular magazines" (Rollins, *Between Women* 53). As a mode of control, formal instruction of both employers and employees preserved social distance in the face of emancipation and black, Irish, and German migration in the North; but, though in the South the racial composition of the servant class changed little until World War I, free-wage labor posed a threat to the antebellum character of service relations in both regions (51). Both acceding to and exploiting this anxiety in an effort to advance his platform for economic uplift, Booker T. Washington and the Tuskegee Normal Institute, which emphasized the industrial arts—including, for women, nursing, teaching, and domestic service—began graduating a generation of "New Negroes."[12]

Domestic service has been praised as a kinder and gentler form of labor, yet what historically makes this trade, regardless of social or racial context, according to Judith Rollins, "an occupation more profoundly exploitative than other comparable occupations" are the personal relationships between employee and employer. What might appear to be the basis of a more humane, less alienating work arrangement allows for a "level of psychological exploitation unknown in other occupations" (156). Intimacy in these work relations is not so much fraudulent as coercive because it is dependent on a tacit distance renewable, ironically, with each gesture of confidence between employee and employer:

> Using a domestic as a confidante may, in fact, be evidence of the distance in even the closest relationships. Employers can feel free to tell domestics secrets they would not share with friends or family precisely because the domestic is so far from being socially and psychologically significant to the employer. As physically close as the domestic may be, she is so existentially distant in the mind of the employer that the employer does not even entertain the possibility of the domestic's divulging secrets to those within the employer's social universe. (167)

Keckley's sharing of Mrs. Lincoln's private letters to her with James Redpath, her literary counselor, and their subsequent publication in the Appendix to *Behind the Scenes* was a scandal precisely because it violated not just public decorum but the existential absence of the employee to which Rollins refers. Whether Keckley herself authorized the printing of the letters, whether she was intentionally misled or simply incompetently served by Redpath, seems moot.[13] The appended letters, coupled with Keckley's reconstructed conversations between the pair, legitimated her claims of intimacy, but that intimacy was a function of Lincoln's certainty that their relations were *il*legitimate within her own racial and social sphere. Thus, although clearly there would have been outrage at any servant who broke faith, as it were, the nature of the public attacks, and Keckley's own rhetorical negotiations within her text, are emphatically and distinctively racialized. Publishing her memoir, whose subject (in no small part) and intended audience were within "the employer's social universe," was taken, in this particular historical instance, as a breach of the very conditions for women's interracial relations. As Jean H. Baker astutely notes, Keckley no doubt became Mrs. Lincoln's "closest friend" "despite or perhaps because of the inequality between an ex-slave, mulatto seamstress and a President's wife." Keckley was, "in the First Lady's view, 'although colored . . . very industrious . . . very unobtrusive and will perform her duties faithfully,'" a reminder of Mrs. Lincoln's "Mammy Sally" (230).[14]

This postwar obtuseness to white emotional and epistemological investment in black unobtrusiveness is exposed as early as Herman Melville's "Benito Cereno" (1855), with its prescient anticipation of narrative insurrections like Keckley's. Captain Amasa Delano's insistent misapprehension of the relationship between the Spanish captain, Don Benito, and his servant Babo leads him to mistake relations on the mutinied ship for a reassuring "spectacle of fidelity on the one hand and confidence on the other." Delano envies Don Benito "such a friend; slave I cannot call him."[15] As his praise suggests, Delano refuses the possibility of economic or physical coercion in what he self-interestedly reads instead as a genteel and fraternal arrangement. Delano misinterprets Babo's plea that he "is nothing: what Babo has done was but duty" ("Benito Cereno" 16) because it reinforces his desire that the good servant never imposes upon white largesse by assuming he or she is "something." Babo *is* in fact "nothing," for what he "has done" is an empty performance of servile duty (although in another sense "duty" refers to his obligation, and that of the others enslaved on board, to dissemble), designed to fulfill Delano's fantasy of the servant who labors for nothing. And the devaluation of his labor is indexed to his lesser existential status under slave law as three-eighths of a person.

Keckley similarly exploits whites' commitment to the economic and ontological hierarchies embedded in domestic labor practices. If, for their respective attempts, Babo's head ended up on a spear and Keckley was skewered in the press, *Behind the Scenes* nevertheless reveals what material advantage Keckley creates within the terms of her position. As Rollins notes, servants do not have to barter their own secrets in exchange for their employers' because the latter are, as a rule, uninterested in the private details of their servants' lives (*Between Women* 156). Keckley, in fact, makes Mrs. Lincoln begin *paying* for the intimate license the latter assumes. When Mrs. Lincoln breaks with their usual arrangement to meet at her own residence and drops in unannounced at Keckley's apartment one day in 1864, she pointedly remarks that "I never approved of ladies, attached to the White House, coming to my rooms. I always thought it would be more in keeping with their dignity to send for me, and let me come to them" (152). Her insistence on the tradition of servile etiquette derived from "associations of her early [slave] life" (133) allows her to condescend to the very woman to whom she caters. When Mrs. Lincoln twice visits Keckley in her own chambers, she is actually indebted to her for the inconvenience, for both parties recognize the visits as an encroachment upon Keckley's privacy requiring additional payment of some kind. After the first visit Keckley asks for and receives a "special favor": a "present of the right-hand glove that the President wears at the first public reception after the second inauguration" (154). The second time Mrs. Lincoln commits this *faux pas,* Keckley obtains permission for herself and a "friend" to hear President Lincoln speak at the White House (175). In both cases Keckley uses Mrs. Lincoln's personal visits as a way to barter social benefit.

### Fashioning the Masculine

Such examples illustrate the way Keckley negotiates female kinship altogether within the narrative, refiguring the affective work on which sentimental fiction depends. One of the clearest examples of her partition from women appears in her alignment with men. In her grieving for the tragic death in battle of Keckley's son, her only child (unnamed in the text), we learn only that it is a "sad blow" (105) to her, but when Willie, the Lincolns' youngest son, dies of fever, Mrs. Lincoln is "inconsolable" (104), a "mater dolorosa"[16] so subject to such "paroxysms of grief" (104) that the president says he will send her to the "lunatic asylum" (104) if she does not control herself. Refusing to allow her eldest, Robert, to enter the military, Mrs. Lincoln is chastised by her husband for elevating maternal propriety over national need: "The services of every man who loves his country are required in this war. You should take a liberal instead of a selfish view of the question, mother" (122). Keckley's self-presentation is fashioned along these less "selfish" lines of masculine restraint rather than feminine display, as I will explain. Identifying more with Mr. Lincoln's solemnity, she is more moved by the "grandeur as well as . . . simplicity" (104) of the silently weeping president at his child's deathbed than by Mrs. Lincoln's conspicuous distress. When the president is murdered, Keckley silently turns away with tears in her eyes and a "choking sensation" (191) in her throat. She is "awed into silence" (192) like another surviving son, Tad, who mourns his father quietly. Mrs. Lincoln, on the other hand, makes an ungodly "scene—the wails of a broken heart, the unearthly shrieks, the terrible convulsions, the wild, tempestuous outbursts of grief" (192). No such narrative convulsions mark the death of Keckley's own son. In fact, her emotional restraint extends to the omission of the "golden words of comfort" in "the kind womanly letter" that Mrs. Lincoln wrote when she heard of her "bereavement" (105), though she seems to have little compunction about publishing verbatim from some of their other private letters, and it might have placed her employer in a better light.

James Olney suggests that Keckley's withholding of vital personal information regarding her ex-husband and only son, a Wilberforce student, while devoting extensive space to the death of William and President Lincoln, grants white lives an importance she cannot claim for herself (xxxiv). But within that substitution of white for black operates also a shift in gender identification that effectively, if unconventionally, lets Keckley claim not only personal but also historic importance for herself. Just as she gains material and rhetorical advantage through preserving distance from Mrs. Lincoln—and from the archetypal feminine that her "hysterics" (200) represent—she also gains by associating herself with the Lincoln men, and briefly with Jefferson Davis. Unlike Mr. Lincoln, who speaks with fraternal generosity of the "soldierly qualities of . . . brave Confederate generals" (137), Mrs. Lincoln apparently has not the proper sororal feelings toward her own brothers in the Confederate army: "How can I sympathize with a people at war with me and mine?" (136). Keckley says at first she is "relieved" that Mrs. Lincoln has "no sympathy for the South," but then compares her with her husband, whose "soul was too great for the narrow, selfish views of partisanship" (136).

Keckley's own efforts at what Olney insightfully calls an "alien apologetics" (xxx)—in which she reunites with her previous owners at Rude's Hill (once occupied, she notes, by General Stonewall Jackson for his headquarters) in a spirit of reconciliation (252)—represent, in William Andrews's terms, revisionism "indicative *of* a historical truth . . . *a* truth emerging in something the writer faces in the present" ("Reunion" 15). In this case her "present" (i.e., postwar) reconciliatory stance creates for her an emotional "truth" akin to Mr. Lincoln's presidential condescension to the national brethren. She even claims she can hail the defeated Jefferson Davis, whom she characterized as "a thoughtful, considerate man in the domestic circle" (69): "Peace!" she writes, "You have suffered! Go in peace" (74). Ironically, this attitude, shared by Mr.—but pointedly not by Mrs.—Lincoln is the basis by which Keckley can also reinvent the bonds between women across the color-line. If her Northern friends, she says, could have witnessed her reunion, in which she is literally "carried to the house in triumph," "they would never have doubted again that the mistress had any affection for her former slave" (250). It is worth noting that it is the attitude Keckley shares with *Mr. Lincoln,* in opposition to that of his wife, that makes possible the erasure of "doubt" about the love of mistresses. This doubt, of course, is one she herself creates in her earlier critical accounts of her mistresses Burwell, who had her beaten (32), and Garland, whose family she almost single-handedly supported at the expense of her health (50). Her narrative suggests that her heart, like the Great Heart, inspires women's love across the color-line.

The rhetorical and economic inversion of mistress and slave in *Behind the Scenes* makes the First Lady a symbolic substitution for Keckley's subjugated position. In Fleischner's perceptive psychoanalytic analysis, Keckley's narrative, "a story of accumulation and debts, the narrator/dressmaker/restrained mourner and the narrated subject/dress buyer/unrestrained mourner Mrs. Lincoln are secret sharers, doubles in mourning and emotional valuation of possessions" (*Mastering Slavery* 102). Keckley both projects the "Otherness" ideologically associated with African Americans on to Mrs. Lincoln, "while at the same time, in light of the two women's interdependent relationship, [retaining] the phantom presence of the Other in her conception of herself . . . [in order to] give linguistic relief to her conflicted sense of self and achieve a narrative reconciliation with her own traumatic past" (102–03). The function of this process of displacement and projection becomes most clear, I would suggest, if we further consider not only the opposition between the women but the triangulation of desire between the two women and the men who feature so prominently in Keckley's text. From one perspective, for instance, Keckley simply usurps the privileged role of mother from the mistress/employer. Although President Lincoln's term of endearment for Mrs. Lincoln is "Mother," Keckley in fact represents the kind of capitalized maternity Mary Todd Lincoln is incapable of, for as both birth and surrogate mother Keckley transcends regional and racial boundaries. Claiming she loves her families "both black and white" (41), Keckley receives letters from those to whom she was once enslaved in which they name her "mother to us all" (259, 264) and name themselves her children (265). But to the degree it is Keckley who aids the women in "pecuniary embarrassment" (222) such as Mrs. Lincoln and the Garlands (238), and to the extent that hers alone are the sheltering arms the women seek in "terrible affliction" (189) or as death approaches (239), she is more like the supporting head of the household, the figure who stands in for an absent or dead husband.

In fact, Keckley repeatedly aspires to public conduct insistently coded in the text as masculine. Her national leadership, as founder of the Contraband Relief Association in 1862, is an immediate success (she takes pains to include an index of substantial donations) and its high-profile support from black and white notables, from Frederick Douglass to Wendell Phillips, is no doubt designed to highlight her social and political influence outside the sphere of the domestic. And in case readers miss the connection, Keckley concludes by strategically echoing Lincoln's title (and second term) with her own: "Mrs. Lincoln made frequent contributions, as also did the President. In 1863, I was re-elected President of the Association, which office I continue to hold" (116). Her work with the Contraband Relief Association, effectively placed between a reprinted memorial tribute to Willie Lincoln by Nathaniel Parker Willis and an account of the White House in decorous mourning for the boy, represents her response to others injured, widowed, or abandoned to "cold neglect" (112): the "relief of suffering soldiers . . . suffering blacks" (113). Like Mr. Lincoln—whom she imagines the Lord advising, like Job, to "'Gird up thy loins now like a man . . .'" (120–21)—Keckley takes action, while Mrs. Lincoln's sphere of vision and movement becomes increasingly constricted: "She could not bear to look upon [Willie's] picture; and after his death she never crossed the threshold of the Guest Room in which he died, or the Green Room in which he was embalmed" (116–17). What Keckley desires, through Mrs. Lincoln, is the potency of Mr. Lincoln, "the Jehovah" (154), the "Moses of my people ... an idol ... a demi-god" (190).

What sympathetic feminine reciprocity exists is linked to her allegiance to her race rather than to her employer, Keckley explains, because Mrs. Lincoln was the wife of the president, "the man who had done so much for my race," and thus she "could refuse or do nothing for her" (269). Racial sympathy is cautiously extended to Mrs. Lincoln by other African Americans for similar reasons. Although Mrs. Lincoln recognizes that "most of the good feeling regarding her straitened circumstances proceeds from the colored people" (Keckley, *Behind the Scenes* 35), the letters from Frederick Douglass and Henry Garnet reveal the extent to which they, too, distanced themselves from a cause that might prove "ridiculous" (319) and jeopardize the pressing interests of the race. Keckley establishes proximity to Mrs. Lincoln, while simultaneously substituting their respective roles, mainly because Mrs. Lincoln exists in closest proximity to the president.

### Metonymies of Desire

This psychic economy of exchange and transference also informs the function of intimate material objects, the giving and collecting of which occupies a disproportionate space of *Behind the Scenes*. Keckley's descriptions sometimes read like a fashion reporter's: "Mrs. Lincoln looked elegant in her rose-colored moire-antique. She wore a pearl necklace, pearl earrings, pearl bracelets, and red roses in her hair. Mrs. Baker was dressed in lemon-colored silk; Mrs. Kellogg in a drab silk, ashes of rose; Mrs. Edwards in a brown and black silk; Miss Edwards in crimson, and Mrs. Grimsly in blue watered silk" (89). Her accounts are in the mode of drawing-room realism, bur her interest in apparel goes beyond its use as a decorative index of social status. If Keckley's narrative is "public history privately experienced," as James Olney cogently puts it, then it is also a history of the public experience of private objects—soiled gloves, blood-stained cloaks, Confederate wrappers, and of course Mrs. Lincoln's wardrobe, carefully described throughout and painstakingly invoiced at the narrative's end. Keckley mediates her personal relations—and her relation to national history—through the sartorial.[17]

Almost all the women's relations are bartered in some way through clothing. Keckley's aunt, Charlotte, for example, is given a silk dress by Mrs. Garland's mother on "condition that her maid look cheerful, and be good and friendly with her," and "to make friends with her" (155) after Keckley's aunt dares to display unhappiness for being punished. As Mrs. Garland describes it:

> A maid in the old time meant something different from what we understand by a maid at the present time. Your aunt used to scrub the floor and milk a cow now and then, as well as attend to the orders of my mother. My mother was severe with her slaves in some respects, bur then her heart was full of kindness. She had your aunt punished one day, and not liking her sorrowful look, she made two extravagant promises in order to effect a reconciliation . . . the mistress told her she might go to church the following Sunday, and that she would give her a silk dress to wear on the occasion. (255)

Mrs. Garland's mother's "extravagant" measures to secure the *appearance* of friendliness from her slave suggest the necessary purchase of deception required to uphold the image of close relations. Her admission that "maid" is a euphemism for slave before the war, though meant to distinguish Keckley's current "condition" as domestic servant, nevertheless exposes the similar affective economy at work in both situations between white and black women. This particular exchange of clothing, however, confounds the racial privilege of largesse, for when Mrs. Garland's mother has nothing to wear for an occasion, "the maid proffered to loan the silk dress to her mistress" and she "made her appearance at the social gathering, duly arrayed in the silk that her maid had worn to church on the proceeding Sunday" (256).

That such largesse is needed to appease is the subject of another tale Keckley relates (with intent to amuse) in which an ex-slave recently come North complains that "'I is been here eight months, and Missus Lingom an't even given me one shife . . . My old missus us't gib me two shifes eber year'" (141). Keckley explains that on Southern plantations the mistress "every year made a present of certain under-garments to her slaves, which articles were always anxiously looked forward to and thankfully received. The old woman had been in the habit of receiving annually two shifts from her mistress, and she thought the wife of the President of the United States very mean for overlooking this established custom of the plantation" (142). Within the humor of the story is the suggestion that combined with the withdrawal of castoffs, which presumably "bought" gratitude from women of color, is the withdrawal also of any semblance of affection: "shiftless" when it comes to others, Mrs. Lincoln is thought "mean." In his chapter "The Clothes Make the Man and the Woman" in *Roll, Jordan, Roll: The World the Slaves Made,* Eugene Genovese notes that "[t]hroughout the South, masters and mistresses distributed clothing in a manner designed to underscore their own benevolence and to evoke gratitude for a supposed gift—a sensitivity to the social significance of clothing that suggests an awareness of the slaves' own positive attitude toward their clothing." Before long, however, "the slaves began to translate these 'gifts' into 'rights' and to let their masters understand as much."[18]

The consequences of any failure to fulfill these unwritten contracts of give and take are apparent also in the narrative's close, when Mrs. Lincoln extends to Keckley frequent promises that she will be "well remembered" (358) if the widow manages to see any profit on her wardrobe, reminders of future rewards that increase as Keckley withdraws after not being reimbursed for all her work sewing and negotiating on Mrs. Lincoln's behalf for several months. According to Keckley, the offers of money, which presume a pecuniary relationship, come hand in hand with appeals for sympathy, which by contrast presume bonds of friendship unsullied by the pecuniary. Even as she defers payment, Mrs. Lincoln desperately pleads in her letters for Keckley to write more, for she feels "as if I had not a friend in the world save yourself" (347). But in response to one of Keckley's letters urgently requesting $500 as partial payment for work to date, Mrs. Lincoln tells her only that when "I get my [wardrobe] back, if ever, from—, I will send you some of those dresses to dispose of at Washington for your own benefit" (360). Shifts too little and too late, apparently, cannot recreate the plantation façade of sororal friendship, especially in the face of a postwar economy in which Keckley has every right to money. Mrs. Lincoln's offer of clothes seems especially antiquated because what need has a seamstress of clothes—the very clothes, in fact, that she had made?

If she rejects the traditional bartering of female ties, however, Keckley still finds old and used clothing immensely valuable for different reasons. Certainly her occupation as seamstress grants her access to the inner domestic circle, and the occasion to comment on the important and mundane events in others' lives: The loss of a lace handkerchief lets her weigh in concerning the Lincolns' son, Tad, who had "displaced" it—he is "mischievous, and hard to restrain" (89), she concludes. Fitting a dress for Mrs. Lincoln and making "the search for a missing article an excuse" (119), she looks over the shoulder of the president to find out what passage in the Bible he is reading. Another time she is "basting a dress" (130) and overhears arguments between Mr. and Mrs. Lincoln about Senator Chase and Secretary Seward; later, listening to a conversation between husband and wife as she fits Mrs. Lincoln, she even finds she shares with Mr. Lincoln, of all things, a powerful love of goats (181).

As Sharon Dean suggests, black female servants can transform their historical invisibility into the "potent angle of vision"[19] of inside outsiders, though I would suggest that Keckley's potency lies not simply in the collection of odd tidbits of personal information, however choice to her readers. From Keckley's vantage point she both creates clothing that attracts the attention of those who observe it (78, 101) and, more importantly, uses her association with an object of clothing to turn *herself* into the object of interest. In 1865, at a Chicago charity fair that displayed a wax figure of Jefferson Davis in the outfit in which he was reportedly captured, Keckley makes the "pleasing discovery" that it was clothed in one of the two "chintz wrappers" she had made for Mrs. Davis in 1860 (74).

Though the exhibition is usually surrounded by a "great crowd" (74), Keckley herself soon replaces the wrapper as spectacle:

> When it was announced that I recognized the dress as one that I had made for the wife of the Confederate President there was great cheering and excitement, and I at once became an object of the deepest curiosity. Great crowds followed me, and in order to escape from the embarrassing situation I left the building. (75)

The wrapper mediates between Keckley and the Davis family, but there is no simple transfer of interest or social worth. The hidden work of the scene is Keckley's initial and necessary attribution of value to the object: She must first point out to others the significance of the wrapper and herself—and in that gesture, their mutual importance. That part of the scene, however, is suppressed through the passive voice; we do not know how or why some person "announced" Keckley's association, nor how or exactly why Keckley informed him or her, and indeed it must be suppressed because if Keckley is to share in the object's interest, the object must first appear self-evidently interesting. From the Latin *interesse*, "having legal claim or title to," "interest" assumes proprietary investment, and Keckley is the most interested party to an object that, she implies, is a phenomenon endowed with a life and intrinsic worth of its own. But it is the crowd's "excitement" that functions as demonstrative speculation, driving up the stock of both the things and her person with its "great cheering" that does not simply acknowledge (as Keckley implies) but actually determines the changeable value of the cultural icons—the wax figure, the chintz wrapper, and the seamstress herself.

Despite her best efforts, this value is deflated even within her account. Davis, Keckley concedes, was in fact wearing a "water-proof cloak instead of a dress, as first reported" when captured, but, she insists, this "does not invalidate any portion of my story" (75). The "story" that she wishes to remain viable involves not simply her claim that the wrapper was indeed the one she had made for Mrs. Davis (she offers the exact month and year when it was contracted) but that the clothing *could have been* involved in romantic circumstances. Since she cannot be the indirect instrument for the celebrated cross-dressing escape attempt by the Confederate president because—to her clear disappointment—the tale is fabricated, Keckley can only insist that the "coincidence is none the less striking and curious" (75). Her belaboring the incident is an effort to stitch together an identity based on associative connection, on the public investment in appearance and possibility, if not fact. Clothes, for this reason, construct personae in Keckley's account. Davis's wrapper is linked to subterfuge (if erroneously), as is Lincoln's plaid shawl, which is "rendered somewhat memorable as forming part of his famous disguise . . . when he wended his way secretly to the Capitol to be inaugurated as President" (309), and as is Mrs. Lincoln's use of heavy black veils when masquerading as Mrs. Clarke in her initial efforts to sell her wardrobe quietly. (Such personae must be tended carefully for, so clothed, they can take on a life of their own. When Keckley insists it would be indelicate of Mrs. Lincoln to leave her hotel at night unaccompanied, she argues that "Mrs. Lincoln has no reason to care what these people may say about her as Mrs. Lincoln, but she should be prudent, and give them no opportunity to say anything about her as Mrs. Clarke" [183].) Like the strategic transvestism so commonly employed by slaves in their flights to freedom, these evasions and escapes dupe because they play off the use of clothing as transparent synecdoche of the self—but in this case cross-dressing is used to signify an alternative public rather than racial self.[20]

It is the public life of objects that most consumes Keckley. The historic resonance of some articles of clothing or accidental objects retroactively creates for her not only a past, but also a prophetic future. She finishes a dressing gown for Jefferson Davis before the Civil War, for instance, "little dreaming of the future that was before it. It was worn, I have not the shadow of a doubt, by Mr. Davis during the stormy years that he was President of the Confederate States" (69). When, after those "stormy years," the presidential party toured the fallen Richmond, they "examined every object of interest" (165), and Keckley makes a point of saying she handled the official papers on desks, and "sat in the chair that Jefferson Davis sometimes occupied; also in the chair of the Vice-President, Alexander H. Stephens" (166). But why the fascination with a piece of furniture whose only claim to fame is that it supported some famous person's posterior?

## Palpable History

In one sense, of course, by setting her seat upon theirs, Keckley both subtly insults and assumes the men's authority. Yet the desire to gaze upon and handle such objects is also an effort to understand and touch history—to make oneself contiguous with the props of historical drama. This desire informs what George Brown Goode, the director of the US National Museum at the Smithsonian Institute at the *fin de siècle,* called the "museum idea." In his *Principles of Museum Administration* (1895), Goode calls for democratic access to objects held in common ownership but previously available only to the socially privileged and the wealthy. As Tony Bennett argues, the "museum idea," deriving from the principles of Benthamist utilitarianism, "rests on the notion that museums should serve as instruments of public instruction"—in other words, "extended circulation"[21] of select national objects among the unwashed masses might reform the lower and working classes into a more refined citizenry. Keckley's inclusion as a black working woman on the presidential tour of "every object of interest" is an exercise in edification for both her and her readers; her actual handling of the resolution prohibiting all free colored people from entering the State of Virginia (166) is intended for her audience as an historical lesson in the ironies of injustice. Keckley views these items in their original material context, but they are already transformed in significance by historical events, and already reserved for "tour" observation. For this reason

Paul Valéry accused exhibitions and museums of being "mausoleums,"[22] entombing objects in an historical vacuum. Indeed, the collected objects function not as a chronology but as a collage of artifacts, as cultural shorthand to a history reassembled in the present. In that sense the objects are made at once familiar and foreign, as the viewers, Keckley included, become tourists of their own culture.

But as in the case of the Davis wrapper, Keckley moves from being a tourist—or tour-guide—to becoming part of the tour. After all, as Keckley's handling of the Virginia resolution suggests, the exhibit is transformed by those who interact with it, and thus in a sense become events and exhibitions themselves. And when she returns to the South to visit the Garlands, she sits in the room that "General Jackson always slept in, and people came near and far to look at it." Each visitor to this "idol" "would tear a splinter from the walls or windows of the room, to take away and treasure as a priceless relic" (253). But in the sentence following this remark, *she* becomes the priceless artifact, the "object of great curiosity" (254). Keckley claims she is "clothed . . . with romantic interest" (254) both because she is associated with Mrs. Lincoln, and because she still has an "attachment" for the Garlands, "whose slave I had once been" (254). Both her presidential connections and her "attachment" to her ex-owners position her as a physical medium to a romanticized past.

Keckley seems to anticipate this construction of a past in her request for objects she believes will become *"sacred"* (367). The white glove that President Lincoln wore on his right hand during the ceremony following his second inauguration is a "precious memento" (154) to Keckley precisely because of the social metonymy of clothing: The glove bears "the marks of the thousands of hands that grasped the honest hand of Mr. Lincoln on that eventful night" (155). Even though Mrs. Lincoln insists Keckley has "some strange ideas" in wanting something "so filthy when he pulls it off [that Mrs. Lincoln] would be tempted to take the tongs and put it in the fire" (155), it is the very fact that the glove is "soiled" (158)—the material used in, and standing for, social exchange—that makes it such a coveted object for Keckley. Of course, in Mrs. Lincoln's case, previously worn clothing can also depreciate in value, as Keckley's reprint of a review of the "exposition of Lincoln dresses" in the New York *Evening Express* makes evident: "'Some of [the dresses],'" the reporter writes, "'if not worn long, have been worn much; they are jagged under the arms and at the bottom of the skirt, stains are on the lining, and other objections present themselves to those who oscillate between the dresses and dollars, notwithstanding they have been worn by Madam Lincoln'" (304).

In fact, after his death, Mrs. Lincoln is increasingly dissociated from her late husband by a critical public, and so while Keckley collects objects of his, the only objects of interest to her associated with her "friend" are things connected to the president: the dress worn by Mrs. Lincoln at the last inaugural address of Mr. Lincoln (368) and the earrings, "the identical cloak and bonnet worn by Mrs. Lincoln on that eventful night. On the cloak can be seen the life-blood of Abraham Lincoln" (367). The cloak, she explains elsewhere, is especially significant because it "bears the most palpable marks of the assassination, being completely bespattered with blood, that has dried upon its surface, and which can never be removed" (311), just like the glove that "bears the marks of thousands who shook his hand on that last and great occasion" (368). The blood, it turns out, proved not to be the president's, suggesting that like Davis's wrapper—Keckley's claims notwithstanding—clothes are not incontrovertible "palpable" connections to the famous events and persons. Despite their materiality—which is meant to testify to the legible presence of history, indeed, to testify to the existence of history itself—things offer at best only emotional, and therefore immaterial, links to the past.

Keckley's description of herself lifting "the white cloth from the white face" (190) of Lincoln lying in state thematizes this process of making raiment legible. Her adjectival equation of fabric and face suggests a doubling of the racial veil: Lifting the white cloth reveals only another racial mask. But upon Lincoln's racially opaque surface, Keckley inscribes his transcendent divinity, the "god-like intellect" that she reads on his "placid" face. This gesture of exposing the public mask (if only to create another of even more mythic proportions) is itself acutely public: The many distinguished people from the Cabinet and army clustered around Lincoln's body make room for and observe her (190). In that parting of the white crowd for a black woman, Keckley, with Lincoln, becomes a "Moses of my people" (190), the historical guide and racial interpreter for her audience. Indeed, the act of writing and publishing *Behind the Scenes* reproduces this exercise in reading "blank" cloth as textual surface and racial shroud, a canvas on and under which she interprets self and history. In Michael Fried's discussion of "upturned faces" in Stephen Crane's story "The Upturned Face," and in *The Red Badge of Courage,* the "pale, horizontal plane of the corpse's face" similarly evokes the "special blankness of the as-yet unwritten page" to create an "allegorization of writing."[23] In Crane's fiction, however, the faces are invariably disfigured, which Fried identifies with the "enterprise of writing," the "force of art" that can only consume or bury, not resuscitate, the natural world ("Realism, Writing" 94–95). Keckley's script does indeed lay Lincoln to rest, but there is no textual pollution of the "white cloth," nor "horror" ("Realism, Writing" 94) at his open casket. Rather, the horror is transformed into poetic opportunity: "Notwithstanding the violence of the death," Keckley writes, "there was something beautiful as well as grandly solemn in the expression . . ." (191). She "gazed long" (191); Lincoln's upturned face is offered up almost willingly as the sacrificial scene of and surface for interpretation, as "the flesh made word."[24]

Or, put another way, the words—*Behind the Scenes*—can only be written after Lincoln's death. Her collection of "valuable relics" (366) has narrative and symbolic significance only when the presidential flesh is no more. The relics' currency is uncoupled from their status as mere commodity; thus she makes a point of refusing the use or exchange value of objects she inherits or barters for. Rather, she donates what is "too sacred to sell" and "what could not be purchased from me, though many have been the offers for it" (367) to Wilberforce University, where her son was educated. Unable to give up all possessions, however, she withdraws the initial offer of the right-hand glove, explaining in a note that she retains the glove as a "precious souvenir of our beloved President" (367). Only as a token and keepsake may such items be privately kept, and whether donated or collected, the objects are out of commercial circulation. "The phenomenon of collecting," Walter Benjamin argues, "loses its meaning as it loses its personal owner."[25] But Keckley, though she capitalizes on her objects' "aura" and the Benjaminian metaphysic of origin, would not consider her donation to a public collection as perfidy to an object's "original" significance or the meaning vouchsafed it by the owner of the private collection. As Tony Bennett suggests, the placing of art (or objects) in a public collection is not "a loss of history—it is not a double betrayal of the history it once had and of another and ideal history it might have had—but, rather, the acquisition of another history, and of the history it *has* had" (889).[26] Keckley's donation, in this sense, lets objects doubly acquire rather than doubly lose history. When she reads the "white cloth" on the "white face" of Lincoln, she grants the inanimate a living history; and by in turn donating what items she does collect, Keckley publicly enshrines the objects' acquisition of this (her) history.

## Marketing Intimacy

Keckley thus takes pains to distance herself from the marketplace traffic that expedited her patron's fall and violates her ethic of collection. But the accumulation of things verifies her position as consumer, and Keckley seems unwilling to entirely forgo her status as market adept. The distinction, after all, between consumer and commodity is especially important because possession (which even the privilege of donation assumes) of objects separates the seamstress from her erstwhile status as personal chattel. Hence her involvement in the scandalous sale of clothes places her at cross-purposes and becomes a tension that Keckley cannot finally resolve. After all, she initially agrees with and publicly defends (307)—is even instrumental in managing—the selling of Mrs. Lincoln's wardrobe, even though by the narrative's end she tries to set herself above the market system to preserve her reputation. A letter to Bishop Payne of Wilberforce University indicating her desire to donate appears not accidentally after a letter from Mrs. Lincoln pleading with her to reject a scheme for money that Keckley had proposed in an earlier letter "announcing that [Mrs. Lincoln's] clothes were to be paraded in Europe" (364–66), but Keckley suggests she never had any plan to traffic in selling and spending. Insisting she holds to a moral economy unlike her employer's, Keckley argues that despite her incriminating actions, she had always thought that Mrs. Lincoln's plans to use her expensive wardrobe as an insurance against poverty was "borrowing trouble from the future" (270).

Critics, however, saw no distinction: *Behind the Scenes* was received as a similarly unforgivable peddling of private wares, especially because Keckley lays bare her own and Mrs. Lincoln's "motives" (xiv) for money as much as for reputation. Bankrupted by her unremunerated alliance with Mrs. Lincoln in the postwar years, Keckley explains in her concluding words that if "poverty did not weigh me down" (330), she would not be writing. Her pleas of poverty, though, worked only against her, for they confirmed the unacceptable obvious: that their employer-employee "friendship" was primarily a function of money. Booker T. Washington had promised whites that "interlacing our industrial [and] commercial" lives would assure them of being "surrounded by the most patient, faithful, law-abiding, and unresentful people the world has seen" (*Up from Slavery* 221); *Behind the Scenes* seemed to breach the contract exchanging employment opportunity for emotional guarantees. Some in the black community feared a white backlash from Keckley's actions and distanced themselves from her (Foster, *Written by Herself* 129). Mrs. Lincoln reportedly refused to speak to Keckley after the narrative's publication. Her other white regulars, too, refused her—not out of sympathy for the late president's widow, bur for the seamstress's racial heresy in expecting payment for "services" that included acts of loyalty and labor that whites hoped need not be bought in the postwar era. Despite her extraordinary ability to manipulate the conditions of her employment to her advantage, in 1868 Keckley crossed a line of which, given the flux of legal and racial renegotiations of labor relations in those early years of Reconstruction, neither she nor her white employers and audience were probably fully cognizant.[27] With the line so clearly drawn across the life and career of Keckley, however, African American writers in her wake were far more circumspect about suggesting that intimacy required reimbursement.

### NOTES

1. Elizabeth Keckley, *Behind the Scenes: Or, Thirty Years A Slave, and Four Years in the White House* (1868). Introduction by James Olney, New York: Oxford University Press (1988), 254, 210. Further references will be to this edition.

2. Olney, Introduction, *Behind the Scenes*, xxx.

3. See Frances Smith Foster, *Written by Herself: Literary Production of African American Women, 1746-1892*. See William Andrews, "The Changing Moral Discourse of Nineteenth Century African American Women's Autobiography: Harriet Jacobs and Elizabeth Keckley" (1991), in *De/Colonizing the Subject: The Politics of Gender in Women's Autobiography*, 225–41. See also William Andrews, "Reunion in the Postbellum Slave Narrative: Frederick Douglass and Elizabeth Keckley," in *Black American Literature Forum*. Andrews persuasively explains Keckley's account of her invited visit to Anne Burwell Garland in 1866 in which she was "carried to the house in triumph" (Keckley 25) as an effort to renew "the slave narrative as a genre that could still be relevant to the new post-slavery era" (15). My aim here is to push this insight even further, to suggest that one way in which Keckley is positioning her narrative's relevance in the post-slavery era is by positioning herself and her writing in the post-slavery market system.

4. Anonymous, *Behind the Seams, By a Nigger Woman, Who Took in Work from Mrs. Lincoln and Mrs. Davis*. National News, 1868, price ten cents.

5. Quoted in Frances Smith Foster, *Written by Herself*, 128.

6. Jennifer Fleischner, *Mastering Slavery: Memory, Family, and Identity in Women's Slave Narratives*, 95. Fleischner's *Mrs. Lincoln and Mrs. Keckly: The Remarkable Story of the Friendship Between a First Lady and a Former Slave* (New York: Broadway Books, 2003) was released after my book went to press and so is unfortunately unavailable for review here.

7. On distinctions between Keckley's notion of self-reliance as cautious embrace of white social norms versus Emerson's anti-conformist definition of self-reliance, see Darryl Pinckney, "Promissory Notes," in *New York Review of Books* (April 6, 1995), 41–6.

8. See Ishbel Ross, *The President's Wife: Mary Todd Lincoln, a Biography*, and Ruth Painter Randall, *Mary Lincoln: Biography of a Marriage*. Keckley in part redefines her position as domestic laborer by frequently contracting outside the home in which she is working, and by elevating her work as a "mantua-maker" to a bona fide profession.

9. Letter to the *New York Citizen* (April 25, 1868). Quoted in John E. Washington's "Behind the Scenes: The Story of Mrs. Keckley's Book," in *They Knew Lincoln*, 4.

10. There are, of course, a few precedents to Keckley's narrative, most notably Eliza Potter's *A Hairdresser's Experience in High Life* (1859). Potter, like Keckley, was very independent and outspoken, but she does not name names and she does not profess loyalty to—and thus expose herself to the same accusations of betrayal of—any one family. Those differences, as well as the volatility of the postwar years, may have accounted for the more hostile reaction to Keckley's work.

The debate over the extent to which Keckley's account was ghostwritten or written in conjunction with her editors seems moot here, except to note that it engages realist demands for authenticity not necessarily invoked in other genres. More noteworthy is the fact that Keckley's self-consciously distinguishes herself from, and yet simultaneously defines, a relatively new literary form. The form does not develop into a tradition, however, because, as I conclude in this chapter, the eclipse of Keckley's career virtually extinguished the possibility of others finding publishers, let alone an audience, for such narratives. Later works seem to take the lesson of her demise. The "barber-poet" James M. Whitfield (1812–71), though passionate about the outrages of racial injustice, never writes of his work or patrons; Frances Harper (1825–1911) worked in domestic service before writing and teaching, but none of her extant poetry, magazine articles, or novels broach the subject of work relations in the same manner; the political writer Maria W. Stewart (1803–79) was a servant girl in a minister's home, but her collection of essays and memoir, *Meditations from the Pen of Mrs. Maria W. Stewart* (1879), mentions working for the clergyman's family only in passing. Mrs. N.F. Mossell's *The Work of the Afro-American Woman* (1894), which argues for the virtues of fiscal and emotional autonomy for black women, makes clear in its catalog of their achievements in literature, journalism, politics, higher education, and medicine that African American women were increasingly no longer content to work only as domestics. Charles Chesnutt's "Sis Becky's Pickaninny," in

*The Conjure Woman* (Durham: Duke University Press, 1993), provides a fascinating example of Keckley's legacy in Uncle Julius's subtle management of interracial intimacy between employer and employee. I give this story extended treatment in "Uncle Julius, Uncle Remus, and the Avuncular Erotics of American Dialect Fiction," American Studies Association paper (Pittsburgh, 1995).

11. Judith Rollins, *Between Women: Domestics and Their Employers*, 59.

12. See Booker T. Washington, *Up from Slavery: An Autobiography*. See especially the reprinted "Atlanta Exposition" speech, 217–33.

For a good discussion of the nursing profession, one of the earliest trades open to black women, see Darlene Clark Hine, *Black Women in White: Racial Conflict and Cooperation in the Nursing Profession, 1890–1950* (Bloomington: Indiana University Press, 1989). For intraracial class relations involving domestics, see June Jordan, "Report from the Bahamas," in *On Call* (Boston: South End Press, 1985).

13. Foster argues that Redpath "indirectly destroyed [Keckley's] business and irreparably harmed her reputation" by publishing *Behind the Scenes* in its final form, though she admits that his impeccable credentials suggest that other factors, which I explore in this chapter, were perhaps more at play in the unexpected, hostile reception of the text. Redpath was "a political activist, a war correspondent, and an advisor to Lincoln on issues such as the independence of Haiti." Redpath was also an abolitionist and a democrat who had edited and published works by Louisa May Alcott, Wendell Phillips, Balzac, Swift, and High in his "Books for the Times" and "Books for the Campfire" series. Perhaps more important to Keckley, Redpath had published William Wells Brown's *Clotelle* and *The Black Man: His Antecedents and His Genius*, a biography of Toussaint Louverture, and his own *Public Life and Autobiography of John Brown*. His *Palm and Pine* had published poems by Frances Harper and the Lyceum Bureau, which he was in the process of establishing during the year that Keckley's book was being published, represented Emerson, Greeley, Beecher, Sumner, and Wendell Phillips (Foster, *Written by Herself* 128).

14. See Jean H. Baker, *Mary Todd Lincoln: A Biography*, 230.

15. Herman Melville, "Benito Cereno," *Herman Melville: Selected Tales and Poems*.

16. Quoted in Ross, *The President's Wife*, 167.

17. Jennifer Fleischner focuses on Keckley's collection of articles as mementos of mourning, suggesting that for Keckley "articles are the children of memory" and their collection "fill[s] familial gaps left through the years." See *Mastering Slavery*, 122. Andrews distinguishes Keckley's "materialist and pragmatic mode of self-valuation" and valuation of things from Harriet Jacobs's idealist moral standard ("The Changing Moral Discourse" 237). My argument here seeks to extend and complicate more than rebut either argument, for clearly Keckley's "materialism" includes but is also more than a commitment to the values of the marketplace or hoarding against a lifetime of losses—though I find especially convincing Fleischner's explanation of the interpolation of private letters and documents into *Behind the Scenes* as a "form of symbolic transference over separations" earlier in her life.

18. Eugene D. Genovese, *Roll, Jordan, Roll: The World the Slaves Made*, 555, 557.

19. Sharon Dean, Introduction, *A Hairdresser's Experience in High Life* by Eliza Potter.

20. In a brief remark about *Behind the Scenes*, Lindon Barrett suggests that Keckley's presentation of "images of white bodies at length ... broached through the synecdoche of dress and fashion, define her text much more fully than images of black bodies." See Lindon Barrett "Handwriting, Legibility and the White Body in *Running a Thousand Miles for Freedom*." My argument aims to elaborate just why and how her text cloaked black bodies in white dress.

21. Tony Bennett, "The Multiplication of Culture's Utility," 862.

22. See Llewellyn Negrin's discussion of Theodor Adorno's analysis of Valéry in "On the Museums' Ruins: A Critical Appraisal," in *Theory, Culture, and Society* 10. 97–125.

23. Michael Fried, "Realism, Writing, and Disfiguration in Thomas Eakins's 'The Gross Clinic,'" in *Representations*, 33–104, especially "Postscript: Stephen Crane's Upturned Faces," 94. We see a fascinating twist on this theme of upturned faces in the burned countenance of the black man, Henry Johnson, in Crane's "The Monster"; I discuss this at more length in "Fear and Loathing in the Classroom; Or, Who's Afraid of Stephen Crane's 'The Monster'?" in *Teaching the New Canon: Students, Teachers, and Texts in the Multicultural Classroom*, 211–23.

24. I am borrowing the meaning of Susan Gubar's words here, for in her discussion of the final scene between Seldon and Lily in Edith Wharton's *The House of Mirth*, she, like Fried, sees a dead body written over, illustrating "the terror not of the word made flesh but of the flesh made word." See Susan Gubar, "The 'Blank' Page and Female Creativity," *Writing and Sexual Difference*, ed. Elizabeth Abel (Chicago: University of Chicago Press, 1982), 82.

25. Walter Benjamin, "Unpacking My Library: A Talk about Book Collecting," in *Illuminations*, trans. Harry Zohn, ed. Hannah Arendt (New York: Harcourt Brace, 1968), 67. Carolyn Sorisio offers another interpretation of the scene of mourning (and of commodity culture) in relation to Keckley's negotiation of the codes of genteel conduct, in "Unmasking the Genteel Performer: Elizabeth Keckley's *Behind the Scenes* and the Politics of Public Wrath" in *African American Review* 34 (2000), 19–38.

26. See also Philip Fisher, *Making and Effacing Art: Modern American Art in a Culture of Museums* (New York: Oxford University Press, 1991). Bennett is making this claim apropos of Philip Fisher's revision of Benjamin's philosophy of collecting. See Bennett, "The Multiplication of Culture's Utility."

27. Harold H. Wyman and William M. Wiecek point out that 1863–67 saw a sea change in judicial review, especially in the area of states' rights to intervene in local city or private affairs as well as the legal and entrepreneurial professions. See Harold H. Wyman and William M. Wiecek, *Equal Justice Under Law: Constitutional Development*, 1834–1875 (New York: Harper and Row, 1982).

Black writers did not begin to critique interracial relations between women, in particular, until the 1950s. After the publication of James Paule Marshall's *Brown*

*Girl, Brownstones* (1959) came James Baldwin's *Another Country* (1963), Allison Mill's *Francisco* (1974), Ann Allen Shockley's *Loving Her* (1974), Al Young's *Who Is Angelina?* (1975), Alice Walker's *Meridian* (1976), Barbara Chase-Riboud's *Sally Hemings* (1979), Alice Childress's *A Short Walk* (1979), and Toni Morrison's *Tar Baby* (1981). For brief discussions of these novels, see Elizabeth Schultz, "Out of the Woods and into the World: A Study of Interracial Friendships between Women in American Novels," in *Conjuring: Black Women, Fiction, and Literary Tradition*, eds. Marjorie Pryse and Hortense J. Spillers (Bloomington: Indiana University Press, 1985), 67–85.

## WORKS CITED

Andrews, William. "The Changing Moral Discourse of Nineteenth Century African American Women's Autobiography: Harriet Jacobs and Elizabeth Keckley." *De/Colonizing the Subject: The Politics of Gender in Women's Autobiography.* Eds. Sidonie Smith and Julia Watson. Minneapolis: University of Minnesota Press, 1992. 225–41.

———. "Reunion in the Postbellum Slave Narrative: Frederick Douglass and Elizabeth Keckley." *Black American Literature Forum* 23:1 (Spring 1989): 5–16.

Anonymous. *Behind the Seams, By a Nigger Woman, Who Took in Work from Mrs. Lincoln and Mrs. Davis.* New York: National News, 1868.

Baker, Jean H. *Mary Todd Lincoln: A Biography.* New York: W.W. Norton, 1987.

Baldwin, James. *Another Country.* New York: Dell, 1963.

Barrett, Lindon. "Handwriting, Legibility and the White Body in *Running a Thousand Miles for Freedom*." *American Literature* 69 (June 1997): 315–36.

Bennett, Tony. "The Multiplication of Culture's Utility." *Critical Inquiry* 21 (Summer 1995): 862.

Benjamin, Walter. "Unpacking My Library: A Talk about Book Collection." *Illuminations*. Trans. Harry Zohn. Ed. Hannah Arendt. New York: Harcourt Brace, 1968.

Birnbaum, Michele. "Fear and Loathing in the Classroom: Or, Who's Afraid of Stephen Crane's 'The Monster'?" *Teaching the New Canon: Students, Teachers, and Texts in the College Literature Classroom.* Eds. Bruce Goebel and James C. Hall. Urbana: National Council of Teachers of English, 1995), 211–23.

Butler, Judith. *Bodies that Matter: On the Discursive Limits of "Sex."* New York: Routledge, 1993.

Chase-Riboud, Barbara. *Sally Hemings.* New York: Ballantine Books, 1979.

Childress, Alice. *A Short Walk.* New York: Putnam, 1979.

Dean, Sharon, ed. *A Hairdresser's Experience in High Life.* By Eliza Potter (1859). New York: Oxford University Press, 1988.

Douglass, Frederick. *Narrative of the Life of Frederick Douglass* (1845).

Fisher, Philip. *Making and Effacing Art: Modern American Art in a Culture of Museums*. New York: Oxford University Press, 1991.

Fleischner, Jennifer. *Mastering Slavery: Memory, Family, and Identity in Women's Slave Narratives*. New York: New York University Press, 1996.

Foster, Frances Smith. *Written by Herself: Literary Production of African American Women, 1746–1892*. Bloomington: Indiana University Press, 1993.

Fox-Genovese, Elizabeth. *Within the Plantation Household: Black and White Women of the Old South*. Chapel Hill: University of North Carolina Press, 1988.

Fried, Michael. "Realism, Writing, and Disfiguration in Thomas Eakins's 'The Gross Clinic.'" *Representations* 9 (Winter 1995): 33–104.

Genovese, Eugene D. *Roll, Jordan, Roll: The World the Slaves Made*. New York: Vintage, 1976.

Goebel, Bruce A. and James C. Hall. *Teaching a "New Canon"?: Students, Teachers, and Texts in the College Literature Classroom*. Urbana: National Council of Teachers of English, 1995.

Goode, George Brown. *The Principles of Museum Administration*. York: Coultas & Volans, 1895.

Gubar, Susan. "The 'Blank' Page and Female Creativity." *Writing and Sexual Difference*. Ed. Elizabeth Abel. Chicago: University of Chicago Press, 1982.

Gwin, Minrose C. *Black and White Women of the Old South: The Peculiar Sisterhood in American Literature*. Knoxville: University of Tennessee Press, 1985.

Harris, Trudier. *From Mammies to Militants: Domestics in Black American Literature*. Philadelphia: Temple University Press, 1985.

Hine, Darlene Clark. *Black Women in White: Racial Conflict and Cooperation in the Nursing Profession, 1890–1950*. Bloomington: Indiana University Press, 1989.

Jacobs, Harriet. *Incidents in the Life of a Slave Girl*. Boston, 1861.

Jordan, June. "Report from the Bahamas." *On Call*. Boston: South End Press, 1985.

Keckley, Elizabeth. *Behind the Scenes: Or, Thirty Years a Slave, and Four Years in the White House* (1868). Introduction by James Olney. New York: Oxford University Press, 1988, 254, 210.

Letter to the *New York Citizen* (April 25, 1868). Quoted in John E. Washington's "Behind the Scenes: The Story of Mrs. Keckley's Book." *They Knew Lincoln*. New York: Dutton, 1942.

Marshall, Paule. *Brown Girl, Brownstones*. New York: Random House, 1959.

Melville, Herman. "Benito Cereno." *Herman Melville: Selected Tales and Poems*. Ed. Richard Chase. New York: Holt, 1950. 16.

Mills, Allison. *Francisco*. Berkeley: Reed, Cannon and Johnson, 1974.

Morrison, Toni. *Tar Baby*. New York: Plume, 1983.

Mossell, Mrs. N[athan] F[rancis]. *The Work of the Afro-American Woman*. Philadelphia: Ferguson, 1894. Reissued by the Schomburg Library of Nineteenth-Century Black Women Writers, 1988.

Negrin, Llewellyn. "On the Museum's Ruins: A Critical Appraisal." *Theory, Culture & Society* 10.1 (February 1993): 97–125.

Pinckney, Darryl. "Promissory Notes." *New York Review of Books* (April 6, 1995): 41.

Randall, Ruth Painter. *Mary Lincoln: Biography of a Marriage*. Boston: Little, Brown, 1953.

Rollins, Judith. *Between Women: Domestics and Their Employers*. Philadelphia: Temple University Press, 1985.

Ross, Ishbel. *The President's Wife: Mary Todd Lincoln, A Biography*. New York: G.P. Putnam 1973.

Saks, Eva. "Representing Miscegenation Law." *Raritan* 8 (1988): 53–54.

Shockley, Ann Allen. *Loving Her* (1974). Boston: Northeastern, 1997.

Shultz, Elizabeth. "Out of the Woods and Into the World: A Study of Interracial Friendships between Women in American Novels." *Conjuring Black Women, Fiction, and Literary Tradition*. Eds. Marjorie Pryse and Hortense J. Spillers. Bloomington: Indiana University Press, 1985. 67–85.

Sorisio, Carolyn. "Unmasking the Genteel Performer: Elizabeth Keckley's *Behind the Scenes* and the Politics of Public Wrath." *African American Review* 34 (2000): 19–38.

Stewart, Maria. *Meditations from the Pen of Mrs. Maria W. Stewart: (Widow of the Late James W. Stewart) Now Matron of the Freedman's Hospital, and Presented in 1832 to the First African Baptist Church and Society of Boston, Mass*. 1879.

Strasser, Mark. "Family Definitions, and the Constitution: On the Antimiscegenation Analogy." *Suffolk University Law Review* 25 (Winter 1991): 981–1034.

Walker, Alice. *Meridian*. New York: Harcourt Brace Jovanovich, 1976.

Washington, Booker T. *Up from Slavery: An Autobiography*. New York: Carol Publishing, 1989.

Young, Al. *Who Is Angelina?* New York: Holt, Rinehart and Winston, 1975.

ELIZABETH HOBBS KECKLEY TIMELINE

1818   Elizabeth Hobbs (Keckley) is born in February in Dinwiddie County, Virginia.

1832   At fourteen, Elizabeth Keckley is given by Armistead Burwell to his oldest son, Robert. She lives with the Robert Burwell family in Chesterfield County, Virginia.

1835   The Robert Burwell family and Elizabeth Keckley move to Hillsborough, North Carolina, where Robert becomes minister of Hillsborough Presbyterian Church.

Harriet Jacobs escapes to her grandmother's attic in Edenton, North Carolina, where she will hide for seven years.

1836   The Burwells arrange for Elizabeth Keckley to be beaten by local schoolmaster William J. Bingham to correct her "stubborn pride."

1837   Anna Burwell opens the Burwell Academy for Young Ladies.

1839   Elizabeth Keckley gives birth to son, George, the result of repeated rapes by Alexander Kirkland, son of a prominent local merchant and planter in Hillsborough; Keckley names the baby George Pleasant Hobbs for her mother's husband and the man she knew as her father.

Keckley is returned to Virginia.

1847   Frederick Douglass begins publication of *The North Star*.

Keckley, her son, and her mother are held by Anne Burwell Garland and her husband Hugh; the Garland family moves to St. Louis.

1849   Harriet Tubman escapes slavery.

1850   Fugitive Slave Act passes.

1852   Elizabeth Keckley marries James Keckley.

After Elizabeth Keckley's repeated requests, the Garlands set the price of her freedom and that of her son's at $1,200 in November.

Harriet Beecher Stowe publishes *Uncle Tom's Cabin*.

1853   Stowe publishes *A Key to Uncle Tom's Cabin*.

1855    Elizabeth Keckley purchases her and her son's freedom from the Garland family.

Frederick Douglass publishes *My Bondage and My Freedom.*

1857    *Dred Scott v. Sandford* is decided by the U.S. Supreme Court, declaring that African Americans, freed or enslaved, are not U.S. citizens, and the federal government has no power to regulate slavery. Elizabeth Keckley's former owner Hugh Garland had been a defense attorney early in the case.

1859    16 October: John Brown leads the attack on the arsenal at Harpers Ferry, Virginia.

Georgia passes a law forbidding owners from manumitting slaves in their wills.

Harriet Wilson publishes *Our Nig: Or, Sketches from the Life of a Free Black.*

1860    Elizabeth Keckley's son, George, enrolls in Wilberforce University.

Keckley moves to Baltimore, then to Washington, DC.

1861    Elizabeth Keckley meets Mary Todd Lincoln on March 4, 1861, the day after Lincoln's first inauguration. Elizabeth Keckley will go on to make approximately sixteen dresses for her in four months.

April 12: Attack on Fort Sumter off the coast of Charleston, South Carolina, signals the beginning of the Civil War.

August 10: Keckley's son, George, is killed in the Battle of Wilson's Creek, Missouri.

Harriet Jacobs publishes *Incidents in the Life of a Slave Girl.*

1862    Elizabeth Keckley founds of the Contraband Relief Association (CRA).

1863    According to the *Christian Recorder,* the CRA's receipts were "$838.68 the first year and $1,228.43 the second year."

January 1: Lincoln issues the Emancipation Proclamation.

November 19: Lincoln delivers the Gettysburg Address.

1865    Thirteenth Amendment passes.

14 April: Lincoln is shot by John Wilkes Booth at Ford's Theatre and dies the following day.

1867    September 18: Old Clothes Scandal begins; Elizabeth Keckley joins Mary Todd Lincoln in New York.

| 1868  | *Behind the Scenes: Or, Thirty Years a Slave, and Four Years in the White House* is published. |
| 1875  | Civil Rights Act of 1875 passes. |
| 1881  | *Life and Times of Frederick Douglass* is published. |
|       | Tuskegee Institute is founded by Booker T. Washington. |
| 1890  | Elizabeth Keckley sells twenty-six of the Lincolns' articles to a collector for $250. |
| 1892  | Elizabeth Keckley accepts a position at Wilberforce University. |
|       | Anna Julia Cooper publishes *A Voice of the South: By a Woman from the South*. |
| 1893  | Elizabeth Keckley organizes a dress exhibit at the World's Columbian Exposition, also known as the Chicago World Fair. |
| 1897  | Harriet Jacobs dies and is eulogized by Francis Grimké, as Keckley will be a decade later. |
| 1898  | Wilmington, North Carolina, Race Riot. |
| 1890s | Elizabeth Keckley suffers a stroke and moves back to Washington, DC. |
| 1907  | Elizabeth Keckley dies of a stroke at the Home for Destitute Colored Women and Children, Washington, DC; is buried at the Columbian Harmony Cemetery. |
| 1960  | Elizabeth Keckley's remains are transferred to the National Harmony Memorial Park in Landover, Maryland. |
| 2010  | Elizabeth Keckley's unmarked grave is located and a marker is placed in her honor. It reads, |

Elizabeth Keckly
1818–1907
Enslaved. Modiste. Confidante.

# FURTHER READING

Adams, Katherine. *Owning Up: Privacy, Property, and Belonging in U.S. Women's Life Writing*. New York: Oxford University Press, 2009.
Ames, Mary Clemmer. "Life in Washington: Stories of the Late Slaves." *Evening Post* 18 April 1862: 1.
———. *Ten Years in Washington: Life and Scenes in the National Capital, as a Woman Sees Them*. Hartford: A.D. Worthington, 1873.
Amireh, Amal. *The Factory Girl and the Seamstress: Imagining Gender and Class in Nineteenth Century American Fiction*. New York: Routledge, 2015 (reprint edition).
Andrews, William L. "The Changing Moral Discourse of Nineteenth-Century African American Women's Autobiography: Harriet Jacobs and Elizabeth Keckley." *De/Colonizing the Subject: The Politics of Gender in Women's Autobiography*. Eds. Sidonie Smith and Julia Watson. Minneapolis: University of Minnesota Press, 1992. 225–41.
Berlin, Ira. *Slaves without Masters: The Free Negro in the Antebellum South*. New York: Pantheon Books, 1974.
Brennan, Charlie. *Amazing St. Louis: 250 Years of Great Tales and Curiosities*. St. Louis: Reedy Press, 2013.
Brown, Elsa Barkley. "African-American Women's Quilting: A Framework for Conceptualizing and Teaching African-American Women's History." *SIGNS Journal of Women in Culture and Society* 14.4 (1989): 921–29.
Carby, Hazel V. *Reconstructing Womanhood: The Emergence of the Afro-American Woman Novelist*. New York: Oxford University Press, 1987.
Chiaverini, Jennifer. *Mrs. Lincoln's Dressmaker*. New York: Dutton Press, 2013.
Crowston, Clare Haru. *Fabricating Women: The Seamstresses of Old Regime France, 1675–1791*. Durham: Duke University Press, 2001.
Domina, Lynn. "'I Was Re-Elected President': Elizabeth Keckley as Quintessential Patriot in *Behind the Scenes: Or, Thirty Years a Slave, and Four Years in the White House*." *Women's Life-Writing: Finding Voice/Building Community*. Ed. Linda Coleman. Bowling Green: Bowling Green State University Popular Press, 1997. 139–51.
Fleischner, Jennifer. *Mastering Slavery: Memory, Family, and Identity in Women's Slave Narratives*. New York: New York University Press, 1996.
———. *Mrs. Lincoln and Mrs. Keckly: The Remarkable Story of the Friendship between a First Lady and a Former Slave*. New York: Broadway Books, 2003.
Foley, Barbara. "History, Fiction, and the Ground Between: The Uses of the Documentary Mode in Black Literature." *PMLA* 95.3 (May 1980): 389–403.

Foster, Frances Smith. "Romance and Scandal in a Postbellum Slave Narrative: Elizabeth Keckley's *Behind the Scenes*." *Written by Herself: Literary Production by African American Women, 1746–1892*. Bloomington: Indiana University Press, 1993. 117–30.

Gimeno Pahissa, Laura. "Former Slaves on the Move: The Plantation Household, the White House, and the Postwar South as Spaces of Transit in Elizabeth Keckley's *Behind the Scenes*." *Revista Alicantina de Estudios Ingleses*. 25: 335–49.

Hoffert, Sylvia. *When Hens Crow: The Woman's Rights Movement in Antebellum America*. Bloomington: Indiana University Press, 2002.

Hutchison, C. "Elizabeth Keckley." *American Literary History*. 19.3: 603–28.

Jones, Lynda. *Mrs. Lincoln's Dressmaker: The Unlikely Friendship of Elizabeth Keckley and Mary Todd Lincoln*. National Geographic Children's Book, 2009.

Karwatka, Dennis. "Elizabeth Keckley and Dressmaking Innovation." *Tech Directions*. 68.4: 12.

Keckley, Elizabeth. *Behind the Scenes: Or, Thirty Years a Slave, and Four Years in the White House*. (1868) Ed. Frances Smith Foster. Urbana: University of Illinois Press, 2001.

Lewis, Catherine, and J. Richard. *Women and Slavery in America: A Documentary History*. Fayetteville: University of Arkansas Press, 2011.

Litwack, Leon F. *Been in the Storm So Long: The Aftermath of Slavery*. New York: Random House, 1979.

Lusane, Clarence. *The Black History of the White House*. San Francisco: City Lights Publishers, 2011.

Painter, Nell. *Sojourner Truth: A Life, a Symbol*. New York: W.W. Norton, 1996.

Petrino, Elizabeth. "Disarming the Nation: Women's Writing and the American Civil War." *Legacy*. 18.1: 112–14.

Rinaldi, Ann. *An Unlikely Friendship: A Novel of Mary Todd Lincoln and Elizabeth Keckley*. New York: HMH Books, 2008.

Roberts, Cokie. *Capital Dames: The Civil War and the Women of Washington, 1848–1868*. New York: HarperCollins, 2015.

Rutberg, Becky. *Mary Lincoln's Dressmaker: Elizabeth Keckley's Remarkable Rise from Slave to White House Confidante*. New York: Walker, 1995.

Schwalm, Leslie A. "'Agonizing Groans of Mothers' and 'Slave-Scarred Veteran': The Commemoration of Slavery and Emancipation." *American Nineteenth Century History*. 9.3: 289–304.

Silber, Nina. "Intemperate Men, Spiteful Women, and Jefferson Davis: Northern Views of the Defeated South." *American Quarterly* 41.4 (December 1989): 614–35.

Smith, Sidonie, and Julia Watson. *De/Colonizing the Subject: The Politics of Gender in Women's Autobiography*. Minneapolis: University of Minnesota Press, 1992.

Steadman, Jennifer Bernhardt, et al. "Archive Survival Guide: Practical and Theoretical Approaches for the Next Century of Women's Studies Research." *Legacy*. 19.2: 230–40.

Sten, Christopher, ed. *Literary Capital: A Washington Reader.* University of Georgia Press, 2011.
Sterling, Dorothy, ed. *We Are Your Sisters: Black Women in the Nineteenth Century.* New York: W.W. Norton, 1984.
Stover, Johnnie M. "African American 'Mother Tongue' Resistance in Nineteenth-Century Postbellum Black Women's Autobiography: Elizabeth Keckley and Susie King Taylor." *A/B: Auto/Biography Studies,* 2003, Volume 18, Issue: 117–44.
Turner, Justin G., and Linda Levitt. *Mary Todd Lincoln: Her Life and Letters.* New York: Alfred A. Knopf, 1972.
Vidal, Gore. *Lincoln: A Novel.* New York: Ballantine Books, 1984.
Williams, Susan S. "Contractual Authorship: Elizabeth Keckley and Mary Abigail Dodge." *Reclaiming Authorship: Literary Women in America, 1850–1900.* Philadelphia: University of Pennsylvania Press, 2006.
Young, Elizabeth. "Black Woman, White House: Race and Redress in Elizabeth Keckley's *Behind the Scenes*." *Disarming the Nation: Women's Writing and the American Civil War.* Chicago: University of Chicago Press, 1999.
Zafar, Rafia. "Dressing Up and Dressing Down: Elizabeth Keckley's *Behind the Scenes* at the White House and Eliza Potter's *A Hairdresser's Experience in High Life*." *We Wear the Mask: African Americans Write American Literature, 1760–1870.* New York: Columbia University Press, 1997.

## ABOUT THE EDITOR

**Dr. Sheila Smith McKoy** is an associate professor of English at North Carolina State University. She holds a BA from North Carolina State University, an MA from the University of North Carolina at Chapel Hill, and a PhD from Duke University. She is the first African American to receive a PhD from Duke's English Department. She is a poet, literary critic, and fiction writer; her work has appeared in numerous publications including the critically acclaimed Schomburg series *African American Women Writers 1910–1940, Callaloo, Contours, Journal of Ethnic American Literature, Mythium, Obsidian: Literature in the African Diaspora, Research for African Literatures,* and *Valley Voices*. Her book *When Whites Riot: Writing Race and Violence in American and South African Cultures* (University of Wisconsin Press, 2001) received critical attention in the US and in South Africa. She has worked extensively in the fields of African, African American, Afro-Caribbean, and other African-descent literatures.

Dr. Smith McKoy focuses on the relationships between Africa and African diaspora counties and cultures. As the director emeritus of both the African American Cultural Center and the Africana Studies Program at NCSU, her work expanded the university's academic and programmatic focus toward a broader understanding of the cultural experiences of peoples of African descent globally. Her global engagement work has taken her to West Africa, East Africa, the Caribbean, and Europe. Dr. Smith McKoy is the co-chair of the North Carolina Community AIDS Fund, a member of the board of Maama Watali, a nongovernmental agency focused on improving health care, educational, and social outcomes in a post-conflict region of Uganda, and a member of the board of the North Carolina Chapter of United Nations Women.

## ABOUT THE CONTRIBUTORS

**William L. Andrews** is E. Maynard Adams Professor of English and Comparative Literature at the University of North Carolina at Chapel Hill. He is the author, editor, or co-editor of forty-five books on a wide range of subjects about African American literature and culture, chiefly before World War I. His titles include *The Literary Career of Charles W. Chesnutt* (1980) and *To Tell a Free Story: The First Century of Afro-American Autobiography, 1760-1865* (1986). He is co-editor of *The Oxford Companion to African American Literature* (1997) and *The Norton Anthology of African American Literature*, Third Edition (2015). He is general editor of "North American Slave Narratives, a Database and Electronic Text Library" http://metalab.unc.edu/docsouth/neh/neh.html.

**Michael Berthold** is an associate professor of English at Villanova University. He has published numerous essays on nineteenth-century American literature and culture. His most recent work examines literary representations of Johnny Appleseed.

**Lynn Domina** is the author of books on the Harlem Renaissance, Lorraine Hansberry's play *A Raisin in the Sun*, and Leslie Marmon Silko's novel *Ceremony*. She is the editor of a collection of essays, *Poets on the Psalms*, and she has written two collections of poetry, *Corporal Works* and *Framed in Silence*. Her articles appear in *a/b: Auto/Biography Studies, Studies in American Indian Literature*, and *African American Literature*. She lives in Marquette, MI, where she serves as head of the English Department at Northern Michigan University.

**Michele Elam,** Olivier Nomellini Family University Fellow in Undergraduate Education, is a professor of English and director of the Interdisciplinary Graduate Program in Modern Thought & Literature at Stanford University. She is the author of *Race, Work, and Desire in American Literature, 1860-1930* (2003), *The Souls of Mixed Folk: Race, Politics, and Aesthetics in the New Millennium* (2011), and editor of *The Cambridge Companion to James Baldwin* (2015). At Stanford she has served as director of the Program in African & African American Studies (2007-10), director of Undergraduate Studies (2006-08), director of Curriculum (2011-13), and has received the St. Clair Drake Outstanding Teaching Award twice.

**Frances Smith Foster** earned her PhD in British and American literature at the University of California, San Diego. At San Diego State University, she helped found the Department of Afro-American Studies and the first Department of Women's Studies in the United States. She was named Charles Howard Candler Professor of English and Women's Studies at Emory University, where she also served as director of the Emory Institute for Women's Studies and chair of the Department of English. As author, editor, or co-editor she has published books such as *Witnessing Slavery: The Development of Ante-Bellum Slave Narratives* (1979), *Written by Herself: Literary Production by African American Women, 1746–1892* (1993), *Norton Anthology of African American Literature*, and *Oxford Companion to African American Literature*. She has received numerous awards and fellowships including an honorary doctorate from State University of New York, Geneseo.

**Regis M. Fox,** an Assistant Professor of English at Florida Atlantic University, holds a BA in English from Clark Atlanta University and a PhD in English from the University of California, Riverside. Her primary research interests include nineteenth-century American Literatures, Feminist Theory, and African-American Literary and Cultural Studies, and she has published in such journals as *Women's Studies: An Interdisciplinary Journal* and the *Journal of American Studies*. She recently served as a McKnight Junior Faculty Fellow, during which time she completed a book manuscript entitled *Unsung, Unwavering: Nineteenth-Century Black Women's Epistemologies and the Liberal Problematic*.

**Aisha Francis** is an independent scholar and nonprofit strategist with expertise in resource development, humanities research, and professional writing. Her eclectic professional background includes several years teaching literature and women's studies at Fisk and Vanderbilt universities, where she received her BA and PhD degrees in English, respectively. In addition to her experience in higher education, she has worked as a successful fundraiser in several sectors including hospitals/health care, the arts/museums, and social services.

**Jill Jepson** is a professor at St. Catherine University in Minneapolis. She is also a linguistic anthropologist, and writing coach. She is the author of three books and over seventy articles on spirituality, history, culture, and writing. She is the founder of Writing the Whirlwind, offering coaching and workshops for writers.

**Janaka B. Lewis** is Assistant Professor of English at University of North Carolina at Charlotte, where she teaches courses in Early African American and American Literature. Her research interests include African American women's narratives of freedom and cultures of sports and play in the nineteenth century. She is completing a manuscript called "Civil Discourse: Black Women's Narratives of Freedom and Nation." She is the author of a children's book *Brown All Over* and also conducts workshops on race and children's literature.

**Nanette Morton** received her PhD from McMaster University in Hamilton, Ontario, Canada in 2000. "Private Spaces, Public Meanings" is an excerpt from her dissertation, "Houses of Bondage, Loopholes of Retreat: Space and Place in Four African American Slave Narratives." She has taught at McMaster University, Brock University, Mohawk College, and Sheridan College. She is currently writing about African American settlers in the Canadian west.

**Janet Neary** is an assistant professor of English at Hunter College, CUNY. Her research examines nineteenth-century African American narrative and visual culture, with a focus on slave narratives. The principal focus of her work is in feminism and critical theory, and she is working on two books on race and visual culture: a monograph, *Fugitive Testimony: Race, Representation, and the Slave Narrative Form*, and a collection of primary texts, *A More Perfect Likeness,* coedited with Sarah Blackwood. Recent essays have appeared in *MELUS* and *ESQ.*

**Clarence "Danny" W. Tweedy III** is an associate professor of English at the University of Mary Washington. His research focuses on how African Americans use both personal and collective trauma to reclaim/redefine identity and bodily subjectivity.

PERMISSIONS

William L. Andrews's essay "Reunion in the Postbellum Slave Narrative: Frederick Douglass and Elizabeth Keckley" originally appeared in *African American Review* (Spring 1989), published by St. Louis University.

Michael Berthold's essay "Not 'Altogether' the 'History of Myself': Autobiographical Impersonality in Elizabeth Keckley's *Behind the Scenes: Or, Thirty Years a Slave, and Four Years in the White House*" originally appeared in the *American Transcendental Quarterly* 13, no. 2 (1999).

Lynn Domina's essay "I Was Re-Elected President: Elizabeth Keckley as Quintessential Patriot in Behind the Scenes" originally published in *Women's Life-Writing*, edited by Linda Coleman, appears here courtesy of the University of Wisconsin Press.

Michele Elam's essay "Dressing down the First Lady: Elizabeth Keckley's *Behind the Scenes: Or, Thirty Years a Slave, and Four Years in the White House*," from her book *Race, Work, and Desire in American Literature, 1860–1930*, appears here courtesy of Cambridge University Press.

Frances Smith Foster's essay "Autobiography after Emancipation: The Example of Elizabeth Keckley" originally appeared in *Multicultural Autobiography: American Lives*, edited by James Robert Payne, and appears here courtesy of the University of Tennessee Press.

Jill Jepson's piece "Disruptive and Disguise in Black Feminine Entrepreneurial Identity" originally appeared in her book, *Women's Concerns: Twelve Women Entrepreneurs of the Eighteenth and Nineteenth Centuries*, published by Peter Lang Publishing.

Janet Neary's essay "Behind the Scenes and Inside Out: Elizabeth Keckly's Revision of the Slave-Narrative Form" originally appeared in *African American Review* (Winter 2014), published by Johns Hopkins University Press.

Clarence Tweedy's essay "Splitting the 'I': (Re)reading the Traumatic Narrative of Black Womanhood in the Autobiographies of Harriet Jacobs and Elizabeth Keckley" originally appeared in *Making Connections*, Vol. 12, No. 2 (2011).

# INDEX

Aberbach, David, 205, 218
Abolition, 44, 61, 96, 105, 108, 111, 113, 125
Abolitionist(s), xiii, xiv, xxii, xxv, xxviii, 27, 28, 39, 63, 95, 108, 132, 165, 169, 174, 179, 221, 242; movement, xiv
Accardo, Annalucia, 165, 181
Adams, Henry, 87
Adams, John Quincy (slave narrator), 31, 32
Adams, Katherine, 251
African(s), xv, 3, xxx, 3, 35, 36, 72, 73, 108, 109, 118, 156, 157, 255
African American literature (Afro-American literature), xii, 21, 30, 31, 34, 41, 75, 115, 161, 205, 206, 214; history (Afro-American literary history), 31, 35, 56; literary criticism, 29. *See also* African American writers
African American men, 116
*African American Review*, 161
African American women, xxiii, 143, 155, 158, 181, 193, 198, 203, 217, 24. *See also* Black American(s): women
African American writers, 37, 110, 203, 204, 240
African Americana, xxx, xv, 154
Agency, xxv, 143, 146, 148, 151, 157, 186, 197, 203, 207, 208, 210, 211, 212, 213, 214, 215, 216, 255
Alcott, Wendell Phillips, 242
Alger, Horatio: *Ragged Dick*, xxviii
Allen, Paula Gunn, 37
American biopower, xxv, 135, 140
American civilization, 194, 196; public, xv, xxvi, xxviii, 36, 49, 157; social structure, 19; society, xiv, 159, 203
American Dream, xxv, xxviii, 8, 38, 39, 41, 56, 69, 73
American history, xv, 14, 157, 185, 193
American liberalism, 127, 135, 136, 138, 139
*American Literary Gazette*, 180
American literature, xv, 34, 56
Ames, Mary Clemmer, 113, 251
Amireh, Amal, 251
Anderson, Benedict, 60, 73
Anderson, Robert, 31, 45, 57; *From Slavery to Affluence*, 45
Andrews, William, ix, xiv, 21–33, 34, 36, 57, 66, 69, 73, 74, 75, 80, 87, 88, 93, 112, 113, 115, 117, 118, 119, 128, 139, 140, 166, 168, 169, 174, 181, 186, 199, 208, 218, 221, 228, 240, 242, 244, 251, 257
Angelou, Maya, 36, 57
Anglo-Americans, 179
Antebellum era, 21, 23, 26, 27, 28, 29, 30, 34, 36, 41, 42, 43, 44, 45, 46, 73, 88, 96, 103, 105, 112, 117, 120, 130, 136, 144, 150, 164, 166, 169, 174, 175, 178, 208, 217, 224, 251, 252
Antiracist, 113, 203
Antislavery, xiii, xxvii, 27, 30, 45, 107, 108, 115, 117, 147, 173
Arlow, Jacob, 205, 216, 218
Asbury, Herbert: *The Barbary Coast*, 18, 19
Assyrians, 35
*Atlantic Monthly*, 183, 184, 199
Aunt Charlotte, 104, 130, 131, 184, 231

Autobiography, xii, xiii, xiv, xvi, xxiv, xxviii, xxix, 1, 2, 6, 7, 8, 9, 11, 21, 23, 26, 30, 34, 35, 36, 37, 39, 40, 41, 47, 54, 56, 60, 62, 67, 74, 75, 87, 88, 92, 96, 112, 116, 174, 186, 207, 208, 211, 212, 213, 217

Babylonians, 35
Baker, Houston, Jr., 80, 88, 211, 218
Baker, Jean H., 126, 140, 225, 242, 244
Baldwin, James: *Another Country* (1963), 244
*Baltimore Sun*, 23
Baltimore, xv, xxi, 4, 127, 248
Balzac, Honoré de, 242
Barnes, Elizabeth, 213, 218
Barrett, Lindon, 99, 100, 116, 117, 118, 119, 243, 244
Bartky, Sandra Lee, 218
Barton, Rebecca Chalmers, 34, 57
"Battle Hymn of the Republic, The," 56
*Behind the Seams*, xxix, xxxi, 6, 94, 109, 116, 120, 221, 240, 244
Bell, Thomas, 18
Benjamin, Franklin, 35, 37, 41, 57
Benjamin, Walter, 238, 243, 244
Benjaminian metaphysic of origin, 238
Bennett, Lerone, Jr., 13, 14, 19
Bennett, Tony, 235, 238, 243, 244
Benthamist utilitarianism, 235
Bergner, Gwen, 205, 206, 218
Berlant, Lauren, 134, 138, 140
Berlin, Ira, 251
Berthold, Michael, ix, 74–89, 213, 218, 257
Bhabha, Homi K., 61, 73
Bingham, William J., xix, 69, 82, 83, 97, 98, 140, 187, 188, 214, 215, 216, 217, 247
Bio-bibliography, 156, 157
Biopower. *See* American biopower
Birnbaum, Michele, 115, 244. S*ee also* Elam, Michele.
Black America, xxvi, 21, 74, 203

Black American(s), 32, 74, 144, 145, 149, 153, 155, 156, 157, 159, 161, 191, 197; community, 7, 9, 21, 39, 40, 90, 91, 147, 152, 159, 240; middle class, 152, 192; Southerners, 25, 28, 32; women, xxviii, 1, 4, 11, 14, 19, 42, 75, 80, 87, 92, 113, 114, 116, 117, 125, 133, 135, 136, 142, 143, 144, 145, 146, 148, 151, 152, 154, 155, 156, 158, 159, 160, 161, 175, 184, 186, 191, 193, 194, 197, 203, 204, 205, 206, 208, 209, 210, 211, 212, 214, 216, 217, 231, 241, 242. *See also* African American women
Black body, 96, 97, 99, 101, 111, 204, 205; female body, 214
Black club women's movement, 155, 156, 160
Black codes, xxvii
Black conduct literature, 143, 145, 146, 150, 151, 154, 156, 159, 160, 161
Black Fashion Museum, 57
Black women. *See* Black American, women
Blackwood, Sarah, 117
Blumin, Stuart, 14, 19
Bondage, xxii, 7, 26, 34, 42, 44, 45, 46, 101, 198
Boston, xxii
Braude, Ann, xxvii–xxviii, xxx
Braxton, Joanne, 75, 82, 88, 131, 140
Brennan, Charlie, 251
Brent, Linda, 42, 57, 199, 208, 209, 210, 211, 212. *See also* Jacobs, Harriet
Broughton, T.L., 88
Brown, Elsa Barkley, 251
Brown, John, 179, 248
Brown, William Wells, 31, 32, 36, 42, 57, 179, 242
Bruce, Henry Clay, 31, 32; *New Man, The*, 32
Bryant, Jerry, 214, 218
Buell, Lawrence, 87, 88

Burger, Mary, 56, 57
Bureau of Labor Statistics, xxx
Burwell School, xxix, 247
Burwell, Anne. *See* Garland, Anne Burwell
Burwell, Armistead, xiv, xx, 127, 185, 186, 221, 247
Burwell, Mary, xvii, 127, 221
Burwell, Robert, xviii, xix, 2, 82, 83, 83, 149, 187, 188, 215, 247; wife (Margaret Anna), xix, 83, 97, 228, 247
Butler, Judith, 244
Butterfield, Stephen: *Black Autobiography in America*, 34, 57

Carby, Hazel V., 251
Cary, Mary Ann Shadd, 160
Chain of being, 109, 118
Chase, Salmon P., 5, 233
Chase-Riboud, Barbara: *Sally Hemings: A Novel*, 244
Chesnutt, Charles, 156, 241; "Sis Becky's Pickaninny," 241; "The Conjure Woman," 242
Chiaverini, Jennifer, 140, 251
Chicago World's Columbian Exposition (1893), xxiv, 7, 155, 249
Chicago, 5, 50, 55, 85, 137, 138, 158, 176, 177, 179, 233
Child, Lydia Maria, xiii, 92
Childress, Alice: *A Short Walk* (1979), 244
Chintz wrapper(s), xv, 85, 233, 234
Citizenship, 72, 118, 127, 143, 145, 152, 155, 157, 159, 207, 212
Civil Rights Act (1875), 249
Civil Rights Act (1866), xxvi
Civil War, xiv, xv, xxiii, xxiv, xxv, xxvi, xxvii, 7, 21, 24, 26, 28, 30, 35, 39, 78, 108, 112, 113, 114, 115, 116, 118, 128, 148, 153, 161, 170, 172, 174, 184, 185, 186, 190, 191, 193, 198, 235, 248; Battle of Wilson's Creek, xxiii

Clifford, James, 86, 88
Collins, Patricia Hill, 134, 140
Colonists, 35
Color-line, 228
Commodity culture, 243
Confederacy, 25, 38, 49, 127, 137, 147, 170, 174; Confederate Army, 227; Confederate Congress, xxvii, 39, 174
Constitution (U.S.), 25, 38, 71, 79, 128
Construction of womanhood, xx
Contraband Relief Organization (Association), xxi, 39, 60, 72, 90, 112, 116, 153, 173, 229, 248
Cooper, Anna Julia, 144, 191, 193, 194, 195, 196, 197, 198, 199, 249; *A Voice from the South* (1892), 144, 193, 199
Covey, Edward, 43, 44, 82. *See also* Douglass, Frederick
Craft, William and Ellen, xiii, xxx, 111, 114, 120, 184, 193, 199
Crane, Stephen, 237, 238, 243, 244; "The Monster," 243, 244; *The Red Badge of Courage*, 237; "The Upturned Face," 237
Criniti, Stephen, 7, 15, 19
Cross-dressing, 234
Crowston, Clare Haru, 251
Crummell, Alexander, Dr., 156, 196

Dame Julian (Juliana): *The Revelations of Divine Love*, 57
Danky, J.P., 161
Davis, Charles T., *The Slave's Narrative*, 34, 57, 120, 182
Davis, Jefferson, xv, xxvii, 4, 25, 38, 49, 50, 69, 72, 79, 85, 147, 170, 174, 185, 221, 227, 228, 233, 234, 235, 236, 237, 252
Davis, Varina Howell, xv, xxiv, xxix, xxxi, 4, 25, 49, 50, 72, 78, 80, 81, 85, 120, 127, 137, 170, 185, 221, 222, 233, 235, 236, 237, 244

de Saussure, Ferdinand, 110, 120
Dean, Sharon G., 19, 233, 243, 244
Delaney, Martin, 156
DeLombard, Jeannine, 116, 117, 119
Democratic Party, xxvi, 125
*Devil in America, The* (1859), 108
"Dixie," 25, 69
Domestic service, 152, 223, 224, 241
Domina, Lynn, ix, 60–73, 112, 113, 115, 119, 181, 251, 257
Douglas, Martha, 5, 176
Douglas, Stephen (Senator), 5, 72
Douglass Frederick, ix, xiii, xvi, xxii, xxx, 21, 23, 24, 25, 26, 27, 28, 29, 30, 31, 32, 36, 42, 43, 44, 45, 55, 57, 63, 73, 77, 82, 88, 91, 100, 105, 106, 114, 117, 118, 119, 130, 133, 140, 141, 147, 149, 153, 156, 163, 164, 165, 166, 167, 173, 174, 181, 187, 189, 192, 222, 229, 230, 240, 244, 247, 248, 249; Auld, Thomas, 23, 24, 26, 30; Auld, Mrs., 106; *Life and Times of Frederick Douglass*, xvi, xxx, 21, 23, 24, 25, 26, 27, 30, 31, 32, 57, 247, 249; *My Bondage and My Freedom*, 164, 165, 181, 248; *Narrative of the Life of Frederick Douglass*, xiii, xvi, xxx, 23, 26, 32, 55, 57, 88, 119, 133, 140, 163, 165, 175, 181, 222, 244; *The North Star*, 247. *See also* Covey, Edward
*Dred Scott* case, xx, 65, 248
Du Bois, W.E.B., 156, 161, 183, 190, 191, 193, 199

Eakin, Paul John, 78, 88
Eighteenth century, 42, 144
Elam, Michele, x, 220–246, 257. *See also* Birnbaum, Michele
Emancipation, ix, 30, 34, 75, 76, 77, 87, 92, 93, 101, 102, 110, 111, 112, 132, 135, 153, 167, 170, 172, 183, 196, 222, 223, 224

Emancipation Proclamation, 68, 90, 174, 183, 248
Emerson, James: *The Madness of Mary Lincoln*, 139, 140
Emerson, Ralph Waldo, 36, 57, 195, 241, 242; "Thoughts on Modern Literature," 57
England, xxii, 16
Enslaved people, xvi, xxii, 153
Enslavement, xii, xiii, xv, xvii, xviii, xxv, xxviii, xxix, 92, 95, 105, 111, 114, 115, 128, 185, 187, 221
Etter-Lewis, Gwendolyn, 207, 209, 218
*Evening Express* (New York), 236
*Evening Press* (New York), 77, 236
*Evening News* (New York), 77

Faulkner, Carol, 199
Female labor, 14, 15, 18, 19, 85
Fifteenth Street Presbyterian Church, xxviii, xxix, 39, 147, 247
Fisher, Philip: *Making and Effacing Art*, 243, 244
Fleischer, Jennifer, xiv, xxiii, xxvi, xxx, 5, 16, 94, 112, 113, 114, 126, 127, 128, 134, 139, 149, 152, 153, 172, 180, 228, 241, 242; *Mastering Slavery*, 19, 113, 119, 182, 241, 242, 245, 251; *Mrs. Lincoln and Mrs. Keckly*, xiv, xxx, 139, 140, 161, 199, 241
Foley, Barbara, 251
Foner, Eric, 199
Foote, Julia A.J., 160
Fort Sumter, 99, 248
Forten, Charlotte (Grimké), 184; *Journals of Charlotte Forten Grimké, The*, 199; "Life on the Sea Islands," 184, 199
Foster, Frances Smith, ix, xiv, xxviii, xxx, 7, 8, 9, 19, 20, 34–59, 62, 73, 93, 112, 128, 139, 140, 145, 150, 160, 161, 166, 179, 180, 182, 221, 222, 240, 241, 242, 252, 257; "Autobiography after Emancipation:

The Example of Elizabeth Keckley,"
7, 9, 112, 119, 166, 182; "Romance and
Scandal in a Postbellum Slave Narrative," 8, 20, 252; *'Til Death or Distance
Do Us Part* (2010), 160, 161; *Witnessing
Slavery,* 57, 73, 182; *Written by Herself,*
139, 140, 180, 182, 222, 240, 241, 242,
245
Fox, Regis M., x, 125–141, 258
Fox-Genovese, Elizabeth, 70, 71, 73, 245
Francis, Aisha, ix, xxx, 142–162, 258
Franklin, Benjamin, 35, 37, 38, 41, 57
Fraser, Isabel, 20
Frazier, Harriet, xxi, xxxi
Fredrickson, George M., 119
Freedmen's Bureau, 183, 190
Freedmen's Village, 39
Freehling, William W., 32
Freud, Sigmond, 207; Freudian thought, 206
Fried, Michael, 237, 238, 243, 245
Fugitive Slave Act of 1850, xiii, xxi, 63, 164, 247

G. W. Carleton and Company, 6, 40, 221
Gaines, Kevin, 161
Garland, Anne Burwell, xx, 24, 25, 50, 103, 104, 105, 130, 131, 137, 168, 175, 189, 231, 240, 247
Garland, Hugh, xxi, 2, 3, 5, 9, 19, 50, 168, 247, 248
Garland, Nannie. *See* Meem, Nannie Garland
Garnet, Henry Highland, xxii, 55, 91,147, 156, 173, 192, 230
Garrison, William Lloyd, xiii, xxvii, xxxi
Gates, Henry Louis: *The Slave's Narrative,* 34, 57, 73, 88, 119, 120, 181, 182, 219
Gere, Ann, 160, 161

Gender, xiv, xvi, xxix, 1, 14, 19, 83, 84, 86, 94, 116, 156, 157, 161, 194, 203, 206, 216, 227
Genovese, Eugene, 232, 243, 245
Gimeno Pahissa, Laura, 252
Goebel, Bruce A., 244, 245
Goldberg, David Theo, 137, 141
Goode, George Brown, 235, 245
Gossett, Thomas, 108, 119
Gilmore, Colonel H., 24, 53
Greeley, Horace, 242
Grimké, Rev. Francis, xiii, xiv, xvi, xxv, xxix, xxxi, 249
Gubar, Susan, 243, 245
Gwin, Minrose, 182, 245

Hall, James C., 245
Hady, Maureen E., 161
Halttunen, Karen, 117, 120
Hammon, Briton, 36, 42, 58
Hampton Negro Conference (1899), 197
Harlem Renaissance, 161
Harper, Frances E.W., 160, 241, 242; Lyceum Bureau, 242
Harris, Joel Chandler, 28
Harris, Trudier, 245
Hartman, Saidiya, 96, 97, 98, 99, 116, 120, 128, 139
Helm, Katherine, 134, 135, 141, 182
Henderson, Carol, 96, 116, 120
Henderson, Mae G., 83, 87, 88
Henke, Suzette A., 206, 218
Hening, William Waller, xvii, xxxi
Henry, George, 36, 58
Henson, Josiah, 22, 23, 31, 32, 33
Higginbotham, Evelyn Brooks, 146, 161
Hillsborough, North Carolina, xv, xviii, xix, xxix, xxiv, xxix, 2, 97, 187, 188, 189, 247
Hine, Darlene Clark, 89, 242, 245
Hobbs, Agnes, xiv, 1, 2, 127, 148

Hobbs, George, xiv, 1, 2, 127, 247; separation from family, 7
Hoffert, Sylvia, 252
Hollander, Anne, 80, 81, 88
Home of the National Association of Colored Women and Children, xxv, 116, 180, 181, 249
hooks, bell, 136, 141, 163, 182, 203, 218; *Ain't I a Woman*, 136; *Rock My Soul*, 203
Howells, William Dean, 36, 37, 58
Hudson, Lynn, 18, 20
Hunter, Tera: *To 'Joy My Freedom* (1997), 160, 161
Hutchison, C. (Coleman), 252
Hyde Park, 52, 106

Illinois, xxi, 3, 5, 68, 137
Inauguration, 4, 62, 101, 137, 173, 226, 236, 248

Jacobs, Harriet, xiii, xviii, xix, 27, 32, 45, 57, 58, 73, 87, 92, 97, 113, 114, 117, 164, 165, 166, 167, 168, 172, 175, 186, 187, 188, 191, 203, 204, 205, 206, 207, 208, 209, 210, 211, 212, 217, 222, 240, 242, 247, 248, 249; *Incidents in the Life of a Slave Girl*, xiii, xiv, xix, 27, 32, 57, 58, 73, 75, 92, 164, 182, 186, 199, 203, 207, 218, 245, 248; Mr. Bruce, 172. *See also* Yellin, Janet
Jackson, Mattie, 31, 113; *The Story of Mattie J. Jackson* (1886), 32
Jackson, Rebecca, 36, 58
Jackson, (General) Thomas Jonathan "Stonewall," 228, 236
Jelinek, Estelle, 35, 37, 57, 58
Jennings, Paul, xxii, xxxi
*Frank Leslie's Illustrated News*, 20
Jepson, Jill, ix, 1–20, 258
Johnson, Andrew, xxvi, 5, 9, 137

Johnson, Eliza, 9
Jones, Lynda, 252
Jordan, June, 242, 245
Jordan, Winthrop, 108, 118

Karwatka, Dennis, 252
Keckley (Keckly), Elizabeth: audience, 46, 52, 53, 62, 65, 94, 113, 145, 154, 158, 169, 172, 186, 194, 204, 225, 235, 237, 240, 241; beating(s), xix, 2, 7, 43, 69, 91, 96, 97, 149, 217; *Behind the Scenes*, ix, xi, xii, xiii, xiv, xv, xix, xxii, xxiii, xxiv, xxv, xxvi, xxviii, xxix, xxx, xxxi, 1, 2, 5, 6, 7, 8, 9, 10, 11, 15, 16, 20, 24, 27, 30, 32, 35, 37, 40, 41, 42, 45, 46, 47, 50, 56, 58, 60, 73, 74, 74, 77, 78, 80, 82, 83, 84, 87, 89, 90, 91, 92, 93, 94, 95, 100, 106, 107, 110, 111, 112, 113, 114, 115, 116, 117, 118, 119, 120, 125, 126, 127, 128, 131, 133, 135, 139, 141, 142, 144, 147, 148, 149, 150, 151, 153, 155, 161, 162, 166, 179, 180. 183, 184, 186, 199, 203, 218, 219, 220, 221, 222, 224, 226, 228, 230, 237, 238, 239, 240, 242, 243, 245, 249, 252, 264; benefactors, xxi, 4, 169; birth, xvi, xi, xiv, xvi, xxiii, xxv, 2, 7, 18, 42, 71, 78, 114, 127, 128, 186, 247; business owner, xi, xxiv, xxvi, xxviii, 2, 3, 4, 5, 6, 7, 8, 9, 13, 14, 15, 18, 38, 40, 48, 68, 72, 134, 137, 145, 147, 148, 152, 153, 155, 157, 158, 159, 167, 169, 170, 176, 177, 178, 179, 180, 242; colored historian, xxix; death of, xxv, 7, 116, 180; dressmaker for Mary Todd Lincoln, xxix, 8, 15, 60, 67, 84, 85, 101, 112, 140, 152, 170, 171, 172, 185, 220, 233, 236, 237, 248; fitting system, 4, 80; freedom, purchase of, xiii, xxi, 4, 7, 9, 19, 38, 50, 63, 68, 71, 76, 127, 169, 222, 248; husband (*see* Keckley, James); letters, xxii, xxiv, xxviii, 7, 39, 40, 46, 48, 50, 54, 55, 76, 77, 81, 83, 86, 93, 115, 129, 149,

150, 153, 160, 169, 179, 221, 222, 224, 225, 227, 229, 230, 232, 239, 241, 242; literacy, xiv, xxii, 106, 211; mantua, 241; memoir, 5, 6, 39, 62, 75, 78, 126, 127, 128, 131, 133, 134, 137, 138, 139, 140, 225; modiste, xxiv, xv, 5, 15, 26, 45, 46, 74, 75, 79, 80, 81, 83, 90, 114, 117, 166, 170, 220, 249; quilt, xxix; son (*see* Kirkland, George [Hobbs]); spelling of name, xiv, xxx, 112, 139; Spiritualism, xxvi, xxviii; Wilberforce University donation, xxv. *See also* Lincoln, Abraham, relationship with Elizabeth Keckley; Lincoln, Mary Todd, relationship with Elizabeth Keckley

Kempe, Margery Burnham, 35, 57; *Book of Margery Kempe, The*, 57

Kent State University Museum, xxix

Kirkland, Alexander, xviii, 31, 140, 247

Kirkland, George (Hobbs), xviii, xxiii, xxiv, 2, 3, 4, 19, 31, 138, 148, 247, 248

Koester, Nancy, xxvii, xxxi

Ku Klux Klan, xxvi

Lander, James, xxvi, xxxi

Lane, Christopher, 218

Laney, Lucy Craft, 197, 199; Hampton Negro Conference (1899), 197

Langston, John Mercer, 45, 58; *From the Virginia Plantation to the National Capitol*, 45

Laplanche, Jean, 207, 218

Law(s), xvii, xxi, xxvi, xxvii, 3, 9, 25, 48, 63, 64, 65, 71, 129, 156, 207, 225, 248

Laub, Dori, 209, 218

Le Bourgois, Mrs. *See* Keckley, Elizabeth; benefactors

Lee, Jarena, 36, 58

Lee, Robert E., 68, 69

Lehman, Amy, xxvii, xxxi

Levitt, Linda, 253

Lewis, J. Richard, 252

Lewis, Janaka, x, 183–199, 258

Lewis, Catherine, 252

Liberalism, 125, 127, 135, 138, 139

*Light from the Spirit World*, xxvii

*Lincoln* (film), 125, 160

Lincoln, Abraham: antislavery position, 125; assassination, xxv, 51, 68, 83, 91, 97, 98–99, 100, 101, 102, 106, 110, 112, 115, 171, 172, 173, 174, 176, 177, 179, 183, 238, 248; Confederates, attitude toward, 68–69, 228; death of son Willie, xxiii, 5, 15–16, 84–85, 172–73, 226–27; Douglass, Frederick, meeting, 62–63, 173–74; emancipation of slaves, 90, 183–84, 248; family, 49; Gettysburg Address, 248; glove (*see* mementoes of); inauguration (1860), 101, 234, 237, 248; inauguration (1864), 62–63, 173–74; Keckley memoir, 41, 87; *Lincoln* (film), 125; mementoes of, xxiv–xxv, 101, 102, 136–37, 230, 236, 237, 238; needs of freed slaves, 80–81, 183–84; politics, 5, 125; relationship with Elizabeth Keckley, xv, xxii, xxiv, 5, 15–16, 39, 50–51, 61–63, 72, 84–85, 125–26, 136–37, 166, 170–71, 185, 229, 233; relationship with wife, 226–27, 228, 233, 237; re-election, 15; reputation, 38, 54, 230, 237–38; Richmond, trip to, xxvii, 173–74; speeches, 50–51, 98–99, 136–37, 170–71; vulnerability, 94, 95, 98–99. *See also* Emancipation Proclamation

Lincoln, Mary Todd: antislavery views, 227–28; behavior, xxvii, 50, 54, 62, 67–68, 83–84, 101, 177–78; death of son Willie, xxiii–xxiv, 10–11, 16, 83, 172–73, 226–27; death of husband, 10–11, 68, 176; financial problems, 16, 18, 66, 67, 90–91, 152, 176–77, 223–24, 239; Keckley, letters to, 7, 79, 115, 149–50, 224–25;

Lincoln, Mary Todd (*continued*)
  Keckley memoir, 7, 10, 18, 40–41, 79, 93, 112, 142, 149–50, 151, 185–86, 191, 192, 220–21, 224–25, 228–29, 240; Old Clothes Scandal, 39, 47–48, 53–55, 101–103, 127, 152, 177–79, 239; relationship with children, 106–108; relationship with husband, 66, 226–28, 229; relationship with Elizabeth Keckley, xii, xiv, xv, xxii, xxiii–xxiv, 2, 4–6, 7, 9, 13, 15, 38, 40–41, 49, 50, 52, 53–55, 60, 67, 79–80, 81, 83–85, 90–91, 101–102, 127, 132, 133–39, 152, 171–73, 174, 175, 176–77, 180, 184, 220–21, 223–24, 226, 228–29, 232, 236, 240, 248; reputation, xxviii–xxix, 10–11, 39, 61, 62, 67, 101–103, 112, 142, 145, 237; Richmond, trip to, xxvi, 174; spending habits, xii, xxvii; spirituality, xxvi; upbringing, 50, 134–35, 171–72; widowhood, 52, 53–54, 68–69, 90–91, 106, 176–79, 180, 223–24, 234
Lincoln, Robert, xxix, 7, 40, 68, 106, 126, 149, 180, 221, 227, 247
Lincoln, Tad, 10, 52, 65, 66, 93, 95, 99, 105, 106, 107, 108, 109, 110, 117, 118, 125, 227, 232
Lincoln White House, xv, xxv, xxvi, 125, 155, 193
Lincoln, William "Willie," xxiii, 5, 10, 11, 50, 83, 85, 172, 226, 229
*List of Free Negroes*, xxi
Litwack, Leon F., 32, 182, 252
Loggins, Vernon, 41, 58
Lowery, I.E., 22, 31, 32
Luciano, Dana, 133, 141
Lundquist, L.R., 49, 59
Lusane, Clarence, 252
Lyon, Nathaniel (General), xxiv

Madison, Dolley, xxii
Madison, James, xxii

Malcolm X: *Autobiography of Malcolm X*, 36, 58
Manuel, Carme, 94, 95, 113, 116, 117, 120
Marrant, John, 36, 58
Marshall, Paule: *Brown Girl, Brownstones*, 243–244
Maryland, 22, 31, 163, 249
Mason, Mary G., 83, 89
McCaskill, Barbara, vii, 120
McClintock, Anne, 85, 89
McClean, Mrs. Mary Ellen Marcy (wife, General George B. McClean), 131, 132, 137, 170
McMaster, Edwin, 5
Meachum, Patsy, xxi
Meem, Nannie Garland, 140, 174, 175
Meier, August, 32
Melville, Herman, 225, 242, 245; "Benito Cereno" (1855), 225, 226
Merish, Lori, 130, 131, 141, 214, 215, 218
Merkerson, S. Epatha, 125
Meyer, Michael, 26, 32
Miles, Diana, 204
Miller, Rosemary E. Reed, xxx
Mills, Allison, 245
Mississippi, 4, 42
Mississippi River, 3
Missouri, xv, xx; St. Louis, xv, xx, xxi, xxvii, 2, 3, 4, 26, 72, 76, 90, 127, 132, 147, 151, 154, 189, 221, 247
Mitchell, Michele, 184, 199
Mixed race, xvi, xvii, 153
Moore, Clement Clark, 118
Morrison, Toni: *Tar Baby*, 244
Morton, Nanette, x, 163–182, 258
Mossell, Mrs. N.F. (Gertrude E.H. Bustill Mossell), x, xxx, 142, 143, 145, 146, 155, 156, 157, 158, 159, 160, 245; *Work of the Afro-American Woman (1894), The*, 142, 144, 155, 157, 158, 159, 241, 245
Mossell, Nathan Francis, 145, 161

Mulatto, 71, 221, 225. *See also* Mixed race
Mullen, Harryette, 117, 120
Murray, Albert, 56, 58

National Harmony Memorial Park, 249
National Home for Destitute Colored Women and Children, xxv, 116, 180
*National News* (New York), 221
Native Americans, xxvi
Neary, Janet, ix, 90–121, 259
Negrin, Llewellyn, 243, 245
Neuman, Shirley, 89
New Negroe(s), 224
*New York Citizen*, 6, 7, 241, 245
*New York Times*, 6
New York, xxii, 6, 25, 50, 54, 67, 68, 91, 126, 132, 152, 163, 169, 177, 221, 236; No. 14 Carroll Place, xi, xxv, 6
Nichols, Charles, 34, 58
Nineteenth century, xv, xvi, xix, xx, xxv, xxvi, xxvii, 1, 10, 11, 19, 23, 37, 38, 75, 80, 81, 86, 87, 94, 107, 108, 115, 117, 131, 133, 142, 143, 144, 145, 146, 147, 151, 152, 155, 156, 157, 158, 160, 161, 165, 193, 203
Niger Delta, 128
Nj-seder-Kai, Princess, 35
North, xxi, xxiv, xxvi, xxvii, 12, 15, 21, 22, 28, 42, 45, 63, 64, 65, 70, 71, 78, 90, 103, 131, 132, 138, 153, 163, 165, 166, 170, 224, 231
North Carolina, xii, xv, xxvi, xxix, 42, 186; Edenton, 247; Hillsborough, xv, xviii, xix, xxix, xxiv, xxix, 2, 97, 187, 188, 189, 247; Wilmington, 249
Northup, Solomon: *Twelve Years a Slave*, 111
Nunley, Vorris, 140, 141

Obama, President Barack and Michelle, xv
Ohio, xv, 8, 171

Old Clothes Scandal, xxiv, 6, 39, 40, 47, 52, 53, 55, 67, 83, 85, 90, 91, 101, 102, 114, 127, 139, 177, 220, 230, 232, 238, 248
Oliver, Kelly, 205, 219
Olney, James, 221
Opelousas Massacre, xxvi
Ottolengul, Daniel, xxix, xxxi, 116

Packard, Jerrold M., 140, 141
Page, Thomas Nelson, 28
Painter, Nell, xiii, xxxi, 252
Pascal, Roy, 47, 58
Payne, Bishop Daniel A., 86, 239
Pennington, J.W.C., 45, 58
Petrino, Elizabeth, 252
Philadelphia, xv, 155
Phillips, Wendell, 229, 242
Picquet, Louisa, 73
Pinckney, Darryl, 241, 245
Pleasant, Mary Ellen, ix, 1, 8, 11, 13, 14, 18, 20
Pontalis, Jean-Bertrand, 207, 218
Port Royal Experiment, 184. *See also* Forten, Charlotte
Portelli, Alessandro, 165, 181
Porter, Dorothy, 41, 58
Post, Amy, xxvii
Postbellum, ix, 8, 21, 22, 23, 24, 25, 26, 27, 28, 29, 30, 31, 35, 37, 38, 41, 42, 44, 45, 56, 73, 92, 93, 101, 102, 103, 105, 111, 112, 113, 118, 129, 135, 166, 167, 168, 169, 221, 223, 240
Potter, Eliza, 1, 11, 12, 13, 14, 16, 17, 18, 19, 20, 241, 243, 244, 253
Preston, Dickson J., 23, 30, 31, 32
Prince, Nancy Gardener, 36
Progressive Era, 144
Pryse, Marjorie, 244, 246
*Publisher's Circular*, 180
*Putnam's Magazine*, 6

Quaker, 155

Race, xvi, 6, 28, 29, 40, 41, 43, 52, 54, 55, 61, 63, 64, 66, 72, 82, 86, 87, 91, 94, 95, 96, 100, 101, 103, 105, 106, 108, 109, 110, 111, 113, 114, 116, 117, 118, 132, 142, 144, 146, 153, 154, 156, 157, 167, 173, 177, 183, 188, 194, 194, 195, 196, 197, 198, 203, 205, 206, 224, 230, 249
Race men, 156
Race rape, xvii
Race woman, 161
Racial identity, 102, 107, 159, 161, 203
Racism, xxi, xxv, 37, 93, 94, 101, 102, 116, 129, 154, 181, 204, 206
Randall, Ruth Painter, 241, 246
Randolph, Peter, 45, 58
Rape, xvii, xviii, xix, xxiii, 2, 7, 140, 148, 188, 209, 247
Rawick, George, 182
Reconstruction, xii, 25, 28, 32, 35, 41, 45, 48, 53, 104, 116, 144, 150, 153, 183, 184, 191, 193, 196, 198, 240
Redpath, James, xxviii, 7, 40, 95, 115, 126, 179, 224, 225, 242; *Public Life and Autobiography of John Brown*, 242
Reef, Catherine, 90, 120
Renza, Louis, 76, 89
Republicans, 78, 125, 152, 179
Reuben, Gloria, 125
Rinaldi, Ann, 252
Roberts, Cokie, 252
Rollin, Frances, 113
Rollins, Judith, 224
Rose, Willie Lee, 27, 32
Ross, Ishbel, 241, 242, 246
Rutberg, Becky, 199, 252

Saks, Eva, 246
Samuels, Shirley, 107, 108, 117, 120
Sandford, John F.A., xx, 248
Santamarina, Xiomara, 14, 20, 93, 93, 120, 160, 161, 162, 199

Sayre, Robert, xiii, xxxi
Scarry, Elaine, 116, 214, 216, 219
Schreiner Jr., Samuel A., 126, 141
Schultz, Elizabeth, 244
Schwalm, Leslie A., 252
Sea Island Experiment, 184. *See also* Forten, Charlotte.
Séances, xxvi
Sekora, John, 34, 58, 112, 114, 120
Seward, William H., 5, 233
Sexism, xxv, 37, 152
Shockley, Ann Allen, 246
Silber, Nina, 120, 252
Slave narrative(s), ix, xii, xiii, xiv, 6, 8, 21–24, 26, 27–31, 35–36, 41, 42, 61, 62, 74–76, 88, 90–96, 99–101, 105–106, 111–118, 139, 144, 163, 203, 213, 217, 221, 223, 240–241; female slave narrators, xix; male slave narrators, xx
*Slave's Friend, The* (1836–1838), 108
Slaveocracy, xv, xx, 25, 26, 28
Smith McKoy, Sheila, ix, xi–xxxi, 255
Smith, Felipe, 156
Smith, James L., 22, 31, 32, 33
Smith, Lydia, 125, 126
Smith, Sidonie, 34, 37, 58, 82, 87, 88, 218, 244, 251, 252
Smith, Valerie, 82, 89, 105, 120, 156, 166, 208, 209, 219
Smithers, Gregory D., xviii, xxx
Smithsonian National Museum of American History Museum, xxix
Sorisio, Carolyn, 10, 11, 20, 161, 162, 243, 246
South, xxi, xxiv, xxvi, xxvii, 12, 21, 24, 25, 26, 28, 29, 31, 42, 45, 64, 69, 70, 73, 78, 103, 114, 138, 153, 163, 166, 169, 170, 173, 174, 183, 184, 185, 191, 196, 198, 224, 227, 232, 236, 249
Spengemann, William C., 49, 59
Spielberg, Steven: *Lincoln*, 125, 126, 160

Spillers, Hortense J., 244, 246
Spiritualism, xv, xxvi, xxvii, xxviii
Spiritualists, xxvi, xxvii; movement, xxvii, xxviii
St. Augustine, 35
Stanton, Domna, 37
Starling, Marion Wilson, 34, 59
Steadman, Jennifer Bernhardt, 252
Sten, Christopher, 253
Stephens, Alexander H., xxvii, 174, 235
Stepto, Robert B., 21, 33, 34, 41, 46, 59, 91, 120
Sterling, Dorothy, 253
Stevens, Thaddeus, 125
Stewart, Maria, 144, 160, 241, 246
Stillers, Richard: *The Spy, the Lady, the Captain, and the Colonel,* 135, 140
Stone, Albert E., 39, 59
Stover, Johnnie M., 253
Stowe Harriet Beecher, xiii, xxvii, 247; *A Key to Uncle Tom's Cabin*, xiii; *Uncle Tom's Cabin,* xiii
Strasser, Mark, 246
Strozier, Charles, 171, 182
Swift, Jonathan, 242
Syncretic belief systems, xxviii

"Tale of Ahuri," 35
Tate, Claudia, 96, 205, 206, 219
Tawawa Chimney Corner, 198
Terrell, Mary Church, 160
Thirteenth Amendment, 125, 248
Thompson, Kathleen, 84, 89
Tuan, Yi-Fu, 163, 182
True Womanhood, 9, 10, 11, 12, 165, 207
Truth, Sojourner, xiii, xiv, xxvii, xxxi, 252
Turner, Nat, 191
Turner, Darwin, T., 34, 58
Tweedy, Clarence W., x, 203–219, 259
Turner, Justin G., 253

Underground Railroad, xv
Union Army, xxiii, xxvii, 68, 153

Valéry, Paul, 236, 243
Victorian, 85, 144, 151, 217; Victorianism 144, 160
Vidal, Gore, 253
Virginia, xiv, xv, xvii, xviii, xx, xxvii, 2, 22, 24, 42, 45, 50, 118, 127, 129, 174, 186, 221, 235, 236, 247, 248; Dinwiddie Court-house, xiv, 127, 247; Richmond, xxvii, 69, 174; Rude's Hill, 24, 129, 228
Virginia Statute 1662, xvii
Vlach, John Michael, 163, 182

Walker, Alice, 244, 246
Wall, Cheryl, 75, 88, 89
War Department, 190
Washington, Booker T., 25, 33, 34, 59, 156, 182, 224, 239, 240, 242, 246, 249
Washington, DC, xiii, xv, xxi, xxii, xxiv, xxv, xxvi, 4, 5, 6, 7, 9, 26, 38, 39, 42, 46, 49, 52, 60, 62, 68, 71, 80, 90, 93, 112, 113, 116, 127, 131, 135, 137, 147, 170, 172, 173, 174, 177, 185, 189, 193, 221, 222, 232, 248, 249
Washington, John E., xxi, 5, 9, 39, 40, 57, 176, 179, 180, 181, 182, 241, 245
Washington, Mary Helen, 191, 199
Webster, Daniel, xxii
Weiner, Marli, 182
Wells-Barnett, Ida, 160
Wheatley, Phillis, 42, 59, 144, 160
White, Deborah Gray, 182
White House, xv, xxii, xxiii, xxvi, 5, 6, 9, 15
White men, 12, 16, 36, 92, 194, 208
White women, xxi, 1, 11, 12, 13, 14, 24, 37, 81, 93, 116, 151, 166, 210, 222, 223
Whitfield, James M., 241

Wiegman, Robyn, 116, 120
Wilberforce University, xxiii, xxiv, 7, 8, 11, 39, 86, 120, 153, 171, 180, 238, 239, 248, 249; Department of Sewing and Domestic Arts, xxiv, 7
Williams, Fannie Barrier, 144
Williamson, Joel, 28, 32, 33
Willis, Fanny Fern (nee Sarah Paron), xiii
Willis, Nathaniel P., xiii, 172, 229. *See also* Lincoln, Abraham: death of son Willie

Wilmington Race Riot, 249
Wilson, Harriet, xxvii, xxxi, 117, 248
Winks, Robin, 22, 33
Wong, Sau-Ling C., 135, 141
Wright, Richard, 36, 59

Yellin, Jean Fagan, xiii, xxxi, 32. *See also* Jacobs, Harriet
Young, Al, 244, 246
Young, Elizabeth, 95

Zafar, Rafia, 92, 93, 121, 253

## ALSO AVAILABLE FROM ENO PUBLISHERS

*Behind the Scenes
Or Thirty Years a Slave, and Four Years in the White House*
Elizabeth Hobbs Keckley
With an introduction by Dolen Perkins-Valdez
Paperback
$10
ISBN: 978-0-9896092-7-2
Also available as an ebook

---

*The Elizabeth Keckley Reader
Volume Two: Artistry, Culture & Commerce*
Edited by Dr. Sheila Smith McKoy
Available in February 2017
Paperback
$17.50
ISBN: 978-0-9973144-4-1

---

www.ingramcontent.com/pod-product-compliance
Lightning Source LLC
Chambersburg PA
CBHW030435300426
44112CB00009B/1009